A CHOOSING PEOPLE

MERCER
UNIVERSITY PRESS

Endowed by
TOM WATSON BROWN
and
THE WATSON-BROWN FOUNDATION, INC.

A CHOOSING PEOPLE

THE HISTORY OF SEVENTH DAY BAPTISTS

Second Edition, Updated and Revised

DON A. SANFORD

MERCER UNIVERSITY PRESS
MACON, GEORGIA

MUP/ H846

© 2012 Mercer University Press
1400 Coleman Avenue
Macon, Georgia 31207

Second Revised, Updated Edition
Originally published 1992 by the Seventh Day Baptist Historical
Society

Books published by Mercer University Press are printed on acid-free
paper that meets the requirements of the American National Standard
for Information Sciences—Permanence of Paper for Printed Library
Materials.

Mercer University Press is a member of Green Press Initiative
(greenpressinitiative.org), a nonprofit organization working to help
publishers and printers increase their use of recycled paper and
decrease their use of fiber derived from endangered forests. This book
is printed on recycled paper.
ISBN   978-0-88146-284-5
Cataloging-in-Publication Data is available from the Library of
Congress

CONTENTS

To Reverend Duane L. Davis (1929–1989)

Duane shared with the author an enthusiasm for the heritage of Seventh Day Baptists from seminary days through forty years of ministry. He was able to bring the historic perspective to every aspect of his ministry, whether General Conference leadership, preaching, teaching, writing, or conversation.

His remembrance of family and church background helped him relate to people and places. One of his unfulfilled dreams was to record for future generations some of the information and understanding of God's presence with "the choosing people" by whom he was nurtured. May this book be a partial fulfillment of his vision.

PREFACE

In the musical *Fiddler on the Roof*, Tevye in a period of personal despair utters a prayer that ends with the lament, "It's true that we are a chosen people. But once in a while can't you choose someone else?"[1] Many Christians believe that God has chosen someone else, and they are convinced that they are that someone! Often this has led either to an intolerant arrogance or an indifferent fatalism. Some of the most unchristian acts have been carried out by those who believe that they, and only they, have been given access to the kingdom of God. Still others have operated under the illusion that as a chosen people, they can do no wrong and hence have shown no responsibility for their actions.

Seventh Day Baptists have generally avoided the claim of being a chosen people. Instead, they see themselves as a *choosing* people, responding to God's call by the choices they make under the guidance of the Holy Spirit through an enlightened conscience. If Abraham is the patron saint of the chosen people, Joshua is the prototype of a choosing people. He was one of the twelve selected to search out the promised land. While ten saw insurmountable obstacles, Joshua, along with Caleb, chose to see the possibilities God could give. When he inherited Moses' mantle of leadership, he continued to recognize man's responsibility to make choices.

> And if you be unwilling to serve the Lord, choose this day whom you will serve, whether the gods your fathers served in the region beyond the River, or the gods of the Amorites in whose land you dwell; but as for me and my house, we will serve the Lord. (Joshua 24:15 RSV)

The history of Seventh Day Baptists is a history of choices made. They have been a minority that has chosen to see the possibilities in following what they believed to be God's will. From the Separatist movement of dissent in seventeenth-century England to life within modern society, choices like those Joshua faced have been ever-present. People have the option to follow the traditionalism of the past, which

---

[1] Jerry Bock, *Fiddler on the Roof* (New York: Crown Publishing, 1965).

treats God as being unable or unwilling to deal personally with each generation. They also find the temptation to easily accommodate the demands of the secular society by following the gods of the land in which they live.

Fortunately, a third option has also been open: "As for me and my house, we will serve the Lord." There is always a recognized danger in choices. Sometimes people make wrong choices. Success is not always guaranteed. This was the chance God took in making man free. But the joy and satisfaction that stem from right choices and the knowledge that, even though we may err, we do not lose our sonship are precious gifts that inspire a choosing people.

ACKNOWLEDGMENTS

To acknowledge all who have contributed to the making and recording of a history spanning nearly four centuries would, in itself, constitute a book. It would include founders of churches, writers of history, and countless men and women who made such a study possible and meaningful. Yet there are certain people whose influence was very personal and direct either in the preparation of the author or the preparation of the manuscript.

Among those who contributed to the author's preparation was Rev. T. J. Van Horn, who, at the time of the author's birth, expressed in a letter a hope that the new life might have a significant role in the denomination. Credit is also given to parents who kept that hope alive. That hope began to focus in seminary, where Dean A. J. C. Bond shared his experiences in the Sabbath and his convictions that Seventh Day Baptists had a unique role in the larger fellowship of Christians. It was here also that Dr. Wayne Rood helped develop a sense of study, research, and recording necessary in the interpretation of history. Introduction to Seventh Day Baptists' history came from Rev. Victor W. Skaggs, who was the instructor in that field. Years later, as president of the Historical Society, he gave further encouragement to the writing of this history. He and his wife, Ardale, offered valuable suggestions as they proofread the manuscript for both style and content.

Several colleagues working at the Seventh Day Baptist Center in Janesville were particularly helpful in the process of organization and writing. Chief among these has been Janet Thorngate, the librarian and archivist for the Historical Society. Her knowledge of denominational history and resources coupled with her literary and writing skills were of incalculable value throughout the whole writing process of research and writing. Rev. Rodney Henry, director of Pastoral Services, was able to give insight into the intended audience and its needs as he made suggestions and gave encouragement. Katrina Saunders prepared the footnotes, checked for accuracy, and entered these and the bibliography into the electronic manuscript. General Conference executive secretary Dale Thorngate and former historian Thomas Merchant were frequent consultants who gave added support.

Appreciation is also given to Rev. Oscar Burdick for his exhaustive research in early-English Seventh Day Baptists. Rev. Burdick also provided research and subject-matter leads in early-American history.

Last but not least, one could not overlook the support of Ilou Sanford, who has patiently lived with her husband's preoccupation with writing concerns, and whose own genealogical fascination and research has added further insight and information to a shared heritage of eleven generations of Seventh Day Baptist ancestry.

INTRODUCTION TO THE SECOND EDITION

By the time *A Choosing People* approached out-of-print status, Don Sanford had retired to focus on his final writing projects. He had conducted most of his research and writing on Seventh Day Baptist history while he worked as a historian for the Seventh Day Baptist Historical Society from 1987 to 2005. As Historian Emeritus, he continued that work and decided, when it was time to reprint the main history, that it deserved updating to a second edition. New information had come to light, and Seventh Day Baptists, he noted, had entered "their seventh half century." He was always counting.

It is not surprising, however, that 15 more years added to the previous 340 did not substantially change the record nor the author's perspective on it. The updates and revisions, though scattered throughout the book, are mainly small changes to correct inaccuracies brought to light by recent research or to bring late-twentieth-century reporting up to date. Two chapters changed the most. Chapter 21, previously "Twentieth Century Missions," is retitled "International Extension" to reflect the growing role of the Seventh Day Baptist World Federation, an association of sister conferences on six continents. The author expanded considerably on Chapter 12, "Associations," to include discussion of the historical relationships between the regional groupings of churches and the General Conference, a topic that has gained interest as Seventh Day Baptists again reconsider the organizational structures of the denomination for a new century. One planned revision Don Sanford was not able to complete involved incorporating new information researched by some of his students on Seventh Day Baptist activity in the seventeenth- and eighteenth-century Great Awakenings. A new development he was particularly happy to add was the decision of Seventh Day Baptists in 2007 to retain their long-term membership in the Baptist Joint Committee for Religious Liberty (see Chapter 22, "Twentieth Century Ecumenical Relations").

Don Sanford died in March 2009. During his final illness he enlisted the help of several colleagues to see the project through to completion. We give grateful thanks to these people who have each had a major role in carrying out his intentions: his daughter Donna Sanford Bond; his successor in the role of historian, Nicholas Kersten; his seminary classmate and fellow-researcher Oscar Burdick; and members of the Historical Society Board, Paul Green and Norma Rudert. Their help is an appropriate memorial. We are honored to make available this update of the only comprehensive history of Seventh Day Baptists.

Janet Thorngate, President
Seventh Day Baptist Historical Society

PART I: HISTORIC ROOTS

PART I TIMELINE:

Date/Reign/Lifespan	Event/Monarch/Person
1320-1384	John Wycliffe
1374-1415	John Huss
1395	Lollards, *12 Conclusions*
1455	Gutenberg Press
1455-1485	"War of the Roses"
1483-1546	Martin Luther
1480-1540	Andreas Fischer
1484-1531	Ulrich Zwingli
1485-1509	Henry VII
1489-1556	Thomas Cramner
1492	Columbus 'discovers' America
1501-1572	John Knox
1509-1547	Henry VIII
1509-1564	John Calvin
1517	Luther, *95 Theses*
1521	Diet of Worms
1525	Tyndale's English New Testament
1534	First Act of Supremacy
1535	Coverdale's English Bible
1539	Great English Bible
1547-1553	Edward VI
1553-1558	Mary I
1558-1603	Elizabeth I
1556-1616	Thomas Helwys
1559	Act of Uniformity
1567-1644	William Brewster

1570-1633	Robert Browne
1570-1612	John Smyth
1581	Brownists Flee
1588	England Defeats the Spanish Armada
1603-1625	James I
1606-	Congregationalists
1611-	Baptists in England
1611	*King James Version*
1620	Pilgrims at Plymouth

1

BACKGROUND OF REFORM

To set an exact date for the beginnings of Seventh Day Baptists is similar to a genealogist's trying to pinpoint his family's exact origins. We can trace our roots as far back as it is possible to find records. The intent of this writing is not to establish any apostolic or documentary succession. Rather, it is to examine the seeds that resulted in the formation of Seventh Day Baptists as a distinct people whose spiritual genesis goes back in time, but whose fruits have blossomed in each succeeding generation.

The first documented Seventh Day Baptist churches were established in England in the middle of the seventeenth century following a period of religiously motivated civil war. Out of this period of dissent, a people gathered to practice and proclaim truths that their study of the Scriptures convinced them were essential for their spiritual worship and development. They chose to follow the dictates of their consciences not only in matters pertaining to the Sabbath and baptism, but also in the freedom to become a choosing people. These choices did not rise out of a vacuum but were the result of centuries of choices made by other people in other times and places.

THE CHURCH OF THE MIDDLE AGES

The fourteenth-century Italian writer Boccacio is credited with the story of the priest who tried to persuade his neighbor to become a Christian. His friend seemed interested but remarked that before he took such a step he wanted to visit Rome to see what the church was really like. The old priest was upset over this procedure, for he knew what the church in Rome was like and was afraid that it would discourage any who looked at it inquiringly. But his neighbor was determined and set off on his investigation. He found what the priest had feared. He saw the contrast between the wealth of the leaders and the poverty of the people. He saw people from all areas come to purchase both political and religious power. There was little that could attract one who was seeking truth.

Upon the neighbor's return home, the priest was surprised that his friend asked for membership in the church. When asked if he had gone to Rome and seen the condition of the church there, the friend responded that he had seen all kinds of sin and corruption in the church, but that only made him more determined to join. The old priest asked him what had persuaded him to join despite all this evil. The man responded that if any institution could exist for so long with such poor leadership and so much sin attached to it, the power of God must be hidden somewhere within it, and he wanted to find that power.[1]

This ancient tale illustrates three significant ideas. There was corruption, but there was also a stabilizing power, and in time people did have a choice.

Corruption

First, the observations of both the priest and his neighbor were correct. The Roman Catholic Church of the time was corrupt. It robbed the poor to support the luxuries, lavish lifestyles, and grandiose buildings enjoyed by Rome's elite. The seven deadly sins of pride, anger, covetousness, lust, envy, sloth, and gluttony could all be found in the church.

The sale of indulgences was particularly offensive. It stemmed from the idea that the keys to the kingdom, promised to Peter in Matthew 16:19, had been transferred to the Pope at Rome. This, they taught, gave him the power to reduce the amount of time a person would have to spend in purgatory. Since there were saints who possessed more than enough merits to free the deceased, these extra merits could be purchased by living relatives. The sacraments of the church, which were intended to aid worship, had degenerated into magical tricks designed to court God's favor and purchase salvation.

Stabilizing Power

In spite of corrupting influences, the power of God in the church enabled it to survive for centuries. The church kept the Christian faith alive while the civilization about it decayed; it provided havens of safety amid times of extreme danger and a measure of stability when governments collapsed. Its scribes copied the Scriptures by hand. The church produced men such as Francis of Assisi, who attempted to imitate Christ's love of all creatures, and Thomas Aquinas, whose writings on Scripture and devotion gave depth to the meaning of faith.

---

[1] "The Second Story," Giovanni Boccaccio, in *Decameron*, 1 vol., trans. John Payne, ed. Charles S. Singleton (Berkeley: University of California Press, 1982; rev., 1986) 1:40-45.

The Option of Choice

A third lesson from the priest's parable is that the neighbor had a choice. He could easily have focused on the church's evil and rejected any of its claim on his life. Instead, he saw within it something that gave him promise and hope. That choice was not made blindly or out of compulsion. He sought the truth and made an informed choice.

The Roman Catholic Church during the Middle Ages might be compared to a dam constructed in an arid region to collect life-giving waters into a reservoir. People who went to it found relief from their thirst. However, there came a time when the climate changed and refreshing rains began to fall on the land. There were many who insisted that, rather than channel this water to the people, they should build the dam higher. To put it in more modern terms, the truth was "sandbagged" or "stonewalled." Even the spillway designed to protect the dam was closed, and the water began to leak out in tiny rivulets. Eventually, the pressure became too great and the dam burst. When such a thing happens there is initial destruction, but eventually the water seeks new channels and is carried to the people downstream.

The change in the climate was created partly by the Renaissance, which began in the early fourteenth century in Europe and continued for the next two centuries. The term *Renaissance* literally means rebirth, and it refers to the rediscovery of the arts, literature, and culture of the ancient Greeks and Romans. The movement created an interest in the translation of ancient writings, including an effort to decipher the Bible in the language of the people. In 1382, John Wycliffe translated the Bible into English and sent out preachers to spread its message. John Huss, who was influenced by Wycliffe, attempted to reform the church in his native Bohemia (now a part of the Czech Republic). He was burned at the stake as a heretic in 1415. The process of rebirth and rediscovery was accelerated in 1450 by Johann Gutenberg's invention of moveable-type printing press, which made it possible for the common people to read the Bible for themselves. When this development enabled the populace to think for themselves, the religious elite lost its tight hold on the revealed will of God. The flood waters that gushed from this breach became known as the Protestant Reformation.

THE PROTESTANT REFORMATION

The term "Protestant Reformation" implies two movements: a protest against all that was wrong within the Roman Catholic Church of the time, and a reform or change to make the church conform to newly discovered truths arising from biblical study. At the beginning of the Reformation, there was no thought of leaving the church, for there was no other church to which people could go. Most accepted the statement of Bishop Cyprian of Carthage, who, around the middle of the third century, wrote: "He cannot have God for his father who has not the Church for his mother. If anyone was able to escape outside of Noah's ark then he also escapes who is outside the doors of the Church."[2]

Luther: A Chooser of Faith

Martin Luther is credited with launching the Protestant Reformation. Luther tried nearly every work of penance the Roman Church prescribed in order to find satisfaction for his soul but ended his quest in utter frustration. His study of the Scriptures led him to discover Romans 1:17, where he found the answer to his search. In the words "The just shall live by faith," Luther saw a sharp contrast between God's promise of salvation through grace and the church's promises that one could buy forgiveness. He was particularly disturbed over the tactics of John Tetzel, who went about the country preaching: "As soon as a coin tinkles in the collection-box a soul straightway flies out of purgatory."

The Ninety-five Theses

One of Luther's common methods of protest was debate. On 31 October 1517, Luther posted on the door of the Wittenberg Castle Church his ninety-five theses, or statements for discussion, which attacked abuses within the church. He did not deny that the church had a role in preserving its children for God. He argued that if the pope possessed the power of remission of sin, he ought to exercise it through intercession, out of most holy charity, and for the great need of souls.[3]

As punishment for his continued attack, Luther was excommunicated in January 1521 and declared to be outside the church's saving grace and protection. In defense Luther appealed to Germany's growing sense of nationalism, showing how the Roman Church had erred, not only in its theology, but also in its misuse of temporal power. Under the protection of Duke Frederick of Saxony, others who had

---

[2] Cyprian, Bishop of Carthage (AD 248–258), *De Catholicae ecclesiae unitate*, sec. 6, in *Documents of the Christian Church*, ed. Henry Bettenson (New York: Oxford University Press, 1947) 102.

[3] Martin Luther, "The Ninety-five Theses," no. 82, in *Documents*, ed. Bettenson, 270.

suffered under Roman authority came to Luther's defense, and the conflict breached the Roman domination beyond repair.

Convicted by Scripture

During the trial at the Diet of Worms in 1521, Luther was ordered to recant or deny his writings. After pointing out the varied nature of his writings, he uttered what has become the classic statement of the Reformation: "My conscience is taken captive by God's word. I cannot and will not recant anything, for to act against our conscience is neither safe for us, nor open to us. On this I take my stand. I can do no other, God help me. Amen."[4]

Thus, once a division was made that permitted people to choose the church through which they might receive God's grace, other voices were heeded.

Zwingli: A Biblical Preacher

Another influential voice of reform was heard in Switzerland, where Ulrich Zwingli preached at Zurich. Zwingli was a great student of the Bible and was particularly well versed in New Testament Greek. His name did not become attached to any major Protestant denomination, for his life was cut short in 1531 during a battle between Protestant and Catholic states in Switzerland. Still, his influence affected many. While Luther would not permit what the Bible prohibited, Zwingli rejected whatever the Bible did not prescribe.[5] Luther began with the Roman Catholic Church and cut away those beliefs and practices that did not conform to the Scriptures. Zwingli and his followers began with the Scriptures and attempted to organize a church as near that of the New Testament as possible.

Calvin: Captive to a Sovereign God

The leadership of the Swiss reform was taken up by a young French student named John Calvin. Forced to leave strongly Catholic France, Calvin left for Basel, Switzerland, where he published the first edition of the *Institutes of the Christian Religion*. This was the most comprehensive and thorough-going statement of Protestantism. Calvin was invited to Geneva City Council, represented by Ami Perkin, where he set up a theocratic government (purportedly a government in which God was the

---

[4] Luther, "Diet of Worms" (18 Apr 1521), in in *Documents*, ed. Bettenson, 285.
[5] Bruce Shelley, *Church History in Plain Language* (Waco TX: Word Books, 1982) 268.

ruler). The officials of the church were the officials of the city. This body, called the Consistory, was responsible for the moral as well as the political supervision of the city and enforced a strict code of ethics. Calvin believed that the church had an obligation under the sovereignty of God to exert its influence over secular government.

In practice, Calvinist rule appears as authoritarian as that of the Roman Church from which Calvin had rebelled, but there was a tremendous theological difference. Calvin believed in God's absolute sovereignty or power over every aspect of life. He had experienced that power in his own life, and he wanted others to share in it. If Luther's guiding text was "The just shall live by faith" (Rom 1:17 RSV), then Calvin's was "Thy will be done, on earth as it is in heaven" (Matt 6:10 RSV).

Election and Predestination

The divine will of God included the doctrine of election and predestination that Calvin defined as "the eternal decree of God, by which he has decided in his own mind what he wishes to happen in the case of each individual. For all men are not created on an equal footing, but for some eternal life is pre-ordained, for others eternal damnation."[6]

Calvin did not believe that anyone could earn salvation by works, but he believed with James that "faith without works was dead" (James 2:17). This notion placed a strong moral responsibility on man to make choices that would be in accord with God's revealed will. If a person is numbered among the chosen, then it follows that, by the very will of the sovereign God, his choices in life will be holy and right.

State Concept of the Church

Both the Lutherans and the Calvinists maintained a state concept of the church similar to that of the Roman Catholic Church from which they broke. This state church concept, like that of the Roman Empire of New Testament days, was geographic in nature, with no part of the empire beyond its jurisdiction. It might be divided into provinces, but the boundaries all fit together so that no one was left outside. By birth, every person became a member of that province. In a church established along geographic lines, a person was considered a part of the family of God as soon as he or she was recognized through the rite of baptism. Thus

---

[6] John Calvin, *Christianae Religionis Instituto* (bk. 3, ch. 21), in Shelley, *Church History*, 302.

members deemed it important that every newborn child be baptized immediately.

THE ANABAPTISTS: DEFENDERS OF COVENANT

The Anabaptists interpreted the church as a colony set in the midst of a state. Following Zwingli's teachings, they recognized that the New Testament church was composed of individual congregations that were established not by decree or by conquest, but by persuasion and testimony wherever the gospel was preached and believed.

Baptism an Issue

The term *Anabaptist* literally means "rebaptized." It was used negatively in connection with the Donatist controversy in the fourth century with the readmission of those bishops who had practiced idolatry by offering incense to the emperor under duress. The term was an epithet, an insult. The code of Justinian in 529 listed rebaptism as one of the heresies punishable by death.

The sixteenth-century Anabaptists did not consider that they were rebaptized because they considered true baptism possible only on belief and confession of faith. Hence they rejected infant baptism, for an infant could hardly make such confession or harbor any religious belief. Conversely, Adult baptism or baptism of believers was impossible to practice within a state concept of the church, for it would leave too many people outside the church and thus deprive them of a chance for salvation. Such a threat to the very foundation of society was considered treasonous.

In 1526 the council in Zurich, Switzerland, decreed that anyone found practicing rebaptism should be put to death by drowning. "If heretics want water, let them have it," they said. It is estimated that between four and five thousand Anabaptists were executed—sometimes by fire, sometimes by sword, but most often by drowning. Such persecution had an effect similar to the persecution experienced by the New Testament church, which dispersed believers in small clusters throughout the known world.

A Community of Believers

The Anabaptists' independence and freedom of thought led at times to excesses that tended to brand the entire movement as revolutionary.

11

In spite of their reputation as heretics, Anabaptists lent several important concepts to the Reformation:

(1) They chose a lifestyle that emulated Christ's example rather than church doctrine.

(2) They were among the first to strictly separate church and state. Their refusal to take oaths or participate in government, along with their pacifist teachings and practices, isolated them from the state.

(3) As a community of believers they developed the congregational view of church authority in which decision-making, including that of the discipline of its members, rested with the entire membership. Even the decision of how to interpret Scripture was made by a consensus of the local congregation as they studied and prayed together.

The Anabaptists were among those who attempted religious reform through the model of restitution, which assumes that something has been lost. They looked to the model of the earliest Christians, those who formed the New Testament church. Daniel Liechty points out that Anabaptists expressed the need for restitution in terms of the "fall" of the church at the time of Constantine, when Christianity became the religion of an empire rather than the religion of personally committed believers.[7]

Some of the early sixteenth-century Anabaptists in central Europe observed the Sabbath of the Bible. They interpreted the decree of Constantine in 325—when the Nicaea Council was summoned, signaling the passing of authority to secular powers—as a sign of the fall of the Roman Church. The most prominent of these was Andreas Fischer, who lived from 1480 to 1540. Of Fischer Liechty wrote, "his Sabbatarianism was an essential and integral part of his whole approach to Christian reform, an approach characterized by the restitutionist pattern of thought."[8]

A more widely known Anabaptist leader was a former priest named Menno Simons from whom the Mennonites received their name. The Mennonites contributed much to the church of the post-Reformation era, particularly to those who followed in the free-church tradition of a choosing people.

---

[7] Daniel Liechty, *Andreas Fischer and the Sabbatarian Anabaptists: An Early Reformation Episode in East Central Europe*, Studies in Anabaptist and Mennonite History, 45 vols., ed. Cornelius J. Dyck (Scottdale PA: Herald Press, 1988) 29:25-26.

[8] Liechty, *Andreas Fischer*, 105.

CONCLUSIONS

The Reformation in Europe was similar to the experience of the Israelites on the threshold of the Promised Land. They had survived centuries of bondage and a generation of wandering in the wilderness as they sought to become God's people. The rediscovery of the Bible in the sixteenth century resembled the mission of the twelve spies in searching out their promised new home. Yet many refused to enter the promised land, preferring the traditionalism of the past.

A full century after the Reformation began, English pilgrim Pastor John Robinson urged that segment of his congregation in Holland that chose to embark for America in 1620 to be alert for "more truths yet to break out of His Holy Word." He lamented the fact that many of the Lutherans would go no further than Luther went, and that the Calvinists were stuck where that great man of God had left them (e.g., they had stopped looking for further revelation from the Word of God). According to Winslow's recollection, Robinson urged them to receive new truths that might emerge from their study of the Bible, and he warned them: "Take heed what we received for truth, and well to examine and compare, and weigh it with other Scriptures of truth, before we receive it; For, saith he, "It is not possible the Christian world should come so lately out of such thick Antichristian darkness, and that full perfection of knowledge should breake forth at once."[9]

The continuing endeavor to understand the Scriptures and their meanings for the Christian's life within the community of believers dominates the history of any choosing people. Later generations were indebted to Luther's insight into the free gift of God's salvation through justification by faith. Zwingli started many toward a rediscovery of the New Testament church. From Calvin's personal experience he infused into the church a new awareness of God's complete sovereignty. To the Anabaptists can be credited the idea of the separation of church and state, in which an individual's choices could be made among a fellowship of believers.

Within this context, attention is now focused on the Reformation taking place in England. Out of this reform arose, among others, a

---

[9] Edward Winslow, "Words of John Robinson: Robinson's Farewell Address to the Pilgrims upon Their Departure from Holland, 1620. The account by Edward Winslow in his "'Hypocrisie Unmasked,' Printed in 1646," in *Old South Leaflets* no. 142, pp. 1-2, reprinted in *Old South Leaflets*, Research and Source Work Search Series # 106 (New York: Burt Franklin, n.d.) vol. 6, leaflet 142, pp. 361-62.

distinctive group of choosing people known as Seventh Day Baptists. The choices of the great reformers affected, but did not limit, the choices that followed. Seventh Day Baptists, like many others of the time, were not convinced that perfection of truth had completely broken out of the anti-Christian darkness. Their concept of the Sabbath was one of the areas on which they shed new light as they chose to interpret and live by the Scriptures.

THE ENGLISH REFORMATION

The Reformation in England, from which Seventh Day Baptists trace their roots, was a movement both political and religious. The political changes provided the climate in which Reformation ideas could develop. The separation of England from Roman Catholic domination could hardly have been successful were it not for seeds of change planted over a century and a half earlier.

POLITICAL CHANGES

At the end of the Middle Ages, England was a country in search of national identity. The British Isles were inhabited by successive invasions of such nomadic tribes as the Celts, the Angles, and the Saxons. The area had become a part of the Roman Empire under the Caesars around the time of Christ. It was conquered by the Normans in 1066, which put it more solidly within the sphere of the Holy Roman Empire. The Normans introduced to England the feudal system whereby the common people gave their labor and freedom in exchange for protection provided by the lord of the manor.

The mixed backgrounds of the people, the establishment of the feudal system, and the inclusion of England in the Holy Roman Empire brought to the political climate three conditions that had lasting effects on both church and state:

(1) Strong national loyalties were slow to develop. Initial loyalties belonged to whichever nobleman was able to offer the most protection and patronage. In a vassal system, an individual's strongest tie was to the person immediately above him in the social and economic class structure.

(2) Intense rivalries existed among the nobility, creating a perpetual struggle for power. The crown of England was worn by the noble who was able to defeat his strongest rival in battle. Yet, that power was never absolute. As early as 1215, the defeated nobles combined in council to force King John to sign the *Magna Charta*, which stated that even a king must obey the law of the land.

(3) In the midst of this constant vying for power, the Roman Catholic Church was the principal force that brought stability to the

country. Princes might come and go, but the church remained from generation to generation, picking up many of the struggles' spoils. Furthermore, the Roman Catholic Church organization was largely feudal in structure, so that loyalty within the church mirrored loyalty within the feudal community.

THE RISE OF THE TUDORS

It was not until 1485 that a dominant royalty emerged in the person of Henry VII, the first of the Tudor line. Henry brought a sense of unity to the nation as he elevated England to the status of a world power. He was skillful in matters of finance, expanding trade and selling appointments to political and religious offices. S. T. Bindoff wrote that prior to England's break from the Roman Church, the crown already had controlling influence over the heads of the English Church, "and bishops who drew their pay from the Church but who earned it by service to the King were unlikely, when the piper played, to refuse to dance the royal measure."[1]

In a further attempt to enhance England's position as a world power, Henry VII turned to one of the most often used, and many times politically disastrous, ploys—matrimony. To consolidate ties with Spain, Henry arranged for the marriage of his oldest son, Arthur, to Catherine of Aragon. After Arthur's untimely death at the age of 16, Henry arranged for his other son, Henry VIII, to marry Arthur's widow, thus enabling him to keep the Spanish family's generous dowry. A quarter of a century later, this alliance caused the irreparable rift between England and Rome.

Henry VIII

Henry VIII, at the beginning of his reign, appeared to champion the Catholic faith. The pope had designated him "Defender of the Faith," a title he continued to use even after his faith changed. He undoubtedly would have died a loyal Roman Catholic had his marriage to Catherine produced a living male heir. When the pope refused to annul his marriage, Henry severed connections with the Church of Rome, established himself as the head of the English Church, annulled his marriage to Catherine, and married Anne Boleyn.

---

[1] S. T. Bindoff, *Tudor England*, The Pelican History of England, 9 vols. (1950; repr., Middlesex, England: Penguin, 1979) 5:82.

In line with the previously accepted practice of allegiance, in 1534 the English Parliament, or governing body of nobility, passed the Act of Supremacy, which declared, "The King's majesty justly and rightfully is and ought to be the supreme head of the Church of England, and so is recognized by the clergy of this realm and their Convocations."[2] This statement signified the official break of the English Church from Roman Catholicism and established King Henry VIII as head of the Church of England. Not all in England accepted this decree, and the struggle continued for many years. Several attempts were made to return England to the Roman fold, but none were successful for long.

Mary I

The most resolute attempt to return England to Roman Catholicism came during the reign of Mary I, the daughter of Henry VIII and Catherine. At stake were strongly held religious views as well as the legitimacy of Mary's claim to the throne. During this reign of about five years, many were martyred by the monarchy for their refusal to give allegiance to Rome. The effect of this continuing struggle can best be understood within the context of the developing religious ideas that would ultimately lead to the Reformation.

CHANGES IN RELIGIOUS THOUGHT IN ENGLAND

Early religious changes in England were less dramatic than those on the Continent. Nonetheless, they were extremely important to the developing reform.

John Wycliffe

One of the earliest voices raised in England affecting the religious thinking and practice of the people was that of John Wycliffe (1324–1384). He deviated from the teachings of the Catholic Church in three areas. First, he spoke of a "dominion of grace" in which lordship, both spiritual and temporary, came directly from God rather than through the feudal concept involving intermediaries. This teaching attacked the whole system built on the Pope's supremacy and the hierarchy of the priesthood.

---

[2] "The Supremacy Act, 1534," *Statutes of the Realm* iii.492, in H. Gee and W. J. Hardy, *Documents Illustrative of English Church History*, ed. Henry Bettenson (1896; repr., New York: Oxford University Press, 1947) 321.

Secondly, Wycliffe accepted the Bible, interpreted literally, as the sole authority of faith. This view rejected the doctrine that the church fathers and church councils were as important as the Scriptures themselves.

These two positions led Wycliffe to the third area in which he questioned the sacraments. He did not conceive of the Mass as the primary act of worship, and he rejected the doctrine of "transubstantiation" (the belief that during the celebration of Mass the bread and wine become the physical body and blood of Christ). Instead, he wrote that "the bread was still bread and the wine was still wine in the Sacrament of the altar."[3] In this belief Wycliffe preceded by nearly a century and a half many of the views held by Luther, Zwingli, Calvin, and the Anabaptists.

Lollards

The religious and political soil was not ready for these seeds to germinate into a full reformation, yet there were some who accepted Wycliffe's teachings. In 1395, a group of his followers, called Lollards, drew up a document known as the "Twelve Conclusions"; its statements comprise one of the earliest examples of what later became fundamental Protestant principles. Their document struck at the very heart of Roman Catholic theology and practice of the time. In addition to rejecting Roman authority and reinterpreting the celebration of the Mass, the document spoke out against such practices as celibacy of the clergy, oral confession, prayers for the dead, consecration of physical objects and images, pilgrimages, and the church's excessive preoccupation with "works of human artisanship" (works by smiths of various kinds—gold, armor, etc.). The political powers opposed the statement that man-slaughter in war or as a punishment for temporal crimes "without spiritual revelation is expressly contrary to the New Testament."[4] The Lollards were met with such opposition and persecution that during the fifteenth century they were nearly eradicated, but one of their contributions had direct bearing on the English Reformation. Their emphasis on preaching rather than the sacraments called for translating

---

[3] "Propositions of Wycliffe Condemned at London, 1382 and at the Council of Constance, 1415," in *Documents*, ed. Bettenson, 246.

[4] "Lollard Conclusions, 1394," Fasciculi Zizaniorum 277-82, in *Documents*, ed. Bettenson, 248.

the Bible into the language of the people.[5] Wycliffe's translations of the Scriptures opened a world of spiritual freedom that previous generations could not have imagined.

A Matter of Authority

The early reformers did not directly influence the English Reformation, for when Henry VIII severed the ties with Rome he did not alter his theology. Attention was focused primarily on changes that would transfer religious authority from the pope to the king. Translations of the Scriptures into English were by the church. William Tyndale was forced to flee England and seek refuge in Germany to translate the Bible into English. Copies of his translations were smuggled into England, where many were burned. Tyndale was eventually condemned as a heretic and burned at the stake. It is reported, that his dying prayer in 1536 was "Lord, open the King of England's eyes."[6]

Miles Coverdale's 1535 translation, and later a 1539 revision known as the "Great English Bible," proved instrumental in making a distinctly English church. However, the *Book of Common Prayer* written by Thomas Cranmer retained much of the Roman Church's traditional ritual and pageantry. The new church continued to uphold the state concept of the church and allowed little freedom of choice. It remained for a later generation to put into practice those distinctively Protestant principles held by Wycliffe and the Reformers on the Continent.

ROLE OF SCRIPTURE IN THE ENGLISH REFORMATION

Each stage of the Protestant Reformation was marked by the rediscovery of the Bible and its application to Christian belief and practice. To stem the flow of reform, rulers often tried to limit the use of the Scriptures. They usually did this either by destroying copies or by silencing those who taught from them. The most dramatic example was the attempt of Queen Mary I, during her short reign from 1553 to 1558, to return England to Roman Catholicism.

---

[5] A. G. Dickens, *The English Reformation* (1964; repr., GlasgowScotland: Fontana, 1967) 44.

[6] Bruce Shelley, *Church History in Plain Language* (Waco TX: Word Books, 1982) 268.

Attempts to Restrict Beliefs

One notable example of an attempt to destroy copies of Scripture is recorded in the diary of Samuel Hubbard, one of the charter members of the first Seventh Day Baptist Church in America. He wrote: "Now 1675 I have a testament of my grandfather Cocke's printed 1549, which he hid in his bed-straw lest it should be found and burnt in queen Mary's days."[7] Although this effort to conceal the Scriptures occurred nearly a century before the establishment of any distinct Seventh Day Baptist Church, it is a part of the denomination's spiritual heritage. Samuel Hubbard's testament is one of the prized possessions of the Seventh Day Baptist Historical Society. Samuel Hubbard's paternal grandparents, Thomas Hubbard and wife, are listed in Fox's *Book of Martyrs* as having been driven out of the town of Mendlesam on the grounds they that held Scripture "to be the sufficient Doctrine unto their salvation."[8]

Sometimes the attempt to silence scriptural teaching ended in martyrdom. The first of some 300 who were put to death during Mary's reign was John Rogers, a biblical translator who was burned at the stake on 4 February 1555 at Smithfield. Queen Mary had expected that the threat of death would weaken Protestantism, but instead it had the opposite effect. Among the most noted martyrs were Bishops Hugh Latimer and Nicholas Ridley. When he was led to the stake, Latimer is reported to have said: "Be of good comfort, Mr. Ridley, and play the man. We shall this day light such a candle, by God's grace in England, as I trust shall never be put out."[9] Such persecutions did much to increase the hatred among the English for anything Roman.

Upon Mary's death, her half-sister Elizabeth became queen. A new Act of Supremacy was passed in 1559 to reaffirm the separation of the church from Rome by again declaring the English monarch head of the Church of England. Another act known as the Thirty-Nine Articles of Uniformity attempted to restrict any practice or belief that did not conform to the Church of England's doctrine. These Articles were Roman in polity and organization, Calvinistic concerning the elect, and

---

[7] Samuel Hubbard, *Register of Mr. Samuel Hubbard* (transcription of excerpts with notes by Isaac Backus, ca. 1775), MSS B136i, p. 32, Rhode Island Historical Society Library, Providence (microfilm copy, MF 1989.4, Seventh Day Baptist Historical Society Library). See also MS 194x.6, p. 29, SDB Hist. Soc. Lib.

[8] John Fox, "Persecution in Suffolk," in *Acts and Monuments of Martyrs…*, 9th ed., 3 vols. (London: Company of Stationers, 1684) 3:590-91.

[9] Fox, *Acts and Monuments*, 3:431.

anti-Lollard in their attitude toward dissenters. They attempted to impose a set of beliefs and practices that permitted the people little chance to follow their own consciences, which by this time had been taken captive by the word of God found in Scripture.

Biblical Interpretations

Reformation in England during the Elizabethan era shifted from the struggle against Rome to struggles within the Church of England itself. In this conflict the Bible became both the defensive armor described in Paul's letter to the Ephesians (6:13-18) and the offensive sword of the Lord mentioned in Hebrews 4:12. During any period of reform, the Bible has been used in three distinctive ways: (1) to proof-text a position already held, often taking passages out of their as foundation for extra-biblical ideas; (2) for "reproof and correction," to refute errors as Paul suggested (2 Tim 3:16); and/or (3) as the sole source for teaching doctrine, reflecting Zwingli's position as he rejected whatever the Bible did not expressly prescribe.

How the Bible was and is interpreted does much to explain the church's basic polity or organization. Differences of interpretation gave rise to such movements within the Church of England as the Puritans and the Separatists, from which all Baptists, including Seventh Day Baptists, trace their origin.

BASIC POLITY LEADING TO SEPARATION

Within the Christian Church are three basic types of organization. Although the following terms have been used to identify specific denominations, they are also generic terms signifying types of church structure. A church may be said to be *episcopal* in form and authority; it may be *presbyterian* in structure; or it may be basically *congregational* in organization. In looking at these forms, one must remember that the church of the New Testament was not a static organization; it was constantly developing to meet the needs within a society that was also undergoing great change. Thus, though each position may have a biblical precedent, we must avoid the temptation to say that any one position, and that alone, is what the church should be like in any other age. The Reformation in England involved many choices as to which polity or combinations of polity best met the church's needs.

Episcopal

The word *episcopal* comes from the Greek word *episcopos*, which is translated in most Bibles as "bishop,"[10] meaning an overseer or a superintendent. The word *connectional* is often used to identify churches with episcopal polity. The idea that power and authority is established by a direct connection with one of the apostles is basic. In the development of the church, overseers were appointed to maintain a connection to such leaders as Paul or Peter and thus assure the purity of church teachings and practices. If the church assumed that Peter was the bishop of Rome, it was natural that whoever followed him in that office would be of supreme importance and be declared the church's ultimate authority. In support of this authority, the Roman Church relied heavily on the statement of Jesus recorded in Matthew 16:18, regarding the Rock on which the church was built, assuming the "Rock" was Peter himself rather than his confession of Christ.

The Reformation broke the power of Rome, but it did not remove the empire's basic authority structure. Power flowed from the top of an administrative pyramid through several levels of intermediaries. This power often included the authority to interpret Scripture and determine doctrine as well as the power to administer both the physical and the spiritual functions of the church. In episcopal polity, traceable apostolic succession is believed to be essential for the proper ordination and administration of the sacraments.

Presbyterian

The word *presbyterian* comes from the Greek word *presbuteros*, typically translated as "elder" in the Bible. It is related to the Old Testament concept of the tribal leader, as in Exodus 12:21, where it refers to the elders of Israel. The New Testament church continued the practice of appointing elders who held positions of respect and authority. The cooperation of appointed elders most clearly identifies presbyterian polity.

John Calvin molded presbyterian polity to Calvinistic doctrine. One of Calvin's disciples, John Knox, carried this concept to Scotland. In 1560, Knox drafted articles of religion that were adopted by the parliament of Scotland, making that country a Presbyterian state. Calvinism entered English politics and religion largely through Scotland.

---

[10] See Acts 1:20, Phil 1:1, 1 Tim 3:1-2, Titus 1:7, and 1 Pet 2:25.

Congregational

Congregational polity stems from the Old Testament concept of the meeting of those who were called together by God. During the Exodus, Israel's place of meeting was called the tabernacle of the congregation (Ex 27:21). Throughout their history, the word "congregation" was used to identify the worshipping body of people of the covenant. In the New Testament, the Christians believed they were the people of the new covenant. Congregationalism places emphasis on the individual Christians who make up a group or congregation. Individuals may be called to exercise particular individual gifts in terms of preaching and other forms of ministry, but the use of these gifts is always for the edification of the entire community of faith.

Congregational polity was seen in the Reformation among the Anabaptists and others who rejected the state or geographic concept of the church. Entrance into the church was by personal acceptance of Christ. Congregational decisions were made by consensus or agreement among the people. Congregations relied on their own reading and study of the Scriptures to make choices in accord with what they understood was the Holy Spirit leading. The freedom exercised was not a freedom for each person to do his or her own thing. Rather, it was, as Franklin H. Littell wrote, "the freedom to participate in the discussions by which discipline was arrived at democratically."[11]

These three lines of thought could hardly exist together for long before conflicts arose that necessitated hard choices. Some believers chose to work within the established church to effect change; others saw no choice but to separate. Those who tried to "purify" and correct abuses became known as Puritans; those who saw no hope of changing the church withdrew and were thus called Separatists. It is from the latter group that the Baptists, including those who chose to worship on the seventh day of the week, emerged.

GROUPS INVOLVED IN CHANGE

Sociologists point to four ways people seek or react to change. These positions are determined by four factors: (a) the degree of change, (b) the direction of the change, (c) the speed of change, and (d) the means used to effect change.

---

[11] Franklin Littell, *The Free Church* (Boston: n.p., 1957) 114, cited by Robert G. Torbet, *A History of the Baptists*, 3rd ed. (1950; repr., Valley Forge PA: Judson Press, 1963) 30.

	Degree of change	Direction of change	Change how fast	Methods of change	Group
Reactionaries	Much	Past	Rapid	Violent if necessary	Catholics
Conservatives	Little or no	Present	Slow	Peaceful	Church of England
Liberals	Some	Future	Gradual	Peaceful	Puritans
Radicals	Much	Future	Rapid	Violent if necessary	Separatists

These questions point out four distinct types of groups:

(1) Reactionaries seek substantial, rapid return to past conditions and, if necessary, will resort to violent means.

(2) Conservatives seek little or no change. They want to preserve the *status quo* as peacefully as possible.

(3) Moderates want some gradual change to a future condition without violence.

(4) Radicals seek considerable, swift change to a future condition and, if necessary, will use rebellion.

In the continuing Reformation in England, all four of these positions can be identified. There continued to be reactionaries who wanted a return to Rome, and at times these rebels would use violent methods to effect that change. Conservatives were represented by the Church of England, which, as reflected in its acts of uniformity and prescribed ritual, wanted as little change as possible. The Puritans were the moderates who wanted to purify the Church of England from within. The fourth group was the radicals or "Separatists," who rejected many of the Church of England's doctrines and practices. These extremists wanted a complete change and were willing to take whatever steps were needed, including separation, to put their ideas into practice.

Because these distinctions are relative, as conditions changed, so did the labels. For example, the Puritans of one age were the conservatives and the reactionaries of another. Many of the Separatists lost their radical tendencies to become the moderates and conservatives of later generations. As one era's radicals became the next generation's moderates, other groups stepped up to take their place. In spite of this constant shift, it is helpful to examine the Puritans and the Separatists in relation to the changes and the choices they made during the critical years of the English Reformation.

Church of England

Religiously, Queen Elizabeth was a conservative. She accepted the role as head of the church she inherited from her father, Henry VIII. She saw the *Book of Common Prayer* as a necessary tool to preserve the integrity of worship. Working through Parliament, she decreed that all parish priests should read in church the exact words of the prayer book, without any omissions. To please some of the reactionaries with ties to Rome, she insisted that all parish priests should wear the vestments and continue much of the outward pageantry of worship. Clergy who did not obey were branded as nonconformists and were punished if they published any criticism of the church. S. T. Bindoff described the Church of England as appealing to the lukewarm multitude and enlisting their lukewarm support. Its chief merits were negative, for it had no pope nor Mass and "it lit no fires to consume men's bodies. The fact that it also kindled no flame in men's hearts, if hardly a merit, was less a defect in that most men's hearts were not inflammable."[12]

Puritans

The hearts of the more moderate and radical members of the church were easily inflamed. They wanted changes that would permit their souls to catch fire. The moderate voice was registered by the Puritans. They had been present from the beginning of the Elizabethan era but were less noticeable than the radical Separatists. It was not until the end of Queen Elizabeth's reign that the Puritans took on the major role that dominated so much of both the English and the American scene in the seventeenth century.

Queen Elizabeth left no direct heir to continue the Tudor line, so in 1603 Parliament turned to a cousin, James VI of Scotland, to take over the reign of both Scotland and England, thus beginning the Stuart reign in England. (He continued to be called James VI of Scotland, along with his title James I of England.) Although his mother, Mary Queen of Scots, was strongly Catholic and had been used by English reactionaries to try to overthrow Elizabeth, James was raised in the Presbyterian Church under the influence of John Knox.

---

[12] Bindoff, *Tudor England*, 224.

Some of the more moderate Anglican ministers saw this as a golden opportunity to make the changes they felt would purify the church. They prepared a long and carefully worded petition that they presented to James. Since it was the ministers' plan to secure the signatures of 1,000 Anglican clergymen, the petition became known as the Millenary Petition. The ministers' moderate position is reflected in their request that, in the case of offenses, "some may be removed, some amended, some qualified."[13] King James convened the Hampton Court Conference to deal with the petition.

Complaints towards the Church of England ranged from the "longsomeness" of the service to the quality of music, from the conduct and maintenance of ministers to discipline within the church. Petitioners asked for changes to the *Book of Prayer* and requested that practices such as the idolatrous use of the cross in worship be abolished, for such acts were not in accord with Scripture. Other requests asked for the dismissal of priests who could not or would not preach, the abandonment of many of the Saints' Days, and the observance of the Lord's Day as a holy day rather than as a holiday.

Some of the Puritans wanted to change the basic polity of the church from the episcopal form headed by the monarch to a presbyterian form with governance managed by small groups of elders within each congregation. James had had enough of this form of government in Scotland and was determined not to give up any of the supreme authority he held in the Church of England. It is reported that he ended the discussion with the reply, "A Scottish Presbytery as well agreeth with a monarchy as God and the Devil…. No bishops, no king…. No! I will make these Puritans reform or I will harry them out of the land, or worse."[14] James kept his word, and many of the Puritans were harried to Holland and eventually to America. This harrying caused many of the moderate Puritans to become radical Separatists.

One positive result of the conference was the decision to prepare a new translation of the Bible. This translation bearing King James's name had a greater effect on reform than any of the carefully worded petitions.

---

[13] "The Millenary Petition, 1603," in *Documents*, ed. Bettenson, 387.

[14] King James I, cited by Reginald D. Manwell and Sophia Lyon Fahs, *The Church Across the Street* (Boston: Beacon, 1947) 123.

Separatists

The Separatist movement in England is often associated with the radical reformer Robert Browne (1550–1633), who professed loyalty to the monarchy but grew impatient with its inability or unwillingness to act on reforms he believed were God's will. He began preaching without ordination and refused the laying on of hands by a bishop, claiming that this act had no meaning or authority. In his booklet *A Treatise on Reform without Tarrying for Any*, Browne called upon his congregation to act immediately, demanding reform rather than waiting for the state-controlled church to abolish its "popish ceremonies." Forced from his teaching position at Cambridge, Browne moved to Norwich, where he met with others who supported him.

At Norwich, Browne's services stood in sharp contrast to worship in the Church of England. He did not use the *Book of Prayer* for either the Scripture passages or prayers, but instead read directly from the Bible and composed his own prayers. He preached at least once a week rather than once a month as was the custom among many priests of his time. After each service he invited the congregation to discuss the message in accordance with the covenant they had drawn up, allowing "any member of the church to protest, appeal, complain, exhort, dispute, reprove, etc., as he had occasion."[15] This gathering is sometimes cited as the beginning of congregationalism.

As so often happens with radical groups, many Brownists far exceeded the radical positions of their leader. They referred to the cathedrals as Temples of the Antichrist and said that a person might worship just as well in barns. They claimed that pulpits were nothing but tubs and discarded anything that bore an emblem of the cross. Meetings were held in fields or in secret places to avoid arrest and persecution. Robert Browne himself was arrested on numerous occasions, and he wrote that he was confined in thirty-two different dungeons, some "so dark you could not see your hand before your face at mid-day."[16] In 1581 he and some of his followers fled to an island off the coast of Holland, which served as a haven for many European religious rebels. After about two years the congregation fell apart, largely over their rule calling for

---

[15] Cited by Manwell and Fahs, *The Church*, 119.
[16] Cited by Manwell and Fahs, *The Church*, 120.

"constant mutual criticism."[17] Browne's name is not revered with that of other Reformers, for he eventually returned to the Church of England and served as one of its priests for forty years.

Many of Brown's followers felt deserted but continued to meet in various communities to study the Bible, listen to sermons, and participate in religious discussions. Two of these communities, Scrooby and Gainsborough, stand out in history, not so much for the uniqueness of their gatherings, but because later churches trace their spiritual roots to these two congregations.

Congregationalists

The Scrooby congregation is considered the mother of the Congregational Churches. William Brewster, William Bradford, and John Robinson were among the congregation who in 1608 migrated to Holland where freedom of worship was granted. At Leyden they formed the group known as the Pilgrims, who sailed for America in 1620 aboard the Mayflower. Among those members of the Scrooby congregation who fled to Holland but did not come to America until a decade later was John Dunham. Nearly a century later in 1705, his grandson, Rev. Edmund Dunham, founded the Seventh Day Baptist Church in Piscataway, New Jersey.

Baptists

Baptist heritage is more closely related to the Gainsborough congregation, where John Smyth and Thomas Helwys were leaders. Their congregation left England around 1607. Soon after they arrived in Holland, they came under the influence of Anabaptist teachings through the Mennonites. Early in 1609, Smyth came to the decision that "infants ought not be baptized" for two scriptural reasons: (1) there is no example in the New Testament that any babies were baptized by either Jesus or the disciples, nor is there any biblical teaching that they should be, and (2) Christ commanded that the disciples were to teach and then baptize.[18] The issue at this point concerned the timing, not the mode, of baptism. Smyth chose believer's baptism rather than infant or paedobaptism. The method used in believer's baptism was effusion or pouring. It was not until several decades later that the practice of

---

[17] Henry Martyn Dexter and Morton Dexter, *The England and Holland of the Pilgrims* (Boston: Houghton, 1905) 199.

[18] See Torbet, *History of the Baptists*, 35.

baptism by immersion became commonly accepted as the mode most nearly reflected in the New Testament teachings.

Smyth's church in Amsterdam, founded on the principle of adult baptism in 1609, is considered the first truly Baptist church. Two years later the congregation split, with part remaining in Holland, where they eventually united with the Mennonites. The other part, led by Thomas Helwys, returned to England, where they settled at Spitalfields just outside of London. Smyth's teachings form the basis of many distinctive Baptist beliefs and practices. However, it is to Thomas Helwys that most English Baptists trace their heritage.

General and Particular Baptists

Helwys accepted Smyth's plea for liberty of conscience but expanded it to include the duty to witness of one's faith. Baptist missionary zeal grew out of the concept of a general or unlimited atonement. In contrast to the strict Calvinist doctrine of predestination, in which some are elected to salvation and some are predestined to damnation (often called particular or limited atonement), the General Baptists believed that Christ's atonement was sufficient for all, even though not all would accept. Helwys asked, "Is it not most equal that men should choose their religion themselves, seeing they only must stand themselves before the judgment seat of God to answer for themselves?"[19] To the General Baptists, the decision for Christ was registered in baptism.

There were, however, many strong Calvinists who chose the concept of adult baptism and congregational polity. Emerging later in the 1630s, this group came to be known as Particular Baptists, for they believed, like other Calvinists, that the work of Christ was intended for particular persons and that they—and they alone—were redeemed. Their position was stated by John Spilsberie, who wrote, "Christ hath not presented to His Father's justice a satisfaction for the sinnes of all men; but onely for the sinnes of those that doe, or shall believe in Him; which are His Elect onely."[20]

The differences between the General Baptists and the Particular Baptists created parallel traditions within the ranks of England's Baptist movement. There were both General and Particular Baptists among

---

[19] Thomas Helwys, quoted in W. T. Whitley, *A History of British Baptists* (London: Charles Griffin & Co., 1923) 33.

[20] John Spillsbury, cited by Whitley, *A History of British Baptists*, 66.

Seventh Day Baptists in England, yet these differences did not prevent fellowship and mutual witness to the distinctive doctrine of the Sabbath. Seventh Day Baptists were Separatists who, in addition to the other principles of congregational polity and believers' baptism, chose to accept the Sabbath of the Bible, the seventh day of the week, as their day of worship.

PART II: SABBATHKEEPING BAPTISTS IN ENGLAND

PART II TIMELINE:

Date/Reign/ Lifespan	Event/Monarch/Person
1599	Nicholas Bownde's *The Doctrine of the Sabbath*–Advocates 1st day Sabbath view
1601-1683	Peter Chamberlen
?-1680	William Saller
1601-1663	Henry Jessey
1603-1625	James I
?-1674	Thomas Tillam
	John Spittlehouse
?-1705	Edward Stennett
	Christopher Pooley
?-1695	John Belcher
1615-1684	Frances Bampfield
1617	John Traske keeping 7th Day Sabbath
1620	Pilgrims in Massachusetts
1625-1649	Charles I
1627-1706	Joseph Davis legacy
1628	Theophilus Brabourne's *Discourse Upon the Sabbath Day*—Advocates 7th day Sabbath view
1640-1649	English Civil War
1649-1659	Commonwealth Period (Oliver and Richard Cromwell)
1650-	James Ockford's *Doctrine of the Fourth Commandment*—1st book on 7th Day Sabbath by a Baptist
1650s	Baptists are keeping 7th day Sabbath
1657	First known Sabbathkeeping Baptist congregations (London- "Mill Yard"; Tillam (Colchester)
1660-1685	Charles II (Restoration of the Monarchy)
1661	John James martyred
1663-1713	Joseph Stennett

1663	Rhode Island Charter
1664	New Jersey to England
1665	Stephen and Ann Mumford emigrate to Newport, Rhode Island
1668	Stennett: "9 or 10 churches in England"
1668	First correspondence between American and English Sabbathkeepers
1679	English-American SDB General meeting proposed
1681	Pennsylvania Charter
1685-1689	James II
1689	Act of Toleration
1689-1702	William & Mary
1702-1714	Anne

3

THE SABBATH IN ENGLAND

As the sixteenth century drew to a close and the Tudor reign gave way to Stuart rule, changes were taking place in the minds of many English people. The reactionary element, which sought a return to Rome, was silenced. The conservatism of the Church of England had been challenged by the moderate forces of Puritanism, which wanted changes to the forms of organization and worship of the church. The radical Separatists took reform a step further as they moved away from the episcopal and presbyterian forms of organization toward a congregationalism that allowed the freedom to worship as one chose. Yet, in spite of these differences, there was one matter on which most Christians of the time appeared to agree. Nearly all took for granted the long-established custom of holding some form of worship or assembly on Sunday, the first day of the week.

A DAY OF WORSHIP

Worship on Sunday had been well ingrained in the habits of the people for over twelve centuries. Some may have questioned its origin, but few voices seemed to challenge its validity for several reasons. First, it served the purpose of providing time for worship and instruction. Most agreed on the need of a day for rest and worship. They felt secure in the fact that God had commanded a day of rest, without questioning which day it should be. William Tyndale (1494–1536), who translated the Bible during the time of Henry VIII, wrote of this need, suggesting that "we be lords over the Sabbath, and may yet change it into the Monday or any other day as we see need,...if we see cause why." He even suggested that perhaps we did not need any holy day "if the people might be taught without it."[1]

Secondly, a strong anti-Jewish attitude had influenced the church since the days of the Crucifixion. So strong was this sentiment that Christian leaders used a few passages of Scripture to support or justify tradition rather than searching for more accurate biblical interpretations,

---

[1] William Tyndale, "Answer to Sir Thomas More's Dialogue," in *The Works of English Reformers: William Tyndale and John Frith*, 3 vols., ed. Thomas Russell (London: Samuel Bentley, 1831) 2:101.

which supported the tradition of Sabbath on Saturday. John Frith, a close associate of Tyndale, described the manner in which the forefathers of the church had substituted Sunday for the Sabbath as an example of Christian liberty. He maintained that it was necessary to set aside a day for people to come together to hear the Word of God, but that the church forefathers had "ordained in the stead of the Sabbath, which was Saturday, the next day following, which is Sunday." He added that they might have retained the Jewish tradition, but it was better to "overset the day and not be bound to any day." In summarizing this thought, which was shared by many others of the time, he wrote:

> We are in manner as superstitious in the Sunday as they were in the Saturday, yea, and we are much madder. For the Jews have the Word of God for their Saturday, since it is the seventh day, and they were commanded to keep the seventh day solemn; and we have not the word of God for us, but rather against us, for we keep not the seventh day as the Jews do, but the first, which is not commanded by God's law.[2]

To be accused of being a Jew during the days of the Tudors and Stuarts could cause a person to lose his citizenship as well as his church membership.

Thirdly, there had grown up in England a great deal of indifference toward any day as being deemed particularly solemn or religious. In a pleasure-starved society, any break from the normal work week was treated as a holiday without serious regard for either its purpose or its origin. However, as the Scriptures became more readily available, and people began to study them as the basis for beliefs and practices, it was only natural that the question of the biblical Sabbath would enter into the collective consciousness.

NICOLAS BOWNDE'S BOOK ON THE SABBATH

The most important writing on the Sabbath during the period, printed in 1595, was a book by Nicolas Bownde titled *The Doctrine of the Sabbath*. Its primary purpose was to secure a biblical basis for a strict, disciplined observance of Sunday. Bownde traced the biblical origin of the Sabbath and emphasized how God blessed and sanctified the Sabbath on the seventh day. He wrote that it was "as needful [sic] for the

---

[2] John Frith, "A Declaration of Baptism," in *The Works of English Reformers*, ed. Russell, 3:294-95.

Lord…to tell us which was the day, as to tell us that there ought to be a day." He ended this portion of the argument by stating that "the Sabbath must needs be still upon the seventh day as it alwais hath beene."[3]

It was at this point that Nicholas Bownde completely reversed himself. He departed from the use of Scripture as the source of doctrine and resorted to proof-texts to support a change in the day of worship. He wrote:

> Concerning this very special seventh day that now we keepe in the time of the Gospell…that it is not the same it was from the beginning which God himselfe sanctifie…all men must keepe holy this seventh day, and none other, which was unto them not the seventh, but the first day of the weeke as it is so called many times in the New Testament, and so it still standeth in force, that we are bound unto the seventh day, though not that very seventh"[4]

In other words, Bownde drew a distinction between *the* seventh day, which is the Sabbath of the Bible, and *this* seventh day, which he held to be the first day.

Aside from two passages of Scripture taken out of context, Bownde's justification for a changed day rests almost completely on traditions and the writings of second- and third-century church fathers. Thus, he demonstrated not only a change of doctrine concerning the day of worship but a change in his source for authority and doctrine. Dr. A. H. Lewis observed that "it is difficult to understand how Mr. Bownde could be so blinded to the legitimate deductions from his own arguments as to talk of a change of day. But so strong were his prejudices against what he calls Judaism that he clings to the Sunday, supporting his claim with a broken reed."[5]

Bownde did rely on the Scriptures for reproof and correction of an almost Sabbathless society. He cited arguments for the necessity of resting on this changed Sabbath with examples of the punishment that came to those who did not rest from their labors. He insisted that the first day must not be called Sunday, for that is derived from paganism as the day of the sun, but should be called "the Lord's Day." In his arguments he seldom used the Lord's Day designation but continued to

---

[3] Nicholas Bownde, *The Doctrine of the Sabbath…* (London: Widdow Orwin, 1595) 32-35.
[4] Ibid., 35.
[5] Abram Herbert Lewis, *Critical History of the Sabbath and the Sunday…* (Alfred Center NY: American Sabbath Tract Society, 1886) 300-301.

refer to the first day as the Sabbath, since he relied on biblical passages that used the term "Sabbath."

The second part of Bownde's work was devoted almost exclusively to specific practices that should mark the Sabbath observance. He favored simplicity of worship and strictness of rest from labor. In elevating the first day of the week to the established day of worship, Bownde insisted that most other festival days should be abandoned, since they had either Jewish or pagan origins.

State Reactions

Bownde's book had considerable impact on seventeenth-century churches. To the Church of England, it confirmed the idea that the church had the power and the precedent to establish doctrine and practice. On the other hand, these established churches opposed the strictness of the day. So restrictive was the "Puritan Sabbath" that in 1618 King James I published *The Book of Sports*, which legalized many of the Sunday activities the Puritans were seeking to abolish. This book recognized the people's complaint that they were "barred from all lawful recreation and exercise on Sunday afternoon after attending divine worship." It raised two main objections. First, the ban deprived the people of "honest mirth" and exercises that might "make their bodies more able for war, when we shall have occasion to use them." Secondly, by providing people no outlet for exercise or recreation, the ban encouraged "tippling and drunkenness."

To offset these potentially dangerous consequences, the king ordered that no lawful recreation should be barred. Lest there be any question as to what might be considered lawful, the king included as lawful recreation such things as dancing, archery, and consumption of Whitsun ale. He prohibited certain unlawful games on Sunday, such as bear- and bull-baiting and bowling.[6] *The Book of Sports* made it plain that no such concessions would be made to those who "abstained from coming to church or divine services." It stipulated that each person must attend his own parish church, that no recreation could begin before the end of all divine services for that day, and that no offensive weapon could be carried or used in the said times of recreation.[7]

---

[6] *The Book of Sports, 1618*, in *Documents of the Christian Church*, ed. Henry Bettenson (New York: Oxford University Press, 1947) 389-91.

[7] Ibid.

Puritan Reactions

To the Puritans, Bownde's book was used to give Scriptural basis for their Sabbath observance, proof-texting ideas they already held. The list of things they could and could not do gave the Puritans the ammunition needed to reprove and correct the daily activities of each individual. This book supported the stern Calvinistic discipline of the time, which promised punishment for all lawbreakers and demonstrated who might be considered among the elect.

However, even among the Puritans, Bownde's book caused problems in its overzealous applications. Thomas Rogers, writing in 1607, stated that such writings "hath been the mother of many heretical assertions and horrible conclusions." He cited examples of sermons that claimed that "to do any servile work or business on the Lord's day was as great a sin as to kill a man or commit adultery"; that "to throw a bowl on the Sabbath was as great a sin as to kill a man"; or that "to make a feast or wedding dinner on the Lord's day is as great a sin as for a father to take a knife and cut his child's throat." Even "to ring more than one bell upon the Lord's day to call people into the church was as great a sin as to commit murder."[8]

As a result of this type of preaching, Bownde's book was banned. Disraeli considered this book to be the source of the conflict that agitated the reigns of both James and Charles, concerning "the mode in which Sunday should be observed, whether with the rigour of a Jewish Sabbath, or with the recreations of a Christian holiday."[9] The banning of Bownde's book did not stop its impact, for as Thomas Fuller noted, the price of the book doubled "and many who hear not of them when printed inquire after them when prohibited.[10]

Separatist Reactions

To the Separatists, who used the Bible as the only source of teaching and doctrine, Bownde's book posed a serious dilemma. His early argument for the Sabbath they could accept, but there were a few who could not justify the change of day nor the use of Scriptures to support

[8] Thomas Rogers, *The Catholic Doctrine of the Church of England: An Exposition...*, ed. J. J. S. Perowne (Cambridge: Cambridge University Press, 1854) 19.
[9] Benjamin Disraeli, *Life of Charles I* (London: Henry Colburn, 1851) 2:17, quoted in Robert Cox, *The Literature of the Sabbath Question*, 2 vols. (Edinburgh: MacLachlan & Stewart, 1865) 1:148.
[10] Fuller, quoted in Cox, *Literature of the Sabbath Question*, 1:147-48.

the change. In succeeding years, the strict observance of Sunday was enforced by civil authorities, making it difficult for those who believed in the seventh-day Sabbath to openly preach or practice their convictions.

EARLY SABBATH PROPONENTS

It was more than a half-century later before any church body separated over the matter of the Sabbath. However, there were individual Christians who began to accept the seventh-day Sabbath and worship on that day, often while they maintained membership in and communion with other churches.

John and Dorothy Traske

The name John Traske has sometimes been associated with the beginning of seventh-day Sabbath observance in England. Around 1617 Traske came to London, where he gained a reputation as a powerful preacher. Among his followers was a tailor named Hamlet Jackson, who had studied the Scriptures on his own. He lacked formal training, but his study of the "plain text" convinced him that many of the Old Testament provisions remained valid and had not been abrogated by the New Testament. He convinced Traske that the seventh-day Sabbath commanded by Scripture was still valid. Traske and most of his followers adopted the seventh-day Sabbath observance.

Traske's acceptance of the Sabbath probably would not have subjected him to the persecution that followed had he not challenged the established churches on other points. He observed other Jewish festivals and followed closely the dietary restrictions prescribed by Jewish law. On 19 June 1618, Traske was sentenced in Star Chamber (an English court of law) for "having a fantasticall opynion of himselfe with ambicion to bee the Father of a Jewish faccion." He was also charged with having written two scandalous letters to the king. He was subjected to many indignities, among them a sentence of life imprisonment, a heavy fine, and expulsion from the ministry.[11]

In prison, Traske chose to live on bread-and-water rations rather than eat the pork that the court had fiendishly prescribed for him. After about a year in prison, Traske recanted and returned to the Church of England. In a writing titled *A Treatise of Libertie from Judaism*, he tried to

---

[11] Quoted in David S. Katz, *Philo-Semitism and the Readmission of the Jews to England*, 1603–1655 (Oxford: Clarendon Press, 1982) 24. For an eyewitness report, see J. Ussher, *Works*, ed. C. R. Elrington and J. M. Todd (Dublin: Hodges & Smith, 1847–1864) 16:359.

dissuade his followers from defending the doctrines he had once advocated. One who was not moved by his writing was his wife Dorothy, who remained in prison for about fifteen years until her death around 1643. Another of Traske's followers, Returne Hebdon, spent about eight years in prison until his death in about 1625.

There is no evidence that Traske was ever associated with any church that later became known as a Seventh Day Baptist church, but he cannot be dismissed as unimportant in the development of Sabbath doctrine. He provided one of the first forums in England to seriously consider the question.[12]

Theophilus Brabourne

King James was succeeded in 1625 by his son Charles, whose marriage to the French Catholic Henrietta Maria made him friendly to Roman Catholics. He strongly opposed the Puritanism that had dominated much of his father's reign. Although James was in many ways very different from the Puritans, he avoided the open clash that in Charles's reign would end in the English Civil War and the execution of the king. James had appointed a Puritan, George Abbot, as Archbishop of Canterbury, but when Abbot died in 1633, Charles appointed an avowed opponent of Puritanism, William Laud. Laud antagonized the Puritans by perpetrating such acts as concentrating worship into one formalized ceremony as prescribed by the *Book of Common Prayer* and by showing no concern for recreation following public worship.

Such a shift in emphasis inevitably led many to reconsider the whole question of the biblical Sabbath and the church's practice of observing the Lord's Day on Sunday. The most prominent voice during this period was that of Theophilus Brabourne, a priest in the Church of England. In 1628, he published *A Discourse upon the Sabbath Day*, in which he attempted to persuade the Church of England to accept the validity of the seventh-day Sabbath.

Brabourne maintained that the Fourth Commandment was still in effect, that it had not changed, and that any meetings of the disciples that may have been on the first day were not to be taken as sufficient grounds for any change unless accompanied by a specific command. His writing stirred such debate within the church that in 1632 he wrote *A Defence Of the most Ancient and Sacred ordinance of God's, the Sabbath Day*, which was directed against "all Anti-Sabbatharians, both of Protestants, Papists,

---

[12] Katz, *Philo-Semitism*, 18.

Antinomians, and Anabaptists."[13] As punishment for publishing this book, Brabourne was imprisoned by the church.

In spite of his strong belief in the seventh-day Sabbath, Brabourne maintained his membership within the Church of England, hoping that acceptance of the Sabbath would reform the church. In calling for reform, he maintained an episcopal polity stating that any reformation must come from the king and Parliament, whom he called the "master builders who lay the stones." He recognized the responsibility of the common people to influence these builders, referring to the common people as helpers who hew the stone and carry them to the building.[14]

Although Brabourne was firmly convinced of the seventh-day Sabbath, he himself did not observe it. Thus, in the aforementioned 1632 defense of the Sabbath, he defended his own position during what he termed a dispensation. He wrote that "a man is not bound in all cases, and at all times, to put in practise what he knoweth should be done." He cited such biblical examples as David's sparing of Joab, his eating of the "shewbread," and the permission Moses granted for divorce.[15]

Throughout his defense, Brabourne stressed the fact that his position was only intended for a season, until the truth of the Sabbath should be accepted by the church as a whole. His writings may have influenced a number to accept the Sabbath, but his rationalizations and personal example may have kept others from fully accepting and completely observing the Sabbath. His hope of general Sabbath reform was never realized in his day, nor has it been in any time following. Yet, the dialogue of this period showed that many people were being challenged by the questions raised. In 1660, Brabourne wrote another book in which he claimed that the Sabbath day debate was the highest controversy in the Church of England.[16]

That the Sabbath should reach such a position of importance in the church is due largely to the efforts of those who historically can be considered Seventh Day Baptists. They are the ones who followed the suggestions of Brabourne to make their teachings known and who took

---

[13] Theophilus Brabourne, *A Defence of...Sabbath Day*, 2nd ed. (London: n.p., 1632) title pg.

[14] Brabourne, "An Exhortation to a Speedy Reformation," in *Defence*, 609-610.

[15] Brabourne, "A Dispensation," in *Defence*, 592.

[16] Theophilus Brabourne, *Of the Sabbath day, Which is now the highest controversie in the Church of England* (N.p., ca. 1660), quoted by Oscar Burdick in "The Great Decade," unpublished manuscript, 1989, Seventh Day Baptist Historical Society Archives, p. 27.

the next step to actually practice their convictions. It is to them that attention is now focused.

4

BAPTISTS IN ENGLAND WHO
CHOSE TO KEEP THE SABBATH

Perhaps no other time or place in history had as great a potential for the wide acceptance of the seventh-day Sabbath as mid-seventeenth-century England. The Sabbath was discussed and debated among the laity and the highest clergy. Even Parliament could not escape the implications of the Sabbath's importance. As in the time of Joshua, people's choices were influenced by tradition and by the political and social conditions of the time.

POLITICAL CLIMATE

Seventh Day Baptists emerged in England near the end of a period of considerable political change. For eleven years (1629–1640), Charles I ruled England without convening Parliament. For nine years (1640–1649), Parliament was engaged in a continuing struggle against the monarchy to regain some of its lost powers. This struggle culminated in civil war and the king's execution. For the next eleven years (1649–1660), Parliament ruled without a king. The monarchy was eventually restored to a leader with Roman Catholic leanings. These political changes had considerable effect on religious thinking and practice.

The English Civil War and execution of Charles I brought Oliver Cromwell to power. Cromwell was a Puritan who believed that the English people were the "chosen people of God." He was anxious to uphold justice and promote Christian well-being. However, having gained power through revolution and the force of an army, Cromwell found it difficult to work within the confines of parliamentary procedure. During his effort to replace the Common Law with the Law of Moses, he had trouble working with those in Parliament who did not share his Puritan views. One of the checks on Cromwell's power was the enactment of a law that granted liberty of Christian worship, yet this law also limited that liberty with the words: "this liberty be not extended to Popery and Prelacy, nor to such as, under the profession of Christ, hold forth and practice blasphemy and licentiousness."[1] Religious liberty, in this case, did not equal religious freedom as we would understand it, as the beliefs of individuals were still subservient to the commonwealth and the Church of England.

FREEDOM OF CHOICE BRINGS SUSPICION

Religious freedom in England encouraged the development of many independent congregations. In theory, people were free to choose their manner of worship without the threat of governmental interference, but it takes more than a proclamation to ensure freedom. B. R. White, in his history of the English Baptists of this period, wrote that the universal toleration held by many, including Baptists, seemed to more conservative churchmen "merely a demand that every man should be free to choose his own road to hell."[2]

Suspicion on the part of the established churches was not without reason. The execution of King Charles was viewed as a religious as well as a political rebellion, for it was considered to be a transgression against God's anointed. This new era of biblical freedom of thought and expression unleashed a hoard of the untrained and often illiterate, who were called "mechanic preachers." Many wild practices and heretical doctrines were advanced causing suspicion concerning any who deviated from the norm.

Vulnerability of Baptists

Baptists were particularly vulnerable to being singled out as enemies of the state for a number of reasons, both real and imagined. Under the monarchy, most Englishmen felt a sense of belonging, for they were a part of a kingdom ruled by one believed to be divinely appointed. During the Commonwealth period, this sense of belonging was transferred to the church into which each individual was born and baptized. Infant baptism neatly tied together the church and community. By contrast, Baptists denied this connection of church and community by birth. They believed the church was a community of believers who entered through personal choice and commitment. In addition to this

---

[1] Maurice Ashley, *England in the Seventeenth Century* (New York: Barnes & Noble, 1980) 109.

[2] B. R. White, *The English Baptists of the Seventeenth Century*, ed. B. R. White, A History of the English Baptists series, 4 vols. (London: Baptist Historical Society, 1983) 1:30.

basic difference in the concept of the church, Baptists suffered from other misconception springing from their core convictions.

Guilt by Association

The diversity of ideas and practices among Baptists gave grounds for opponents to unfairly judge them by associating with a number of unpopular causes. First, Baptists were often called Anabaptists because the two groups shared some similarities in basic beliefs. The English Baptists, however, did not want to be identified with the Anabaptists on the Continent for two main reasons: (1) The name tended to associate them with some of the more radical Anabaptists, such as the participants of the 1535 Munster rebellion in Germany that, for over a century, had stood for wild-eyed religious fanaticism, and (2) Baptists wanted to make it plain that their doctrines and practices were based on the study of the Bible itself, rather than doctrinal reliance on other movements.

Second, there were Baptists who became involved in social and political movements that were considered a threat to the government. As early as 1649, a Baptist named James Toppe wrote to a friend about "Christ's monarchial and personall reign uppon earth over the kingdoms of the world...in wych is also shewed the tyme when this kingdom shall begin and where it shall be."[3] In 1652, an eclipse of the sun was seen as a sign that there would be a "glorious rising of the Fifth Monarch" in fulfillment of a prophecy in Daniel, which these "Fifth Monarchists" interpreted to mean the ushering in by force of the reign of Christ. The Fifth Monarchy movement was never large, but it was seen as a threat to both Cromwell and, later, after the restoration of the monarchy, Charles II. Fifth Monarchists believed that the Second Coming was due at any moment and that, until that event occurred, the Fifth Monarchists were the men entitled to rule.

A number of Baptists were associated with this movement, including a sufficient number of Sabbathkeepers, leading some historians to conclude that Seventh Day Baptists were an offshoot of the Fifth Monarchists.[4] The movement reached its peak in January 1661 when one of its leaders, Thomas Venner, led an unsuccessful uprising to overthrow Charles II, who had just returned from exile in France. A

---

[3] Quoted by W. T. Whitley, "SDBs in England," *Baptist Quarterly* 12/8 (Oct 1947): 252.

[4] W. T. Whitley, "A Century of Sabbath Doctrine, 1595–1695" (1911), ms. copied by Charles Henry Greene (C. H. Greene Papers, notebook 10, pp. 80-178, SDB Hist. Soc. Lib.). A later version was published by W. T. Whitley as "Men of the Seventh Day."

Seventh Day Baptist preacher, John James, was martyred in 1661 for his Fifth Monarchist views.

Third, the suspicion directed toward all Baptists was especially intense against Seventh Day Baptists because of their supposed association with the Jews. The admission of Jews into England during the general tolerance under the Commonwealth caused many to become wary of any who kept the seventh day as a Sabbath. Most Christian writers of the period who championed the Sabbath of the Bible made specific denial of being Jewish, although some believed that the ultimate aim of the admission of Jews into England was to convert them. Many believed that once the Jews were exposed to the clear Christian light of the Protestant Reformation, they would embrace Jesus. Some later Seventh Day Baptists targeted Jews for evangelism since they were already Sabbathkeepers and needed only to accept Jesus as the Messiah.

SEVENTH DAY BAPTISTS EMERGE DURING
THE GREAT DECADE, 1650–1660

In spite of suspicions and opposition, the period of the Commonwealth following the beheading of King Charles I was a decade of religious as well as political change. After years of authoritarianism on the part of the crown and the established church, there existed a period of relative freedom during which the populace could find and develop personal identity both politically and religiously. Seventh Day Baptists trace their beginnings as a separate denomination to this decade.

Some events in history can be dated precisely by decisive events or actions. There are, however, some movements within history that have no clear beginning, but came as a result of ideas that took root and slowly matured. Several factors in the process of maturing have made it difficult for historians to place an exact date on the origins of Seventh Day Baptists as a distinct people. Among these factors were anonymity of authorship of materials that were clearly Seventh Day Baptist, volatility of religious convictions during this period, and the similarity of doctrine with the doctrines of other religious groups.

To avoid suspicion and danger of persecution, some Seventh Day Baptists wrote anonymously or used initials rather than full names. Some records—such as those of the Tewkesbury Baptist Church, which contain the names of Stephen and Anne Mumford, the first Seventh Day Baptists in America—were written in code. Varied name spellings have also complicated efforts to identify the authors. For example, James

Ockford's name was sometimes spelled "Oakeford"; Peter Chamberlen can be found as "Chamberlain"; and William Saller's name appeared as "Salter," "Seller," or "Sellers."

Second, beliefs underwent change as people began to experience freedom of thought and expression. B. R. White observed that many people's convictions changed "at breakneck speed" so that a person might be "a loyal adherent to his parish church in 1644 and then by turns a Presbyterian, an Independent, a Baptist, a seeker and, before the restoration of Charles II in 1660, a Quaker." He cautioned that it was unwise to assume that a person remained in a particular group "at the moment when some fragment of evidence brings him to the historian's notice."[5]

A third difficulty in establishing specific dates for the formation of local churches is the fact that although individuals may have held distinctive beliefs concerning the Sabbath or baptism, they shared most other tenets of faith with other churches. Thus, a number of those whom historians might claim as Seventh Day Baptists by virtue of doctrine were actually participating members of churches that worshipped on Sunday. Some even served as pastors of other churches while maintaining private or small-group worship on the Sabbath.

THE FIRST SEVENTH DAY BAPTISTS

In spite of these difficulties, there is sufficient evidence to claim a date in the early years of the 1650s as the birth date for Seventh Day Baptists. This information comes from two sources: (1) their own writings and records, and (2) the writings and actions recorded by opponents who attempted to refute their positions.

James Ockford

The first known document to support the seventh-day Sabbath by a Baptist was written by James Ockford. In 1650 he published a book in London that bore the title *The Doctrine of the Fourth Commandment, Deformed by Popery, Reformed & Restored to its Primitive purity.* Its publication caused such concern in Salisbury that the mayor asked the Speaker of the English Parliament what should be done, since the book undermined the observance of the "Lord's day." The mayor referred the matter to a committee of Parliament, which recommended that all copies

---

[5] White, *English Baptists*, 31.

be burned and the author punished. Only one copy is known to have escaped the flames.

Ockford assured his readers that he was fully Christian, saying, "I am no Jew, nor inclined to any Jewish opinions; I seek not righteousnesse by the Law, but by faith in the Son of God, according to the Gospel."[6] He saw the Sabbath as a delight and a joy, stating, "happy shall the Church be, that worshippeth God according to his Law, and giveth him his due, by placing on the Seventh day, the honour which God requireth to be performed on it."[7]

Ockford had no chance to defend his writing at the time it was condemned. Other writers, however, took up the issues he raised. Daniel Cawdry, in a book titled *Sabbatum*, devoted several pages to refuting Ockford's book. Theophilus Brabourne, who continued to write on the Sabbath from within the Church of England, made note of Ockford's book in a response to Cawdry. Even Parliament took steps to strengthen the observance of Sunday by passing new laws.

An Anonymous Writer

It is possible that the burning of Ockford's book caused others to write anonymously. One such anonymous book is the first known work on the Sabbath that also calls for believers' baptism by immersion. This work, published in 1652 under the title *The Moralitie of the fourth commandment*, pointed out the inconsistent beliefs of those who rejected the Sabbath as Jewish while using the rite of circumcision to support infant baptism. The author called for baptism by immersion, writing, "First see the heart Baptized in the blood of Christ, then bring the body to be washed in pure water, the whole body, not a part, washed, not sprinkled."[8]

This anonymous writer displayed the tolerant attitude that has generally marked Seventh Day Baptists in their relations to those who keep Sunday. While most of the book speaks strongly for the seventh-day Sabbath and refutes Sunday as being contrary to the Bible, he calls for readers to remember "that God hath called us into Peace and Love,

---

[6] James Ockford, *The Doctrine of the Fourth Commandment...* (London: n.p., 1650) 71. Only one known copy exists at Christ Church College, Oxford, England (microfilm, MF 1986.76, SDB Hist. Soc. Lib.).

[7] Ockford, 58.

[8] *The moralitie of the fourth commandment* (1652) M26171A, UMI, National Library of Scotland, Edinburgh, p. 86.

not to Contention and Bitterness; and let everyone walke, not offending other Brethren in their practice."[9]

William Saller

The first pastor of record to lead a Seventh Day Baptist church was probably William Saller of the congregation later known as the Mill Yard Church in London. About the year 1653, writing under the name W. Salter, he published a booklet titled *Sundry Queries tendered to such as are, or profess themselves to be Ministers of Jesus Christ, for clearing the Doctrine of the Fourth Commandment. And the Lord's Sabbath Day.*[10] Saller is mentioned as pastor by Thomas Tillam of Colchester, who in 1657 reported a communication from London confirming that congregations were meeting every Sabbath and that a Brother Saller was a part of one.[11] The first record book of that church was destroyed in a fire, but the second book (now in the possession of the Seventh Day Baptist Historical Society) begins with the date 1673 and indicates that Saller was then, and had for some time been, the pastor. This record book identifies Saller and his congregation with a church that has become known as the Mill Yard Seventh Day Baptist Church.[12]

In 1657, Saller and John Spittlehouse wrote an appeal to the chief magistrates. They were concerned that laws requiring cessation of labor on Sunday would cause hardship to those who would be forced to give up work on a second day each week if they observed the seventh day as a day of Sabbath rest. Thus, out of economic necessity, some who believed in the seventh day had "to break the Lords Sabbath, and to observe that of Mans erecting."[13] For close to three decades, Saller continued to write and preach his convictions. Twelve of his books have been identified, eleven of which are known to still exist today.[14]

---

[9] Ibid., 6.

[10] William Saller, *Sundry Queries tendered to such as are, or profess themselves to be Ministers of Jesus Christ, for clearing the Doctrine of the Fourth Commandment. And the Lord's Sabbath Day* (N.p., ca.1653).

[11] Thomas Tillam, *The Seventh Day Sabbath Sought Out and Celebrated* (Regents Park, Oxford/British Library, London: n.p., 1657 ed.).

[12] Mill Yard, London, Eng. SDB Church Records, 1673–1845, ms., CRR 1932.1, SDB Hist. Soc. Lib.

[13] Wm. Saller and John Spittlehouse, *An Appeal to the Consciences...* (N.p., 1657) 12, cited by Burdick, "Decade," 19.

[14] Oscar Burdick, "Sleuthing the Origins of English SDBs in the 1650s: A Bibliography," in *Summary Proceedings of the 38th Annual Conference of the American Theological Library Association*, ed. Betty A. O'Brien (Holland MI: Western Theological Seminary, Jun 1984) 139.

Henry Jessey

Associated with Saller was Henry Jessey, pastor of a famous London dissenting church known as the Jacob-Lathrop-Jessey church; the church had been founded as an independent church in 1616 by Henry Jacob. Its second pastor was Reverend John Lathrop, who served the church for eight years. In 1632 Lathrop was apprehended along with about forty others for dissenting and refusing to take an oath. After two years in prison, Lathrop was released on the provision that he leave England. In 1634 he sailed for Massachusetts, where he pastored churches in Scituate and Barnstable.[15] Several families from these churches, including Lathrop's own descendents, were later associated with the Seventh Day Baptist church founded in 1705 at Piscataway, New Jersey.

The history of Jessey's church is important in the development of belief and practice concerning baptism. In polity, the church was congregational and supported open membership, accepting individuals who had been baptized as infants as well as those baptized as adults. (Jessey himself was baptized in 1644.) Some of its members chose to emphasize believers' baptism as an essential sign of the elect, which in the 1630s caused several groups to split from the church to form the first Particular Baptist congregations.

Henry Jessey's acceptance of the Sabbath, probably around 1653, did not cause him to leave the pastorate of his church. His biographer has written that for two years he "kept his opinion much to himself" and observed the day in his own Chamber with four or five others but "on the first day he preached as before."[16]

Jessey seldom attempted to force his doctrines on others. He published a *Scripture Almanac* whose calendar bore the word *Sabbath* on each seventh day. Although Jessey was among the pastors linked to the Fifth Monarchy movement, he was listed with those who used the impending approach of the Lord's return to spur evangelism.

Dr. Peter Chamberlen

One of the best-known names associated with early Seventh Day Baptists is that of Dr. Peter Chamberlen, personal physician to James I,

---

[15] See: Amos Otis, *Genealogical Notes of Barnstable Families*, 2 vols. (Barnstable MA: F. B. & F. P. Goss, 1888) 2:170-88.

[16] Edward Whiston, *The Life and Death of Mr. Henry Jessey* (N.p., 1671) 87, quoted by Burdick, "Decade," 7.

Charles I, and Charles II. He wrote extensively in the fields of medicine, public health, and social and economic reform. His tombstone dates his death at 1683 and states that he had kept the seventh-day Sabbath "above 32 years." This would place his conversion to the Sabbath at about 1651. In one of his last writings, published in 1682, he claims to have been the first to endeavor to rescue the Sabbath, but in light of evidence now available about others' earlier writings, this might imply, as Oscar Burdick has suggested, "an elderly man of strong personality writing less than precise history...."[17]

One of Dr. Chamberlen's strongest stands on the Sabbath occurred as he participated in a 1659 debate held at the Stone Chapel beside St. Paul's Cathedral in London. Jeremiah Ives spoke against the Saturday Sabbath, while Dr. Chamberlen, Thomas Tillam, and Matthew Coppinger spoke for the Sabbath. Ives published an account of the debate in his book *Saturday No Sabbath*, which was addressed to "The Believers in Christ, especially they who are in bondage to the Jewish Sabbath, and more particularly those in Colchester." His report of "hundreds of people" at the debate showed the extent to which the question was being raised during that decade.

Before the Stone Chapel debate was over, the House of Commons appointed a subcommittee "to consider how to suppress the meetings of Quakers, Popists...and the setters up of the Jewish worship." Some historians interpret this statement as being specifically directed against the increasing interest Christians were showing in the Sabbath during this time of renewed Bible study and independent worship.

That same year, a meeting of the Abingdon Baptist Association reported two members who observed the seventh-day Sabbath yet did not forsake the church. A church at Watford cast out eight members who apparently had accepted the Sabbath, neglected the church meeting, and refused communion. The Abingdon Baptist Association called another meeting involving three churches to decide how far they could walk together with those who held to the seventh-day Sabbath or in what instances they could have communion together. Those at the meeting recommended "that in case nothing else should be found amiss but the bare observing of the 7th day Sabbath, then the saying of the apostle in Ro.14.1,5f, might be well minded." (Romans 14:1ff reflects the Apostle Paul's conviction that those who worship on different days should be convinced in their own minds.) One church reported that it had been

---

[17] Burdick, "Decade," 5-6.

spared from "the spreading errours of the time, viz.,...quakers and of those that hold the Seventh-day Sabbath."[18]

Thomas Tillam

Another person involved in the Stone Chapel Debate was Thomas Tillam, a minister from Colchester, a city about 45 miles northeast of London. Records indicate that in May 1656, Tillam had requested of Oliver Cromwell and the Council of London a place for a congregation to meet in Colchester. Since the council had received a good report of Tillam's piety and ability, they urged the mayor and aldermen of Colchester to provide a suitable place for Tillam and his group to meet. This action shows that churches still depended on the state considerably for support. The city apparently gave Tillam a parish church in which to hold meetings. In 1660, Tillam wrote that the Sabbath church of Colchester met in a "steeple house," a derogatory term Dissenters used for parish (Church of England) buildings usually called "churches."

Tillam's book, *The Seventh Day Sabbath sought out and celebrated,*[19] published in 1657, is significant for two reasons. First, it contains the reference to the letter mentioned in connection with Saller that is the first actual documentation of Sabbath congregations in London. Second, two versions of the book, both carrying the same date, show that Tillam was shifting in his thinking. The earlier edition shows support for both Saturday and Sunday as days of worship; in this edition Tillam stated that he hoped Christians could embrace the opportunities and privileges the first day offered for worship. In the later edition, he stated that even though it was true he had "pleaded the first dayes preheminence as a rejoycing day," he admitted that his "affection had out run judgement."[20] He cautioned against celebrating communion on Sunday but did not object to persons attending preaching services, so long as it did not hinder the six-day labor requirement.

By the end of the decade, Tillam's position had changed so much that he wrote of the Sabbath that "tis time to withdraw from such as cannot endure to hear of it."[21] He had earlier observed that Jews were

---

[18] Abingdon Baptist Association, *Association Records of the Particular Baptists of England...*, 4 vols., ed. B. R. White (London: Baptist Historical Society, 1971–1974) 3:190-95.

[19] Tillam, *The Seventh Day Sabbath Sought Out.*

[20] Tillam, *The Lasher Proved Lyar* (London: n.p., ca. 1658) 9, cited by Burdick in "Decade," 17.

[21] Tillam, *The Temple of Lively Stones* (N.p., 1660) 386, cited by Burdick in "Decade," Jun 1984, MS 1992.42, SDB Hist. Soc. Lib., 20.

attracted to the Sabbath worship of the Sabbatarian Christian groups. He may have been influenced by these Jews as he became more legalistic in his practice. The combination of strict legalism, growing intolerance of others, and Fifth Monarchist connections ultimately led Tillam to prison. In 1664 after being released, he headed a group of Dissenters and established a colony near Heidelberg, Germany, where he set up a church that was free to follow the biblical teachings he felt were required of all who wished to enter Christ's kingdom on earth.[22]

Tillam is particularly important as an example of one whose developing Sabbath convictions drew opposition to the whole movement. In 1667, a document signed by a number of leading Seventh Day Baptists formally disavowed Tillam's legalistic beliefs and practices.[23] A 1674 letter from Joseph Davis of London to Samuel Hubbard in Rhode Island gives a final word on Tillam: "I hear he died in Germany; a very great blemish to the truth he was, I fear he went out as a snuff. The holy sabbath hath been the more slighted by such that have lived out of the power."[24]

---

[22] Oscar Burdick, "Research Trip to England and Germany 1988," MS 1988.56, SDB Hist. Soc. Lib.

[23] *A Faithful Testimony Against the Teachers of Circumcision and the Legal Ceremonies...lately gone into Germany* (1667) signed "on behalf of the rest" by seven men including Stennet(t) and John Belcher. This work was originally bound as an appendix to Edward Stennett's *The Royal Law...*, 2nd ed. (London: n.p., 1667), "Pamphlet X 240," John Rylands Library.

[24] Joseph Davis, letter to Samuel Hubbard, 5 Aug 1674, transcription in *Register of Mr. Samuel Hubbard* (manuscript of excerpts with notes by Isaac Backus, ca. 1775), MSS B136i, p. 80, Rhode Island Historical Society Library, Providence (microfilm copy, MF 1989.4, SDB Hist. Soc. Lib.). See also MS 194x.6, p.76, SDB Hist. Soc. Lib.

5

SEVENTH DAY BAPTISTS UNDER A RESTORED MONARCHY

At the beginning of the 1650s, there were only a few scattered voices in England calling for the observance of the seventh-day Sabbath, but during that decade the country's rulers granted individuals enough freedom to participate in the local congregations of their choosing. The records of the period are scanty, but there is evidence of at least two Seventh Day Baptist churches with origins dating to that decade: Mill Yard and Colchester. During the next decade, as the monarchy curtailed freedoms, many of those who had chosen to accept the Sabbath gathered together into covenant groups or churches. Thus, in February 1668, Edward Stennett was able to write to a "remnant in Rhode Island" that there were in England at that time about nine or ten churches that kept the Sabbath "besides many scattered disciples, who have been eminently preserved in this tottering day."[1] A few years later, in 1671, this Rhode Island "remnant" organized the first Seventh Day Baptist Church in America.

The Great Decade of the 1650s, which had offered such hope for a general acceptance of the seventh-day Sabbath, ended with the Sabbathkeepers' realization that the Sabbath doctrine would have to become a distinctive tenet of a select group. This change was partly a result of the restoration of the monarchy in May 1660 under Charles II, the son of the executed Charles I, and partly due to the restrictive attitudes of those who called for the monarchy's restoration.

RESTRICTIVE LAWS OF PARLIAMENT

The Declaration of Breda spelled out the terms by which Charles II could return to England. In addition to granting considerable power to Parliament, the agreement promised liberty "in matters of religion which do not disyturb the general peace of the kingdom."[2] It did not take long

---

[1] Edward Stennett, letter to Sabbath-keepers in RI, 2 Feb 1668, transcription in "The Seventh-day Baptist Church in Newport, R.I.," *SDB Memorial* 1/1 (Jan 1852): 27-28.

[2] *Declaration of Breda*, quoted by B. R. White, *The English Baptists of the Seventeenth Century*, A History of the English Baptists, 4 vols., ed. B. R. White (London: Baptist Historical Society, 1983) 1:93.

for people to discover how elastically Parliament could interpret the "disturbance of the general peace." A series of laws collectively called the Clarendon Code was enacted against Dissenters. Among these were the Corporation Act, which prevented anyone from serving on municipal bodies who refused to take communion according to the Church of England; the Act of Uniformity, which required all clergy to use the revised *Book of Common Prayer* or give up their assigned parish; the Conventicle Act, which provided penalties against people who attended services not conducted according to the *Book of Common Prayer*; and the Five-Mile Act, which banned nonconformist preachers from living in or even visiting any place in which they had formerly officiated.[3]

Underpinning these acts was England's hierarchical social structure. Those in power in Parliament believed that a restored Church of England, backed by a restored monarchy, could best cement society and support political stability. Many believed that the rapid growth of dissenting churches and sects had been one of the main causes of the English Civil War and the execution of the king. They viewed freedom of religion as a challenge to authority, which might cause another civil war or lead to total anarchy.

CHANGED ATTITUDES

The changed religious climate fostered the shift from a generally free and open discussion of the Sabbath to more sharply divided debate. It became more difficult for persons to remain in an established church and hold Sabbath convictions. Brabourne's dream of general acceptance of the Sabbath was dashed. Tolerance of dissenting views was replaced by persecution.

John Milton defended the "no Sabbath" position, holding that the seventh-day Sabbath is strictly Jewish and that there is no command in the New Testament for observing any particular day. He did state strongly that it is only on the authority of the church that Sunday is observed, and any who claim scriptural authority are on dangerous territory and should be aware of the consequences likely to follow from their interpretation of Scripture. In conclusion Milton stated that if the time of public worship were regulated "by the prescriptions of the decalogue, it will surely be far safer to observe the seventh day,

---

[3] Cited in Maurice Ashley, *England in the Seventeenth Century* (1952; London: Hutchinson & Co. Ltd., 1978) 133-35.

according to the express commandment of God, than on the authority of mere human conjecture to adopt the first."[4]

SEVENTH DAY BAPTISTS IN THE RESTORATION PERIOD

In the years following the Restoration, in spite of persecution, a number of Sabbathkeepers rose to positions of responsibility. John Belcher was arrested for both religious and political reasons. John James was martyred. Francis Bampfield came to accept the Sabbath while in prison and eventually died in the Newgate prison for his devotion to the Scriptures. Edward Stennett spent time in prison and chose to make vocational sacrifices for his Sabbath convictions. Members of the Stennett family exercised their choice by accepting leadership positions in Baptist churches while holding personal Sabbath beliefs. Whether through persecution, reaction to the excesses of Tillam's colony, or changes in theological beliefs, some others chose to leave the Sabbath during this time. Among these was John Cowell, an elder in the Tewkesbury Baptist Church who, after promoting the Sabbath for thirteen years, gave up personal observance and even wrote against it.

John Belcher: A Prisoner for the King of Kings

John Belcher, a bricklayer by profession, was the pastor of the Bell Lane congregation in London for most of the church's existence. Previously he had been imprisoned for suspected Fifth Monarchist beliefs.[5] In 1671 he was again imprisoned, this time for both his political and his nonconformist religious persuasions. The State Papers refer to him and members of his congregation as "Sabbatarians and Fifth Monarchy men." Belcher and three others were taken to the Tower while thirty others were imprisoned elsewhere. Their meeting place was ordered destroyed by the state.[6] This was probably the imprisonment mentioned in a 1672 letter from the Bell Lane Church addressed to the church at Newport, Rhode Island. In this letter they referred to the

---

[4] John Milton, *A Treatise on Christian Doctrine: Compiled from the Holy Scriptures Alone*, trans. Charles R. Sumner (Boston: Cummings, Hilliard & Co., 1825) 326-41.

[5] *1910–1911*, vol. 2 of *Transactions of the Baptist Historical Society* (London: Baptist Historical Society, 1911) 269. See also W. T. Whitley, *A Baptist Bibliography* (London: Kingsgate Press 1916) 68.

[6] W. T. Whitley, *A Baptist Bibliography* (London: Kingsgate Press, 1916) 96, reprinted in *Sabbath Recorder* 82/19 (7 May 1917): 581.

imprisonment of most of the congregation, and though not "now in hold," they were still prisoners whose fate was not known.[7]

Some of the correspondence from Belcher and others in the church gave encouragement to the Sabbathkeepers in Newport, which led to their separation from the Baptist Church in 1671. In 1668, members of the Bell Lane church wrote to the Newport congregation, encouraging them to persevere and be true to their convictions, but the letter also urged the congregation to set a good example and promote open-mindedness by showing tolerance to those whose beliefs differed.[8]

John James: A Political Martyr who Kept the Sabbath

One of the most dramatic and best documented incidents involving a Seventh Day Baptist minister was the martyrdom of John James on 27 November 1661. A book in the British Museum, printed in 1661, carries the title *The True and Perfect Speech of John James, a Baptist, and Fifth-Monarchy-man*. The author of this book gave a detailed account of John James's execution, revealing the authorities' fear of treason and sedition following the restoration of Charles II. The author spoke of the people that "go under the name of Fifth-monarchy men, whose principles to Monarchy are both dangerous and pernicious"; it also described how one of them, John James, "a pretended Preacher of that Society, a Silk Weaver by Trade," was arrested at White Chappel on Saturday, 19 October 1661. James was accused of preaching from Psalm 8:2, "from whence he raised several doctrines which alluded to Sedition and Rebellions."[9]

Previously, in January that same year, Thomas Venner and his Fifth Monarchy followers had participated in an unsuccessful uprising designed to advance the kingdom of Christ on earth by force. This gave the court a pretext for suspending the declaration of indulgences the restored monarchy had initially promised. John James was tried, condemned, and executed. His body was quartered and the remains placed in strategic spots around the city as a warning to others.

Nothing in the report of either the initial charges or the trial accused James of being a Sabbathkeeper or a Nonconformist. The fact that he was

---

[7] Quoted by Corliss F. Randolph, "Correspondence between London and Newport, 1669–1685," *Sabbath Recorder* 152/13 (31 Mar 1952): 151.

[8] Quoted by Ernest Payne, "More about the Sabbatarian Baptists," *Baptist Quarterly* 14/4 (1951–1952): 163.

[9] "The True and Perfect Speech of John James…" (London: 1661), Ann Arbor MI: UMI, Wing (2nd ed.), J431, British Library, London.

preaching on Saturday may have drawn attention to his message, prompting those who reported him to the authorities. In his final speech beneath the gallows, he defended his heritage as an Englishman but left no doubt that his ultimate loyalty was to God. In speaking of his personal religious beliefs, he acknowledged that he was a baptized believer who accepted the principles in Hebrews 6:1-2 and such doctrines as faith in God, repentance from dead works, baptism, the laying on of hands, the resurrection of the dead, and eternal judgment. He ended by affirming that he owned the Commandments of God, the Ten Commandments as expressed in Exodus 20, and did not dare willingly to break the least of those to save his life. He also declared, "I do own the Lord's holy Sabbath, the seventh day of the week to be the Lord's Sabbath."[10]

John James was not martyred for his Sabbath convictions. Yet, his willingness to stand firm and the forgiving nature he displayed toward those who persecuted him are traits that define other great figures over the course of Seventh Day Baptist history.

Francis Bampfield: Convinced while Convicted

In his book *Saints and Rebels: Seven Nonconformists in Stuart England*, Richard L. Greaves includes a chapter titled "Making the Laws of Christ His Only Rule; Francis Bampfield, Sabbatarian Reformer." Greaves states in his introduction that Bampfield was a committed Royalist during the English Civil War but that he never held radical political views, even though he was imprisoned for his nonconformity. Greaves calls Bampfield's religious life "a perfect illustration of the classical spiritual pilgrimage, which ranged from fidelity to Anglican principles all the way to the advocacy of Seventh-Day Baptist tenets." Although he falsely links Bampfield with the Fifth Monarchists because of his Saturday Sabbath convictions, Greaves makes it plain that Bampfield did not share their political ideology: "Indeed, his advocacy of sabbatarianism was an outgrowth of his approach to Scripture as the source of all knowledge as well as the boundary and foundation of religious experience."[11]

---

[10] "The Trial of John James at the King's-Bench for High-Treason, November 14, 1662," in *A Complete Collection of State-Trials, and Proceedings…*, 2nd ed., 6 vols. (London: n.p., 1730) 2:473. (The correct year was 1661; this date has been corrected in later editions of this publication.)

[11] Richard L. Greaves, *Saints and Rebels: Seven Nonconformists in Stuart England* (Macon GA: Mercer University Press, 1985) 179.

The Bampfields were a prominent family that held a number of political offices. One brother, Thomas, was a member of Parliament and Speaker of the House of Commons in 1659. Francis Bampfield prepared for the ministry, graduating from Oxford with Bachelor and Master of Arts degrees. Later, he looked on these educational years as "void spaces" with little Scripture learning. Because his initial loyalty was to the monarchy and the established church, his services were interrupted by the troops of Cromwell. Yet, by the time of the Restoration, Bampfield had gone through a religious experience that placed him among the Nonconformists.

After a popular ministry at Sherborne, where he attracted a congregation numbered in the thousands, Francis Bampfield was dismissed along with hundreds of others for refusing to conform to the *Book of Common Prayer*. On 19 September 1662, while conducting a worship service in his own home, soldiers barged in and arrested Bampfield along with about twenty-five of his followers. He was released after five days but was arrested again the following week for conducting an illegal service. After Bampfield spent a year and a half in prison, arrangements were made for his release on condition of "good behavior," but Bampfield refused because he interpreted the terms as a confession of guilt. He remained in Dorchester prison for just less than nine years.

While in prison Bampfield organized his own church, preaching as often as sixteen times per week to other prisoners and visitors who came to worship with them. It was during this time (around 1665) that he accepted the doctrine of the Sabbath, believing it to be mandated by both Scripture and nature. At first he observed the Sabbath in private, but after gaining a few converts, he proclaimed his belief openly.[12]

During this imprisonment, Bampfield and two others were convinced of the validity of believers' baptism by immersion. Since the prison had no facility suitable to perform baptism, they resolved to be baptized as soon as they were released. Bampfield's own account records the men rowing up the Thames to Battersea, where they worshipped on a Sabbath morning. Later, Bampfield traveled to Salisbury and reported that in the manner of John Smyth, one of the Baptist movement's

---

[12] Greaves, *Saints and Rebels*, 189-90.

founders, he baptized himself in the Avon River "as by the Hand of Christ himself."[13]

During his time in Salisbury, Bampfield was again imprisoned for a period of eighteen weeks. Upon his release he went to London, where in 1676 he established the Pinner's Hall Seventh Day Baptist church.[14] Bampfield's final imprisonment was in 1683, when he was committed to Newgate prison for failure to take the oath of allegiance and supremacy. By this time his health was so broken that he died the next year in Newgate prison. Edmund Calamy wrote, "He was one of the most celebrated preachers in the West of England, and extremely admired by his hearers, till he fell into the Sabbatarian notion, of which he was a zealous asserter."[15] This "falling into the Sabbatarian notion" was but the logical result of the conviction that underlies all of his writings and preaching: "The Scriptures of Truth are a perfect Library of all saving Knowledge, and profitable Science."[16]

Apart from his writings and witness to the Sabbath, Bampfield is significant to Seventh Day Baptists as one of the first to propose an association of Sabbatarians to include churches on both sides of the Atlantic. His proposal was not implemented at the time, but his statement shows concern for improving education for both children and ministers, sponsoring a more accurate translation of the Bible, and studying means to convert the Jews.[17] He was also significant as the primary founder of the Pinner's Hall Seventh Day Baptist church, which continued into the mid-nineteenth century. In this church several of the Stennett family were nurtured and gave service to the cause of Christ.

THE STENNETT FAMILY

For over a century, the name Stennett was associated with the cause of both Baptists and Seventh Day Baptists in England. Through their writings, their hymns, and their representation of the free-church tradition, their influence has extended to modern times.

---

[13] Francis Bampfield, "*Shem 'achar*," *A Name, an After-one* (London: n.p., 1681) 14, 16-17, quoted by Greaves, *Saints and Rebels*, 192-93.

[14] Edward Calamy, *The Nonconformist's Memorial: Being an Account of the Lives, sufferings, and Printed Works of the Two Thousand Ministers Ejected from the Church of England, chiefly by the Acts of Uniformity, Aug. 24, 1662*, 3 vols. (London: n.p., 1802) 2:151.

[15] Calamy, *Nonconformists's Memorial*, 2:152.

[16] Francis Bampfield, *Cal-Toshiah Pangeosia. Pantechia. Pansophia. All in One* (London: n.p., 1677) 1.

[17] Greaves, *Saints and Rebels*, 201.

The four generations of Stennetts represent the wide spectrum of practice found among some later Seventh Day Baptist families. Edward was a strong contender for the Sabbath, and because of his belief he suffered persecution. His son, Joseph, served as pastor of the Pinner's Hall Seventh Day Baptist Church while also preaching at other churches on Sunday. In the third generation, Joseph II was primarily a pastor of the Little Wild Street Baptist Church but maintained a close relationship with his father's church and often preached there. In the fourth generation, Samuel held Sabbath convictions but primarily associated with the Baptists.

Edward Stennett: A Contender for the Sabbath

Edward Stennett was a Baptist in Abingdon who accepted the Sabbath during the latter half of the 1650s. In 1658, he wrote a short book titled *The Royal Law Contended for...*, in which he attempted to prove scripturally that the Ten Commandments were still in force and that the seventh-day Sabbath should be kept.[18] His opponents raised questions, which he answered with scriptural parallels.[19]

Throughout his life, Stennett held services wherever he lived. Around 1670, he moved from Abingdon to an old castle in Wallingford, where he held services. John Belcher held membership in that congregation into the 1680s. Others, upon moving to London, became members of the Pinner's Hall church. The records of Pinner's Hall reveal that Edward was invited to serve on occasion as pastor until 1690, when his son became its pastor. Edward is also known to have preached in the Baptist Church at Reading, about 15 miles southeast of Wallingford. The Wallingford church ceased to exist soon after Stennett's death in 1705, but the church he pastored at Watlington, Oxfordshire, continued for another century.

Edward Stennett was singled out for persecution during the Restoration for violating the restrictions of the Clarendon Code. He took up the study of medicine because he was barred from preaching. For over thirty years, he was a leading voice for the Seventh Day Baptists in England. His correspondence with Seventh Day Baptists in America shed considerable light on some of the persecutions and problems

---

[18] Edward Stennett, *The Royal Law Contended for or, Some brief grounds serving to prove that the Ten Commandments are yet in full force, and shall so remain, until heaven and earth pass away*, 2nd ed. (London: n.p., 1667) A2-3.

[19] Edward Stennett, "The Penalty for Sabbath-Breaking," *The Seventh Day is the Sabbath of the Lord* (London: n.p., 1664), partially repr. in *Sabbath Recorder* 1/44 (24 Apr 1845): 172.

Sabbathkeepers on both sides of the Atlantic experienced. His letter dated 6 March 1670 contributed to the establishment the following year of the first Seventh Day Baptist church in America.[20]

One of the greatest contributions of Edward Stennett to Christ's cause was what he gave to his family. Education was a distinguishing mark of the Stennett family for over a century.[21] Joseph paid tribute to his parents as he prayed, "Thou didst season my tender years with a religious education; so that I sucked in the rudiments of Christianity as it were with my mother's milk, by the gracious admonitions and holy discipline of my godly parents."[22]

Joseph Stennett: Chooses to Pastor a Sabbath church

Joseph Stennett was born in 1663 at Abingdon. He was considered extremely well educated for one whose family association as Dissenters excluded him from schools such as Oxford or Cambridge. He "mastered French and Italian and became a critic in Hebrew and other oriental tongues, successfully studied the liberal sciences, and made a considerable proficiency in philosophy," which augmented his study of the Scriptures and works of the church fathers. His biographer also notes that he was not ashamed of any notion in religion that might be out of fashion, claiming to be "the better satisfied with his principles, because they were formed on a diligent and impartial study of the holy scriptures themselves."[23]

Joseph Stennett came to London in 1685 serving as a teacher who "had a true sense of the value of English liberty." He began to write verse and published several pieces that encouraged the "spirit of liberty in the people." Some of this work he did anonymously for political reasons. He was influential in stirring public opinion during the latter days of Charles II and throughout the reign of James II, who succeeded Charles in 1685.[24]

---

[20] Edward Stennett, letter to Sabbath-keepers in RI, 6 day 1 month 1669, transcribed in Samuel Hubbard, *Register of Mr. Samuel Hubbard* (transcription of excerpts with notes by Isaac Backus, ca. 1775), MSS B136i, pp. 66-67, Rhode Island Historical Society Library, Providence (microfilm copy, MF 1989.4, SDB Hist. Soc. Lib.). See also MS 194x.6, pp. 58-59, SDB Hist. Soc. Lib.

[21] Joseph Stennett, *The Works of the Late Reverend and Learned Mr. Joseph Stennett*, 5 vols. (London: n.p., 1732) 1:7.

[22] Stennett, *Works of Joseph Stennett*, 1:7-8.

[23] Ibid., 1:8-9.

[24] Ibid., 1:9-10.

In 1690, Joseph was ordained as pastor of the Pinner's Hall
congregation; he served them faithfully for the rest of his life, even
though the church was not able to give him much financial support. His
biographer wrote that even though he had a number of offers more to his
temporal advantage, "he preferred the invitation of this small people by
reason of his agreement with them in principles." In addition to his
pastorate on the seventh day, it is recorded that "he preached to divers
other congregations constantly on the first day."[25] This and his
representation of all Baptists, through such services as drafting a letter
on their behalf to congratulate the king upon his deliverance from an
assassination plot, has provided grounds for all Baptists to claim Joseph
Stennett as their own.

Joseph Stennett is remembered for his poetic skills. He published a
number of hymns relating to the sacraments of communion and baptism,
as well as hymns on the Sabbath. His most noted hymn, "Another Six
Days Work Is Done," is still printed in a number of hymnbooks. Oscar
Burdick suggests that by writing popular hymns and because of his solid
reputation as a Baptist leader in London, Stennett helped
Nonconformists overcome their early reluctance to sing hymns. Before
this, many sang only the Psalms.[26]

Joseph Stennett II: A Sabbatarian Pastor of a Baptist Church

Joseph Stennett II was born in 1692 during the reign of the tolerant
Protestant rulers, William and Mary, who had been called to take over
the throne after the "bloodless" revolution had toppled James II in 1689.
At age fifteen, Stennett II was baptized and joined the Pinner's Hall
Seventh Day Particular Baptist Church, but most of his ministry was
with Baptist churches in Exeter and London.

While serving a Baptist church at Exeter, he received a call to
become the pastor of the Mill Yard Seventh Day General Baptist Church
in Goodman's Fields, London. An entry in their record book dated 5
March 1720 states that an invitation be made to Mr. Joseph Stennett so
that he "might bee usefull for the promotion of the Sabbath; to come to
preach amongst the Sabbath keepers." The records also state that it was
"agreed by the Church to Invite him in Love: Trusting to his Moderation

[25] Ibid., 1:11-12.
[26] Oscar Burdick, "The Stennett Family," master's thesis, Alfred University School of
Theology, 1953, MS 195x.3, p. 61, SDB Hist. Soc. Lib.

hee knowing our Principles about Generall point."[27] Even though at the time Stennett was serving a church that worshipped on Sunday, the congregation at Mill Yard still recognized that he believed in the Sabbath and felt that this conviction would outweigh the theological differences between General and Particular Baptists. The records give no indication as to why Stennett declined the invitation. They merely show that on 24 April 1721, the church received his response in a letter.[28]

In 1737, when Stennett did return to London, it was as the pastor of the Little Wild Street Baptist Church, though he maintained a close relationship with the Seventh Day Baptist church. In 1753, Rev. Samuel Davies, who later became president of Princeton, wrote in his diary, "Preached yesterday P. M. for Dr. Stennett, in a small congregation of Seven Day Baptists, who seem very serious people."[29]

Joseph Stennett II died in 1758, having served for forty-four years as a Baptist minister, preaching at times in the church of his origin, the Pinner's Hall Seventh Day Particular Baptist Church. Oscar Burdick observed that "as to his personal religion, he was a Seventh Day Particular Baptist, but vocationally, he always served first-day Baptist churches. Historians of both denominations claim him as an important person."[30]

Samuel Stennett: A Champion for Baptist Principles

Samuel Stennett, like his father, maintained a dual relationship between the Baptists and the Seventh Day Baptists. His main ministry was with the Little Wild Street Baptist Church, where he lacked just three years of serving for half a century. Although his membership was always with that Baptist church, his service was never limited to it. The Pinner's Hall record book indicates that he "freely and chearfully offered his services till such time as the church could obtain...[a pastor] of its own."[31]

For nearly twenty years, Samuel Stennett served the church on a part-time basis but did not choose to make it his full-time vocation. During a literary debate Samuel Stennett revealed his position on the

---

[27] Mill Yard London, Eng. SDB Church Records, 1673–1845, ms., CRR 1932.1, SDB Hist. Soc. Lib., 234.

[28] Mill Yard, London, Eng. SDB Church Records, 1673–1845 (7 May 1721) 235.

[29] "President Davies in London," Sabbath Recorder 12/8 (2 Aug 1855): 29.

[30] Burdick, "Stennett Family," 167.

[31] Pinner's Hall, London, Eng. SDB Church Records, 1686–1863 (1763), ms., CRR 1951.9, p. 128, SDB Hist. Soc. Lib.

Sabbath by stating that "not having yet met with any passage in the New Testament that appears to me to have repealed the fourth commandment, I cannot think myself sufficiently authorized to renounce that and to keep this."[32] About two months before Samuel Stennett's death in 1795, John Evans wrote that he "passed a most agreeable day with him at Muswell Hill. As he kept the 'seventh-day Sabbath,' enquiries were made respecting the principles of the Sabbatarians…."[33]

Seventh Day Baptists of the twentieth century identify Samuel Stennett as a hymn writer. His hymn "Majestic Sweetness Sits Enthroned" is still found in some hymnals, while the old gospel hymn "On Jordan's Stormy Banks I Stand" may occasionally be found in collections of old gospel songs. For the most part, contemporary hymnals have bypassed the treasury of verses written by the Stennetts.

Although the Stennetts were the most noted family of those connected with Seventh Day Baptists in England, in later years there were others who in their own ways contributed to the distinctive witness of Seventh Day Baptists. Among these were men such as Edmund Townsend, who succeeded Joseph Stennett at the Pinner's Hall Church; William Henry Black and William Mead Jones, who served the Mill Yard Church during the nineteenth century; and Benjamin Purser, who purchased and endowed a meetinghouse for the Natton Church. Despite valiant effort and dedication, the Seventh Day Baptist churches in England never fulfilled the hopes and expectations of their seventeenth-century founders. Yet, in their history are found clues that give a message to later generations.

CLUES FOR THE FUTURE: CONCLUSIONS

The early third-century theologian Tertullian, in commenting on the persecution of Christians by the Roman emperors, wrote, "Nor does your cruelty, however exquisite, avail you; it is rather a temptation to us. The oftener we are mown down by you, the more in number we grow; the blood of Christians is seed."[34]

---

[32] Samuel Stennett, *An Answer to the Christian Minister's Reasons for Baptizing Infants…* (London: J. Buckland, 1775) 177-78.

[33] John Evans, sermon preached at Worship-Street, Sorditch, "October 18, 1795; being a sincere tribute to the memory of Rev. Samuel Stennett…" (London: C. Whittingham, 1795) iv.

[34] Tertullian, "Apology," *The Ante-Nicene Fathers*, 10 vols., ed. Alexander Roberts and James Donaldson (Buffalo NY: Christian Literature Publishing Company, 1885) 3:55.

Persecution can make inspirational reading and can lead to the scattering of seeds and formation of new Christian centers, but it does not always follow that persecution is conducive to growth. The history of Seventh Day Baptists in England demonstrates that the sufferings of men such as John James, Francis Bampfield, and Edward Stennett were not sufficient seed to produce the kind of yield that Sabbathkeepers had envisioned during the Great Decade of the 1650s.

Charles Henry Greene and James Gamble, in their 1910 account of the Seventh Day Baptists in the British Isles, *Seventh Day Baptists in Europe and America,* listed thirty-two churches that had existed in the period from the mid-seventeenth century to the beginning of the twentieth century.[35] Some of those listed represent small clusters of Sabbathkeepers whose only evidence of their existence may be a chance reference in correspondence of individuals or the records of other churches. In a few cases, a single church may have had more than one place of meeting at different times throughout history. The number of viable churches probably did not exceed sixteen, with three in London, (Mill Yard, Bell Lane, and Pinner's Hall), two in the neighboring shire or county of Essex (Colchester and Braintree), and others scattered from the North Sea coast at Norfolk to the English Channel at Dorset and north to Natton (near Tewkesbury) in Gloucestershire. By the 1980s, only two Seventh Day Baptist churches remained in England: the Mill Yard church located in Tottenham, a section of Greater London; and a relatively new church in Birmingham, which more recently fostered a branch in the city of Bristol. These churches are not the direct fruit of seeds sown by seventeenth- and eighteenth-century Sabbathkeepers, even though the organization of the Mill Yard church has remained intact for over three centuries. They are largely transplants from the Jamaican Seventh Day Baptist Conference.

Attempts have been made to explain the decline of Seventh Day Baptist churches in England. Greene and Gamble stated three reasons: "(1) lack of organized fellowship among the churches; (2) dependence on charitable bequests that developed weakness in individuals and churches; and (3) employment of first-day pastors which necessarily blockaded all aggressive Sabbath work."[36] There appear to have been

[35] James Lee Gamble and Charles Henry Greene, "The Sabbath in the British Isles," *Seventh Day Baptists in Europe and America,* 3 vols. (Plainfield NJ: American Tract Society, 1910) 1:139-63.
[36] Gamble and Greene, "The Sabbath in the British Isles," in *SDBs in Europe,* 1:63.

other more basic factors that underlay these three reasons and further contributed to the decline in membership among the English Seventh Day Baptist Church until a more recent resurgence from migrations of Seventh Day Baptists from the West Indies.

Lack of Organized Fellowship

First, the lack of organized fellowship may have been a symptom of basic theological, scriptural, and political differences. For example, for a time in the seventeenth and eighteenth centuries, there were three congregations in London. The Mill Yard congregation was General Baptist, which held that Christ's atonement was sufficient for all even though not all would accept. The Pinner's Hall church was a Particular or Calvinistic Baptist church, which held that Christ's work was intended for particular persons known as the elect.

The minutes of the Mill Yard Church for 4 June 1721 indicate that two congregations "now meeting together on the Sabbath day have agreed to communicate together though as two."[37] In 1727, there was a rift in the Mill Yard Church. Several of the Particular Baptists objected to pastor Robert Cornthwaite's Socinian (Unitarian) views and withdrew, selecting Edmund Townsend as their pastor. They met in Curriers' Hall.[38]

A second difference was in the interpretation of Scripture. The church at Colchester, under the leadership of Thomas Tillam, tended to be much more legalistic in the matter of Jewish law. Other members had different views over the specific requirements of Sabbath observance. The legalism of Tillam and Christopher Pooley of the Norwich church may have been instrumental in the decision of John Cowell to desert the Sabbath after serving as pastor for the Sabbathkeepers of Natton. His book *The Snare Broken*, written in 1677, caused considerable disturbance in the churches, for when a person rejects the Sabbath after having spent years championing it, the effect on other Sabbathkeepers can be devastating.

A third barrier to closer fellowship among the churches was political. The Bell Lane Church in London, under the leadership of John Belcher, contained a number who were regarded as Fifth Monarchist and were imprisoned for their political beliefs. Some Seventh Day Baptists

---

[37] Mill Yard London, Eng. SDB Church Records, 1673–1845 (4 Jun 1721) 235.

[38] Unnumbered footnote, *Minutes of the General Assembly of the General Baptist Churches in England*, 2 vols., ed. W. T. Whitley (London: Kingsgate Press, 1909–1910) 2:49.

were supporters of the monarchy, while others were prominent in the Commonwealth. The government of the time did not always endeavor to prove their target's culpability. Guilt by association was common ground for persecution. For safety's sake, individuals and congregations were often scattered.

Thus, though later historians may see the lack of organization and fellowship as one of the reasons for the decline of Seventh Day Baptists, the differences that separated them may have been greater than the doctrine of the Sabbath that united them. William Mead Jones, a late-nineteenth-century English Seventh Day Baptist pastor, wrote that "they did not subordinate their Calvinism, Arminianism, and other theoretic and controverted matters to the necessities of the teaching and practice of a tenet that requires sacrifice, push, and devotion, fifty-two times a year, every year of one's life.[39]

Reliance on Endowment

Second, historians cite the dependence on endowments as a contributing cause for the churches' decline. W. T. Whitley, in his book *The Baptists of London*, wrote about endowments and changing conditions in London, which seemed to occur at fifty-year intervals. With respect to 1691 he wrote: "Three Seventh-day churches walked apart, but a rich draper in the Minories was about to bequeath his wealth to them and ensure some kind of existence."[40] The rich draper was Joseph Davis, a member of the Mill Yard Church. A generous man, he endowed the churches but, over a century later, caused untold problems of jealousy and litigations as various people fought over the endowment he provided. As the number of male members of the Mill Yard church slowly decreased due to death and a failure to bring in new members, trustees were appointed from members of the General Baptists, who were not as sympathetic to the cause of the Sabbath. After lengthy litigations over the rightful recipients of the trust, the Seventh Day Baptists were left with only a token of the original intent of the Davis legacy—a lasting, meaningful support of their congregations.[41] In

---

[39] William Mead Jones, "English SDBs," in *Jubilee Papers* (Westerly RI: Board of Managers of the SDB Missionary Society, 1892) 18.

[40] W. T. Whitley, *The Baptists of London, 1612–1928* (London: Kingsgate Press, n.d.) 36.

[41] For a fuller account, see William Henry Black, ed., *The Last Legacy…* (London: Mill Yard Congregation, 1869), and *Report of the Commissioners Appointed in Pursuance of An Act of Parliament…Mr. Humphrey's Report on "Joseph Davis Endowment for Sabbatarian Protestant Dissenters"* (London: W. Cloves & Son, 1840).

addition to the loss of funds, the internal friction caused by the administration of the trust, and the amount of time, energy, and money expended in trying to reclaim the inheritance, took its toll.

Yet, it is important to understand that in England, as in most countries that have had state churches, the clergy were supported largely by the state. This support came either from direct taxation or through endowments, many of which had been created during the Reformation under Henry VIII by the confiscation of land owned by the Roman Catholic Church. The custom of the church using voluntary contributions to support the minister who served them was not commonly practiced at this time. Thus, Edward Stennett was considered "a faithful and laborious minister: but his dissent from the established church deprived him of the means whereby to maintain his family" and forced him to take up the study of medicine for a living.[42] John Belcher was known as a bricklayer, and John James was a ribbon weaver (making ribbon using a special loom). Although John Ridley left a Baptist church to become a Seventh Day Baptist minister (in Ingham, Colchester), there were a number who embraced the Sabbath yet retained positions in other churches. This led to a third diagnosis for the decline of Seventh Day Baptists in England.

Reliance on First-Day Ministers

The third major reason historians cite for the decline of Seventh Day Baptists in England was the employment of first-day pastors, a practice that hindered aggressive Sabbath work. Most of the Sabbathkeeping churches in England grew out of other churches and often retained leadership ties with them. In an 1845 editorial in the *Sabbath Recorder*, George B. Utter attributed the decline of the church at Natton to the ministry of Thomas Hiller, who was a Sabbathkeeper in opinion and practice and was invited to serve the Sabbathkeeping church at the same time that he remained pastor of the first-day Baptist Church. Although he was held in esteem by both congregations, the membership declined, leading Mr. Utter to write, "A minister of the Gospel, who is at the same time pastor of one church worshipping on the seventh day of the week, and another church worshiping on the first day of the week, can never be faithful to them both."[43]

---

[42] J. Stennett, *Works*, 1:4.

[43] George B. Utter, "The Sabbath-keeping Church at Natton, Eng.," *Sabbath Recorder* 2/1 (26 Jun 1845): 1.

On the other hand, it is possible that there were factors other than economics that caused men like Samuel Stennett to preach for other churches. It may be, as Oscar Burdick suggested, that "the later Stennetts 'apartness' from other Seventh Day Baptists was a judgment on that denomination's Christianity."[44] Judging from the books written by Seventh Day Baptists of the period, many felt the defense of the Sabbath was a primary consideration. The Stennetts, on the other hand, thought that Christian living was more important than controversy.

This highlights a dilemma faced by Seventh Day Baptists of many generations, who have had to choose between limiting their service to those with whom the Sabbath distinctive is shared, or to cooperate and minister to those who differ on the doctrine of the Sabbath but share in most other doctrines. The experience of the English Seventh Day Baptists is inconclusive, for even those ministers who served but one congregation fared little better than those who split their ministries.

Persecution and Discrimination

A minority group within a society dominated by a powerful majority faces tremendous odds that many are not able to overcome. The case of the Joseph Davis legacy illustrates the fact that a group of people, small in number, had little standing in the court system. Many of the Sabbathkeepers in England during the nineteenth century reported difficulty finding employment that left them free to worship on the Sabbath. Despite the services many had given to the state in various capacities, some who kept the Sabbath were looked upon as enemies of the state or suffered equally the continued discrimination against the Jews, who also observed the Sabbath.

W. T. Whitley commented in relation to the example made of John James: "The lesson struck home, and men saw that they had to choose between submission, exile, passive resistance, rebellion; for the parliament would do nothing to help them. All four alternatives were taken by Baptists."[45] Some Seventh Day Baptists did choose to submit; some chose to leave England and migrate to America; a number offered passive resistance that left little opportunity for aggressive Sabbath promotion. Few were in any position to rebel successfully.

Still, in spite of the Sabbathkeepers' troubled history, the words of Tertullian remain true: "the blood of Christians is seed." The seed that

---

[44] Burdick, "Stennett Family," 300.
[45] Whitley, *A History of British Baptists* (London: Charles Griffin & Co., 1923) 110.

was sown produced meager fruit in England but was carried to America, where it took root and continued to give men and women the opportunity to "choose ye this day whom you shall serve." Seventh Day Baptists have continued through over three centuries to be a choosing people within a new "promised land," one not on the other side of the river but on the other side of an ocean.

PART III: SEVENTH DAY BAPTISTS IN AMERICA BEFORE 1800

PART III TIMELINE:

1794   "Blue Laws" in Pennsylvania
1797   Brookfield, New York SDB Church

6

COLONIAL AMERICA

The seed that was carried from England to America found fresh soil in which to germinate. Still, as in England, external conditions determined the choices available to the people who established Seventh Day Baptist churches during America's colonial period. William Sweet, in his *The Story of Religion in America*, suggests several conditions that greatly influenced the development of American religious history.[1]

CONDITIONS IN COLONIAL SOCIETY

First, most of colonial America was settled by those considered to be political, social, economic, and religious radicals. Rather than submitting to authoritarian rule or registering only passive resistance, many chose exile.

Second, a majority of the colonists came from the poorer classes who were dissatisfied with their economic status and thus were easily swayed by radical ideas. Many of these colonists may have known what they were against, but not necessarily what they were for. Attempts to implement new ideas were often executed by heavy-handed political means. Such attempts failed to recognize that these means were the real problem. Puritans, for example, instituted a rigid political and cultural model to implement their ideals as opposed to the inflexible monarch and Church of England, creating further religious strife in New England.

A third factor was the expansion into the western frontier. This westward migration was particularly important for Seventh Day Baptists, whose movements closely paralleled those of the population in general. This movement, first inland from the coastal areas and later westward across the Appalachian mountains, caused the planting of new congregations and the necessity of communication between congregations.[2]

Fourth, only a small percentage of the population in the American colonies were members of colonial churches. Since many surviving records of the period come from churches, the emigration of groups such

---

[1] William Warren Sweet, *The Story of Religion in America* (1930; repr., New York: Harper, 1950) 1.

[2] For a more thorough discussion of the frontier's influence, see Don A. Sanford, A *Free People in Search of a Free Land* (1976; repr., Janesville WI: SDB Historical Society, 1987).

as the Pilgrims in 1620 and the Quakers in 1682 led many to conclude that most of the people who sailed to America came in search of religious freedom. The historical fact is that many shiploads of settlers came for reasons far removed from any religious consideration.[3] According to William Sweet, "there were more unchurched people in America, in proportion to the population, than could be found in any other country in Christendom. It was the large number of unchurched that made necessary the development of revivalism to win people to the Christ and resulted in an aggressive American Christianity."[4]

A fifth observation is the parallel between American political and religious history. The nationalism that led to the Federal Constitution was found in the development of religious organizations. Not only were denominations developing national organizations, but they were also forming ecumenical groups to signify the national scope of their perceived mission. Alexis de Tocqueville, a noted French writer, contrasted the spirit of religion and the spirit of freedom, which he saw as marching in opposite directions in France, whereas in America he saw them united and reigning together.[5]

This relationship became particularly evident in the establishment of the American Constitution. Many of the basic concepts of that document grew out of the tradition of the religious covenants that had been in existence in the colonies since the 1620 signing of the Mayflower Compact. Even the opening words, "We the people," and the unusual step of affixing signatures at the end, "In witness whereof," suggests the covenantal nature of the document.[6]

Within this environment, Seventh Day Baptists took root in the New England colony of Rhode Island and the Middle Colonies of Pennsylvania and New Jersey. There they found the freedom to choose beliefs according to their individual consciences and were permitted to enter into covenant relationships.

---

[3] John Winthrop, *Winthrop's Journal: History of New England, 1630-1649*, 2 vols., ed. James Kendall Hosmer (New York: Scribner's, 1908) 1:274.

[4] Sweet, *Religion in America*, 5.

[5] Alexis de Tocqueville, *Democracy in America*, ed. Phillips Bradley (New York: A. A. Knopf, 1945) 308, quoted by Sweet, *Story of Religion*, 7.

[6] See Norman Fiering's preface in Donald S. Lutz and Jack D. Warren, *A Covenanted People: The Religious Tradition and the Origins of American Constitutionalism* (Providence RI: John Carter Brown Library, 1987).

Champions of Religious Freedom

Religious freedom for many of the early settlers of America meant merely the right to worship according to the dictates of their own particular practice; it was not intended to grant similar rights to those who differed. The state church concept was well ingrained in the minds of even those who had rebelled against the application of the episcopal polity in the European churches from which they had come. Religious liberty in colonial Massachusetts has been defined as the liberty to conform to Puritan orthodoxy. Nathaniel Ward expressed this sentiment in his statement, "All Familists, Antinomians, Anabaptists and other Enthusiasts shall have free liberty to keep away from us."[7]

There were three areas in early colonial America where freedom of religion was permitted: Rhode Island, Pennsylvania, and Maryland. The first two colonies listed provided the environment in which Seventh Day Baptists had their colonial American beginnings and from which they spread as the nation expanded.

Rhode Island Baptists

By the end of the colonial period (about 1750), religious toleration was widespread. The diversity of religious beliefs and the vast numbers who held no religious convictions, coupled with the colonies' desire to attract settlers, forced a relaxation of religious requirements. However, the colony of Rhode Island, from its very beginning, was established on the principle of separation of church and state. It was one of the first civil governments in the world to grant complete religious freedom. Although Roger Williams has often been credited with establishing this heritage in Rhode Island, there were others who did more to determine the nature of that freedom.

Roger Williams

Roger Williams came to Boston in 1631 at the age of thirty. His separatist views kept him from joining the Puritan church at Boston, which he argued had not completely separated from the Church of England. He was called to the church at Salem by its congregation, but the General Court interfered. For two years he worked among the Native Americans at Plymouth and studied their language. His acquaintance

---

[7] Lutz and Warren, *A Covenanted People*, 29.

79

with the Narraganset chiefs paved the way for his later settlement among them.

In 1634, Williams again was called to serve the church at Salem, where he made serious charges that struck at the very heart of both the civil and religious authorities. First, he charged that Salem's royal charter was not valid, since the true owners were the natives. Second, he claimed that civil power extended only to the bodies and property of men and not to their spiritual beings. He was banished from the colony and made his way to the area around Providence, where he found shelter among the natives. In 1636, he purchased land from the natives that became the foundation for the colony of Rhode Island.

In 1638, a church of rebaptized members formed in Providence. Roger Williams served as its pastor for only a few months. His contribution to Baptist thought was in the area of polity, which stemmed from his political philosophy. The practice of immersion or "dipping" was probably brought to the colonies by Mark Lucar, who came to Newport in 1648 from the Particular Baptist church of John Spilsbury in London. The modern historian Edwin Gaustad noted that "Baptist zeal in Rhode Island was immeasurably heightened by a direct infusion of English Baptists from abroad."[8]

Dr. John Clarke

The second major settlement in Rhode Island was on the island of Aquidneck, which later took the name of Rhode Island. The most important figure in this colonization was Dr. John Clarke. In 1637 he came to Boston, where he observed differences concerning the covenant; some held to a covenant of works for sanctification while others "prest as hard for the Covenant of grace that was established on better promises, and for the evidence of the spirit."[9] Clarke became associated with the movement led by Anne Hutchinson, who taught a covenant of grace. When she was banished from the Massachusetts colony on charges of heretical teachings, Clarke was among those who followed.[10]

---

[8] Edwin S. Gaustad, ed., *Baptist Piety: The Last Will & Testimony of Obadiah Holmes* (Grand Rapids MI: Christian University Press, 1978) 17.

[9] John Clark, *Ill Newes from New England* (London: n.p., 1652), quoted by Thomas William Bicknell, *The History of the State of Rhode Island and Providence Plantations*, 3 vols. (New York: American Historical Society, Inc., 1920) 1:274-75.

[10] John Russell Bartlett, ed., *Records of the Colony of Rhode Island and Providence Plantations, in New England*, 10 vols. (Providence RI: A. Crawford Green & Brother, 1856) 1:52.

There was considerable contrast between the settlements of Providence and Aquidneck. Many who followed Williams were poorly educated and owned few personal possessions. They had little personal theology and simply sought a place where they could escape persecution. Except for Roger Williams, none had any practical experience in civil affairs.[11] Providence was slow to establish any form of government beyond that related to land and land ownership. Even the charter, which Williams secured from the English crown in 1644, offered no guarantee of religious freedom. On the other hand, the settlement at Aquidneck was formed by a group of families from the Boston area who were united by a "solemn compact" or covenant dated 7 March 1638, nearly six months prior to their migration to Rhode Island.[12]

Dr. John Clarke spent twelve years in England from the period of the British Commonwealth to the beginning of the Restoration working to secure a charter for the Rhode Island colony. He is credited with much of the wording of the charter, which was granted in 1663. Among other provisions, the charter confirmed the Native Americans' claims to the land and set up a democratic government under three branches: legislative, judicial, and executive. This was the first such charter to specifically state that freedom of worship and of conscience were basic individual rights.

In this climate of political freedom, Seventh Day Baptists and others in America were able to exercise choices based on their interpretation of the Scriptures. The earliest official records for the Newport Baptist Church under the leadership of Dr. John Clarke date from 1644, although it is possible the group met earlier.

An event took place in 1651 that Gaustad described as having created a disturbance in which "the structures of the New England way clashed directly with the turbulence of a Rhode Island way, with results that reverberated all the way to London and back." On 16 July 1651, three men from Newport—John Clarke, Obadiah Holmes, and John Crandall—went to Massachusetts to minister and serve communion to a blind fellow Baptist named William Witter. Witter had previously been called before the grand jury for saying that "they who stayed while a child was baptized do worship the devil." A number of converts were baptized and the sacraments were served, which incited the authorities to arrest the three men. The most serious charge was that of

---

[11] Bicknell, *History of Rhode Island*, 1:354.
[12] Bartlett, *Rhode Island Colony Records*, 1:52.

"rebaptizing" others. The men defended their actions on the grounds that they had not rebaptized anyone, since infant baptism was not a valid ordinance. The penalty for breaking this law directed against the Anabaptists was banishment, but, they argued, how could one be banished who was already living in another jurisdiction?

All three were fined and committed to prison until the fines were paid. The alternative to paying the fines was to be "well whipped." Some friends paid the fine for Clarke and he was released. Crandall was allowed to return home to raise money for his fine. Holmes refused to pay or let others pay it for him, choosing instead the alternative punishment at the whipping post. Thirty lashes were laid on him while he continued in prayer and testimony.[13]

This episode had considerable effect on the cause of religious liberty in the colonies. About a year later, while John Clarke was in England negotiating for the Rhode Island charter, he published a book with the full title *Ill Newes from New-England: or A Narrative of New-Englands Persecutions. Wherein is Declared That while old England is becoming new, New-England is become Old*. When this book appeared in 1652, Oliver Cromwell was in power and there were many Baptists in England who held prominent positions in the Commonwealth. Publication of religious persecutions in Massachusetts swayed political and public opinion against the intolerance of Puritan practice in America and paved the way for granting greater religious freedom in the colonies. Ironically, Obadiah Holmes and John Clarke were among those who later opposed the Sabbathkeepers in their Newport congregation, a move that led to the establishment of the first Seventh Day Baptist Church in America. John Crandall, on the other hand, became closely associated with the Sabbathkeepers, performing pastoral functions on their behalf.

Middle Colonies

The Middle Colonies in America contained the greatest mixture of peoples and beliefs of any of the New World settlements. Included were such religious groups as the Dutch Reformed, English Quakers, Swedish Lutherans, German Reformed, Mennonites, Dunkers, Schwenkfelders, Welsh Baptists, German Lutherans, Moravians, and Scotch-Irish Presbyterians.[14] In addition, there were settlements of Roman Catholics in Maryland and Delaware. The attraction of this territory was due to

---

[13] Gaustad, *Baptist Piety*, 22-30.
[14] Sweet, *Religion in America*, 83.

religious toleration stemming from both theological and practical motivations.

William Penn

William Penn, who founded Pennsylvania in 1681, held strong religious convictions concerning a person's individual rights. He held that persecution was a sin against God, since it attempted to limit the "inner light" (a key doctrine in Quaker theology) as well as limit the "sphere of action" of God's grace. His *Frame of the Government of the Province of Pennsilvania in America* contained provisions for freedom of religion, but it was not an unrestricted freedom.[15] No freedom was granted to an unbeliever, and restrictions were placed on others, which caused undue hardships for generations. Article XXXVI proved particularly restrictive to those who chose to worship on the seventh-day Sabbath, for it required them to abstain from common daily labor "every First Day of the Week called the Lord's Day."[16]

Lord Baltimore

The first statement of religious toleration in America was made in Maryland, where a proprietary colony was granted to Cecil Calvert (Lord Baltimore) in 1631. Initially he wanted to provide a sanctuary for Roman Catholics who were not permitted to practice their religion in England. He realized that he would not be able to recruit enough Catholics to adequately settle a colony and that to call the colony Catholic would invite persecution. By granting freedom of worship to all, he could provide a safe refuge for Catholics as well as Protestants. In 1649, the Act Concerning Religion made toleration part of Maryland's laws. Not only did the act grant tolerance, but it levied a fine on anyone who called another a "Heretick, Schismatic, Idolator, Puritan, Independent, Popish Priest, Jesuit, Lutheran, Calvinist, Anabaptist, Antinomian, Barrowist, Roundhead, Separatist, or any other name or terme in a reproachful manner relating to matters of religion."[17]

---

[15] William Penn, Article XXXV, *The Frame of the Government of the Province of Pennsilvania in America...* (London: n.p., 1682), repr. in Lutz and Warren, *A Covenanted People*, 32.

[16] Penn, Article XXXVI, *Government of Pennsilvania*, repr. in Lutz and Warren, *A Covenanted People*, 32.

[17] "The Act Concerning Toleration" (1649), quoted by Lutz and Warren, *A Covenanted People*, 29.

Elias Keach

Within this setting of broad toleration, a great number of settlers came from Europe, bringing with them diverse religious ideas. Of particular significance to Seventh Day Baptists was the immigration centered in Philadelphia, where Baptists from England and Wales found a haven. In 1688, Elias Keach, the son of a prominent London Baptist pastor, founded a Baptist Church at Pennepek near Philadelphia on the bank of the Delaware River. Keach was not a professing Christian when he came to America but posed as a minister. In the midst of a sermon, he became convicted of his deception and begged his congregation for their forgiveness. It was remarked that he was converted under his own preaching. H. Leon McBeth, in his book *The Baptist Heritage*, commented that this conversion greatly blessed the Baptists of the Middle Colonies, for Keach brought youth, vigor, and organizing skill, as well as a vigorous evangelistic outreach, throughout the area where several new churches were established.[18]

Keach extended his preaching into New Jersey. Assisted by Thomas Killingsworth, three separate churches in New Jersey grew from the outreach of the Pennepek church. One gathered at Piscataway in Middlesex County in 1689, another was organized in Middleton in Monmouth County, and a third grew in Southern New Jersey at Cohansey. Thus, by 1690, there were Baptist churches in each of the four areas of the Middle Colonies where Seventh Day Baptists were to have churches in the succeeding decades. At least four separate Sabbath churches were established in the Philadelphia area of the Pennepek church in southeastern Pennsylvania, beginning with a church at Newtown around 1700. The Piscataway Seventh Day Baptist Church, established in 1705, was composed initially of members from the Piscataway Baptist Church. The Shiloh Seventh Day Baptist church was established in 1737 near Cohansey, and it was in Monmouth County near Middleton that the Shrewsbury Seventh Day Baptist Church had its beginning around 1745. The presence of Baptist churches in these areas provided the climate in which Seventh Day Baptists could take root and grow.

---

[18] H. Leon McBeth, *The Baptist Heritage* (Nashville: Broadman, 1987) 146.

7

THE FIRST SEVENTH DAY
BAPTIST CHURCHES IN AMERICA

There are three distinct centers in America from which Seventh Day Baptists trace their origins: Newport, Rhode Island; Philadelphia, Pennsylvania; and Piscataway, New Jersey. Each congregation formed under different circumstances and from differing backgrounds. The Newport Church was an outgrowth of people who moved to Rhode Island to escape the religious intolerance of the Puritan Massachusetts Bay colony. Those in the Philadelphia area were mostly immigrants with Quaker backgrounds who came in search of political and economic freedom. The Piscataway church was greatly influenced by the Pilgrims of the Plymouth colony.

Although a number of people contributed to the founding of these three churches, each church identified a single individual as "the first." These three founders stand as representatives of three methods by which other churches have been established. Stephen Mumford of Newport was a Sabbath observer when he came to America. He shared his beliefs among a nucleus of people within an established Baptist congregation. Abel Nobel is credited with establishing a church in Pennsylvania as a result of controversy among segments of the Quaker community. Doctrinal disputes over revelation and inspiration, coupled with administrative problems, led some to establish a New Testament Church according to scriptural teachings. Edmund Dunham was a leader in the Baptist Church at Piscataway who was challenged over his observance of Sunday. Through Bible study, he and several others became convinced of the Sabbath and formed their own congregation.

These same methods have continued in the propagation of the Sabbath. Some, moving to a new location, readily share their faith. Others seek to establish a more perfect church according to biblical principles and cannot ignore the implications of the seventh-day Sabbath. Still others who are very content in their faith may become convinced of an error in their previous position and choose to follow the dictates of conscience as God reveals truth to them.

NEWPORT, RHODE ISLAND

The first Seventh Day Baptist Church in America was established in Newport, Rhode Island, on 23 December 1671 (Julian calendar). The church took root when five members of the First Baptist Church joined Stephen and Anne Mumford in covenant together.

Stephen Mumford

The first known Seventh Day Baptist in America was Stephen Mumford, who arrived in about 1664. Correspondence between the Seventh Day Baptists in Rhode Island and the Bell Lane Church in London led some to conclude that the Mumfords had been members of that church prior to coming to America. However, decoded records of the Tewkesbury Baptist Church in Gloucestershire list Stephen Mumford and Sister Mumford among the congregation's Sabbathkeepers in 1663. Many of the early Sabbathkeepers in England did maintain membership in other churches for a number of years.

The Mumfords left a mixed congregation of both Sabbath and Sunday observers. The same practice existed in the Baptist church established by Dr. John Clarke in Newport. There is no record, however, of the Mumfords having joined that church in Newport. In fact, John Comer's history of the church states that "Stephen Mumford and his wife were never joined because of ye non observation of the 7th Day (e.g., Mumford would not join because the First Baptist Church was not Sabbatarian)...."[1]

Little is known of Mumford's life in England or the reason for his coming to America. Within ten years he had attained considerable status in the Newport community, where he was listed as a freeman in the year 1671, giving him the right to participate in town government. Presumably through his influence, several members of the Baptist church in Newport accepted the Sabbath. Among those were Samuel and Tacy Hubbard and their family.

Samuel and Tacy Hubbard

Few people in colonial times left as complete a record as did Samuel Hubbard. Much of his journal and many of his letters were copied, and extracts have been used to exemplify colonial thought in this period.

---

[1] Rev. John Comer, "A History of the Baptist Church in Newport," n.d., Isaac Backus Papers, MSS 273, B1, F21, p. 4, Rhode Island Historical Society.

Samuel was born in 1610 in Mendelsham, England, and emigrated to Salem, Massachusetts, in 1633. The following year he moved to Watertown, Massachusetts, where he joined the church in 1635 "by giving account of my faith." Tacy Cooper came to Dorchester in 1634 and joined the church there. Samuel and Tacy married in 1636 in Windsor, Connecticut. The Hubbards made several moves during the next few years. At Springfield they were instrumental in gathering a church. In 1647 they moved to Fairfield, where they subscribed to Baptist ideas.[2] Samuel gave his wife credit for taking the lead in this enlightenment as he wrote: "God having enlightened both, but mostly my wife, into his holy ordinance of baptizing only of visible believers, and being very zealous for it, she was mostly struck at and answered two times publickly; where I was also said to be as bad as she, and are threatened with imprisonment to Hartford jail, if not to renounce it or to remove; that scripture came into our minds, if they persecute you in one place flee to another: and so we did."[3]

In 1648 they settled in Newport, where they were baptized by John Clarke and joined the church. Almost from the beginning, Samuel was recognized as a leader. In 1665 the Hubbards accepted the seventh-day Sabbath, an event Samuel recorded in his journal: "My wife took up keeping of the Lord's holy 7th day Sabbath the 10 day March 1665. I took it up 1 day April 1665. Our daughter Ruth 25 Oct. 1666—Rachel—Jan. 15 day 1666. Bethiah—Feb. 1666. Our son-in-law Joseph Clarke 23 Feb. 1666."[4]

The circumstances of the Hubbards' coming to the Sabbath are not recorded. Since this happened shortly after the arrival of Stephen Mumford and his family, it is assumed that the Mumfords were instrumental in bringing them to an acceptance of the Sabbath. Yet, Seventh Day Baptists are not dependent on an "apostolic succession" for the Sabbath. The question of the Sabbath debated in England during the Great Decade of the 1650s could hardly have escaped the notice of people in the colonies who were in communication with the mother country. In a 1669 letter to the church in Bell Lane, London, Samuel Hubbard made reference to books of Stennett, Cowell, and probably

---

[2] Ray Greene Huling, *Samuel Hubbard, of Newport: 1610–1689* (N.p.: n.p., n.d.), repr from *Narragansett Historical Register* 5/4 (Dec 1887): 1-15.

[3] Samuel Hubbard, *Register of Mr. Samuel Hubbard* (transcription of excerpts with notes by Isaac Backus), ca. 1775, Isaac Backus Papers, MSS 273, B1, F27, Rhode Island Historical Society. See also MS 194x.6, pp. 7-8, SDB Hist. Soc. Lib.

[4] Hubbard, *Register of Mr. Samuel Hubbard*, 9-10. See also MS 194x.6, 9-10.

Saller.[5] Stephen Mumford may have introduced members of the congregation to some of this writing, but it was the study of Scriptures that confirmed this belief.

By the end of the decade, there were eleven people in the congregation who had embraced the Sabbath. In addition there were others, including Dr. John Clarke's nephew Joseph Clarke, who had moved to the western part of the state where a portion of the Hubbard family had settled. The growth of Sabbath convictions created a concern within the First Baptist Church.

A Church Is Born

Although the date 1671 is given as the birth date for the first Seventh Day Baptist Church in America, there was a considerable gestation period accompanied by discomfort and labor pains. Edwin Gaustad, in his biographical sketch of Obadiah Holmes, pointed out that the six years between Tacy Hubbard's first acceptance of her Christian duty to the separation at the end of 1671 "were years of painful decision and almost daily discomfort." Four questions were raised from the Sabbatarian side: (1) How much proselytizing of others within the church was appropriate? (2) Could one still take communion with non-Sabbatarians? (3) How much loyalty did the Hubbard family owe to the church of Clarke and Holmes? (4) How should one behave toward those who became Sabbatarians and then changed their minds?[6]

It was the last question that in the end forced a separation from the mother church. Two couples, Mr. and Mrs. Nicholas Wyld and Mr. and Mrs. John Salmon, had been among the earliest to accept the Sabbath, but early in 1669 they stopped observing the Sabbath and spoke against it. The anxiety and discouragement that accompanied this "apostasy," as it was viewed, is revealed in correspondence with Sabbathkeepers in England and with members of Hubbards' family in Westerly. To the church at Bell Lane in London, Samuel Hubbard wrote, "It is a very hard exercise to us, poor weak ones to lose four so suddenly out of the 11 of us."[7] Edward Stennett advised the remaining Sabbathkeepers to seek dismissal, and, if they were refused, to withdraw themselves. The church in Bell Lane gave similar advice, adding that they should "have love to

---

[5] Hubbard, *Register of Mr. Samuel Hubbard*, 50 (3 Jul 1669). See also MS 194x.6, 41.

[6] Edwin S. Gaustad, *Baptist Piety: The Last Will & Testimony of Obadiah Holmes* (Grand Rapids MI: Christian, 1978) 52.

[7] Hubbard, *Register of Mr. Samuel Hubbard*, 48-49 (3 Jul 1669). See also MS 194x.6, 40-41.

all saints holding up general communion with them, as prayer & prophesie, lest it be those you have the particular offence against."[8]

This division in the church over the Sabbath had its effect on others in the New England area. A letter from the Baptist Church in Boston urged Sabbatarians to remain in the First Baptist Church of Newport and "get along as well as they could."[9] Letters also showed that the church at Providence became involved. The attitude there was different from that found in the Puritan colonies, where differences of doctrine were met with imprisonments, corporal punishments, and banishments. Gaustad noted that the effort made among Baptists was "to counsel, guide, convince and reprove with love."[10]

In spite of every effort at reconciliation, the Sabbatarians met a seemingly inflexible opposition from men such as Obadiah Holmes. Their position is understandable, since about a decade before the controversy over the Sabbath arose, the church in Newport had been racked by a split over the doctrine of the laying-on-of-hands and other principles drawn from the sixth chapter of Hebrews. Out of a church membership of under fifty members, twenty-one had withdrawn from the Newport Baptist church to form a "Six Principle Baptist Church." Holmes and Clarke were undoubtedly fearful that another doctrinal dispute might further weaken the church.

The debate reached a crisis in 1671 when Obadiah Holmes preached that the teaching of the Sabbath was causing people to "leave Christ and go to Moses."[11] Dr. John Clarke took a more conciliatory position, but after prolonged discussions it became apparent that a separation was necessary. Although the keeping of the Sabbath was the underlying difference, the sharing of communion as a sign of covenant relations was the final issue that forced the withdrawal.

Actual records of the two churches prior to 1690, if such existed, are lost, but the Baptist church's pastor during the early part of the eighteenth century, John Comer, took great pains to collect and preserve authentic information on the church's early years. A descriptive narrative of the controversy within the church included the debate between Obadiah Holmes and William Hiscox, who became the pastor

---

[8] Hubbard, *Register of Mr. Samuel Hubbard*, 67 (7 Feb 1667–1670). See also MS 194x.6, 60.
[9] Gaustad, *Baptist Piety*, 53.
[10] Ibid., 60.
[11] "The Seventh-day Baptist Church in Newport, R.I.," *SDB Memorial* 1/1 (Jan 1832): 38.

of the Sabbathkeepers.[12] About the only reference in that portion of Samuel Hubbard's journal still available simply states: "We entered into a church covenant the 23 day Dec., 1671, Wm. Hiscox, Stephen Mumford, Samuel Hubbard, Roger Baster, Sister Hubbard, Sister Mumford, Sister Rachel Langworthy."[13] (The actual separation took place on 7 December 1671, and the covenant was signed sixteen days later on 23 December, according to the Julian calendar. The dates according to the calendar generally adopted in America around 1750 places the dates at 18 December 1671 for the separation and 3 January 1672 for the signing of the covenant.)

A John Comer manuscript among the Isaac Backus papers at the Rhode Island Historical Society library contains the content of that church covenant.

> After serious Consideration and seeking God's face among our selves for the Lord to direct us in a right way for us, & our Children, so as might be God's glory and our Souls good and others Example, We Entered into Covenant with the Lord and with one another, and gave up our selves to God and to each other, to Walk together in all God's Holy Commandments and the Ordinances according to What the Lord had Discovered & Should Discover to us, to be his Mind for us to be obedient unto; with Sence upon our Hearts of great need to be watchful over one another, Did promise so to do, and in Building and Edyfying each other in our Most Holy faith.[14]

Some of Holmes's fears over the loss of the Sabbathkeepers were realized in the decades that followed. During the six years following the organization of the first Seventh Day Baptist Church in America, thirty members were added, although not all resided in Newport. Samuel Hubbard reported that there were in 1678 twenty in Newport, ten in New London, and seven in Westerly. A list of members in 1692 contains seventy-six names of individuals who had entered into covenant

---

[12] "A Brief and faithful relation of the Difference between those of this church and those who withdrew their Communion from it with ye causes and reasons of the Same...," *Newport, RI First Baptist Church Records, 1725*, ms., book #1167, Newport Historical Society, Newport RI, 137-53. See also *Newport, R.I. SDB Church Records, 1692–1846*, MS 19x.78, pp. 109-136, SDB Hist. Soc. Lib.

[13] Hubbard, *Register of Mr. Samuel Hubbard*, 10. See also MS 194x.6, 10.

[14] Comer, "A History of the Baptist Church in Newport," 2. See also: MS 1989.30, p. 2 SDB Hist. Soc. Lib. Note: There are slight variations between the two extant copies of the Newport SDB covenant.

relationship. At the same time, the First Baptist Church from which they separated showed considerable decline. Between the time of Obadiah Holmes's death in 1682 and the coming of John Comer in 1725, the church was often without a pastor. Around 1694, the church's membership of ten men and nine women voted to place themselves for a time "under the ministry of the Rev. Mr. William Hiscox of the 7th day Church."[15]

In 1726, the Baptist Church of Newport invited Seventh Day Baptists to send pastor Joseph Crandall to assist in the ordination of their newly chosen pastor, John Comer. The letter of invitation was addressed "unto you beloved in our Lord-Jesus-Christ desiring your assistance herein, though in some points we are differing from you."[16] The answer from the Seventh Day Baptists was cordial, acknowledging the importance of the event, but it concluded with the note that in consideration of the Scriptures requiring observation of the seventh-day Sabbath, and their "neglect to observe the fourth Commandment," they could not grant the request.[17]

In spite of this rejection, there continued to be cordial relationship between the Seventh Day Baptists and their Baptist brothers. When John Comer was pastor of another Baptist church in Newport, he wrote in his diary of several occasions when he worshiped with the Seventh Day Baptists, preaching for them on occasion and having Joseph Crandall preach in his church. He also implied membership in a Newport Association of Baptist Churches[18], which made use of a chapel known as Green End. Several Baptist churches owned a small meetinghouse at the head of the cove north of Easton's Beach, where baptisms were held. The records of the Newport Seventh Day Baptist Church show that from 30 April 1753 to 28 November 1785, meetings were held at Green End during which a sermon was given and then candidates were "baptized and passed under hands, and were received into the church."[19] The building, which may have been the meetinghouse in which Clarke and

[15] Gaustad, *Baptist Piety*, 106.
[16] Newport Church of Christ, letter to Seventh Day Baptist Church of Newport, 24 April 1726, Isaac Backus Papers, MSS 273, B1, F5, Rhode Island Historical Society.
[17] Seventh Day Baptist Church of Newport, letter to Church of Christ in Newport, 6 May 1726, Isaac Backus Papers, MSS 273, B1, F5, Rhode Island Historical Society.
[18] C. Edwin Barrows, ed., *The Diary of John Comer* (Newport RI: John P. Sanborn & Co., 1893) 7:49-53, collections of the Rhode Island Historical Society Library?, Newport RI.
[19] Newport, R.I. SDB Church Records, 1692-1846, ms. copy by Joseph Stillman, MS 19x.78, pp. 201-237, SDB Hist. Soc. Lib.

Holmes preached and thus where the split took place[20], became "very much decayed before the commencement of the Revolutionary War, and was destroyed shortly after the close of that War."[21]

In time, the vitality and witness of the Newport Seventh Day Baptist Church shifted to daughter churches in the western part of the state. Still, Newport is considered the birthplace of the denomination in this country.

PHILADELPHIA AREA

About thirty years after the organization of the Newport church, a second group of Sabbathkeepers had its beginning in Pennsylvania near Philadelphia. Like Rhode Island, Pennsylvania was a colony founded on principles of religious freedom. Unlike Rhode Island, which was a haven for colonists direct from England or from neighboring states, Pennsylvania acted like a magnet, attracting settlers from among the persecuted on the continent of Europe. Many of them came from countries with state churches, deeply rooted traditions, and customs that made it difficult for a minority group such as Seventh Day Baptists to attain the strength needed to survive beyond the colonial period.

The influences that led to the establishment of churches in the Philadelphia area are not as clearly defined as in Newport. At times the leadership was less stable because it was provided by persons who chose not to fully identify with the churches they founded or temporarily led. Among the members there was considerable diversity. Many of these leaders came from a Quaker background in which meetings and worship were less structured and less dependent on pastoral leadership than in the traditional churches. Some united with Seventh Day Baptists, not because of strong doctrinal convictions, but because their services offered an alternative to less meaningful worship elsewhere. This was particularly true where services were held in German or Welsh rather than English.

Nonetheless, by the end of the eighteenth century there were several Sabbathkeeping groups in Pennsylvania with branches that extended into New Jersey, Delaware, and western Virginia. None of the Philadelphia area churches existed long into the nineteenth century,

---

[20] C. Edwin Barrows, *History of the First Baptist Church in Newport, R.I.* (Newport RI: John P. Sanborn & Co., 1876) 27.
[21] "The Seventh-day Baptist Church at Newport, R. I.," *SDB Memorial* 2/2 (Apr 1853): 72.

except for the German Seventh Day Baptist community at Ephrata. Yet, the names of members of these churches echo in countless churches to which some of the families migrated.

Abel Noble

The first record of the acceptance of the seventh day as the Sabbath in the Pennsylvania colony centers on Abel Noble, who was born in 1655 in Bristol, England. His father was a prosperous Quaker merchant who raised his son in the tradition of George Fox and William Penn. In 1684, Abel Noble came with other Quakers who fled from persecution in England and settled on the western banks of the Delaware River in "Penns Woods," or Pennsylvania. Although Quakers did not believe in a professional clergy, they recognized that certain individuals exhibited gifts of exhortation; Abel Noble was one such individual.

Abel Noble was an itinerant preacher and agitator who championed the causes of the Sabbath and baptism without assuming the responsibilities of a pastor. He felt as much at home on the courthouse steps addressing any who might listen as he did in the pulpit. His influence extended beyond fellow Quakers with whom he found disagreement. Noble had close contacts with some of the German Pietists who had emigrated to this area in search of freedom of worship. He, along with a number of others who held to the seventh-day Sabbath, corresponded with leaders such as Johannes Kelpius. They contributed to Conrad Beissel's acceptance of the Sabbath and the formation of the first German Seventh Day Baptist congregation in 1728. Beissel and his followers later settled at Ephrata, Pennsylvania, where the semi-monastic community known as the Cloisters began in 1733.

It is not possible to isolate the paths by which ideas and issues come to individuals or churches. There is no evidence that Abel Noble was a Sabbath observer long before 1697, when, according to Morgan Edwards, Noble baptized the first Keithian and won over several people to the observance of the seventh day.[22] Charles H. Greene wrote that Abel Noble made a business trip through New Jersey in about 1696. While in Cohansie Country, he met Thomas Killingsworth, who converted him to Baptist opinions. There were members of the Newport Seventh Day Baptist church living in the Cohansey area as early as 1684 and on Long Island, where Abel Noble did some preaching. Possibly their influence

---

[22] Morgan Edwards, *Materials toward a History of Baptists*, 2 vols. (Danielsville GA: Heritage Papers, 1984) 1:30

convinced him of the Sabbath.[23] On the other hand, it is possible that he came to the Sabbath on his own.

In addition to Abel Noble, four other men challenged the Quakers' hold in Pennsylvania during the last decade of the seventeenth century. Two of them could not be classified as Seventh Day Baptists, but nonetheless they influenced the formation of Seventh Day Baptist Churches in the area.

George Keith

George Keith raised his voice against "the Devil and the seductive spirit of Quakerism." He had been trained as a Presbyterian minister in Scotland. Around 1662, he became a Quaker and vigorously promoted that denomination's faith. After several imprisonments and much persecution, he emigrated in 1682 to East Jersey, where he was appointed Governor General. In 1689 he taught school in Philadelphia, where his "turbulent and contentious nature" involved him in a dispute with his Quaker brethren. He had denied the teaching of Quaker orthodoxy, which held that each person had within himself sufficient divine grace for his own salvation. Joining with Keith, forty-eight people signed a confession of faith and a statement of the reasons for their separation from the Quakers. Abel Noble, along with a Welsh immigrant named William Davis, were among those who supported George Keith.[24]

Rival meetings were set up in Burlington, New Jersey, and in the house of Thomas Powell in Upper Providence, about 10 miles from Philadelphia. These meetings drew many Quakers as well as adherents of other denominations. George Keith did not formally join any of these splinter groups, but he seemed to enjoy stirring up religious ferment. He returned to England in 1694 and eventually joined the Church of England. In 1702, he returned to America as an Episcopal missionary. Keith never provided the leadership that normally would be expected from one whose name is attached to so important a movement. The religious climate may not have been ripe for such a radical person as Keith, but it was ready to foster the growth of some of the ideas he expressed in his 1691 statement of dissent.[25]

The Keithian statement of faith gave particular prominence to the Bible and the commandments of God. This statement specified that in

---

[23] Charles H. Greene, "The Keithians," *Sabbath Recorder* 63/14 (7 Apr 1907): 235.
[24] Charles H. Greene, "The Keithians," MSS 19x.178.1-5, SDB Hist. Soc. Lib.
[25] Ibid.

accord with the Scriptures, the days of the week and names of the months should be numbered, such as first, second, third, etc., rather than bearing names of pagan origin. With such attention to the biblical basis for all phases of life, it was inevitable that some would see the inconsistency of observing the first day when the Bible stressed the seventh day.

Henry Koster

A second influence leading to the formation of Sabbath congregations in the Philadelphia area came from Heinrich Bernhard Koster, a German Pietist with strong Lutheran ties. When he came to America in 1694, Koster found the state of religion at a very low point. Putting aside some of his mystical doctrines, he preached the plain gospel with untiring energy among the English, Welsh, and Germans. He brought to the religious revival in the colony two elements the Quakers neglected: formal worship, including preaching, and personal study of the Scriptures. At his own expense, he purchased and distributed a large stock of English Bibles. Many of the Keithians turned to Koster for leadership following George Keith's defection. Koster saw among the Keithians the need for ordained ministers to perform the ordinances of baptism and the Lord's Supper. Even though he had been raised as a Lutheran, he announced that he would publicly baptize by immersion any who would present themselves for this purpose. Among those who were baptized were the nuclei of two Seventh Day Baptist churches, including William Davis and Thomas Rutter.[26]

There is evidence that Koster considered joining the Seventh Day Baptists, but he was too deeply grounded in the Lutheran faith to make the move. One of his Lutheran colleagues, Jonas Auren, accepted the Sabbath while serving as pastor of a Lutheran church. Auren published his reasons for accepting the Sabbath in 1700, after which he was called to appear before the governor. It is recorded that "so ably did Auren defend his position, that he was permitted to return as pastor, with the understanding that he was to preach the Orthodox Lutheran doctrine on Sunday to his congregation, while he and his family were at liberty to keep the seventh day."[27]

---

[26] Julius Friedrich Sachse, "Henrich Bernhard Koster," *The German Pietists of Provincial Pennsylvania (1694-1708)* (Philadelphia: P. C. Stockhausen, 1895) 251-98.

[27] Sachse, "Jonas Auren," 127-28.

William Davis

Another voice that challenged the hold of Quakerism in Pennsylvania was that of William Davis, sometimes called the "erratic missionary" because of his tendency to stir up controversy. He was born in 1663 in Wales and attended Oxford University, intending to go into the ministry. At Oxford he became interested in Quaker doctrines and left the University before graduating. In 1684 he traveled with other Quakers to Pennsylvania, where he began speaking publicly on doctrinal issues. In 1691 he joined George Keith in separating from the Quakers, but he and Keith soon had a falling out over doctrinal issues. Around 1696 he, like Abel Noble, came in contact with Rev. Thomas Killingsworth and accepted many of the beliefs of the Baptists. He joined the Pennepek Baptist Church, where he was chosen as pastor, but in less than two years the church banished him for expressing what they considered a heretical view on the person of Christ, thinking he denied the Christ's divinity.

Davis's contacts with Abel Noble during the Keithian dispute convinced him of the supremacy of the Moral Law and man's necessity to observe the seventh day of the week as the Sabbath. He became a Seventh Day Baptist and pastored the church gathered in Pennepek before moving to Rhode Island and later to Shrewsbury, New Jersey. His loyalty to the denomination has never been questioned, although both his temperament and certain unorthodox views caused considerable controversy not only among the Pennsylvania churches but in Rhode Island and New Jersey as well. Some of his descendents constituted the core, nearly a century later, of a religious migration to what is now West Virginia.

Thomas Rutter

A fourth name important to Philadelphia's Seventh Day Baptist history is Thomas Rutter. He had been baptized in 1696 by Henry Koster and was among the group made up of Koster, William Davis, and Thomas Boyer, who challenged many of the Quakers' beliefs and practices. Both Rutter and Koster published tracts to which a German Lutheran named Pastorius responded with a book titled *Henry Bernhard Koster, William Davis, Thomas Rutter and Thomas Bowyer: four boasting disputers of this world briefly rebuked and answered according to their folly.*[28] Rutter, who was considered an effective evangelist, traveled throughout the region, with many baptisms to his credit. He was one of those who delivered the concept of the Sabbath to Conrad Beissel and the German Seventh Day Baptists.

C. H. Greene described Thomas Rutter as "a man of sound judgment and excellent doctrine. Whenever there came any trouble amongst the Pennsylvanian Sabbatarian churches, and they had their full share of trouble, Thomas Rutter was the man who was always called on to straighten things out."[29]

CHURCHES IN THE PHILADELPHIA AREA

The rejection of the Quaker doctrines which led to individualized interpretations of Scripture left a number of people receptive to Baptist principles and to the acceptance of the Sabbath. Much of the information concerning the early Baptist and Seventh Day Baptist churches of this period and area comes from the work of Morgan Edwards, who researched and published *Materials towards a history of the Baptists.* In the first volume, published in 1770, Edwards used material on the Pennsylvania Baptists to identify four Seventh Day Baptist churches established in the Philadelphia area and to demonstrate that these churches had formed as a result of those who had come from Quaker Baptist traditions.[30]

Upper Providence or Newtown

The society at Newtown in Upper Providence, Chester County, about 24 miles west of Philadelphia, first met as Keithian Baptists in the house of Thomas Powell. The society organized in about 1700 and chose Thomas Martin, whom Abel Nobel had baptized, to minister to the group. During its first two years, the church experienced regular growth, in part because it offered an English-speaking place of worship in a strongly Welsh settlement where services were often held only in the Welsh language. The church meeting in the Powell home offered services

---

[28] Francis Daniel Pastorius, *Henry Bernhard Koster, William Davis, Thomas Rutter & Thomas Bowyer, Four Boasting Disputers of this World briefly Rebuked and Answered according to their Folly..., which they themselves have manifested in a late pamphlet, titled, "Advice for all professors..."* (New York: W. Bradford, 1697), cited by Sachse, *German Pietists,* 280-81.

[29] Charles H. Greene, "Chester Co. Pa. biography," MS 1918.2.6, pp. 85-86, C. H. Greene Papers, SDB Hist. Soc. Lib.

[30] Edwards, *Materials,* 1:28-30.

in English, which the non-Welsh members more easily understood. In 1698 George Keith, now a member of the Church of England, returned to the area accompanied by a very persuasive and aggressive Episcopal minister, Evan Evans, who offered services in both Welsh and English. Several townspeople were drawn to them, including Thomas Powell, in whose home they met.

Morgan Edwards recorded that "in 1700 a difference arose among them touching the sabbath which broke up the society. Such as adhered to the observation of the seventh day kept together at Newtown."[31] The group continued to meet in the house of David Thomas, but the church soon declined and the principal voice for the Sabbath shifted to other churches.[32]

Pennepek (Philadelphia)

The Seventh Day Baptist church located at Pennepek in the Lower Dublin County of Philadelphia has sometimes been identified with the Keithian congregation meeting in Philadelphia. Charles H. Greene suggested that the small log meetinghouse the Keithians had built in 1692 at Spruce Street, below Mulberry would become the meetinghouse of the "Philadelphia Sabbatarian Baptist Church in 1698."[33] Julius Sachse wrote that the Keithian congregation under Koster, which grew convinced of the Sabbath, eventually became a distinct church, known as the Seventh-day Baptist Church of Philadelphia with Thomas Rutter as the first pastor.[34]

The church records of the Mill Yard church in London reference correspondence in 1701 from the Baptist quarterly meeting at the home of Thomas Rutter, "8 miles from Philadelphia," stating that many of them had become Sabbathkeepers.[35] This detail is consistent with Edwards's mention of the Seventh Day Baptist church at Pennepek about "9 miles NebN [northeast by north] from the city," which the Keithian Baptists had formed in about 1701.[36] Thomas Graves donated a plot of

[31] Ibid., 1:28.
[32] William L. Burdick, "The Eastern Association," *SDBs in Europe and America*, Seventh Day Baptist General Conference (Plainfield NJ: American Sabbath Tract Society, 1910) 2:670-71.
[33] Greene, C. H. Greene Papers, MS 1918.2.6:82-84.
[34] Sachse, *German Pietists*, 126.
[35] Mill Yard, London, Eng. SDB Church Records, 1673–1845, ms., CRR 1932.1, p. 120, SDB Hist. Soc. Lib.
[36] Edwards, *Materials*, 1:30.

ground on which to build a meetinghouse. The church experienced some growth until Evan Evans attacked the church with such force that Thomas Graves was won back to the Church of England (known in America as the Episcopalian church). Graves deeded the lot over to the Episcopalians, depriving the Sabbatarians of their place of meeting. Julius Sachse wrote that these proceedings were made possible "through the simplicity of the Sabbatarians, who trusting in their faith had neglected to take a deed for the ground."[37] The meetings continued in the homes of some of the members, but little growth is recorded.

The next few years were marked by a bitter controversy in which the Baptists and the Seventh Day Baptists joined forces in meeting the challenge of Keith and Evans. The Baptists were represented by their most capable leader, Thomas Killingsworth, while the William Davis was the mouthpiece for the Seventh Day Baptists. Out of this controversy, the Episcopalians appeared to gain ground while groups such as the Quakers and Baptists experienced a growing intolerance toward dissenting doctrine.

In 1711, William Davis again was involved in a doctrinal dispute over the nature of Christ (Davis contended that Jesus' two natures had mixed and were no longer distinct). He left the Philadelphia area for Rhode Island, leaving the church without an effective leader. Several of its members fellowshipped with the Newtown church or moved on to other locations. The Newtown church's later history involved a cemetery plot known as the Sparks Burial Ground in the very heart of Philadelphia. (A commemorative memorial to its history is now to be found at Shiloh, New Jersey.)

Nantmeal or French Creek

A branch of the Newtown church was formed in 1722 at East Nantmeal in Chester County, about 32 miles from Philadelphia. In some records this branch appears by the name of French Creek. It received an influx of members from the Great Valley Baptist Church who had accepted the Sabbath. Numerically, it was the largest Seventh Day Baptist Church in the area and the only one to have its own church building, which its congregation built in 1762. From this church several families went to establish short-lived churches in such places as Broad River, South Carolina, and Tuckaseeking, Georgia.

---

[37] Julius F. Sachse, "Sabbath Keepers of the Seventh Day Baptists of Chester County" (1888), PP 1916, pp. 5, 7, SDB Hist. Soc. Lib.

Considerable mystery surrounds another possible church in this area known as the Conogocheage. A letter written in 1748 is prefaced with the greeting: "The Church of Christ, observing the commandments of God in ye faith of Jesus Christ, meeting at Conogocheage, in Lancaster county, in Pensilvania, sendeth greeting to our beloved brethren at Piscataway, in New Jersey."[38]

Morgan Edwards recorded that Jonathan Dunham was ordained at the Conogocheage in 1745.[39] Charles Henry Greene's manuscript dealing with churches in the area makes a possible identification with George Adam Martin, who, mainly through a study of Scriptures, embraced the Sabbath and along with about sixty others was banished from the Dunkard church, where he had been preaching. Greene dates this church's organization to 1735 and states that Martin was the pastor until 1757, when he joined the Ephrata community. Greene wrote that Martin was succeeded by Rev. John Horn.[40] During Horn's pastorate, the church probably merged with the French Creek church. Yet, neither of these names appears on the 1748 letter to the Piscataway Church. One name that does appear is Jonathan Curtis, whom the Piscataway Church had ordained deacon in 1714.[41] Also signing the letter were William James and Lewis Williams, who are listed among those who came from the Great Valley Baptist Church to the French Creek church in 1726.[42]

Nottingham

Another Seventh Day Baptist church in the Philadelphia area was located in the southwestern part of Chester County near the Maryland border at Nottingham. Its principal leaders were Samuel and Richard Bond, in whose Cecil County, Maryland, home the congregation often met. The church suffered directly from the state Sunday laws of 1794, which were designed to strengthen the observance of Sunday. These laws proved discriminatory against Sabbathkeepers, whose beliefs required them to refrain from work on the Sabbath and, because of the new laws, on Sunday. The church's numbers were never large, and the

---

[38] "Correspondence of the Churches—1740–1750—Extracts," sec. IV, *Sabbath Recorder* 37/45 (10 Nov 1881): 3.

[39] Edwards, *Materials*, 1:136.

[40] Charles H. Greene, "The Keithians," MS 19x.178.4, pp. 55-56, SDB Hist. Soc. Lib.

[41] See: "The Seventh-day Baptist Church at Piscataway, N. J.," *SDB Memorial* 2/3 (Jul 1853): 121.

[42] "Extinct Seventh-day Baptist Societies in South-Eastern Pennsylvania," *Sabbath Recorder* 45/27 (4 Jul 1889): 422. See also Edwards, *Materials*, 1:30.

migrations into the western regions of Virginia, to such areas as Lost Creek, brought it to an end.

In 1788, well-known Baptist theologian Elhanan Winchester visited both the English and the German Seventh Day Baptists in southeastern Pennsylvania. In his journal, Winchester described them with these words:

> Such Christians I have never seen as they are, who take the Scriptures as their only guide, in matters both of faith and practice…. They are industrious, sober, temperate, kind, charitable people, envying not the great nor despising the mean. They read much, they sing and pray much, they are constant attendants upon the worship of God; their dwellings are all houses of prayer; they walk in the commandments and ordinances of the Lord blameless, both in public and in private,… Whatsoever they believe their Saviour commands, they practice without inquiring or regarding what others do.[43]

Morgan Edwards summed up the status of the Seventh Day Baptists in Pennsylvania by saying that by 1770 there were "(1)…26 families containing about 130 souls; whereof 34 were baptized; (2) they originated from the Keithian Baptists about the year 1700 by means of Abel Noble; (3) they have two yearly meetings with one meetinghouse; and but one minister, Rev. Enoch David."[44]

New Jersey Beginnings

The third birthplace of Seventh Day Baptists in America was in the colony of New Jersey. Initially, New Jersey had been a part of the Dutch colony of New Amsterdam. With the restoration of the Stuart monarchy in 1660, the English claims to the entire eastern seaboard from Nova Scotia to Georgia were renewed. To consolidate their claim, the English encouraged settlement in this territory by granting 150 acres to every freeman who would settle in the colony, "provided the immigrant equipped himself with a good musket."[45] Liberty of conscience was guaranteed to all who became subjects of the English crown, and permission was granted to maintain such ministers as they might prefer. The unsettled conditions that accompanied the Restoration in England

---

[43] Elhanan Winchester, quoted in "Extinct SDB Societies," *Sabbath Recorder* 45/28 (11 Jul 1889): 438.

[44] Edwards, *Materials*, 1:31.

[45] Francis Bazley Lee, *New Jersey as a Colony and as a State*, 4 vols. (New York: Publishing Society of New Jersey, 1903) 1:132.

under Charles II prompted many willing recruits. Puritans, Congregationalists, Baptists, and Quakers, as well as men of no religious convictions, responded. Of greater significance with regard to Seventh Day Baptists was the migration that came from Puritan New England, where Baptists were facing increased discrimination and persecution.

Piscataway

In December 1666, Hugh Dunn, John Martin, Hopewell Hull, and Charles Gilman, together with their families, secured land in New Jersey between the Rahway and Raritan Rivers. They were Baptist refugees who had settled on the banks of the Piscataqua River that separated New Hampshire from Maine. Thomas Griffiths, in his *A History of Baptists in New Jersey*, suggests that they called their home in New Jersey by the name of their New England home, "linking thus the memories of persecution and of escape from bondage and that of freedom." Maine was then a part of Massachusetts Bay colony, and "Puritan intolerance could as well reach them in their hiding in the wilds as in the nearer dwellings."[46] Within three years other settlers came from this area, including John Drake, who would serve as the first pastor of the Piscataway Baptist Church.

Two dates have been given for the founding of this Baptist church in Piscataway. In 1686 the town meeting agreed that a meetinghouse should be built and appointed a committee to see to its construction. Thomas Griffiths concludes that this was the church's beginning, since the building committee was made up largely of Baptists who were reported "to have swarmed into it and preached."[47] Other records show that Hugh Dunn, John Drake, Nicholas Bonham, John Smalley, Edmund Dunham, and John Randolph formed a gospel church in spring 1689 with the help of Rev. Thomas Killingsworth.[48]

From the original Baptist church, the Piscataway Seventh Day Baptist Church split in 1705. One Sunday when Edmund Dunham was on his way to services, he saw his brother-in-law Hezekiah Bonham performing forbidden "servile labor." Thinking it his Christian responsibility to reprimand those who broke God's command to cease from labor on the Sabbath, he urged Bonham to stop. In response,

---

[46] Thomas S. Griffiths, *A History of Baptists in New Jersey* (Hightstown NJ: Barr, 1904) 252.

[47] Griffiths, *History of Baptists in New Jersey*, 253.

[48] Edwards, *Materials*, 1:85.

Hezekiah Bonham demanded scriptural proof that the first day of the week was holy by divine authority. It is generally presumed that Bonham's work on Sunday was more a matter of indifference than of any conviction concerning the seventh day as a Sabbath. But there was no indifference on the part of Edmund Dunham. He accepted the challenge and not only searched the Bible himself for proof, which he had assumed must be there, but enlisted others in the church to join in the investigation.[49]

Out of this study, Dunham became convinced that the fourth commandment was still morally binding and that he ought to take the seventh day as God's holy Sabbath. Seventeen others followed his lead and met with Edmund Dunham in his home. Most continued their membership with the Baptist church for a time, but the subject was so serious that it pitted minister against minister, deacon against deacon, brother against brother. Even to this day, there is a grammar school in the Piscataway community that bears the name "Quibbletown," and a marker bears the inscription: "Quibbletown—A colonial hamlet which was so named because of dissension as to whether Saturday or Sunday is the Sabbath. New Market, N.J., 1830."[50]

For the sake of peace, the Sabbathkeepers withdrew and entered into a covenant agreement on "the 19th day of August, 1705." They chose Edmund Dunham to be their pastor and sent him to Rhode Island, where he was ordained at Hopkinton in the Newport Church "by prayer and the laying on of hands by their elder, William Gibson."[51]

Plymouth Connections

Although the date 1705 may be taken as the beginning of the Piscataway Church, its direct roots go back to the Plymouth colony in Massachusetts. No less than twelve of the church's charter members were descended from the Pilgrims settled at Plymouth, Scituate, and Barnstable in Massachusetts. These descendants brought with them a heritage of religious independence. Among them were the Fitz Randolph

---

[49] "The Seventh-day Baptist Church at Piscataway, N. J.," *SDB Memorial* 2/3 (Jul 1853): 119.

[50] John Bevis, "Quibbletown," editorial, *Sabbath Recorder* 198/5 (May 1976): 23.

[51] *Piscataway, N. J. SDB Church Records, 1705-1836*, MS, CRR 1956.9.1, p. 22, SDB Hist. Soc. Lib.

family, which traces its direct lineage to Deacon Blossom of Plymouth.[52] The Bonham and Dunham families trace their lineage to both the Mayflower Fullers and Rev. John Lathrop, the second pastor of the famous Jacob-Lathrop-Jessey Independent Church in London.[53] Several of the children of Nicholas and Hannah Bonham were to play important roles in the formation of both Baptist and the Seventh Day Baptist churches in New Jersey. Edmund Dunham also had roots going back to Scrooby, England, which is often considered the birthplace of Congregational churches.[54] Six of Edmund Dunham's immediate family were charter members of the church. A younger son, Jonathan, was only eleven at the time the church organized, but he had the distinction of being the first male member to join after the day of organization. Upon his father's death in 1734, Jonathan was licensed to preach. In 1745, he was ordained and served as full pastor for thirty-two years, until his death in 1777 at age eighty-three.[55]

For over 250 years, the Piscataway Seventh Day Baptist Church gave witness before it succumbed to increased urbanization and migrations. Yet, its influence continues through a number of daughter churches as well as the countless descendents of those who were reared within its covenant relationship.

---

[52] Oris H. F. Randolph, comp., *Edward Fitz Randolph Branch Lines, Allied Families, and English and Norman Ancestry:* A Family Genealogy, 860–1976 (Ann Arbor MI: Edwards Brothers, 1976) 1.

[53] Isaac Watson Dunham, comp., *Dunham Genealogy: Deacon John Dunham of Plymouth, Massachusetts, 1589–1669, and His Descendants* (Norwich CT: Bulletin Print, 1907) 250.

[54] Dunham, *Dunham Genealogy,* 4-9.

[55] John H. Bonham, referencing Oliver B. Leonard's notes, in *Notebooks of John H. Bonham, Shiloh, N.J., 1880-1952*; see sections tagged "Hugh Dunn Family" and "Piscataway Church."

8

REACHING OUT IN COVENANT
AND ASSOCIATIONAL RELATIONS

A covenant is a formal document by which consenting believers enter into an agreement with one another in the sight of God to obey God's laws. Seventh Day Baptists, as they spread out from their centers of origin, continued to maintain a covenant theology. As new churches were organized and new covenants established, attempts were made to maintain the covenantal spirit through correspondence, family ties, visiting ministers, and periodic meetings attended by representatives of the churches.

The emphasis on independence and local autonomy, which later generations claimed as essential to the workings of the Holy Spirit, is not found in the early history of these churches. They believed that the Holy Spirit worked in community. There existed a close relationship between churches such as Newport and Westerly (later Hopkinton), or Piscataway and Shiloh, where family ties and marriages linked the churches together. These relationships were religious as well as familial and social.

NEWPORT AND ITS COVENANT OUTREACH

By 1660, members of the Newport Baptist Church had settled in the Narraganset country comprising the western part of the Rhode Island colony. Although this land had been purchased from the Indian chief Sosoa in 1660, ownership of this area (sometimes called Misquamicut, or Squamicut) was disputed by Connecticut, Massachusetts Bay, and Rhode Island as well as various Indian tribes who did not accept Sosoa's right to sell. Jurisdictional disputes led to imprisonments, including that of several men who were later identified with Seventh Day Baptists.

The King Philip's War of 1675–1676 forced a number of settlers to seek safety among their Christian brothers in Newport. Samuel Hubbard records in his journal, "My daughter Burdick and her 8 children and my daughter Clarke and her 3 children and their husbands came to this Island for fear of the wars July 1675."[1]

Westerly (First Hopkinton)

The date of the first church services in Westerly is uncertain. A sermon given by John Callender on the occasion of the 1738 Rhode Island Centennial celebration gave 1665 as the date when a number of members of the church under Mr. J. Clarke settled at Westerly and selected John Crandall as a preacher and an elder. "They afterward did generally embrace the seventh-day Sabbath, and their successors are now a very large and flourishing church."[2]

According to Samuel Hubbard, three of his daughters, Ruth, Rachel, and Bethiah, all accepted the Sabbath in 1666. Ruth married Robert Burdick; Rachel, a charter member of the Newport Seventh Day Baptist Church, married Andrew Langworthy; and Bethiah married Joseph Clarke, who also accepted the Sabbath in 1666. These families were among Westerly's early settlers. They maintained close family and covenant relationship with the Sabbathkeepers in Newport and representing over thirty years of Sabbathkeeping in Westerly prior to the church's formal organization in that area in 1708.

In a 1678 letter, Samuel Hubbard noted that seven of the thirty-seven members of the Newport Seventh Day Baptists Church lived in Westerly.[3] In 1692, the membership numbered seventy-six, but there was no separation of members by location; they were all considered part of a single covenant church.[4] These early records show much concern over the proper administration of the sacrament of communion. At a meeting in July 1692, the congregation agreed on a definite rotation whereby communion would alternate every four weeks between Westerly and Newport.[5]

In 1708, the church separated into two distinct congregations. The minutes of the yearly meeting at Westerly for 17 July 1708 read, "by the

---

[1] Samuel Hubbard, *Register of Mr. Samuel Hubbard* (transcription of excerpts with notes by Isaac Backus), ca. 1775, Isaac Backus Papers, MSS 273, B1, F27, p. 10, Rhode Island Historical Society. See also MS 194x.6, p. 10, SDB Hist. Soc. Lib.
[2] Mr. Callender, "Century Sermon," (Newport RI: S. Kneeland and T. Green, 1738), cited in "The Seventh-day Baptist Church in Newport, R. I.," *SDB Memorial* 1(Apr 1852): 76.
[3] Hubbard, *Register*, 100. See also MS 194x.6, 97.
[4] "The Seventh-day Baptist Church in Newport, R. I.," *SDB Memorial* 1/3 (Jul 1852): 121.
[5] Newport, R.I. SDB Church Records, 1692–1846, ms. copy by Thomas B. Stillman and Joseph Stillman (1850), MS 19x.78 (3 Jul 1692), p. 1, SDB Hist. Soc. Lib.

mutual agreement of the Church, that part of the congregation in and about Westerly shall be hence forward a distinct congregation by themselves...provided the brethren and sisters at Newport that were not present at said meeting do consent thereto."[6] At first the church at Newport did not approve the action taken at Westerly, but after considerable correspondence it approved the separation into distinct churches with the agreement that Bro. Joseph Crandall administer baptism at both places.[7] A comparison of extant membership lists reveals a Westerly membership of seventy-two at the date of organization in 1708. In 1712, ten others had professed the seventh-day Sabbath and were baptized but had not received the laying on of hands, a practice that quite generally accompanied baptism during the church's colonial days.[8]

The two groups continued to think and act as one fellowship. They consulted often on matters of both faith and practice and continued in their periodic meeting for communion. They were united in their correspondence with Seventh Day Baptists in New Jersey and Pennsylvania. The clerk of the old Newport Church lived in Westerly so that, when the separation occurred, the minutes of the Westerly Church were simply added to those that had filled the previous pages of the Newport church record book.

Some of the early records show the deep concern the corporate body had over members who had broken the covenant by actions or attitudes. Members who absented themselves from the breaking of bread or from Sabbath worship were "labored with" in attempts to restore them to fellowship. The church records describe some of these transgressions in detail. A number of entries involve efforts to settle a disagreement that arose in the Philadelphia area churches over the teachings and practice of William Davis, who had come to Rhode Island and asked for membership in the Westerly church. Concern was also shown over the branch of the church residing in New London, Connecticut, some of whose members were called "Rogerenes" after their principal leader, John Rogers. Although still listed as members of the Newport Church, this group differed on several issues. They refused

---

[6] Newport Records (17 Jul 1708), 34.
[7] Newport Records (19 Oct 1708), 145.
[8] "The Westerly Seventh-day Baptist Church," SDB Memorial 3/1 (Jan 1854) 38-40. Note: The 1712 list is included in the Newport Records copied by Stillman, 103-105.

medical attention when ill or injured and sought persecution in order to dramatize their distinctive beliefs.

Doctrinal questions were considered and often voted on by the entire church. One such record dated 25 June 1713 records a minority opinion concerning the rite of baptism for "such persons that are not under the observation of the seventh day Sabbath." The majority voted against baptizing them but John Maxson, Joseph Crandall, Joseph Clark, and several others "declared they were not of that opinion, but that persons might be admitted to that ordinance which had true repentance and faith, though they might not see that particular truth."[9]

As people moved to other locations, most kept their membership in the home church until a new church might be formed. Even then, the covenant concept continued. By the end of the eighteenth century, there were 764 members of the old Westerly Church (by this time called First Hopkinton). By 1816 the number had grown to 947, in spite of the fact that several daughter churches had taken many of Westerly's members in the migration to the West.

PENNSYLVANIA AND NEW JERSEY COVENANT OUTREACH

The covenant relationship that existed among the Pennsylvania and New Jersey churches, like that in Rhode Island, encompassed many family ties. Because of the distances involved, the meetings were less frequent. Some members were newer to the faith and came to the Sabbath through independent scriptural study. Thus, they were more dependent on one another for leadership and the administration of the sacraments and ordinations.

Seventh Day Baptists in the Middle Colonies during the colonial period were centered in four areas: Philadelphia, Piscataway, Cohansey (Shiloh), and Shrewsbury. Baptists in these four areas had been united in a form of covenant relationship from about 1690 onward, but there was no direct connection between the Baptist associational connections and those of Seventh Day Baptists. The trend showed, however, that Seventh Day Baptists were not unique in their covenant relations, and that the religious climate of the region encouraged a sharing relationship.

C. H. Greene's description of an annual May meeting held at the spacious stone home of David Thomas reveals the Seventh Day Baptists' dedication in maintaining lines of communication among their brethren. Greene wrote of their coming from all over New Jersey and parts of

---

[9] Newport Records (25 Jun 1713), 95.

Chester County. The bridle paths and bad roads led through sparsely settled and dangerous territory. The Thomas Mansion became the scene of unbounded hospitality, since the travelers remained for several days. Many of the meetings attracted "neighboring Friends, Baptists, Churchmen and others."[10]

Shiloh: A Church with Many Roots

The church that is now known as Shiloh was constituted as "The First Congregation of Seventh Day Baptists residing in Hopewell in the County of Cumberland and the State of New Jersey." The congregation that formed this church in 1737 was previously identified by the Cohansey name. It had close ties with Newport, Piscataway, and the Philadelphia area churches as well as the local Baptist church.

Some of the earliest settlers in this territory near the north shore of Delaware Bay were members of the John Myles Company of Baptists from Glamorganshire, Wales, who came to Massachusetts in about 1662 and settled at Swansea near the Rhode Island border. In 1675 a series of Indian raids, which led to King Philip's War, caused a number of the company to seek refuge on the island where Newport is located. The combination of Indian raids and persecution by the Puritans persuaded some that a return to Swansea was not advisable. Many, including members of the Ayars and the Bowen families, settled in Newport and Westerly, where they became acquainted with Seventh Day Baptists.

Robert Ayars first bought land on the Cohansey River in 1685. To this original holding he added other land, including a tract of 2,200 acres on which the current town of Shiloh is located. In 1687 and 1690, Rev. Timothy Brooks led two separate migrations conducted by the expeditionary group known as the Bowen Company to this property. Soon other settlers, including some from Wales, came to this location, where the government had guaranteed that no man would be molested on account of beliefs or religious practices.

Soon after the Bowen Company made their settlements at Bowentown, they built a meetinghouse and began to hold regular Sabbath services. A close relationship existed between them and the Cohansey Baptist Church. In 1710, Timothy Brooks and two of his daughters united with Cohansey; two other daughters remained with the Sabbathkeeping congregation and were among the charter members of the Shiloh church when it was officially constituted in 1737. In

[10] Charles H. Greene, "The Keithians," MS 19x.178.5, p. 28a-b, SDB Hist. Soc. Lib.

addition to such local ministers as Timothy Brooks and Samuel Bowen, these churches were also served by itinerant ministers. These circuit riders included Rev. Thomas Killingsworth, who also preached at such places as Pennepek in Pennsylvania and Trenton, Piscataway, and Middleton in New Jersey, where Sabbathkeeping Baptists were located.

The Seventh Day Baptist evangelist Jonathan S. Davis, affectionately known as the "Great High Priest of Trenton," frequently visited the congregation, which included several of his Davis family relatives. In addition, his wife Elizabeth was one of the Bowens who had arrived with the Swansea migration. Despite the familial connections, the journey must have been difficult. As the written history of the Shiloh church notes, "only a sense of duty to his Master can ever account for those long, hard horseback journeys which were made through a forest country, then but sparsely settled."[11]

Jonathan S. Davis proposed that the congregation sign nine "Articles of Faith" that would bind them in a covenant relationship based on biblical beliefs and principles. That these articles were almost identical to the statement of faith used by the Piscataway Church shows the close relationship between the New Jersey churches. Eighteen people signed this document on 27 March 1737.[12] Among the signers was Jonathan E. Davis, the nephew of Jonathan S. Davis. The following year he was ordained by the church and served as its pastor for thirty years.

The third pastor, who was also named Jonathan Davis (but with the middle name "David"), was from a different family. His father, David Davis, was the pastor of the Welch Baptist Church in Welch Tract, Delaware. He had married Margaret Bond, whose family had been members of a Seventh Day Baptist Church in Chester County, Pennsylvania. Margaret chose not to compromise her position on the Sabbath to join her husband's church but traveled some distance to be baptized and join the group at Cohansey. In time, her husband joined in her convictions and served as pastor at Shiloh for seventeen years.

[11] John Bonham, "Early Years, 1687–1785," repr. in John H. Camenga, comp., *History of the SDB Church of Shiloh, New Jersey, Prepared for the Two Hundred-Fiftieth Anniversary, 1737–1987* (Shiloh NJ: Shiloh SDB Church, 1987) 22, MS 1988.2, SDB Hist. Soc. Lib.

[12] "Articles of Faith," repr. in Camenga, comp., *History of the Shiloh Church*, 29. See also "Articles of Faith," *Piscataway, N.J. SDB Church Records, 1705–1836*, MS, CRR 1956.9.1, pp. 4-7, SDB Hist. Soc. Lib.

Shrewsbury

The third church established in New Jersey was at Shrewsbury in Monmouth County, near the Atlantic Ocean. Like Piscataway and Cohansey, this was the site of considerable Baptist activity. It was not far from Middletown, where Elias Keach and Thomas Killingsworth had preached during their circuits. Of the thirty-six people named in the patent giving them title to the colony founded in the mid-1640s, eighteen were Baptists, and the wives of several others were also of Baptist persuasion. Their charter contained a pledge of freedom to all who would plant or inhabit the land. It stated that "they shall have free liberty of conscience, without any molestation or disturbance, whatsoever, in their worship."[13] This differed from the charter for a Congregational colony at Newark, New Jersey, granted in 1666, which provided that no one but members of the Congregational churches could be admitted as freemen, and any who might differ in religious opinion must keep their views to themselves or be compelled to leave the place.[14]

The first Baptist church in the area of Shrewsbury formed in 1668. Some of its members were immigrants from England, but names such as Jonathan Holmes and Obadiah Holmes, Jr. show the presence of settlers from Newport. The guarantee of freedom of worship and close ties with the Newport community encouraged Seventh Day Baptists to relocate in Monmouth County. Accordingly, about fifteen members of the Westerly (Hopkinton Church) congregation, who lived in the area of Stonington, Connecticut, moved to Shrewsbury in 1745. They were led by the Rev. William Davis, who had been one of the leaders among the Seventh Day Baptists in the Philadelphia area and who later moved to Rhode Island. With him came three of his sons, John, Thomas, and Joseph, together with their families. Other families included Maxson, Stillman, Babcock, and Brand. A 1750 letter written to the churches in Rhode Island regarding the practice of foot washing reveals these members' sense of covenant relation through the practice's continual usage of familial, loving relational language to describe the relationship between the congregations.[15]

---

[13] Thomas S. Griffiths, *A History of Baptists in New Jersey* (Hightstown NJ: Barr Press, 1904) 17.

[14] Ibid.

[15] Corliss Fitz Randolph, *A History of the SDBs in West Virginia* (Plainfield NJ: American Sabbath Tract Society, 1905) 14.

The Shrewsbury record book still exists, but it contains many gaps where no entries were made.[16] There was concern for discipline within the church, and its leaders made efforts to reclaim those who had broken the covenant. Pastors from Piscataway and Shiloh occasionally visited the congregation to administer the sacraments when the church lacked pastoral leadership. In September 1789, this church migrated as a body to western Virginia to become the nucleus of the Salem, West Virginia, Seventh Day Baptist Church. Even after their reorganization in Salem, the members continued to use the old leather-bound record book they had carried with them from New Jersey.

The records of these early Seventh Day Baptists demonstrate a sense of covenant that existed from the very beginning. Names that appear on the membership rolls show direct relation to families already prominent in churches in other areas. There was much intermarriage among these families, which helped unite the churches in Rhode Island, New Jersey, and Pennsylvania. This pattern of intermarriage has continued through much of the history of Seventh Day Baptists. Also holding them together were ties of common conviction and the desire to help each other and encourage each other's faith. Out of this mutual concern came a strength that allowed them during the following century to meet adversities and extend the Gospel into many new areas.

---

[16] *Shrewsbury, N. J.–Salem, W. Va. SDB Church Records, 1745-1834*, MS, CRR 19x.121, SDB Hist. Soc. Lib.

9

CHURCHES AND THE STRUGGLE
FOR INDEPENDENCE

Donald Lutz and Jack Warren, in their book *A Covenanted People*, point out that the Constitution of the United States had its roots in the covenant traditions of Protestantism. Its peculiar characteristics of government by consent of the governed, reliance on a written constitution, and belief in a higher law were all derived from the dissenting church polities of the seventeenth century.[1]

In addition to these theological contributions, the churches became directly involved in the struggle for freedom. It is estimated that in the years leading to the Declaration of Independence and the Revolutionary War, New England ministers as a whole were delivering over 2,000 sermons a week; many of these sermons reflected the idea of the covenant that God had made with the colonists as a special people. "This belief," wrote Lutz, "provided them with a way of making sense of the sometimes bewildering events of the pre-Revolutionary crisis and, ultimately, with a justification for resistance, revolution, and Independence."[2]

EARLY SEVENTH DAY BAPTIST ATTITUDES

Few, if any, copies of sermons from Seventh Day Baptist pulpits of the pre-Revolutionary era survive today, but there is considerable evidence that the covenant theology had an impact on the churches' attitudes and involvement in matters of state. According to one written history of the Westerly (Hopkinton) church, "The most of the church, in the true spirit of patriotism, endorsed the principles of the revolution."[3]

This attitude had been demonstrated previously, during the period of the French and Indian War, when the Newport church, in a 1758 letter to the Piscataway church, expressed mutual sympathy with them "in all the troubles and afflictions that we are meeting withall in our Christian

[1] Donald S. Lutz and Jack D. Warren, introduction, *A Covenanted People: The Religious Tradition and the Origins of American Constitutionalism* (Providence RI: John Carter Brown Library, 1987).
[2] Ibid., 38.
[3] "The Westerly Seventh-day Baptist Church," *SDB Memorial* 3/3 (Jul 1854): 136.

Cause whether from friends or Enemies."[4] About a year later, a letter from the Newport church addressed to the churches in both Piscataway and Cohansey carried similar expressions of God's special relationship to the colonists struggling for freedom. This letter even expressed the concept of "Manifest Destiny," which nearly a century later was used to justify the nation's westward expansion during the Mexican War. The letter ends with a prayer that God would "carry on his triumphs through ye northern Regions till he Extends his Empire from the Eastern to ye Western Sea and from the River of Canada to the Ends of America."[5]

The unsettled conditions of this struggle had deep and long-lasting effects on Seventh Day Baptist individuals and churches. Many became directly or indirectly involved in the struggle for freedom from British rule. Some were politically involved; some were involved with the military; and many fell victim to occupation troops and patriot forces that marauded in search of provisions. Still others suffered for conscience's sake over the struggle itself, which seemed to violate the commandment "Thou shalt not kill." While later generations may look with pride on these early Seventh Day Baptists' commitment and contribution to the cause of liberty, there is no escaping the fact that several churches never fully recovered from the losses they suffered.

POLITICAL INVOLVEMENT

From colonial days to modern times, Seventh Day Baptists have taken citizenship responsibilities seriously. Many have served the government in capacities that ranged from justice of the peace to chief justice of a state supreme court, from councilman to member of the General Assembly, and from mayor to governor. The most prominent among these public servants was the Ward family of Rhode Island.

The Wards of Rhode Island

Thomas Ward and his wife Amy were members of the Newport Seventh Day Baptist Church in 1692, and most of their family were members either of that church or the Westerly church. Their son Richard was governor of Rhode Island from 1740 to 1742. A detailed letter from

---

[4] Letter, 10 Jun 1758, signed by John Tanner, John Maxson, et al.; repr. in *Newport RI SDB Church Records, 1708–1817*, book #1400 (Jun 1758), 118-19, Newport Historical Society Library, Newport RI. See also negative microfilm copy, MF 1957.10, SDB Hist. Soc. Lib.

[5] *Newport RI SDB Church Records, 1708–1817* (17 Jul 1759) 120, MF 1957.10, SDB Hist. Soc. Lib.

Governor Ward to the Board of Trade remains a primary source for tracing the historical burden the use of paper money placed on the colonies.[6] Richard Ward was considered a member of the congregation at Newport even though it was not until 1753, at the age of 64, that he was baptized and joined the church as a "communicant" (member who could participate in the Lord's Supper).[7] It was not uncommon in the Newport church for persons to assume official leadership responsibilities and worship with the church prior to becoming covenant members. Henry Collins, one of Newport's most distinguished and philanthropic citizens and half-brother to Richard Ward, did not join the church until age thirty; his father, Arnold Collins, was listed as a church trustee even though his name does not appear on the list of covenant members.

Several of Richard Ward's family were prominent in both the political and military arenas of the colonial struggle for freedom. One son, Thomas, served as the colony's secretary of state from about 1747 until his death in 1760. A younger son, Henry, succeeded Thomas in that position, serving until his death in 1797. Two grandsons, Charles and Samuel, Jr., were officers in the Revolutionary War, the latter rising to the rank of lieutenant colonel.[8]

The most noted of the Ward family was Richard's son Samuel, who was born in 1725. In 1756, Samuel was elected to represent Westerly in the General Assembly. In 1761, he became chief justice of the colony and in the following year was elected governor. Three things distinguished his career as governor. First, he ordered the arrest of British sailors who had committed various crimes after landing at the Newport harbor. His subsequent correspondence with Great Britain affirmed the sovereign rights of the Rhode Island colony to ensure order and justice inside its borders. Second, he was the only governor in the colonies who refused to sign an oath in support of the Stamp Act. Third, he organized a committee of intelligence in each Rhode Island community to secretly secure intelligence on the actions and whereabouts of British militia.

---

[6] "Report of Governor Ward to the Board of Trade, on paper money," 9 Jan 1740, repr. in *Records of the Colony of Rhode Island and Providence Plantations in New England,* ed. John Russell Bartlett, 10 vols. (Providence RI: Knowles and Anthony & Co., 1860) 5:8-14.

[7] "The Seventh-day Baptist Church at Newport, R. I.," *SDB Memorial* 2/1 (Jan 1853): 37-38.

[8] John Ward, "Genealogy of the Ward Family," appended to John Ward, *A Memoir of Lieut.-Colonel Samuel Ward* (New York: n.p., 1875) 16-20. See also Bartlett, ed., *Records of the Colony of Rhode Island,* 5:215, and John Ward, *The Life and Services of Governor Samuel Ward* (Providence RI: J. A. and R. A. Reed, 1877).

Yet, Samuel Ward is best remembered as one of two Rhode Island representatives to participate in the First and the Second Continental Congresses, which met in Philadelphia in 1774 and 1775. He was elected chairman of the all-important Committee of the Whole (he presided over the congresses). He nominated George Washington for general of the Revolutionary Army, and correspondence between Washington and Ward indicated that the general considered Ward his personal emissary to the Continental Congress. In one of his letters to General Washington Ward wrote, "I have dedicated to you my life, my fortune, and my sacred honor." A short time later, some of these same words were echoed in the closing lines of the Declaration of Independence.[9]

Samuel Ward persistently urged the patriots to create a navy in the colony's struggle against British dominance of the sea. His concern for this cause may have contributed to his death just months prior to the signing of the Declaration of Independence. A smallpox epidemic broke out in Philadelphia while the Continental Congress was in session. The only protection against this dread disease was inoculation, which produced severe and painful side effects. Ward postponed inoculation, believing that he could not afford to lose precious time he needed for his naval campaign. On 15 March 1776, while presiding over the Continental Congress, he was suddenly stricken with telltale symptoms of smallpox and died ten days later at the age of fifty-one. Had he lived just a few months longer, he could have affixed his name to that 4 July 1776 document that memorialized his convictions.

Like his father, Samuel was not baptized until relatively late in his life. On 5 August 1769, at the age of forty-four, Samuel Ward was baptized and joined the Westerly church, although he had identified with the church from a much earlier age. We can only speculate as to the reasons for his delay, but his letters and his testimony clearly indicate his commitment. In his written confession addressed "To the Sabbatarian Church of Christ in Westerly & Hopkinton," he affirmed his belief that baptism was a Christian duty and asked to be admitted to that ordinance. After confessing his sins and declaring his reliance on "the unbounded Goodness and Mercy of God and his only begotten Son," he promised to walk in all the commandments and ordinances of the Lord.[10]

---

[9] Kenneth E. Smith, *Sam Ward, Founding Father* (Plainfield NJ: SDB Hist. Soc., n.d.) n.p.

[10] Samuel Ward, "Samuel Ward to the Hopkinton Church, 1769" (3 Aug 1769), in *Church Letters to the Seventh-day Baptist General Conference, and Other Papers, 1746–1835,*

When duty called him from his home, Samuel Ward wrote of his desire to join his family in worship.[11] Much of Ward's correspondence reveals his sense of God's presence with the colonists in their struggle for freedom. While in the Continental Congress he wrote, "I cannot think that God brought us into this wilderness to perish; or what is worse, to become slaves, but rather to make a great and free people."[12] A great-granddaughter of Governor Ward, Julia Ward Howe, penned the words of the Civil War hymn "The Battle Hymn of the Republic."

The Ward family were not the only Seventh Day Baptists to express the idea that God chose America for a covenant relationship and who worked politically for the colonists' separation from England. Sixteen Burdicks were among the Hopkinton patriots who signed the Test Act on 19 September 1776, which declared that the "the War, Resistance and Opposition in which the United American Colonies are engaged against the Fleets, and Armies of Great Britain is, on the part of the Colonies, Just and necessary...."[13] Some were Seventh Day Baptists who served actively in the army.

Greenwich Tea Party

Farther to the south, a short distance from Shiloh at Greenwich, New Jersey, the cause of freedom was shown in a protest against the tax on tea. The British unloaded a shipment of tea at the mouth of the Cohansey River and stored it at Greenwich, awaiting overland transport to Philadelphia. They were fearful that the Philadelphia patriots might follow the example of the previous year's Boston Tea Party. On 22 November 1774, forty men disguised as Indians removed the chests of tea to the village square, where the chests "accidentally caught fire," destroying more tea than had been overthrown in the harbor at Boston. Some who participated in this act of defiance were from Shiloh. How many were members of the Seventh Day Baptist Church is uncertain, since only part of those involved were identified by name. However, history does record that the group gathered at the home of Ebenezer and Sarah Bond Howell, the latter of whom was a staunch member of the

---

bound ms., MS 19x.181, SDB Hist. Soc. Lib., 9. (Note: transcript copy, BX6393.C57, SDB Hist. Soc. Lib.)

[11] Samuel Ward, quoted in "Religious Views and Character of Samuel Ward," *Sabbath Recorder* 47/20 (14 May 1891) 310-11.

[12] Ibid., 311.

[13] Test Act," *Narragansett Historical Register*, in Nellie Johnson, comp., *The Descendents of Robert Burdick of Rhode Island* (Norwich NY: Syracuse Typesetting Co., 1937) 1296.

church. Two of her sons, Richard and Lewis, were among the Greenwich tea party participants. Richard later distinguished himself in the Revolutionary War and eventually became governor of New Jersey.[14]

Military Involvement

It is unknown how many Seventh Day Baptists served militarily in the Revolutionary War, but most churches had members in the army. Walter B. Gillett, the sixth pastor of the Piscataway Church, noted that church members differed their thinking as to whether the war was justified, but nonetheless "all the patriots were either in the regular army, or enrolled in the militia and were liable to be called at any moment."[15]

The Effect of the War on Migrations

One direct effect of the war was increased migration west. Economic losses and disruptions, newly claimed territory, and military roads through the mountains encouraged and enabled many to seek new homes on the frontier. One patriot from Piscataway, Samuel Fitz Randolph, was commissioned an ensign in the Second Regiment of Sussex County. His contacts and travels in this capacity influenced the migration of Seventh Day Baptists from Piscataway and Shrewsbury. They followed a military road through the Allegheny Mountains to Woodbridgetown, Pennsylvania, before moving south to western Virginia, where in 1792 the Shrewsbury church was reestablished as the Salem Seventh Day Baptist Church.[16]

Among those who participated in that migration were other Revolutionary veterans, including Rev. Jacob Davis, the first pastor of the Salem church. He had been a chaplain in the army while pastoring the Shrewsbury church, returning home on frequent furloughs to tend to his flock. His father James Davis had owned a shipyard at the beginning of the war and sided with the British. A brother, William, guided the British fleet through Hell Gate Channel into New York City at the time of its capture. However, after his shipyard was burned, James became a

---

[14]*Historic Roadsides in New Jersey* (Plainfield NJ: Society of Colonial Wars in the State of New Jersey, 1928). See also John H. Camenga, comp., *History of the SDB Church of Shiloh, N.J.* (Shiloh NJ: Shiloh SDB Church, 1987) xxv.

[15] Gillett, "The Seventh-day Baptist Church at Piscataway, N. J.," *SDB Memorial* 2/3 (Jul 1853): 123-24.

[16] Corliss Fitz Randolph, *A History of SDBs in West Virginia...* (Plainfield NJ: American Sabbath Tract Society, 1905) 16ff.

loyal supporter of the colonists until he was "killed by a stray British bullet as he rode out to watch the Battle of Monmouth" near Shrewsbury. According to tradition, his horse carried him back to his home. William also switched allegiance and fought with the Americans. He was among the early settlers of Salem, where he bought all of the bottom land east of Salem, thus earning the designation "Bottom Billy" to distinguish him from the other William Davises in the area.

Other veterans of the Revolutionary War who came during the migration from New Jersey included the second pastor of the Salem Church, Reverend John Davis, and the father-and-son team of Thomas William Davis and William "Greenbrier Billy" Davis.[17] Several other churches, as they were constituted, received as members those who had served actively in the Revolutionary War. Richard Bond of Lost Creek had been a major in the army. Edward J. Greene, Luke Maxson, and Judge Edward Greene were among the early members of the Alfred Seventh Day Baptist Church who had fought in the Revolutionary War.[18]

A Chaplain in the Army

Ebenezer David, the son of Philadelphia-area pastor Rev. Enoch David, attended Rhode Island College, which later became Brown University. While still a student in 1770, he was baptized and joined the Newport Church. Shortly after his graduation in 1772 the church licensed him to preach, and in 1775, a little over a month after the first Revolutionary War shots were fired at Lexington and Concord, he was ordained to the ministry. By the end of the year, David had enlisted in the army as a chaplain, serving first with troops near Boston and later with those in the New York City area at Ticonderoga, Peekskill, and Valley Forge. During his terms in the chaplaincy he returned to Providence to study medicine, but he soon returned to his troops. In 1778, he contracted typhus while at a hospital in Lancaster and died on 19 March of that year.

Most of the information about Ebenezer David's public life comes from a collection of letters he wrote to a friend in Providence. Most of the letters contain details of military life and action, but some reflect David's sense of God's covenant with the nation. In January 1776, he wrote:

[17] Susie Davis Nicholson, *Davis: The Settlers of Salem, West Virginia: Their Ancestors and Some of Their Descendants* (Strasburg OH: Gordon Printing, 1975) 6, 7, 10.

[18] Silas C. Burdick, "Alfred," in *A Centennial Memorial History of Allegany County, New York*, ed. Georgia Drew Merrill (Alfred NY: W. A. Ferguson & Co., 1896) 625-26.

"What GOD is about to bring to pass in the Kingdome of His Providence is known by him alone. It behoves us to view his hand discharge our Duty & Leave the event with Him."[19]

At times David questioned whether America deserved God's favor. In March 1776, he spoke of some who thirsted for military glory and he pleaded that both the men and the country put more trust and confidence in God, closing, "But who can behold the profanity of our Camp & reflect upon the awful security of our Land, & not fear least GOD should frown upon us."[20] Later that month, he reflected on the uncertainty surrounding the revolution, concluding, "I realize that the Lord reigns, that the Government is upon Emmanuels shoulders—Who can but rejoice at this? May God's judgments be sanctified to a stiff necked people who as yet appear to wax wors & wors."[21] Although he asked that "the God of armies the Founder & Upholder of States declare in our favor,"[22] he wept over the overall lack of cooperation and the leaders' ineptness. "May America's GOD interpose & save our Country when those set for the defence of it are at swordspoints."[23]

Passive Involvement

Not all Seventh Day Baptists of the Revolutionary period were committed to the covenant concept of a just and holy rebellion. A few, particularly in the northern New Jersey area of Piscataway and Shrewsbury, sided with the British and were labeled as Tories. This divided loyalty caused considerable disruption in the churches and forced some to move to safer areas. Still others interpreted any form of fighting as a violation of the Ten Commandments and the teaching of Jesus and chose to remain neutral. However, in the midst of fighting and occupation, it was difficult for anyone to remain completely unaffected by the war.

Conscientious Objectors

A majority of the members of the Westerly (Hopkinton) church sided with the colonial army, but the records show that in 1777, when

---

[19] Ebenezer David, "Letter IV" (29 Jan 1776), *A Rhode Island Chaplain in the Revolution: Letters of Ebenezer David to Nicholas Brown, 1775–1778*, ed. Jeannette D. Black and William Greene Roelker (Providence: Rhode Island Society of the Cincinnati, 1949) 10.

[20] David, "Letter V" (1 Mar 1776), 14.

[21] David, "Letter VI" (10 Mar 1776), 16.

[22] David, "Letter VII" (12 Aug 1777), 40-41.

[23] David, "Letter XVII" (11 Nov 1777), 64.

Amos Burdick was asked why he "did not walk with the church," he cited as one of the reasons that the church "approves the taking up of arms and learning of war, which was contrary to his opinion." The church gave him "liberty to act his own opinion as to bearing arms, but did not think it right for him to labor to hinder others at this difficult and distressing time." When he asked the congregation that a note be made in the church record book that he be "given liberty to speak and act his liberty in full on said matter," he was refused.[24]

A different situation existed among Seventh Day Baptists in Pennsylvania, where many of the members took a noncombatant stand. C. H. Greene noted that the Sabbatarians as a class refused to bear arms in the Revolutionary War. They retained enough of their Quaker heritage to consider that contention either at arms or at law was inconsistent with Christian character. Yet, in spite of their noncombative stand, they did not escape the war's consequences. The home of David Thomas was the first stop made by the British raider Tarlton after his 1777 defeat by Captain Henry Lee ("Light Horse Harry Lee") at Easttown. The house was looted and stripped by Tarlton and his men.[25]

The difference between the pacific Quaker leanings and the Wayne family's military background may account for the separated burials of General Anthony Wayne's parents. His mother Elizabeth is buried with the Iddings and Thomas families in the Newtown Seventh Day Baptist Cemetery (now marked as the Baptist Cemetery), while his father Isaac lies at St. David's Episcopal Cemetery several miles away.[26]

The refusal to bear arms caused other troubles during the war and afterwards. Some noncombatants were fined and imprisoned when the state militia had been organized and they chose not to report. As late as 1785, the fine for the military delinquency of John Horn, a Seventh Day Baptist minister, was appealed to a council over which Benjamin Franklin presided. The verdict ended with the words, "it is the opinion of the Council that John Horn be exempt by law from military service, and that he be released from that which has been imposed upon him."[27]

---

[24] *Westerly, R.I. SDB Church Records, 14 Sep 1777*, repr. in "The Westerly Seventh-day Baptist Church," *SDB Memorial* 3/3 (Jul 1854): 136.

[25] Charles H. Greene, "The Keithians," transcript draft, MS 19x.178.4, p. 29, SDB Hist. Soc. Lib.

[26] Ilou M. Sanford, "Tale of the Lonesome Tombstones: Do They Tell It Like It Was?" *Sabbath Recorder* 211/8 (Sep 1989): 24-25.

[27] Greene, "The Keithians," 29.

Pacifists Become Involved at Ephrata

The German Seventh Day Baptists of the Ephrata Cloister were also directly involved in noncombatant ways. Ephrata, a haven for pacifists, was suspected of harboring Tories, for anyone not actively supporting the Revolution was considered a traitor. James Reed wrote a letter of inquiry and warning to Ephrata. Peter Miller, the cloister leader at the time, answered the letter on 10 October 1776, stating a basic premise of many who chose the pacifist position: "We ought to abhor all War, for to subject all Men without Distinction to the Civil Law, is injurious to the Christian Cause, as some may be under a higher Magistrate, and also consequently emancipated from the civil Government.... In the present struggle there is a third Party, who observe a strict Neutrality."[28]

Two episodes illustrate Peter Miller's devotion to the "higher magistrate" concept. When Washington's army was in need of paper for shot wadding, it learned of a large paper supply at Ephrata. Wagons sent to pick up the needed supplies were met by Miller, who told the captain that, as this would contradict their neutrality, they would not consent unless Washington took the supply by force. The captain ordered six men from the hospital on the cloister grounds with fixed bayonets to load two wagons full. Miller concluded the account, "The captain afterwards settled with us, paying us honestly, and we parted in peace; though we never asked from him a certificate, but trusted to providence."[29] The confiscation was a severe blow to the community's economy, for the paper supply contained unsold copies and unbound printed sheets of the *Martyrs' Mirror*, one of the community's greatest published works. A few of the bound copies were returned, but for the most part the potential sales proceeds were lost.[30]

Another depiction of Miller's character is the story of his intercession on behalf of Michael Widman, a notorious Tory who had heaped considerable abuse on Peter Miller. Widman was arrested for treason and sentenced to be hanged. Upon hearing of the arrest, Peter Miller set off by foot to Valley Forge to request a pardon from Washington. The general refused on the grounds that the cause of liberty required that an example be made, but he added, "otherwise I should

---

[28] E. Gordon Alderfer, *The Ephrata Commune: An Early American Counterculture* (Pittsburgh: University of Pittsburgh Press, 1985) 163.

[29] Ibid., 166.

[30] Ibid.

most cheerfully release your friend." Miller responded: "Friend! He is my worst enemy—my incessant reviler. For a friend I might not importune you; but Widman being, and having been for years, my worst foe, my malignant, persecuting enemy, my religion teaches me "To pray for those who despitefully use me." The story reveals that Washington was so moved by this demonstration of Christian charity that he granted the pardon on the provision that Miller carry the order back to the executioner. Miller walked another 18 miles to deliver the note, arriving just in time to save Widman's life.[31] Efforts to completely document this story from contemporary historical records have thus far been unsuccessful. However, the fact that such a story would exist and be believed for two centuries gives insight into Peter Miller's impeccable reputation and faultless character.

The reputation of the Ephratans' strong Christian character was sufficiently known that following the Battle of Brandywine in September 1777, Washington suggested that the wounded be transported by wagon to the Cloister at Ephrata, where he knew they would receive compassionate care. It is estimated that about 500 wounded were brought to Ephrata and that about 150 died there, either of their wounds or the dreaded camp fever and typhus that afflicted the soldiers as well as many of the order's brothers and sisters. The Cloister never completely recovered from the losses in personnel, supplies, and facilities. Two of their finest buildings, Kedar and Zion, had to be burned to rid the settlement of infection and contamination.[32]

Effects of Occupation

The two churches that suffered most severely from the effects of British occupation were Piscataway and Newport. It is estimated that at least one-third of the houses in Piscataway were pillaged, with countless tales of horror. Governor Livingston, in a speech before the General Assembly in 1777, declared that the English soldiers, while in New Jersey, "warred upon decrepit age and defenseless youth, plundered friends and foes, destroyed public records and private monuments, and

---

[31] Julius Friedrich Sachse, *The German Sectarians of Pennsylvania, 1742–1800: A Critical and Legendary History of the Ephrata Cloister and the Dunkers*, 2 vols. (Philadelphia: n.p., 1900) 2:340-342.

[32] Julius Friedrich Sachse, *The Moment on Zion Hill: An Address Delivered at Ephrata, Lancaster, P.A., on Patriots' Day, Wednesday September 11, 1895* (Lancaster PA: New Era Book and Job Print, 1895) 6-9. Bound with Sachse, *Benjamin Furly, "An English Merchant at Rotterdam," Who Promoted the First German Emigration to America* (Philadelphia: n.p., 1895).

violated the chastity of women, disfigured private dwellings of taste and elegance, and in the rage of impiety and barbarism profaned edifices dedicated to Almighty God."[33] Piscataway was situated in the midst of this devastation. Several from the Dunham and the Dunn families of the church were among those whose houses and barns were burned. Although Reverend Jonathan Dunham was treated with respect and the church building spared destruction, services were neglected and the church never fully recovered.

Many of the churches in Newport were used by the British for quartering of soldiers or stables for horses. The Seventh Day Baptist church was spared, perhaps as has been suggested, because of the two tablets of the Ten Commandments that adorned the wall. Many members fled to more secure locations. Others were forced to take British soldiers into their homes, giving them bed and board. Elder William Bliss was one of those forced to quarter troops in his home. Although there was no evidence of personal harm to his family, the action of his daughters Elizabeth, Barbara, and Mary clearly demonstrated the family's sentiments.

On the embankment on either side of the Bliss home, the occupying army planted its flags. One day, while the attention of the British was drawn elsewhere, the two older sisters took down the colors and tore them into thirteen strips before returning them to their places. When the soldiers returned, they began a search and offered a reward for the culprits' arrest. The young ladies managed to escape detection. Had they been found, they might well have been executed. Mary is credited with taking one of the finest swords of a British officer quartering there while he was at dinner and thrusting it through a hole in the plastering so that it would drop between the ceiling and the clap-boarding. It remained there until after the war, "when it was taken out and kept as a trophy of female valor, till it was destroyed by the conflagration of the house of Elder Bliss."[34]

When one considers that the total membership of Seventh Day Baptists in 1776 can be numbered in terms of a few hundred with less than a dozen churches, it is doubtful any comparable group of citizens were more involved in, or contributed more to, the cause of liberty than those who called themselves Seventh Day Baptists. Their sense of

[33] Charles H. Greene, "Middlesex and Piscataway in the Revolution," MS 1918.2.9, pp. 71-72, C. H. Greene Papers, SDB Hist. Soc. Lib.
[34] Unnumbered footnote in "Arnold Bliss," *SDB Memorial* 3/2 (Apr 1854): 57-58.

covenant placed them in the mainstream of those who yearned for the political freedom for which they had labored and tied to their practice of religion for over a century.

Not only did Seventh Day Baptists contribute to this struggle for independence; they also were vitally affected by it. The expansion of territory resulting from the 1783 Treaty of Paris opened up whole new regions into which they could venture. Many chose to settle in these areas, where they could establish their own communities of faith. At the same time, this expansion challenged them to develop ways to maintain the close covenant relationship of clustered churches. It is to this associational relationship and the desire to do collectively what they were incapable of doing individually that attention must now turn.

PART IV: SEVENTH DAY BAPTISTS IN 19TH CENTURY

PART IV TIMELINE:

Date/ Lifespan	Event / Person
1783	Treaty of Paris
1785	Northwest Territory opened
1787	Shrewsbury, NJ SDB congregation migrates to Virginia
1795	Second Great Awakening
1802	Seventh Day Baptist General Conference established
1803	Louisiana Purchase
1810	American Board of Foreign Missions established
1811	Henry Clarke's *History of the Sabbatarians*
1812	War of 1812 begins
1818	Board of Missions of the SDB General Conference established
1821-1825	*SDB Missionary Magazine*
1825	Erie Canal opened
1826	*Psalms & Hymns*
1828	American SDB Missionary Society established
1830-1839	*The Protestant Sentinel*
1835	First SDB *Expose of Faith*
1835	SDB General Tract Society
1835	First SDB Associations form
1835	American SDB Education Society
1836	Texas declares independence
1836	Alfred Select School, New York
1837	DeRuyter Institute, New York
1840-1844	*Seventh Day Baptist Register*
1842	New York City Sabbath Tract Society
1843	American SDB Missionary Association/Society
1844-	*The Sabbath Recorder*
1846-1848	Mexican-American War
1847	Missionaries to China

1849-1866	SDB Publishing Society
1851-1860	*The Sabbath Visitor*
1852-1854	*Seventh Day Baptist Memorial*
1855	SDB Education Society
1855	Missionaries to Palestine
1857	Alfred University, NY charter
1861-1865	American Civil War
1862	Homestead Act
1863	SDB General Conference Historical Committee
1866	Bailey's *History of the SDB General Conference*
1867	Milton College, WI
1871	School of Theology, Alfred University, NY
1872	Sabbath School Board
1872	SDB Memorial Board
1872-1895	SDB Publishing House, Alfred, NY
1880	Second SDB *Expose of Faith*
1881	Christian Endeavor movement begins
1882-1897	*The Outlook*
1884	SDB Women's Board
1885	*The Helping Hand in Bible Study*
1886	Student Volunteer Movement/Foreign Missions
1888	Salem College, WV
1889	Young People's Committee
1890	Chicago Council
1895	SDB Publishing House moves to Plainfield, NJ
1898	Spanish-American War
1900	Fouke School, AR

10

POST-REVOLUTIONARY AMERICA

The close of the Revolutionary War brought about great changes that profoundly affected the American people's religious lives. The concept of covenant theology, which brought settlers to America's shores and contributed to the wartime belief that theirs was a holy crusade, gave way to the concept of the individual's independence. The spiritual revival of the early eighteenth century known as the "Great Awakening" lost much of its vitality during the century's last quarter and was sometimes mockingly termed the "Great Asleepening."[1]

DECLINE IN RELIGIOUS FERVOR

Several environmental, as well as theological, factors contributed to a decline in religious fervor and the struggle for national identity during the decades following the Revolutionary War. Two major factors, the fallout from the war and theological shifts, can be credited for this decline.

Direct Effects of the War

First, many who were actively involved in the fighting experienced the disrespect for life and property that accompanies any war. Families and churches were disrupted and sometimes uprooted. A generation of potential leaders was diminished by war-related casualties.

Second, the war exposed many people to conditions and attitudes that were not conducive to spiritual values. A biographical sketch of one of the most influential Seventh Day Baptist pastors of the early nineteenth century, William Satterlee, notes that his father lived on the direct route of travel between Boston and the Hudson River military stations. Troops passing through often camped on the Satterlee farm. Some of the influences were not calculated to strengthen his religious profession, for the language "filled his thoughts with their corrupt imaginings, and soon dispelled the former seriousness of his mind."[2]

---

[1] Peter Marshall and David Manuel, *From Sea to Shining Sea* (Old Tappan NJ: Fleming H. Revell Company, 1986) 48.

[2] "William Satterlee," *SDB Memorial* 1/4 (Oct 1852): 167.

A third factor in the decline was the migration to the West. The Treaty of Paris signed in 1783 fixed the western boundary of the United States at the Mississippi River, more than doubling the area of the thirteen colonies. Many of the settlers in this new territory were typical frontiersmen who pushed west in search of adventure or economic gain. Many settled in isolated areas far removed from church influence. If they happened to settle in communities, it was more for protection than for worship. The struggle to carve out a living in an often hostile environment left little time for what some considered an unnecessary trappings of civilized society.

A fourth factor was the change in the economic and social climate. The embargo on imports from England stimulated the development of American industry. The steam engine perfected by Isaac Watts in 1769 and the spinning jenny and power loom encouraged the development of a textile industry in New England. Eli Whitney's 1793 invention of the cotton gin revolutionized Southern agriculture and made it possible for the South to provide the raw material for this growing industry. The revitalized slave trade caused theological and moral divisiveness as it brought attention to the issue of slavery and its implications for man's relation to both God and fellow men.

In 1798, Eli Whitney's second major contribution, the concept of interchangeable parts, enabled the division of labor in factories. Unskilled jobs became available for young people squeezed off the small family farms and for a steady stream of immigrants. Since most of these factories operated on a six- or even seven-day work week, Seventh Day Baptists found it difficult to expand into urban areas. Many either gave up the Sabbath or joined the migrations to the West, where farming and lumbering offered more flexibility.

A fifth cause of religious decline was administrative organization. William W. Sweet noted that the breaking of Old World ecclesiastical ties, for some churches, created the need for "creating new ecclesiastical machinery" that occupied the attention of the religious leaders, thus delaying the revitalization of the religious life.[3] This had less direct impact on Baptists, who were already independent of foreign ties, yet there were two divergent consequences. On the one hand, in setting up new machinery for the propagation of their particular church, some used political power such as the Blue Laws to gain an advantage over

---

[3] William Warren Sweet, *Religion in the Development of American Culture* (New York: Scribner's Sons, 1952) 53.

minority groups. On the other hand, many Baptists reacted to the organizational machinery they saw being developed among other churches by spurning any type of denominational organization.

Theological Changes

Challenge to the religious thinking of the time came from the writings of continental philosophers such as Voltaire. The so-called "Age of Reason" had many followers among America's political and intellectual leaders. In this philosophy, reason replaced faith and philosophers emphasized happiness and fulfillment in this life. Thomas Paine, who had contributed so much to the cause of the Revolution with his pamphlet *Common Sense*, continued his writing with such works as *The Rights of Man* and *The Age of Reason*. In these essays, he rejected all revealed religion and declared that pure morality is founded on "natural religion." In 1804, Paine ridiculed Christianity by claiming it to be the "strangest religion ever set up," because "it committed a murder upon Jesus in order to redeem mankind for the sin of eating an apple."[4]

Several of the framers of the Constitution were Deists who restricted their belief in God to that of a divine Creator. Their emphasis on man's innate goodness is expressed in the Declaration of Independence, which proclaims "that all men are created equal, that they are endowed by their Creator with certain unalienable rights."[5] Among the Deists, the sinfulness of man and the need for a Savior had little meaning. Some of this thinking led either to Unitarianism, which basically holds that man is too good to be condemned, or to Universalism, which teaches that God is too good to condemn man. In either case, the motivation for strong missionary zeal or personal repentance and conviction was lacking.

INDUCEMENTS TO CHRISTIAN EXPRESSION

The closing decades of the eighteenth century brought several positive influences from which Baptists profited in their mission. A renewed interest in evangelism, along with the opportunities provided by the migration to new territories and a developing national consciousness, proved powerful assets to Baptists.

---

[4] Sweet, 91-93.
[5] "Declaration of Independence," (1776) 2nd par.

Evangelical Christianity

William Brackney, in his book *Baptist Life and Thought: 1600–1980*, points out that by 1750 a new sense of optimism and piety, which grew out of the First Great Awakening, brought renewed zeal for evangelistic work.[6] Baptists' emphasis on personal religion and commitment to Christ made them particularly receptive to the revivalism, which was marked by the preaching of Jonathan Edwards in New England and John Wesley in England. Their renewal of faith made them less receptive to the rationalism and Deistic teachings that had dominated the political scene. When a Second Great Awakening emerged after 1795, Baptists were ready to take full advantage of it with both a home mission movement and a global foreign missions vision stirred by William Carey's work in India.[7]

New Territory Brings New Opportunities

The newly opened Appalachian region may have attracted some irreligious settlers, but others chose this territory as a place to plant new churches. The migration of the Shrewsbury Seventh Day Baptist Church to Salem in western Virginia (now West Virginia), beginning in 1789, was but one example of the practice of claiming land in new territories for the establishment of covenant communities. Members of the First Hopkinton Church in Rhode Island provided the nucleus for new churches across the state of New York. Berlin Church in Rensselaer County was constituted in 1780, First Brookfield in Madison County in 1797, and Alfred in Allegany County by 1816.

The 1785 Land Ordinance provided for the survey and sale of land in the territory north of the Ohio River and west to the Mississippi River. The Northwest Ordinance of 1787 provided guidelines for the settlement and a form of a Bill of Rights that preceded the one attached to the Constitution. It specified that no person "shall ever be molested on account of his mode of worship or religious sentiments" and added that "Religion, morality and knowledge being necessary to good government and the happiness of mankind, schools and the means of education shall forever be encouraged." Slavery was also prohibited within the territory.

---

[6] William H. Brackney, ed., *Baptist Life and Thought: 1600–1980* (Valley Forge PA: Judson Press, 1983) 149.

[7] Ibid.

This ordinance also promised "good faith" toward the Indians, promising that their lands and property would not be taken without their consent "unless in just and lawful wars authorized by Congress." Nevertheless, the Native Americans' defeat at Fallen Timbers in 1794 made settlement much safer and encouraged the migration of church-related families to the area. Beginning in about 1805, a fairly steady stream of Seventh Day Baptist families began to move down the Ohio River then north up the Little Miami River. Churches were established at such places as Todd's Fork, Mad River, North Hampton, and Jackson Center in Ohio before they gave way to further migrations into the West.

National Consciousness

The sense of a national identity extended to the churches, both on an interdenominational and a denominational level. A stronger national government, with safeguards against the establishment of a state church, lessened suspicions among denominations. An embargo on imports from England stopped the flow of Bibles from abroad and forced Protestant churches in this country to cooperate in the printing and distribution of Bibles. With the end of the war came an increase in emigration from France and other predominantly Catholic nations. Many Protestants shared a common fear of Catholicism and made a united effort to claim the frontiers for Protestantism.

The trend toward the organization of churches on the denominational level was reflected in cooperative missionary activity. Robert Torbet observed that churches that relied on voluntary contributions needed a "central organization for the efficient dispensing of funds, particularly in missionary enterprises."[8] As early as 1707, five Baptist churches in Pennsylvania and New Jersey had joined together in what became known as the Philadelphia Baptist Association, which acted primarily as an advisory council for local churches. However, this association also served in such matters as ordination of ministers and cooperative evangelistic or missionary activity.[9] Other associations were formed from New England to the Carolinas. In 1814, the Baptists created a national missionary organization, the General Missionary Convention of the Baptist Denomination in the United States for Foreign Missions

---

[8] Robert G. Torbet, *A History of the Baptists*, 3rd ed. (1950; repr., Valley Forge PA: Judson Press, 1963) 244.
[9] Ibid., 211-214.

(also known as the Triennial Convention) to carry out missionary activity on a national scale.[10]

Because of their small numbers, the interrelatedness of members, and years of close communications, Seventh Day Baptists did not experience the sectionalism that marked many of the other American churches. Nonetheless, as a part of the mainstream of Protestantism, they were affected by the political, social, and theological environments of the age. In responding to the conditions of the new century, they made choices that were to chart the path of denominational development through the next two centuries.

---

[10] Ibid., 230.

11

SEVENTH DAY BAPTIST GENERAL CONFERENCE

President Jonathan Allen of Alfred University, in an article in the *Sabbath Recorder*, stated that the time of the origin of General Conference is "a sliding scale of some four years—from 1801 to 1805."[1] The quote reflects a process by which the Seventh Day Baptist General Conference evolved after being foreshadowed by cooperation for many years by American Seventh Day Baptists. Once formed, the conference required additional time to determine its mission, function, and organization, a process that has continued in the years since.

BIRTH OF GENERAL CONFERENCE

On 11 September 1801, the first formal action to organize a conference was taken at an annual church meeting held at Hopkinton, Rhode Island. Elder Henry Clarke of Brookfield, New York, presented an open invitation to all Seventh Day Baptist churches "to unite in an institution for propagating our religion in the different parts of the United States, by sending out from the various churches in said Union missionaries, on the expense of the several churches who may fall in with the proposition."[2] A circular letter was sent out in the name of "The Sabbatarian Baptists in their General Conference assembled at Hopkinton" asking each church to consider this proposition so that formal action might be taken by the responding churches at the next annual meeting.

The following year, when the Yearly Meeting of the Hopkinton Church was held, four churches agreed to the proposition either via letter or by a representative in attendance: the Hopkinton and Newport churches in Rhode Island, the Waterford church in Connecticut, and the church at Brookfield, New York. Piscataway, New Jersey, and Petersburg (Berlin), New York, sent letters that they did not concur "at present." Cohansey (Shiloh), New Jersey, made no mention of the proposition in their letters, and Bristol, Connecticut, sent no letters. In a separate

---

[1] Jonathan Allen, "Conference—Its Origin," *Sabbath Recorder* 37/5 (3 Feb 1881): 3.
[2] Henry Clarke, *Proposition given at Yearly Meeting at Hopkinton, R.I., Sept. 11, 1807*, repr. in *Seventh Day Baptist Conference*, comp. Corliss F. Randolph (Newark NJ: Committee on Denominational History, 1907) 8.

meeting, a committee composed of at least one member from each of the churches represented presented a plan for the cooperative support of missions activity with the provision that the annual conference circulate to three places—Hopkinton, Petersburg, and Piscataway. September 1802 is thus considered the birth month of the General Conference, for it marked the change from action undertaken by a single church to action on behalf of a General Conference.[3] The constitution was not adopted until 1805; thus that date is sometimes chosen as the conference's birth year.[4]

Forerunners of General Conference

If 1802 is considered the birth date of the General Conference, then 1696 may be taken as the date of its conception. The first recorded Yearly Meeting was held that year between the Newport and Westerly (Hopkinton) churches when the latter was only a branch of the former. Some form of this Yearly Meeting continued for over 100 years before the conference formally organized. In 1705, the church at Piscataway was admitted to the union and fellowship. Subsequently, other churches or branches joined. Jonathan Allen noted that the Hopkinton church, by virtue of its location and numerical strength as well as its religious vigor, was considered the "Mother Church"; others "swarmed out from her as bees from a parent hive; and the home gathering that took place at her Yearly Meetings and General Communion was the great religious event of the year."[5] The minutes of the Hopkinton church for 23 August 1763 indicate how important these gatherings were for the congregation. The previous year, a motion to dispense with the Yearly Meetings was defeated because many church members felt that it was necessary to meet together "to provoke one another to Christian love and unity, that the weak might become more strong, that God might have glory, and our souls peace."[6]

Similar gatherings brought the brethren together in both Pennsylvania and New Jersey. In 1763, a letter from the annual meeting

---

[3] "General Conference Second Annual Session, 1802," in Randolph, *SDB Conference*, 13-18.

[4] James Bailey, *History of the Seventh-day Baptist General Conference: From Its Origin, September, 1802, To Its Fifty-third session, September, 1865* (Toledo OH: S. Bailey & Co., 1866) 37-51.

[5] Allen, *Sabbath Recorder* 37/5 (3 Feb 1881): 3.

[6] Hopkinton, *R.I. SDB Church Records, 23 Aug. 1763*, repr. in "The Westerly Seventh-day Baptist Church," *SDB Memorial* 3 (Jul 1854): 130.

of the Cohansey, Piscataway, and Pennsylvania churches lamented the omission of the church letter from the Rhode Island meetings.[7] A similar letter in 1770 expressed regret that the Rhode Island yearly meetings were dropped, depriving them of the fellowship "which used to subsist between us."[8] Throughout these years, messengers and letters circulated freely among various gatherings, as well as with individual churches on both sides of the Atlantic. They might well have continued in this fashion were it not for the desire among Seventh Day Baptists to send out missionaries and evangelists.

The Missionary Imperative

Rev. James Bailey, in his *History of the Seventh-Day Baptist General Conference* published in 1866, wrote that the central idea that determined the organization of the General Conference was embodied in the proposition for concerted action in missionary labors. He noted that several Yearly Meetings would have served all the purposes of social and spiritual reunion, of home gatherings, and of seasons of worship at the common altar; but a united effort, under some established rules, seemed necessary to carry out the church brethren's benevolent designs.[9]

Even though the churches seemed to agree on the need for missions outreach, there was no unanimity on how that should be carried out. The Petersburg (Berlin), New York, church stated that the plan proposed "was a little out of the line and form of the primitive custom of Christ sending his missionaries." They argued that Christ had told his disciples to "carry neither purse, nor scrip, nor shoes."[10] The Waterford, Connecticut, church questioned whether "we as a people are ripe for such a business, considering the variety of sentiment among us."

---

[7] "Piscataway, 1763," letter from Cohansie and Piscataway SDB churches to the Newport RI SDB church, 17 Oct 1763, in *Church Letters to the Seventh Day Baptist General Conference, and Other Papers, 1746–1835*, bound MS 19x.181, pp. 5-6, SDB Hist. Soc. Lib. Note: transcript copy, with corrections, BX6393.C57, SDB Hist. Soc. Lib.

[8] "Yearly Meeting of New Jersey Churches to Rhode Island Churches. 1770," in *Church Letters to the Seventh Day Baptist General Conference, and Other Papers, 1746–1835*, transcript copy, with corrections, BX6393.C57, pp. 11-12, SDB Hist. Soc. Lib.. Note: the original is catalogued as MS 19x.181, SDB Hist. Soc. Lib.

[9] Bailey, *History of the SDB General Conference*, 50.

[10] Jonathan Allen, "General Conference—Second Session, 1802," *Sabbath Recorder* 37/8 (24 Feb 1881): 3.

Waterford's members then urged elders and brethren to visit from place to place, "not for filthy lucre's sake, but of a ready mind."[11]

The Cohansey, New Jersey, church stated that they had "reason to believe that an approved administrator would be an useful blessing to our congregations." Having requested that a minister be sent to them, they added, "We trust you will not fail to supply every destitute church and society, as far as your power and opportunity may enable you; for we understand that to be the design of the General Conference."[12]

The General Conference constitution contained no provision for sending or supporting any missionaries. References to this original intent were effectively omitted because of disagreement, either on the method or on the grounds stated by the Bristol, Connecticut, church: "We are all republicans in church as in state government. Hence we doubted the propriety of the elders and brethren, not being delegated for that express purpose, taking the liberty of changing the customs and usages of the church in establishing a new constitution."[13] In 1811, when a plan for the support of traveling ministers was requested by delegates, the conference voted, "Agreed that the same lie in file at present, and afterwards by vote the same is dismissed from further consideration."[14] It was not until the General Conference session of 1817 that any direct effort was made to carry out the missionary designs of the original proposal that gave birth to General Conference.

Other Baptists faced similar problems in organized missions activity. Robert G. Torbet points out that the first controversy to split the ranks of Baptists, particularly in the South and West during the first quarter of the nineteenth century, arose over the denomination's missionary ventures. Some were called the "anti-effort" forces, for they were opposed to centralized authority, an educated and salaried ministry, and any number of man-made organizations including missionary societies.[15]

The direction in which effort was exerted changed from that envisioned by men such as Henry Clarke. There was division concerning

---

[11] Allen, "General Conference, Third Session, 1803," *Sabbath Recorder* 37/9 (3 Mar 1881): 3.

[12] Cohansey, West Jersey SDB Church, letter to the General Conference, Oct 1804, in *SDB Conference*, ed. Randolph, 34.

[13] Bristol CT Sabbatarian Church, letter to the General Conference, 1805, in *SDB Conference*, ed. Randolph, 45.

[14] "Conference Minutes," *SDB Yearbook* (1811) BX 6390, 54 Y92 1807–1840, p. 3.

[15] Robert G. Torbet, *A History of the Baptists*, 3rd ed. (1950; repr., Valley Forge PA: Judson Press, 1963) 268.

responsibilities and a hesitation in relinquishing local autonomy in favor of any centralized power, but there was no lessening of the missionary imperative. The General Conference provided much of the impetus for the spread of the Gospel and advancement of the churches. From approximately 1,119 members in eight churches located across four states in 1802, there was an increase to 9,098 members in 100 churches across 23 states by the end of the General Conference's first 100 years.[16]

FUNCTIONS OF EARLY GENERAL CONFERENCE

The General Conference in its organized form served five major functions during the nineteenth century. (1) It gave the people a sense of identity; (2) it helped define doctrine; (3) it served as a communicating agent; (4) it provided a means for education; and (5) it instigated some programs (discussed below).

1. Identity. A major function of the General Conference was to give the denomination a collective identity so that it could act on behalf of the churches. The first article of the 1805 constitution specified the name "Sabbatarian General Conference," which was retained until 1817, when the name "Seventh Day Baptist General Conference" took root.[17] A sense of identity was important to conduct business and communicate with those both outside and within the fellowship.

In 1815, a dispute arose over property near the center of Philadelphia that had been given by deceased Seventh Day Baptists as a burial ground. The city was interested in acquiring this property for commercial purposes. Since there no longer was a Seventh Day Baptist church in the city with which it could negotiate, the General Conference provided an agency that could represent Seventh Day Baptists.[18] The General Conference also provided a unified entity to communicate with other religious bodies. The 1816 minutes acknowledged that the conference had received copies of the annual report of the Baptist Board of Foreign Missions for the United States. The recognition of Seventh Day Baptists as a distinct denomination has been important in ecumenical relations.[19] The General Conference has often acted on behalf

---

[16] "Fifth Annual Session, 1805," in Randolph, *SDB Conference*, 30. See also *SDB Yearbook* (1902) 65-70.

[17] Article I, General Conference Constitution (1805), repr. in Henry Clarke, *A History of the Sabbatarians or Seventh Day Baptists in America...* (Utica NY: Seward & Williams, 1811) 69. Compare *SDB Yearbook* (1817) 1.

[18] Conference Minutes, *SDB Yearbook* (1815) 4.

[19] Conference Minutes, *SDB Yearbook* (1816) 6.

of Seventh Day Baptists in relation to both state and national government.

2. Doctrine. Closely related to the establishment of an identity is the defining of Seventh Day Baptist corporate beliefs. In three specific ways, the conference has acted directly in influencing doctrinal standards. (1) It has set guidelines for membership; (2) it has at times examined and ordained ministers; and (3) it has developed statements that have reflected the basic beliefs of member congregations.

Guidelines for Membership—The constitution of General Conference was specific in its guarantee of local autonomy, stating "that all things transacted in such General Conference be done by way of advice, counsel or recommendation, and by no means to affect or alter the government or discipline of the churches, in their individual capacity."[20] Nonetheless, in order to accept new churches into membership, the General Conference established certain criteria to define its members' distinctive identity. The conference specified that "no church in our union can receive into their fellowship a person, except they observe the seventh day for a Sabbath: neither such as have not been baptized by immersion."[21]

Although they were careful to avoid any formal statement of faith for close to thirty years, some of the conference's actions and correspondence indicate concern for maintaining purity of faith. For example, in 1808 three churches in what is now West Virginia applied for membership in the General Conference. The Lost Creek and the New Salem churches were accepted with little question, but the request from the church on the West Fork of the Monongahela River was denied because its congregation communed with the First Day Baptists. The letter that was sent on behalf of the General Conference urged holding fast the pure faith of a church through "external fellowship," while cherishing with others the "internal fellowship" and "life-power" of religion.[22]

Questions concerning doctrine and polity were occasionally referred to the General Conference. In 1810, Henry Clarke laid before the conference questions as to whether a church was fully officered without a pastor or watchman; whether it was consistent with the gospel for a

---

[20] Article III, Constitution, Clarke, *A History of the Sabbatarians*, 70.

[21] Article IX, Clarke, *A History of the Sabbatarians*, 71.

[22] Letter to the SDB church residing on the west fork of the Monongahela River VA, 11 Sep 1808, *SDB Yearbook* (1808) 18-19.

church to retain as a wholesome member one who has the ability, and refuses, to bear any part in the expenses of the church; and whether a pastor was obligated by Scripture to continue his pastoral services to a church in case such church refuses to give him a living in proportion to his time in attending the services of said church.[23]

For several years these questions were discussed both at General Conference sessions and in individual churches. The General Conference concluded by saying that the individual churches were best qualified to determine what and how many officers were necessary. "We are further of the opinion," said the conference, "that discussing nice and delicate points in Conference are likely to tend to strife and had better be omitted."[24]

Examination of Ministers—For many years, the General Conference defined doctrine by its examination and ordination of persons recommended by the churches as ministers. From 1824 to 1855, a council called a presbytery was set up at the conference to consider a candidate's statements and recommend ordination. The records do not show the composition of this presbytery, but in 1822 and 1823 these matters were referred to a committee or a council composed of the elders and deacons present at the General Conference sessions.[25] In 1889, the conference responded to the request of the Jackson Center, Ohio, church for the ordination of L. D. Seager with the suggestion "that the power for good to the Jackson Centre Church would be much greater if Bro. Seager's examination and ordination (if determined upon) could be held at that church."[26]

Ordinations are no longer held as a part of General Conference sessions, but denominational representatives are generally included in the examination and ordination of persons entering the ministry. The conference does set the criteria for official recognition of ministers.

Statements of Faith—With the reception of new churches at the rate of about one per year, the conference was often called on to review statements of faith and make recommendations. Since a number of members and even some of the ministers were from other denominations, it seemed advisable to have some statement of general faith as a safeguard against possible doctrinal and theological errors. In

---

[23] Conference Minutes, *SDB Yearbook* (1810) 5.

[24] Hopkinton SDB Church, letter to the General Conference, 30 Aug 1811, repr. in *Church Letters*, MS 19x.181.120, p. 120 (transcript, p. 97).

[25] Conference Minutes, *SDB Yearbook* (1822) 3; "8th," (1823) 4; "20 Sep" (1824) 4.

[26] Conference Minutes, *SDB Yearbook* (1889) 9.

1831, the General Conference appointed a committee to draft an exposé of faith. In 1833, an "exposé of the doctrinal sentiments of the denomination" was submitted for consideration and printed with the minutes.[27] Only five churches voted to accept, but in 1835 Conference voted that the exposé "is in our opinion the sentiments of the connection."[28]

This exposé served virtually unchanged for nearly twenty years as a testimony of the faith generally held by Seventh Day Baptists, but it was never intended as a test of orthodoxy. In 1852, a few minor changes were made and a general explanatory note was added stating that "this Exposé is not adopted as having any binding force in itself, but simply as an exhibition of the views generally held by the denomination."[29]

In 1874, a resolution was adopted by the conference expressing the idea that some of the newer members might benefit from a more "full and explicit system of doctrine." Conference resolved that a committee be appointed to draft such an exposé "consisting of seven of the most aged Seventh Day Baptist ministers present, and five of the most aged deacons present."[30] The motion to strike the words "most aged" was defeated, and six years later, in 1880, a new statement was adopted. This statement remained for over fifty years until 1937, when a new statement was adopted. Another statement was adopted in 1987 as a result of renewed scriptural study by churches and individuals.

In 1843, the General Conference decided that it was "advisable to make an appeal to the various orders of Christians in reference to the Sabbath of the Bible, urging them to a thorough examination of the subject."[31] Thomas B. Brown, Nathan Hull, and Paul Stillman drafted a letter and issued it in the name of the General Conference to the Baptists throughout the United States. About a century and a half later, Baptist historian H. Leon McBeth wrote of the message, "One would be hard put to find a better defense of the sabbath; the address is calmly stated, biblical in emphasis, and fraternal in tone. The authors appeal for first

---

[27] "The Following Expose Was Submitted for the Consideration of the Churches...," Conference Minutes, *SDB Yearbook* (1833) 8-12.

[28] Conference Minutes, *SDB Yearbook* (1835) 10.

[29] "Second-day Morning," Conference Minutes, *SDB Yearbook* (1852) 11.

[30] Conference Minutes, *SDB Yearbook* (1874) 27.

[31] Conference Minutes, *SDB Yearbook* (1843) 8.

day Baptists to adopt seventh day views and, failing that, to show more understanding for their sabbatarian brethren."[32]

This letter was directed at three positions held by Baptists: (1) those who acknowledged the obligation of the Sabbath, but changed the day from the seventh to the first day of the week; (2) those who regarded the sabbatic law as having been nailed to the cross and considered the first day as an institution entirely new; and (3) those Baptists who considered neither the Old nor the New Testament to impose any obligation of rest, and advocated one on the grounds of expediency.[33] The letter acknowledged similarities, stating that "your baptism is our baptism; your church government is our government; your doctrinal principles are ours; and there is nothing which constitutes any real ground of separation, except the great and important subject we now urge upon your attention."[34]

3. Communication. The General Conference functioned as a communicating agency in such services as circular letters, statistical reporting, and sessions of General Conference. In this role, the General Conference undertook the responsibility of reporting to its constituent members the status of congregations and the official business enacted by the conference in session on their behalf.

Circular Letter—The practice of sending a circular letter addressed to all of the churches replaced separate letters from one church to another. This circular letter was included with the General Conference minutes until 1840. A Committee on the State of Religion reported some of the same information each year from 1836 until 1901, when the committee reported that "all the duties of value along the line of our work is contained in the Corresponding Secretary's Report."[35]

The content of both the circular letters and the state-of-religion messages ranged from doctrinal and biblical studies to social and moral issues of the time. Most called for greater consecration and devotion to the task at hand. Many expressed pleas for continued and expanded dissemination of the Sabbath cause, not least through the dedicated

---

[32] H. Leon McBeth, *A Sourcebook for Baptist Heritage* (Nashville: Broadman Press, 1990) 543.

[33] Thomas B. Brown, ed., *An Appeal for the Restoration of the Bible Sabbath: in an Address to the Baptists, from the Seventh-day Baptist General Conference* (New York: American Sabbath Tract Society, 1852) 5.

[34] Brown, ed., *An Appeal*, 22.

[35] Report of the Committee on the State of Religion, Conference Minutes, *SDB Yearbook* (1901) 45.

living of individual Seventh Day Baptists. The state-of-religion reports were often responses to communications from individual churches and were not intended as reports of the General Conference's actions.

Statistical Reporting—The periodic tabulation of statistical information normally included the name and address of each church, the pastor, the number of members added or removed, and the total number of communicants (members in good standing). For a few years, the report also listed the schedule of communions. These statistics, which were printed and distributed in the minutes of General Conference sessions, increased the sense of community among member churches. If a church did not have a representative present at a session of the General Conference, one of the other ministers was delegated to visit that church to keep open the lines of communication.

General Conference Sessions—The fact that the churches gathered in the General Conference proved one of the most effective means of communication. In 1907, Dr. J. Nelson Norwood spoke of the power of conference to educate, inspire, spiritualize, unify, and provide timely leadership. The personal meetings were important, for as he said: "Having seen one another face to face, heard one another's voices, eaten at the same table, we should be better able to differ and still keep sweet."[36] Ninety years later, the cafeteria manager at one of the colleges that often hosted the General Conference was quoted as saying, "Seventh Day Baptists love to eat. Seventh Day Baptists love to talk. Seventh Day Baptists love each other."

4. *Education.* Sessions of General Conference served an educational role in creating an enlightened people. Conference reports helped keep churches and individuals informed. Many of the programs were designed to stimulate people's thoughts and actions.

Reporting of History and Activity—One of the first recorded actions of the General Conference was the recommendation in 1806 to publish a book on "the rise and progress of the Sabbatarian Churches in North America printed in a brief, historical manner." Henry Clarke was appointed to conduct the research and secure subscriptions to cover the cost of printing. In 1811, he published a book under the title *A History of the Sabbatarians or Seventh Day Baptists, in America, Containing Their Rise and Progress to the Year 1811, With Their Leaders' Names, and Their*

---

[36] J. Nelson Norwood, "The Power of Conference—Its Nature and Sources," *Sabbath Recorder* 63/37 (16 Sep 1907): 1004.

Distinguishing Tenets, etc.[37] Not only did this book communicate the past history of the individual churches and the organization of the General Conference, but its content served to mold the thinking of Seventh Day Baptists for several generations.

Clarke identified Seventh Day Baptists with other Christians in affirming that the Bible contains God's holy will as revealed to man and by showing agreement with other fundamental Christian principles. He maintained that the Seventh Day Baptists were generally between the Calvinists and Arminians; that they were good citizens who bore their share of responsibilities to the state; and that in nearly 140 years of existence there was not an instance of one of their elders being guilty of scandalous immorality. Clarke's chapter on "External Fellowship" identifies a cooperative spirit with other Christians while maintaining a close covenant relationship within the denomination. This is followed by discussions of the distinctive beliefs on Baptism and the Sabbath.

The societies and agencies of the denomination have used the General Conference as a means of educating local congregants about their programs and learning from them what needs they can meet. For many years, the annual meetings of these societies took place in conjunction with sessions of the General Conference.[38] This practice continued until about 1903, when it was determined that the societies should hold their annual meetings in the states of their incorporation.[39]

Even after the societies no longer held meetings at the time and place of the General Conference, the conference provided the means to share reports and make suggestions. With the adoption of a unified budget, the power of the purse greatly affected the work of Seventh Day Baptists through its agencies. Most of the leaders and those attending sessions of the General Conference were also leaders and active participants in the societies.

Conference Helps Mold Thought and Action—The General Conference exerted direct education in doctrine and ethical beliefs and practices. Many of the early conferences were in the form of "what-to-think" seminars instead of the more modern "how-to-do" seminars. The 1809 minutes reported that the discourses were solemn and impressive, and

---

[37] Henry Clarke, *A History of the Sabbatarians or Seventh Day Baptists, in America* (Utica NY: Seward & Williams, 1811).
[38] Conference Minutes, *SDB Yearbook* (1884) 13.
[39] Report of the SDB Education Society, *SDB Yearbook* (1903) 155.

that even "the youth behaved uncommonly modest, and scarce one person but what appeared instructed by the solemn truth delivered."[40]

One of the General Conference's standing committees for many years was the Essay Committee, which selected writers to prepare and present papers at the next session. Topics ranged from theology to social issues, from church polity to science and evolution, from questions of morality to biblical interpretation and Sabbath observance. Of particular concern were various aspects of the Sabbath, including such items as activities permitted on the Sabbath, communion with non-Sabbathkeepers, Sunday legislation, and questions concerning the time of day when the Sabbath begins. In 1863, James Bailey wrote an essay on "The History of Our General Conference," which was later printed in book form. It served later generations as a primary source on the General Conference's early history.[41]

Several topics were given extensive treatment year after year, while others were strong issues for shorter periods of time. The question of temperance was an issue throughout much of the General Conference's early years. The question of whether a person could be a member of a secret society, such as the Masonic Lodge, and still be in good standing in the church first appeared on the floor of the conference in 1827 and reappeared periodically for over fifty years until it no longer was a major issue.[42] At times the topics for consideration were rather minor, such as the issue debated in 1836 concerning the wearing of black clothing for funerals. (The practice was declared to be "very burdensome and expensive and without an example or precept from scripture."[43])

During the pre-Civil War days, topics dealing with slavery, the use of force, and war in settling differences were considered. Some resolutions show shifts of attitudes as conditions changed. In 1858, the General Conference declared "that the practice of resorting to war for the settlement of national difficulties is barbarous, unjust, and unchristian; and that it is the duty of the Church to bear its solemn protest against

---

[40] Conference Minutes, *SDB Yearbook* (1809) 5.

[41] Bailey, *History of SDB Conference.*

[42] The following question was proposed at the 1827 Conference: "Would it not be advisable, under existing circumstances, for this Conference to request those brethren in the different churches, who are members of the Masonic fraternity, to withdraw from that connexion?" The question was decided in the affirmative. See Conference Minutes, *SDB Yearbook* (1827) 5. One of the last resolutions was passed in Sep 1874 requesting ministers to present the subject before the people. See Conference Minutes, *SDB Yearbook* (1874) 23, 26.

[43] Conference Minutes, *SDB Yearbook* (1836) 10-11.

it."[44] Yet, in 1864, near the end of the Civil War, the conference affirmed its support for the war, declaring, "No compromise with, no surrender to, rebels, let the war be three years or thirty; that we are fighting in the interest of a holy cause, for which no suffering or sacrifices are too great."[45]

With increased interest in scientific investigation during the last quarter of the nineteenth century, essays were prepared to inform or challenge thinking on related topics. In 1876, A. H. Lewis wrote an essay on "Evolution," while D. H. Davis considered the broad topic of the "Conflict of Science and Religion."[46] Of such importance were some of these topics that in 1879 the General Conference recommended that the Executive Board select the list of topics to be considered and that a limited time be allowed for general discussion.[47] In 1891, the question of biblical criticism came before the conference.[48]

One can only speculate on the effects of these essays and discussions given on the floor of the General Conference and sometimes printed in the minutes or in the *Sabbath Recorder*. George Tomlinson's 1874 essay on the topic "New Testament doctrine of the political, moral and ecclesiastical status of woman"[49] may have influenced the establishment of the Woman's Board about a decade later. Similarly, O. U. Whitford's 1887 topic "Our young people—how to train them in religious and denominational work?"[50] contributed to the establishment of the Young People's Board in 1889.

5. Development of Programs. The constitution the General Conference adopted in 1805 limited its transactions to those of "advice, counsel or recommendation."[51] The revision proposed in 1838 specified that "It shall be the duty of this General Conference, to receive all communications made to them from the churches or Associations,

---

[44] Conference Minutes, *SDB Yearbook* (1858) 6.

[45] Conference Minutes, *SDB Yearbook* (1864) 6.

[46] Report of the Committee on Essays and Essayists, Conference Minutes, *SDB Yearbook* (1876) 5.

[47] Report of the Executive Board, Conference Minutes, *SDB Yearbook* (1879) 12.

[48] Conference Minutes, *SDB Yearbook* (1891) 12.

[49] Conference Minutes, *SDB Yearbook* (1874) 16.

[50] Conference Minutes, *SDB Yearbook* (1887) 17, 24-25.

[51] Article III, General Conference Constitution (1805), repr. in Clarke, *A History of the Sabbatarians*, 70.

relative to their welfare, and give such counsel and assistance as they deem proper."[52]

Through its power of advice, the General Conference has at times helped heal divisions between or within churches. In most cases, the conference was reluctant to interfere with internal differences within churches. However, there were occasions when some external advice was needed, as in matters affecting other churches or the denomination as a whole.

The General Conference also provided the facility for bringing together special interests, how to best select or publish a hymnbook suitable for use in all the churches. The first such hymnbook was published in 1826, with others following in 1832 and 1847. In 1878, the conference approved a plan for adapting the hymnbook *The Service of Song* for use by Seventh Day Baptist churches. The alterations involved changing a single line of one hymn and replacing five or six hymns that made reference to Sunday. *The Seventh Day Baptist Praise Book* published by George Utter in 1879 resulted from this plan of hymnbook adaptation, though the resolution also noted, "by this vote the Conference does not assume any financial responsibility, but promises to use its influence to procure for the book as extensive a circulation as possible."[53]

Through its power of recommendation, the General Conference has initiated a number of programs. During the first half of the nineteenth century, it was instrumental in the organization and support of the Missionary Society, the Tract Society, and the Education Society. As needs were perceived it responded to requests for a Sabbath School Board, a Woman's Board, a Young People's Board, a Historical Board, and a Memorial Board. The General Conference contributed to the creation of regional associations and has struggled with ways to make these associations more effective in the denomination's collective efforts.

[52] Article 8, "The Amended Form of the Constitution," Conference Minutes, *SDB Yearbook* (1838) 11.
[53] Conference Minutes, *SDB Yearbook* (1878) 4.

12

REGIONAL ASSOCIATIONS OF CHURCHES

Perhaps nowhere is the concept of a "choosing people" better demonstrated than in regional associations. As poets have professed, no man is an island unto himself. Seventh Day Baptists sometimes use the term *lone Sabbathkeepers* to describe those who live some distance from a church, but few can maintain their faith without maintaining some form of association with those who share common convictions. Likewise, isolated churches usually flounder without the advantages of a wider fellowship.

When the General Conference was organized, nearly all Seventh Day Baptist churches were located in a narrow strip of land near the Atlantic Ocean. Brookfield, in central New York, and the New Salem and Lost Creek churches, in what was then western Virginia, were the only churches in the Appalachian region. The Revolutionary War pushed the boundary west to the Mississippi River and added to the new nation such inviting areas as the Old Northwest Territory. The Louisiana Purchase in 1805 more than doubled the area of the United States and made the entire Mississippi River system available for inland transportation. A few military roads had been carved through the mountains during the war and settlers began to flow into the frontier areas. The defeat of the Indians by forces under Gen. Anthony Wayne and victory in the War of 1812 opened the Great Lakes region for settlement. The opening of the Erie Canal in 1825 provided stimulus for further expansion. Not only did the new routes provide access into the region, but they also made it possible to send goods from the West to markets in the East.

Seventh Day Baptists followed this westward migration so that from the eight constituting churches in 1802, by 1835 the denomination had expanded to over five times that number. Most of the new churches were located in central and western New York and western Virginia, with a few in Pennsylvania and Ohio. Some of these settlers enjoyed the homecoming atmosphere of the annual sessions of the General Conference, but the vast majority were unable to spend the time and expense to undertake such long and tiresome journeys. Maxon Green's journal details his horse-and-buggy voyage from Alfred, New York, to the 1829 conference at Ashaway, Rhode Island, beginning with his departure from Alfred on 2 September and ending with his return on 13 November. Green spent approximately nine weeks traveling to and from the conference. Granted, he visited some family and churches on the way, but with no public transportation, not many people could devote that much time and expense to attend an annual session of conference. As early as 1815, the General Conference considered the possibility of having two conferences, one for those on the coastal regions and a second for those beyond the Appalachian Mountains to the west, though ultimately this did not come to pass. By 1830, over twenty churches had been established in the regions on the western side of the Appalachians.

THE DEVELOPMENT OF ASSOCIATIONS

When the General Conference met in Hopkinton, Rhode Island, in 1835, it recommended that three associations be formed that would appoint delegates to represent them at the General Conference and that "such delegates form the active body of such General Conference when in session."[1] A committee was appointed to draw up a plan of organization calling for three regional associations—Eastern, Middle, and Western—to meet each year a few weeks prior to the General Conference session. For this purpose, each association was to appoint twelve delegates.[2]

Eastern Association

The Eastern Association was composed of the churches in Rhode Island, New Jersey, and Connecticut. Its name has not changed, and its boundaries have been altered little during the succeeding years. Some churches adjacent to the area in Pennsylvania and New York (and more recently Washington D.C., Maryland, and northern Virginia, have since been included. For a time, the Salem and Lost Creek churches in western Virginia (now West Virginia) were members of the Eastern Association.

The Eastern Association was organized in May 1836 at a meeting in Piscataway, New Jersey. Only four churches—Piscataway and Shiloh in New Jersey, Waterford in Connecticut, and Second Hopkinton in Rhode Island—reported to the new organization at its first annual meeting in 1837. The Shiloh church did not meet with the association after that first meeting until 1846, when it was admitted to membership (the people

---

[1] Conference Minutes, *SDB Yearbook* (1834) 8.
[2] Conference Minutes, *SDB Yearbook* (1835) 9-10.

were not convinced that it was necessary to meet). Several of the other churches appeared unconvinced of the need for an association. Some feared an association might break the strong mother-daughter relationship that existed between the First Hopkinton Church and the new churches on the frontier. The annual homecoming was a celebration they did not want to see replaced by other meetings.

These churches that were already at the center of denominational activity were less likely to understand the effect geographic isolation and extended travel had on other churches that longed for closer fellowship and renewal of covenant relationship. It is also possible that the same reluctance that caused Rhode Island to delay ratification of the federal constitution fifty years earlier still lingered, causing some to fear federalism or shared power and authority within religious organizations. Article VIII of the Eastern Association's constitution specified: "The Association shall adopt no measures, and pass no resolutions that shall interdict or infringe upon the connections of the churches with the General Conference, and nothing in these articles shall be construed as in the least, affecting the connection of the churches with that body."[3]

The delay of some of these churches to participate fully in the associational organization forced changes that affected the operations of the General Conference for generations. From the very beginning of the association plan, some of the churches reported to the General Conference through their respective associations while others reported directly. We can only speculate as to whether the structure, and possibly the effectiveness, of the General Conference might have been different if those first churches had all agreed to a subordinate associational structure.

Central Association (Central New York)

The Central Association was designated to include those churches in New York State west of the Hudson River and east of Allegany County. It first reported to General Conference in 1836 using the name Central Association, a name it retained until about 1956, when it became known as the Central New York Association. The churches in New York east of the Hudson River were free to choose whether they wished to be

---

[3] William L. Burdick, "The Eastern Association," in Corliss Fitz Randolph, ed., *Seventh Day Baptists in Europe and America*, 3 vols. (Plainfield NJ: American Sabbath Tract Society, 1910) 2:705.

included in the Eastern or the Central Association. The churches in the Berlin and Petersburgh areas opted for the Eastern Association.

Although this was the smallest association in area, during the nineteenth century it was one of the most influential. The very concept of a General Conference is attributed to Henry Clarke, who served the Brookfield, New York, church. Through migrations, as well as strong missionary and evangelistic efforts, a total of eighteen churches had been organized within the General Conference's boundaries by 1850. A number of the churches in other associations on the frontier were daughters of the churches in central New York, since the best routes across the Appalachian uplands led through this area.

Many of the early printing efforts that influenced the entire denomination came from this association. Its most successful educational endeavor, DeRuyter Institute, produced leaders of the denomination in missions, education, and finances. The first officers of the Young People's Board were from this association. It took an active role in social reforms and Sabbath promotion. Perhaps it was this concern for Sabbath that prompted one of its members, Rachel Oakes Preston of Verona, New York, to share her Sabbath conviction with those who were instrumental in the founding of the Seventh-day Adventist denomination.[4]

Western Association (Allegheny)

The Western Association, at the time, was composed of the churches in Allegany County, New York, and areas both to the west and south of that county. The churches in western New York and northern Pennsylvania retained that name until 1968, when they became the Allegheny Association. In 1980, the Seventh Day Baptist Church of Toronto, Ontario, in Canada joined the association.

The churches that initially comprised this association represented the second stage of migration from Rhode Island, for many were branches of Central Association churches. About forty churches were organized during the nineteenth century in western New York and Pennsylvania. In addition, churches in western Virginia (later West Virginia), Ohio, and Wisconsin were at one time assigned to the Western Association.

The Western Association was also active in the denomination's printing and educational development. The first denominationally

---

[4] Russell J. Thomsen, *Seventh-day Baptists—Their Legacy to Adventists* (Mountain View CA: Pacific Press, 1971) 41-42.

owned printing house was located in Alfred, New York, which became the center of denominational theological education for over a hundred years. Many of the association's sons and daughters were actively engaged in evangelism and missions throughout the nineteenth and twentieth centuries.

The Western Association was a base for the third stage of the basic migration to the West. Many of the Seventh Day Baptist settlers in the southern part of Wisconsin Territory came from western New York. They brought with them ideas and institutions that were extensions of the environment from which they traveled.

Southeastern Association (Appalachian and South Atlantic)

With the migrations into the West and the South, other associations were carved out of territory once an extension of the Eastern and the Western Associations. In 1839, the areas of western Virginia, southwestern Pennsylvania, and Ohio were collectively organized as the South-Western Association. In 1850, this association was divided into the Virginia and the Ohio Associations. The Virginia Association was dissolved in 1855 "upon the apparent deleterious effects of inharmonious views and movements, evinced at past meetings of this body."[5] There were both theological and social disagreements on issues, including slavery, the nature of man, sin, and death.

In 1871, upon the invitation of the Salem, West Virginia, church, a council of churches was called to reorganize an association in that area. A constitution was drafted that reactivated the association on January 15, 1872. This time the name South-Eastern Association (later spelled Southeastern) was taken to more accurately identify its geographic location. Invitations to join were sent to the church at Jackson Center, Ohio, and to the German Seventh Day Baptists at New Enterprise, Pennsylvania, "if it should be found that they were in doctrinal harmony with the association." Two years later, the Jackson Center church was admitted. In 1886, the church at Salemville, Pennsylvania, which had been organized from the German Seventh Day Baptists, asked for admission and was accepted.[6] In 1969, the German Seventh Day Baptist Church of Salemville, known as the "Brick Church" due to its edifice, became a member of the association, even though it was not a member of

---

[5] "The Virginia Association," *Sabbath Recorder* 12/33 (24 Jan 1856): 130.
[6] Corliss Fitz Randolph, *A History of the SDBs in West Virginia* (Plainfield NJ: American Sabbath Tract Society, 1905) 281ff.

the General Conference.[7] In 1999, because of growth in the Carolinas, Georgia, and Florida, churches in these states withdrew from the Southeastern Association to form the South Atlantic Association. The remaining churches adopted the name Appalachian Association.

Because of its geographic isolation, the Southeastern Association was less prominent in denominational leadership until near the end of the nineteenth century, when Salem College had been established at Salem, West Virginia. However, the presence of such family names as Davis, Van Horn, Bond, and Randolph in churches across the nation give testimony to the convictions of those early families, whose sons and daughters provided leadership to the denomination as they moved westward through Ohio, Illinois, Iowa, and beyond.

Northwestern Association (North Central and Mid-Continent)

In 1838, Seventh Day Baptists began to migrate to the Wisconsin Territory (now Wisconsin), where a church was established in 1840 at Milton. Other churches were established at nearby Albion in 1843 and Walworth in 1847. Movements out of this area, as well as further migrations from the East, led to the organization of churches in several states in the West and Midwest and created a need for another association.

At first this organization was called the Wisconsin Association, but in 1849 its name was changed to the Northwestern Association to include churches established in Illinois, Iowa, and Minnesota. By the end of the century, through migrations, evangelistic work, and a wider interest in the Sabbath, churches were organized in an ever-widening circle. Thus, this Northwestern Association had, at one time or another, included churches in seventeen states from Ohio, Kentucky, and Tennessee in the East to Colorado, Idaho, Oregon, and California to the West; and from Michigan, Wisconsin, Minnesota, and South Dakota in the North to Arkansas and Texas in the South. In area it embraced a territory several times that of all the other associations combined.

As an association, it gave form to organized women's work and direction to the denomination's early youth activities. It established an academy at Albion, Wisconsin, and gave encouragement and support to other educational institutions that had been organized by individuals or

---

[7] Executive Council Report, Southeastern Association Minutes (1970), E-File folder 27, MS 19x.703.064, SDB Hist. Soc. Lib.

churches. It was active in evangelism on the home field and encouraged the observance of the Sabbath among the emigrants to the West.

Following the Civil War, this association was active in promoting colonization in locations "where the blessings of the Sabbath might be enjoyed."[8] In 1874, an attempt was made by the association to establish a colonization board of the Seventh-day Baptist North-Western Association "to direct the emigration of our people to the West that those thus emigrating may at once secure religious and educational advantages."[9] In 1871, a colonization association of the Dakota, Wisconsin, church led to the establishment of a church in Nebraska at North Loup.[10] Similar efforts were made to encourage settlers to locate in Nortonville, Kansas, in southern Illinois at Villa Ridge, and at other locations in the South and West.[11]

Because of its size, the Northwestern Association encouraged the formation of sub-groups, although there was never any organizational connection. The churches in southern Wisconsin met in quarterly meetings until the 1980s, and churches in northern Wisconsin and Minnesota formed a semi-annual meeting. Other groups met in southern Illinois, in Michigan and Ohio, in Kansas and Nebraska, in Colorado, and in Arkansas and Texas. In time, new associations grew out of these geographic and cultural groups.

In 1947, several churches in the Northwestern Association requested a regrouping of the churches. The General Conference approved a plan that resulted in the creation of three associations from the Northwestern Association: the Northern Association with churches in Michigan, Ohio, and Indiana; the North Central Association comprised of churches in Illinois, Wisconsin, and Minnesota; and the Mid-Continent Association made up of churches in Nebraska, Kansas, and Colorado. With more efficient means of travel and its members' growing affluence, in 1969 the Northern Association was able to merge with the North Central Association. At about the same time, a new church was established in Columbus, Ohio. By 1990, however, that church had joined the Southeastern Association, and the Stonefort church in southern Illinois joined the Southwestern Association.

---

[8] Northwestern Association Minutes (1865) 11
[9] Northwestern Association Minutes (1874) 15.
[10] Hosea W. Rood, *A Historical Sketch of the Thorngate-Rood Family* (Ord NE.: Horace M. Davis, 1906) 70-80.
[11] C. M. Lewis, "Southern Illinois," *Sabbath Recorder* 27/62 (21 Dec 1871): 206.

Southwestern Association

The first division of the old Northwestern Association occurred in 1888, when the Southwestern Association was organized. James F. Shaw described the incentive to organize as "the hunger which the human soul, inflamed by the fires of religion within, feels for communion with those of like faith."[12] The intense opposition to Sabbathkeeping in the area tended to draw the small, scattered churches into a covenant group to strengthen their work in evangelism and Sabbath reform. In January 1888, even before they had officially organized as an association, this group began publishing a small newsletter titled *Sabbath Outpost*, which they continued to publish for eleven years. Response to this evangelistic effort provided the basis for eight churches from the states of Texas, Mississippi, Missouri, and Arkansas to constitute the Southwestern Association, which was accepted into General Conference membership in 1889.[13] Churches in Alabama were later included in the association but have more recently affiliated with the Southeastern/Appalachian Association.

The Southwestern Association was less influenced by migration than the other associations. It relied heavily on converts to the Sabbath for growth and support. Throughout the early years of its existence, it the Southwestern Association's territory was considered a primary mission field; other churches provided considerable support to finance its evangelistic, tract, and educational efforts, including the formation of a mission school at Fouke, Arkansas.

Pacific Coast Association (Northwest)

The Pacific Coast Association was the natural result of the fellowship that existed among Seventh Day Baptists living near the west coast in the early years of the twentieth century. The first church in California to become a member of General Conference was the Tustin Seventh Day Baptist Church in Orange County, which was accepted in 1892. Its membership never grew beyond a few families, some of whom united with a church organized at Colony Heights in 1896. By 1902 several factors, including difficulties over sustaining the colony's water supply, forced the church to abandon the project. Most of its members

---

[12] James F. Shaw, "The Southwestern Association," in Corliss Fitz Randolph, ed., *Seventh Day Baptists in Europe and America*, 3 vols. (Plainfield NJ: SDB General Conference, 1910) 2:920.
[13] Ibid., 2:920-31.

moved to Riverside, California, where they adopted the name of the city for the church.[14]

The Riverside Church recognized its responsibility to other Sabbathkeepers along the West Coast and consequently organized the Pacific Coast Association. This new group was basically an association of individuals scattered among the western states served by a single church; it could not be recognized at that time as an association because the General Conference was an organization of churches, not individuals. At Riverside's fourth annual meeting in 1906, Pastor Eli Loofboro reported that, on behalf of the church, he had visited Sabbathkeeping members of the association in Idaho, Oregon, Washington, and California. A number of these individuals were members of the Riverside Sabbath School, and they received study materials from the school's Home Department.[15]

With the organization of the Los Angeles, California, church in 1910, the old Pacific Coast Association disbanded and a new one organized along somewhat different lines. It retained the same name, but the membership, instead of being composed of individuals, included churches. Membership was also granted to "scattered individual Sabbath keepers, not members of churches, who may desire to become members."[16] Prior to this action, the Riverside Church and its predecessors, Tustin and Colony Heights, each had been considered a part of the Northwestern Association. In 1911, the Pacific Coast Association took its place alongside the others. As the association grew northward, it established churches in the Bay Area and eventually in Seattle and Portland and beyond. In March 2007, the new Northwest Association came into being to represent churches in Washington, Oregon, Idaho, and Montana.[17]

RELATIONSHIP OF ASSOCIATIONS TO THE GENERAL CONFERENCE

From the beginning, the relationship of associations to the General Conference has been advisory, with each retaining its own autonomy. The committee of the General Conference, which reported in 1835 on the

---

[14] Daisy Furrow Allen and Elizabeth Bonham, "Section I, 1893–1949," *History of the Riverside SDB Church*, ed. Bernice B. Chapman and Maleta O. Curtis (Riverside CA, 1979) 5-13.

[15] Eli F. Loofboro, letter to Pacific Coast SDB Association, *Sabbath Recorder* 62/47 (19 Nov 1906): 741.

[16] "Mountain Tops at Riverside," *Sabbath Recorder* 70/3 (16 Jan 1911): 73-76.

[17] Rob Appel, "...and Northwest makes 10," *Sabbath Recorder* 229/5 (May 2007): 23.

organization of associations, envisioned a type of organization based on the principle of federalism, defined as "a form of government in which power is distributed between a central authority and a number of constituent territorial units."[18] Several churches did not choose to be represented through associations but continued to appoint delegates directly to the conference. Thus, in 1837 it was voted that "those churches who are members of any association shall be represented by the delegates from the associations, and those churches that are not members of an association shall have direct representation."[19]

The 1838 constitution stated that the General Conference "shall consist of churches and associations."[20] A conflict of autonomy was created when some churches had direct representation, while others were represented indirectly through the associations. This dual form of representation remained in the constitution for over thirty years, but there are few references to delegates sent by associations. An effort was made in 1852 to encourage churches that had withheld connection with an association to reconsider the matter and "connect themselves with the association within the bounds of which they are respectively located."[21]

A new constitution proposed in 1868 listed membership by churches and added the provision: "The Associations shall be considered auxiliaries to the General Conference, and their officers as delegates ex officio"[22]; however, in 1870 the proposal failed to get the necessary two-thirds vote.[23] By the time a constitutional revision was adopted in 1875, it did not mention associational representation.[24] Care was taken, however, that vice presidents were elected each year from the different associations, even though no power or duties were assigned to them. When new associations were added, one more vice president was added to the General Conference's list of officers. Subsequent revisions to the constitution failed to include associations as an organic unit of the General Conference despite major proposed changes in 1882 and 1953. A recommendation in 1955 that each association elect two members to the conference's nominating committee, though not codified at the time, was

---

[18] "Federalism," *Webster's New Collegiate Dictionary*, 1966 ed.

[19] Conference Minutes, *SDB Yearbook* (1837) 5.

[20] Article 2, "The Amended Form of the Constitution," Conference Minutes, *SDB Yearbook* (1838) 10.

[21] Conference Minutes, *SDB Yearbook* (1852) 8.

[22] Article 3, Constitution, Conference Minutes, *SDB Yearbook* (1868) 5.

[23] Conference Minutes, *SDB Yearbook* (1870) 11.

[24] Article 2, Constitution, Conference Minutes, *SDB Yearbook* (1874) 18-19.

actually implemented for the next fifty years until 2007, when the conference approved an official constitutional change: "Each member of the Committee on Nominations shall be a member of a member church of the General Conference. The Committee on Nominations shall consist of six members appointed by General Conference President, and two members appointed or elected by each Association to serve a one-year term" (Article X).[25]

WORK OF ASSOCIATIONS IN AND THROUGH GENERAL CONFERENCE ACTION

Although there was little organic relationship between the associations and the General Conference, there was considerable interaction between them. For many years, the associations directed the reporting of statistics and activities. Actions of the General Conference have often been initiated by ideas and programs generated within associations. Some of the General Conference's recommendations have been channeled through the associations for implementation.

Much of the denomination's evangelistic work during the nineteenth century was carried out by the missionary societies within the associations. Even when a denominational society existed, it often worked through the association's auxiliary societies. The Northwestern Association, in 1853, affirmed its responsibility to work in the home field and "especially to care for the feeble sabbath settlements within our borders."[26] Four years later, that association became involved in the foreign field and resolved to cooperate with the General Board in missionary work but would "never rest satisfied until we ourselves, through its agency, shall have sent out a missionary family from our midst, to some foreign field, and support it there."[27] By 1865, amid growing denominational interest, the role of the denominational missionary agency increased to the point where the Northwestern Association resolved that in its opinion all missionary matters of the denomination should be managed by a General Board.[28]

Attempts have been made over the years to involve associations in various denominational programs. Some subcommittees of boards and agencies have been located in associational areas. The headquarters of

---

[25] Conference Minutes, *SDB Yearbook* (1882) 15; (1953) 21; (2007) A2.
[26] Northwestern Association Minutes (1853) 6.
[27] Northwestern Association Minutes (1857) 7.
[28] Northwestern Association Minutes (1865) 11.

the Woman's Board has been rotated on a geographic basis often connected with an association. Young people's camps have generally been organized on an associational level. Ordinations have historically involved representation from sister churches in the association, and in 1990, the General Conference recommended that each association create an Ordination Preparation Committee to examine the credentials of ministerial candidates and make recommendations to the local churches.

Some of the associations have remained active in both home and foreign missions work. They have provided churches encouragement and fellowship. They have been active in camping programs for young people, often owning and maintaining their own facilities. At times they have served as auxiliary units to the denomination, and they have often hosted General Conference sessions.

Thus, though the General Conference has remained a conference of churches, it has worked through the associations to carry out much of its mission. Likewise, the associations have had a direct voice in the selection of the personnel appointed to denominational leadership.

13

THE RISE OF SOCIETIES: MISSIONS

Norman Maring and Winthrop Hudson, in their book A *Baptist Manual of Polity and Practice*, observed that a fresh awareness of the church's missionary and evangelistic responsibility early in the nineteenth century brought new forms of cooperation among churches and denominations. Among Baptists, this led to the development of two conflicting models for organization: (1) the associational principle and (2) the societal principle.[1]

ASSOCIATIONAL PRINCIPAL

The associational principle as applied to churches refers to organization based on a common interest for mutual benefit. Dr. Wayne Rood wrote that among Seventh Day Baptists there has been a constant search for balance between local autonomy and the associational principle. "Seventh Day Baptists are largely agreed that in a balance between the two principles is to be found the best relationship."[2]

The General Conference began as an association. Like other Baptists of the time, Seventh Day Baptists responded to a missionary and an evangelistic responsibility. Yet, unlike many other Baptists, whose fear of losing local autonomy delayed any national organization, Seventh Day Baptists were able to form a national association in the establishment of the General Conference. At the same time, some of the same attitudes that kept other Baptists from uniting had a direct effect on the General Conference's efforts to adapt the societal principle to an associational organization.

SOCIETAL PRINCIPLE

In contrast to the associational organization formed by churches, a society is composed of individuals banded together by specific interests. Membership is voluntary and often open to persons of any or no

---

[1] Norman H. Maring and Winthrop S. Hudson, *A Baptist Manual of Polity and Practice* (Valley Forge PA: Judson Press, 1963) 167.
[2] Wayne R. Rood, ed., *A Manual of Procedures for SDB Churches* (Plainfield NJ: SDB General Conference, 1972) 19-20.

denomination upon payment of dues. The popularity of societies grew among those who feared centralization of authority and power. There were both advantages and disadvantages to the societal principle as it developed in the churches.

An association of churches is largely advisory. Before it can act, it has to get consensus or agreement from individual churches containing members who are not particularly interested in missions, or tracts, or education. A society, on the other hand, has limited membership made up of people who already hold a common interest. It can respond almost immediately to a need. Furthermore, since the society is made up of individuals who support the work directly, members do not feel that they are giving up their local church autonomy in the decision of where and how their money is being spent.

In a paper titled "The Two Structures of God's Redemptive Mission," Ralph D. Winter used the terms "modalities" and "sodalities" to differentiate between the two concepts of church structure. Modality is a structured fellowship such as a congregation or denomination that has little distinction as to age or sex. Sodality involves an adult second decision beyond membership in a church or denomination, such as that found in a missions agency or a local men's or women's club.[3] Winter maintained that "the vehicle that allowed the Protestant movement to become vital was the structural development of sodality, which harvested the vital 'voluntarism' latent in Protestantism, and surfaced in new mission agencies of all kinds, both at home and overseas." Most of the missions activity in the nineteenth century began from members' initiative "independent of the ecclesiastical structures to which they were related."[4]

Among Baptists, this formation of sodality or society was found in the experience of Luther Rice and Adoniram Judson, whom the Congregational Board of Missions had sent to India. In 1813, while en route to India, they became convinced of the Baptist position regarding believer's baptism. Both resigned from their appointment with the Board of Missions. Judson and his wife went to Burma to establish a Baptist mission there, while Rice returned to America to raise money for this new venture. Rice had hoped to enlist support from associations, but

---

[3] *Address to the All-Asian Consultation, Seoul '73, Korea, Aug. 27–Sept. 1, 1973*, quoted by Ralph D. Winter, *The Two Structures of God's Redemptive Mission* (South Pasadena CA: William Carey Library).

[4] Winter, *Two Structures*, 132-33.

since the need was too urgent to work through the modality structure of denominations, he went directly to the people. The missionary enthusiasm of interested people led to the formation of a society called the American Baptist Missions in the Far East.[5]

The success of this society led to the establishment of other societies to support special work in other areas. Those interested in printing and tract distribution, in education, in history, in women's work, in youth, or in other special interests formed their own societies. As the number of societies multiplied, the competition for support from virtually the same people increased. The lack of overall planning and coordination led to duplication of effort, inefficiencies in administration, and the serious disadvantage Maring and Hudson expressed as the divorcing of the "missionary and educational agencies from responsibility to the churches," thus hampering the development of a coherent and efficient denominational organization in the United States.[6]

Even though Seventh Day Baptists had a denominational organization in the form of the General Conference, which was established on an associational basis for missions, it was not able to function in "harvesting the voluntarism" it needed within the churches to carry out a strong missionary effort. It could advise churches to send out missionaries, and it could help coordinate programs, but most of the work was done through societies established for those purposes.

THE CHOICE OF SOCIETIES TO WORK IN MISSIONS

In 1813, the General Conference recommended that every member church send out itinerant preachers.[7] The 1817 conference requested "the systematical arrangement of sending out missionaries, or travelling preachers," calling on a united effort in encouragement and support of local societies for "the promulgation and spread of the gospel in its purity." The General Conference proposed that its annual sessions "be considered the central society of the Seventh Day Baptist order in North America," with responsibility in designating persons to be sent on such missions, and that a committee to consist of one member of each local missionary society, if practicable, be formed as the Board of Trustees and Directors of Missions of the Seventh Day Baptist order in America.[8] The

---

[5] Robert G. Torbet, *A History of the Baptists*, 3rd ed. (1950; repr., Valley Forge PA: Judson Press, 1963) 248-49.

[6] Maring and Hudson, *A Baptist Manual*, 171.

[7] Conference Minutes, *SDB Yearbook* (1813) 3.

[8] Conference Minutes, *SDB Yearbook* (1817) 5.

effect of the suggestion was to promote communication and cooperation between the autonomous missionary societies and groups that already existed in local congregations. In effect, this was promoting a consortium/congress representing the local churches already engaged in this work at the conference level.

Conference recommended that the board solely control the funds, direct the itinerary of the missionary, and require a "correct journal of his travels, expenditures, and donations received by him in his tour." They stated that it was "thought not advisable for any one society to send out any missionaries, even at their own expense, unless by first obtaining the approbation of the General Conference, for the person sent out."[9]

Board of Trustees and Directors of Missions

In 1818 the recommendation was adopted, and after the adjournment of conference business, the delegates organized a Board of Managers to implement the recommendation. Matthew Stillman was appointed the leader and Amos R. Wells an assistant.[10] It was in this capacity that Wells made a missionary journey in summer 1819 through New Jersey, western Virginia, Ohio, and Pennsylvania, concluding his travels at the session of the General Conference in Brookfield, New York. At that 1819 session, a constitution was drawn up that included most of the provisions that had previously been recommended along with such checks and balances as: "No salary or sum shall be agreed upon between this board and any missionary in their employ, until he shall have completed his mission and made his returns to this board and shall have no voice in fixing his own pay."[11]

In 1819, William Satterlee, Amos R. Wells, and William B. Maxson were commissioned as missionaries for the ensuing year.[12] Over the next four years, such missionaries as Amos R. Wells, John Davis, William Maxson, John Greene, Amos Satterlee, Daniel Babcock, Richard Hull, Lewis A. Davis, Job Tyler, and Matthew Stillman described their adventures in detailed reports. These are all recorded with the General Conference minutes or in the *Seventh Day Baptist Missionary Magazine*,

---

[9] Ibid., 5-6.
[10] Conference Minutes, *SDB Yearbook* (1818) 5-6.
[11] Constitution, Articles 3 & 5, Conference Minutes, *SDB Yearbook* (1819) 9, 10.
[12] Conference Minutes, *SDB Yearbook* (1819) 11.

which was published under the patronage of that early Missionary Board from August 1821 to September 1825.[13]

The reports of Amos R. Wells show the extent of some of those early missionary endeavors. The committee that audited his report in 1820 recorded that he had collected $80.22, had spent $33.55, and had a balance in his hands of $46.67. It recommended that he be allowed $112 for his services for the year past.[14] On one of his tours he was gone for 5 months and 8 days, traveled 1,055 miles, preached 111 sermons, and baptized 9 people. His traveling expenses were $14.55, while donations amounted to $14.04.[15] A second tour lasted about 4 months, during which he traveled 1,566 miles, preached 69 times, baptized 24 persons, assisted in the organization of 2 churches, spent $19, and received donations of $41.31.[16] A more detailed report in the *Missionary Magazine* lists the specific amounts individuals and collections contributed, ranging from 13 cents to $13.50. It also listed several fringe benefits, including "one pair of woolen socks, a pair of flannel drawers, a handkerchief, a cambrick neckhandkerchief and cotton cloth for overalls."[17]

This first step by the General Conference in coordinating the missions through a Board of Trustees and Directors of Missions set a pattern for an aggressive home missions program that was to highlight a period of expansion and growth. However, there were some who favored an organization more independent of the General Conference, so in 1821 the Missionary Board resolved that the portion of the General Conference's constitution relating to the nomination of missionaries be dispensed with for the present year.[18]

Some of the management may have been turned over to the emerging societies, but the General Conference continued to respond directly to requests for help. In 1826, the conference appointed William Maxson and Joel Greene to organize a church, if they deemed it advisable, in Fox Township, Pennsylvania, adding that the conference bear the expense of such a journey.[19] The 1827 conference minutes report

---

[13] *Seventh Day Baptist Missionary Magazine* 1:1–2:7 (Aug 1821–Sep 1825).

[14] Conference Minutes, *SDB Yearbook* (1820) 12-13.

[15] "A Summary of Amos R. Wells' Journal in 1819 & 1820," Conference Minutes, *SDB Yearbook* (1820) 17.

[16] "Summary," Conference Minutes, *SDB Yearbook* (1820) 17.

[17] *SDB Missionary Magazine* 1/6 (Nov 1822): 200.

[18] "Missionary Intelligence," *SDB Missionary Magazine* 1/2 (Nov 1821): 45.

[19] Conference Minutes, *SDB Yearbook* (1826) 4.findme

that Maxson visited and helped plant a church in Cuba, New York. (Joel Greene was unable to attend.) The church in Cuba is now known as Little Genesee and is still in existence.

Seventh-day Baptist General Board of Missions

A new constitution in 1824 adopted the name Seventh-Day Baptist General Board of Mission and made the board more responsive to local missionary societies. Annual meetings were held at the time and place of the General Conference, but the board was composed of delegates from "the several Missionary, Bible, or Mite Societies, which may be disposed to vest their funds in the Board." (A "mite" was a small amount of money donated for a purpose—in this case, missions.) Each society that contributed annually to the funds was entitled to one vote. The main object of the Board was the employment of missionaries, but the printing or purchase and distribution of tracts and religious books were also stated goals.[20]

There was little change in the missionaries' operating procedures. They were required to be regular ministers of some church within the denomination; their routes were prescribed in detail; and no salary was to be agreed on until the completion and review of their tours. Many of the same missionaries continued under the new board. Seven new churches were added, largely as a result of the board's labors.

The American Seventh-Day Baptist Missionary Society

A new and more independent society organized in 1828 to generate interest in missions among Seventh Day Baptists and to increase the efficiency of missions work.[21] The basis of membership was the payment of dues amounting to $1 per year or a $10 lump sum for lifetime membership. Missionary, mite, and Bible societies that contributed annually were entitled to one vote for every $2 contributed. This new society assumed the missionary work of the denomination and, according to O. U. Whitford, "From this date the management and direction of our missionary work are more separate from the General

---

[20] Constitution, Articles 1, 2, & 5, *SDB Missionary Magazine* 2/3 (Aug 1824): 80-81.

[21] O. U. Whitford, "Historical Sketch of Our Home and Foreign Mission Work for One Hundred Years," in *Seventh Day Baptists in Europe and America*, 3 vols., ed. C. F. Randolph (Plainfield NJ: SDB General Conference, 1910) 1:335.

Conference, and hence its history is more separate from that of the Conference."[22]

Most of the new society's work was to continue sending missionaries to the home field. Twenty-three new churches were established during the decade of the 1830s. Not all of this expansion was the direct result of Missionary Society activity, for there was also considerable western migration during this period. However, many of the new churches were within regions of New York state and areas of what is now West Virginia and neighboring Ohio, where the Missionary Society lent the most encouragement and support to local churches and associations. Pastors of established churches often spent time with scattered members in neighboring communities in a pattern similar to the circuit riders who characterized the Methodists of the time.

CHOOSING AREAS FOR MISSIONS GROWTH

Basically, there were four choices open to Seventh Day Baptists for growth: (1) strengthening scattered members; (2) going to other Christians; (3) taking the gospel to Sabbathkeeping Jews; or (4) breaking new ground in missions.

1. Strengthen Scattered Members. The early missionary societies chose biological growth as a primary focus. The constitution of the early societies carried mottos such as "to promote pure and undefiled religion, by employing missionaries and sending them to the destitute and scattered brethren in our fellowship."[23] In 1828 the Missionary Society defined its purpose more sharply: "to aid in sending the Gospel to the destitute and scattered of the Seventh Day Baptist denomination." The itineraries of most of the missionaries sent out by the early societies were established to visit "the scattered brethren" who had moved to new locations with a primary mission to strengthen and encourage them. However, the possibility of taking the gospel to others, where the door might be opened, was always an option.[24]

2. Go to Other Christians. On the frontier, doors frequently opened onto the second growth area: convincing other Christians of the validity of the Sabbath. Amos R. Wells reported that during his missionary tour of 1821–1822, he preached in schoolhouses, in courthouses, in numerous

---

[22] Whitford, "Historical Sketch," 1:336.
[23] Constitution of the Board of Trustees and Directors of Missions...," Conference Minutes, *SDB Yearbook* (1819) 9.
[24] Constitution of American SDB Missionary Society, Article 2, *SDB Yearbook* (1828) 13.

churches—eight Baptist, five Methodist, four Presbyterian, one Episcopal, and two Lutheran churches—as well as in several unidentified meetinghouses. Normally he gave a gospel message that the listeners eagerly sought, "like cool water to a thirsty soul." He did not hesitate to identify his denomination and answer questions concerning the Sabbath. A few chose to become Seventh Day Baptists as a result of the doors Wells opened and through his winsome sharing of his Sabbath convictions, as gleaned from the Scripture.[25]

Alexander Campbell recalled his own experience in choosing to become a Seventh Day Baptist through one of these "open doors." In 1821, he heard that a Jew was preaching 4 miles from his home. He had never seen a Jew and was anxious to meet one of that people about whom he had read so much in the Bible. He soon discovered that this man, Russell Wells, was not a Jew but a Seventh Day Baptist missionary from Rhode Island who preached the Gospel "not merely in word, but with melting power." He recalled that, though Wells had said nothing about the Sabbath, he was impressed that such a "spiritually minded, honest and able minister of the Gospel must, at least in his own judgment, have some good Scriptural reasons for keeping the Seventh-day Sabbath."[26] As a result of this encounter, Seventh Day Baptists gained a most powerful evangelist and leader who was particularly active in both the printing and educational work of the denomination during the next sixty years, as Campbell himself became a prominent Seventh Day Baptist.

The 1843 open letter from the General Conference to members of the Baptist denomination, mentioned in the preceding chapter, was a deliberate attempt to recruit denominational growth from among those who were already Christian. The Sabbath Reform movement of the latter part of the century also targeted this second area for growth.

3. *Take the Gospel to Sabbathkeeping Jews.* In 1834, members of the Missionary Society chose to expand their mission into the third growth area, conversion. In New York City alone there were thousands of Jews who were observing the biblical Sabbath. Converted to Christianity, they could find a ready home among Seventh Day Baptists, since there already existed a common bond in shared Sabbath observance. There

---

[25] "Elder Amos R. Well's Journal of a Missionary Tour," *SDB Missionary Magazine* 1/6 (Nov 1822): 180-84.
[26] Alexander Campbell, *Autobiography of Rev. Alexander Campbell,* ed. Charles Alexander Burdick (Watertown NY: Post Printing House, 1883) 8-9.

was also the reasonable hope that a Christian denomination preaching about Christ in a way that maintained the law and the prophets might receive a favorable hearing.[27]

Since some feared that the interest in this new area would detract from the primary purpose of the missionary societies, a separate society was established in 1838 and named "The American Seventh-day Baptist Society for the Promotion of Christianity among the Jews." Their work was short lived, for they experienced difficulties in six areas: (1) the great proportion of foreigners among the Jews was not sufficiently fluent in English to understand the preaching; (2) there was a general lack of spirituality among those who had little regard for their own worship on the Sabbath; (3) the Jews' inherent bias favored their own religion; (4) those who understood Hebrew rejected the English translations of the Scriptures; (5) the doctrine of the divinity of Jesus appeared as blasphemy involving strange gods; and (6) there was strong prejudice against the Christian religion induced by the Jews' great suffering under Christian powers.[28]

In 1840, the emphasis of missions work among Seventh Day Baptists shifted from employing missionaries to publishing tracts and other works, and the society reenvisioned itself as the "American Evangelical Board of Directors for Disseminating Religious Truth among Jews."[29] This new organization met with the same difficulties others experienced, so by 1843 its work—but not its interest in missions to Jews—ceased.

About a decade later, interest was rekindled in a different direction. During the 1840s, denominational missionary interest was centered on foreign missions, leading to the establishment of work in China. At a meeting of the Missionary Society in 1852, it was proposed that a mission to Palestine might not face the same problems encountered with the American Jewish immigrants. The following year, the Missionary Society resolved to establish such a mission, with Rev. William Jones serving as the missionary.[30] It was decided to link this mission in Palestine with an industrial or agricultural development mission. Mr. and Mr. Charles Saunders were chosen to head this part of the mission. In 1854, Rev. and Mrs. Jones and Mr. and Mrs. Saunders settled temporally in Jaffa while

---

[27] William C. Daland, "Our Work for Jews," in *Jubilee Papers* (Westerly RI: Board of Managers of the SDB Missionary Society, 1892) 85.

[28] William B. Maxson, quoted in ibid., 87.

[29] Daland, "Our Work for Jews," in *Jubilee Papers*, 88.

[30] Missionary Society Minutes, *SDB Yearbook* (1853) 16-17.

they looked for a favorable spot to hold the agricultural mission. The agricultural element encountered insurmountable odds because of the limited budget and the political, social, and cultural barriers that existed. William Jones had limited success in Jerusalem until ill health and other circumstances prevented the establishment of a permanent mission there. In 1859, lack of support forced the mission effort to close, and the missionaries were called home.[31]

About twenty-five years later, Seventh Day Baptists again became involved in a mission to Jews. Theophilus Lucky, a Christian Jew, met some Seventh Day Baptists while in seminary and joined the New York City church. Though working independently, he received some support from Seventh Day Baptists in his publishing efforts. For a short time, William C. Daland edited a monthly paper titled *The Peculiar People*, which Lucky had begun.[32] By 1890, nearly all missionary efforts directed toward the Jews had been discontinued.

4. Breaking New Ground in Missions. A pivotal year for missionary interests was 1842, when the question was raised whether the General Conference, as presently organized, was "a suitable vehicle for the diffusion of the benevolence of the denomination," or whether an entirely new organization was necessary.[33] It was reported that the Missionary Societies were "so crippled in their operations, that their influence is scarcely felt, and their existence hardly known beyond the precincts of our own denomination." There was hesitation to form any new organization because "many of our aged brethren whom we regard with fond affection, are not prepared for any great change in its features, and we would not without sternest necessity recommend any course that would be to their grief."[34]

Reorganization for Expanded Missions—Rather than creating a new society, it was proposed by a special committee to promote missions on an associational *principle*, with each church in the denomination considering itself a missionary society. Each association would then establish a central missionary society, and a general society would include the central societies as auxiliaries that would meet annually to take charge of the funds contributed. An executive board of the general society was given authority to appoint missionaries, select the field of

---

[31] O. U. Whitford, "Jewish Mission," *Seventh Day Baptists in Europe and America*, 1:348-49.

[32] Daland, "Our Work for Jews," in *Jubilee Papers*, 90.

[33] Conference Minutes, *SDB Yearbook* (1842) 17.

[34] Conference Minutes, Appendix 1, *SDB Yearbook* (1842) 21.

labor, disburse the funds, and perform other work of the organization. Although this plan was primarily intended for home missions, it was proposed that the same organizational plan could apply, if needed, to a foreign mission society.[35]

Thus, in 1843 there were three missionary societies: (1) the American Seventh-day Baptist Missionary Society, (2) the Hebrew Missionary Society (or Board of Directors for Disseminating Religious Truth among the Jews, a name that later changed to the Seventh-day Baptist Jewish Missionary Society), and (3) the newly constituted Seventh-day Baptist Missionary Association. In 1846, the first of these societies merged with the latter new association; the Hebrew mission societies ceased their operations, and their interests were later taken up by the merged society.

Seventh Day Baptist Missionary Association/Society—The General Conference recommendation called for a Missionary Association, but the constitution when adopted retained the societal principle of individual membership on payment of dues. In 1849, a resolution was passed stating that "hereafter the term 'Society' instead of 'Association' be used in the name of this body."[36] It is this Missionary Society that has continued to the present day in Seventh Day Baptist missions at home and abroad.

The initial work of the Missionary Society continued to be among the "destitute and scattered brethren" on the home field. Several ministers were employed to make visits to various locales ranging from a few weeks to close to a year in length. It was to this society that James Leander Scott reported through his book, *A Journal of a Missionary Tour*, printed in 1843.[37] The book details Scott's travels as a missionary on behalf of Seventh Day Baptists and this new Missionary Society. His is among the earlier accounts of Seventh Day Baptist work on the American frontier.

In 1844, the Missionary Society's constitution was amended to add the words "and other parts of the world" to the statement of its objective in the dissemination of the gospel. This was the beginning of a conscious

---

[35] Ibid.

[36] Missionary Society Minutes, *SDB Yearbook* (1849) 2.

[37] James Leander Scott, *A Journal of a Missionary Tour*, March of America Facsimile series 80 (Ann Arbor MI: UMI, 1966), repr. from 1843 edition. University Microfilms republished this work in 1966 to represent that important phase of frontier America. Cathy Luchetti excerpted large portions in *Under God's Spell: Frontier Evangelists, 1772–1915*, published by Harcourt Brace Jovenovich in 1989.

choice to take the gospel to the pagan world outside the Judeo-Christian culture.

Rejecting the Choice of Africa—The Missionary Association in 1844 expressed concern over the report by Samuel Davison that there were millions of Sabbathkeepers in a number of different nations of Eastern Africa "sunk in ignorance and superstition, without suitable means of instruction and improvement." It was recommended that the Missionary Board investigate opportunities for establishing a mission among these communities.[38]

The Missionary Board took steps the following year to raise money and procure one or more individuals who were willing and qualified to engage in such work.[39] In 1846, Rev. Solomon Carpenter and his wife Lucy agreed to serve and were instructed by the board to prepare for the work by obtaining a knowledge of medicine and surgery as well as other studies related to foreign missions.[40] Reasons the board gave for selecting Abyssinia in Eastern Africa as the site for their initial foreign missionary operations included the tremendous numbers of heathen in the area, the fact that the area was "entirely unoccupied by any other missionary body," and the understanding that many there had been keeping the seventh day of the week since the days of Solomon.[41]

The following year, the Executive Board reported the necessity of having a second missionary couple accompany the Carpenters. Nathan Wardner, a seminary student at Alfred University, indicated his willingness to serve on the foreign missions field, so a call was issued to him and his wife even though he had not completed his studies. Both couples were willing to go wherever sent, although in their preparation questions were raised concerning East Africa as the best field.

Upon further investigation, the board decided to change the location of the mission from Abyssinia to China, acknowledging that, in the selection of Abyssinia, "zeal went beyond prudence." The area chosen in Abyssinia was not easily accessible; some of the tribal lands through which they would have to travel were hostile to foreigners; the government would not welcome them; and the climate was unsuited to the "frail and delicate constitutions" of the accepted missionaries.

---

[38] Missionary Association Minutes, *SDB Yearbook* (1844) 14
[39] Special Meeting of Directors, Missionary Association Minutes, *SDB Yearbook* (1845) 10.
[40] Missionary Association Minutes, *SDB Yearbook* (1846) 4.
[41] Missionary Association Minutes, *SDB Yearbook* (1846) 5-6.

Equally important was the board's recognition that some previous "benevolent operations had been mismanaged," so that it was necessary to invest their efforts in an area where activities and successes could be more easily and quickly reported. They reported that "A successful experiment, first made in some accessible region, would reanimate the drooping faith of the denomination, so that we should be better prepared for a more difficult work."[42]

China Mission—China offered many opportunities. It had a vast population, fulfilling the demand that their first duty was "to proclaim the gospel where it can be made to bear upon the greatest number of minds at once." The Chinese were also recognized as being "a shrewd and intelligent race and likely to exercise a greater influence upon the world than other heathen nations." Added to this was the ease of communication, which would give early information of the arrival and work of the missionaries and enable them "to attend to their wants more promptly."[43]

On 5 January 1847, Solomon and Lucy Carpenter, along with Nathan and Olive Wardner, set sail for China. They initially stopped in Hong Kong while Mr. Carpenter went on to Shanghai to find a desirable location to begin their mission work. In 1849, they reported the first converts, and by July 1850 the Shanghai Seventh Day Baptist Church was organized. From the beginning, education was a vital part of their mission; Mrs. Wardner opened a day school for Chinese children.

The Tai-Ping rebellion in 1850 and a local insurrection in Shanghai in 1853 forced the missionaries to seek safety, as their home had been partially destroyed. With some help from the government, repairs were made and in 1855 their work resumed. The next year, sickness made it necessary for Mrs. Wardner to return to America with her boys. The following year, Mr. Wardner was granted leave to return.

Poor health also took its toll on the Carpenters, forcing them to return to America in 1858, thus leaving the little church of eleven members without pastoral leadership. Yet, when the Carpenters returned in 1860, they found the members of their little flock "steadfast in the faith," in spite of unrest caused by revolutionists.[44] It is to the

---

[42] Report of the Executive Board, Missionary Association Minutes, *SDB Yearbook* (1847) 6-7.

[43] Report of the Executive Board, Missionary Association Minutes, *SDB Yearbook* (1847) 9.

[44] Solomon Carpenter, letter to the Missionary Society Executive Board, 16 Jul 1860, Missionary Society Minutes, *SDB Yearbook* (1861) 16.

credit of the work of those early missionaries that the China mission was able to overcome many difficulties with only minimal assistance from America. The American Civil War, during the period of the Carpenters' second tour of duty, further burdened the Missionary Board's resources. The Carpenters met their needs through Mr. Carpenter's employment as an interpreter at the United States Consulate in Shanghai.[45] In 1864, the family returned to America again for reasons of health.[46]

In 1873, the board reported that "the denomination had almost lost its interest in this far-off field, its faith in foreign missionary work, and its consciousness of obligation to engage in the work of preaching the gospel to every creature." A common plea expressed, and repeated many times since, was "charity begins at home." The board answered, "Experience shows that if we could revive and successfully prosecute our foreign missionary work, we should do, not less, but more in labors at home besides, duties are ours—the results, we are willing to leave with God."[47]

In spite of the fact that the mission was able to continue with little help from abroad, the board considered action to liquidate some of its property. It did this in part to test the denomination's concern for the mission's future. The maneuver had its desired effect. Interest in foreign missions picked up, some churches resumed their missionary prayer meetings, and the Carpenters agreed to return to China one more time.[48] It was to be their last trip, for the lingering effects of cholera took its toll on Mrs. Carpenter; she died the next year on 21 September 1874. When Mr. Carpenter's own health deteriorated, his doctor advised a change of climate. In summer 1876 he returned to America, thus ending the first phase of the China mission.[49]

In 1880, the board sent a new missionary team to China. Rev. David H. Davis, pastor of the Shiloh, New Jersey, church, along with his wife and Miss Eliza Nelson, formerly a teacher from Alfred, New York, accepted the call to go as missionaries.[50] Two years later Lizzie Nelson married John Fryer, a professor at the Kiangnam Arsenal in Shanghai, and gave up direct work in the mission. The following year, 1883, Dr.

---

[45] Carpenter, letter to the Executive Board (1862), Missionary Society Minutes, *SDB Yearbook* (1863) 24.
[46] Missionary Society Minutes, *SDB Yearbook* (1864) 19.
[47] Missionary Society Minutes, *SDB Yearbook* (1873) 15-16.
[48] Missionary Society Minutes, *SDB Yearbook* (1873) 16.
[49] Missionary Society Minutes, *SDB Yearbook* (1876) 12.
[50] "China," Missionary Society Minutes, *SDB Yearbook* (1880) 16.

Ellen F. Swinney arrived in Shanghai to fulfill a different role, beginning the medical mission work that would become an integral part of the China mission continuing through the first half of the twentieth century.[51]

Rev. and Mrs. G. H. F. Randolph and Miss Susie Burdick began work as missionaries in 1889, assisting particularly in educational work.[52] In 1894, Dr. Rosa Palmborg joined the mission. She arrived just prior to the serious illness of Ella Swinney, which necessitated Dr. Swinney's return to the United States for a period of recovery.[53] During the century's closing year, Rev. and Mrs. Jay W. Crofoot agreed to head the growing work of the schools they established in Shanghai.[54]

The work of foreign missions during the nineteenth century was slow and often hampered by lack of personnel and financial support. It was often difficult to motivate the missionary spirit of a people whose major concern was still for the "scattered and destitute" Seventh Day Baptists in the American frontier. Yet, by the end of the nineteenth century, the China mission had expanded to include not only a church and housing for missionaries, but also boarding schools for both boys and girls in Shanghai; the mission had also acquired land in Lieu-ho that it would later use to build a hospital.

During the first half of the twentieth century, while membership was declining in the United States, the church in China was growing. A number of other leaders responded to the call to take the gospel to the Chinese people. Among these leaders were Rev. and Mrs. H. Eugene Davis (1902–1943), Dr. Grace Crandall (1911-1947), Anna West (1920–1942), Mabel West (1920–1949), Nettie West (1920–1949), Dr. and Mrs. George Thorngate (1924–1950), Miriam Shaw (1930–1939), and Sarah Becker (1947–1948).[55]

In spite of the disruption caused by the Japanese invasion, the church at Shanghai reported its 1949 membership to be 670, making it the largest Seventh Day Baptist church in the world at that time. The political changes in post-World War II China, with the Communist

---

[51] "A Medical Mission," Missionary Society Minutes, *SDB Yearbook* (1883) 14.
[52] "School Work," Missionary Society Minutes, *SDB Yearbook* (1889) 17-18.
[53] "The China Mission," Missionary Society Minutes, *SDB Yearbook* (1896) 1-2.
[54] "Reinforcements," Missionary Society Minutes, *SDB Yearbook* (1899) 5.
[55] Thomas L. Merchant, "Our China Missions—A Legacy of Service," *Sabbath Recorder* 201/4 (4 Apr 1979): 16-17. See the series on China missions, *Sabbath Recorder*, vols. 201–202 (Apr 1979–Apr 1980).

takeover and the Cultural Revolution, effectively closed the Missionary Society's direct involvement in China.

The Seventh Day Baptist Church's first major effort to reach beyond the Judeo-Christian culture taught several valuable lessons. First, it demonstrated the importance of ministering to people's physical and educational needs along with their spiritual needs. Second, it showed the value of developing native leaders who could continue the mission's work without assistance from abroad. Finally, it expanded the vision of many who realized that the Great Commission of Christ was to actually go to all the world and make disciples. They saw meaningful mission work beyond the American frontier, many for the first time, and it opened their eyes to the wider world.

14

THE PUBLISHING INTERESTS
OF SEVENTH DAY BAPTISTS

The missionary spirit that gave rise to the various missionary societies also gave rise to the desire for better means of communication. In the publishing field, Seventh Day Baptists chose four mediums: (1) periodicals, (2) tracts and pamphlets, (3) lesson materials, and (4) books. Associational and societal organizations were both used to generate these publications. In addition, much printing was done independently by individuals.

PERIODICALS

In 1819, several individuals living in the Schenectady, New York, area attempted to establish a stock company to publish a denominational periodical and other publications. The project failed for lack of financial backing, but the interest continued and found expression in other ways.[1] With the exception of four years during the effort's first decade, the Seventh Day Baptists have continuously published periodicals since 1821.

The Seventh Day Baptist Missionary Magazine

The first Seventh Day Baptist periodical was a quarterly titled *The Seventh Day Baptist Missionary Magazine*. It was published by the Board of Trustees and the Directors of Missions from 1821 to 1825, with Henry Clarke, Eli S. Bailey, and William B. Maxson as editors. Its stated purposes were:

> (1) to acquaint the public with the sentiments and religious observances which distinguish this people from other Christian denominations;
> (2) to circulate religious and missionary information among the societies of our denomination;
> (3) to cultivate harmony among all evangelical Christians; and

---

[1] Arthur L. Titsworth, "The American Sabbath Tract Society: Including All Seventh-day Baptist Publications and Sabbath Reform Work," *Seventh Day Baptists in Europe and America*, 3 vols., ed. C. F. Randolph (Plainfield NJ: SDB General Conference, 1910) 1:421-22.

(4) to unite with others in the laudable work of holding up the doctrine of the cross.[2]

The magazine included articles covering each of the stated purposes, including such topics as the Sabbath and baptism, the history of the denomination, reports of the Missionary Board, and missionary journals. Denominational news included accounts of newly organized churches, ordinations, revivals, and obituaries. News from other Baptist missions included correspondence from Adoniram Judson in Burma. The range of general articles ran from poetry to the support of ministers and the education of children, and from Bible study and prayer to theological issues, especially salvation. The final issue, published in September 1825, listed the reasons for discontinuing the magazine, including the rising cost of postage and the delinquency of subscribers in settling their accounts.[3]

The Protestant Sentinel

At the 1829 session of the General Conference, John Maxson presented a proposition for "publishing a weekly paper devoted to subjects of general interest, and particularly the discussion of the distinguishing tenets of this denomination."[4] The first issue of the *Protestant Sentinel* appeared on 14 April 1830, with John Maxson as editor. Except for greater emphasis on distinctive doctrines, its purposes were similar to those of the *Missionary Magazine*.[5] Like its predecessor, the *Sentinel* received only moral backing from the General Conference. In 1830, the conference approved the editor's labors and urged "all friends of the sabbath to use all reasonable exertions to extend the patronage of that paper."[6]

During its nine years of existence, the *Protestant Sentinel* faced a number of problems that ultimately led to its discontinuance and thus provided an example of problems faced by other publishing enterprises. (1) It never had adequate support from any sponsoring body. The General Conference wanted a publication but was not in a position to

---

[2] "Editors Address to the Patrons and Friends of This Magazine," foreword, *SDB Missionary Magazine* 1/1 (Aug 1821): 3.

[3] "To the Patrons of This Work," editorial, *SDB Missionary Magazine* 2/7 (Sep 1825): 189.

[4] Conference Minutes, *SDB Yearbook* (1829) 10.

[5] John Maxson, "The Protestant Sentinel," editorial, *Protestant Sentinel* 1/1 (14 Apr 1830): 1.

[6] Conference Minutes, *SDB Yearbook* (1830) 7.

offer more than moral encouragement. (2) The responsibility largely fell on one man, so that any discontent and opposition was focused on that person. (3) Its location was a handicap, for any news covered by the paper appeared several weeks after people in the East or South had already heard it. (4) The name did not adequately capture the periodical's content. (In 1838, the words *and Seventh Day Baptist Journal* were added to the name.) (5) Finally, a large enough financial base was simply not available.[7] The sale of advertisements brought in some money, but with a circulation of less than 800, the advertising market was too small to attract lucrative ads.

The last edition of the *Protestant Sentinel*, dated 21 May 1839, contained a brief history of Seventh Day Baptist publishing to that date, as reviewed by John Maxson. He summarized the intent of the *Sentinel* as being grounded "in the Temperance Reform," the Sabbath, the purpose of Sabbath Schools and Bible classes, missions, a more effective system of ministerial support, "the cause of the Aborigines of our own country, and exposed the awful sin of slavery."[8]

The Seventh Day Baptist Register

In September 1839, within four months of the last issue of the *Protestant Sentinel*, the General Conference recommended that the brethren at DeRuyter publish a prospectus for a paper, "provided that a permanent publication of the same can be secured to the denomination—if not, that the same be recommended to the Brethren in New Jersey and New York, provided that the pecuniary responsibility rest upon those publishing the same."[9]

On 10 March 1840, the first edition of the *Seventh Day Baptist Register* appeared with Joel Greene and Alexander Campbell as editors. Its stated objective was "to promote the interests of religion, by discussing and defending its doctrines and enforcing its duties." The editors intended to "conform implicitly to the sentiments and spirit of the Bible" but devote a portion of their columns to literary and scientific subjects to promote "a correct taste, and a love for solid information." Approved narratives, moral essays, and historical sketches were to be included for the young mind "in such a manner as to draw it away from such journals as contain

---

[7] John Maxson, section on Removals in "Brief History of the Seventh Day Baptist Press," editorial, *Protestant Sentinel* 8/52 (21 May 1839): 1.
[8] Maxson, "Brief History," 1.
[9] Conference Minutes, *SDB Yearbook* (1839) 13.

light reading only." Recognizing that many readers subscribed to no other periodical, a synopsis of Congressional and legislative proceedings would be included without favoring or opposing any political party.[10]

At the end of the first year, Rev. James Bailey became editor and proprietor and continued the publication for three more years. The *Register* was able to meet its expenses but the profit margin provided the editor little compensation. The final issue, dated 13 March 1844, carried a "valedictory" in which the editor stated that one reason for discontinuing the publication was the physical demand it placed on him: "The sole care of publishing and editing has been ours. The Editor's task must be performed, whether sick or well, in company or alone, under every possible circumstance and condition, and the number of those who know how to excuse his lack is exceedingly small."[11]

A second reason for discontinuing the periodical revealed the effects and influence of the developing national consciousness of urban centers. Bailey cited three effects location had on the publication of any denominational periodical:

(1) The majority of the readers depended on the *Register* for news of the day. From DeRuyter he could not get the news to the people in less than one to two weeks after those who took a city paper received it.

(2) New York City was the center of religious intelligence and action. Almost all denominations had their publications there. The city also gave the editor a chance for more stimulation as he came in contact with men of influence and action. Separated from this stimulation in his rural setting, the articles tended to become monotonous and lack interest.

(3) There had always been an anxiety on the part of some for the denominational press to be located in New York City, and this anxiety would remain until the change was made. For the sake of unity, Bailey recommended a change of location and gave his blessing to a new effort.[12]

The Sabbath Recorder

The change of location to New York City gave rise to the birth of the *Sabbath Recorder*, which for more than a century and a half has been recognized as the communicative voice of the Seventh Day Baptist

---

[10] "Our Plan," editorial, *SDB Register* 1/1 (10 Mar 1840): 2.

[11] James Bailey, "Valedictory," editorial, *SDB Register* 5/2 (13 Mar 1844): 2.

[12] Bailey, "Valedictory," 2.

denomination. For most of those years, the publication's existence has been only indirectly tied to the General Conference, which could only offer moral support and encouragement. With the implementation of a unified budget early in the twentieth century, the conference assumed part of the financial burden. Still, the ownership and management of the *Sabbath Recorder* for most of its existence rested with private individuals or with an independent society.

In 1844, eleven Seventh Day Baptists in the New York City area assumed responsibility for publishing a denominational paper. George B. Utter was editor and financial agent of the first issue of the *Sabbath Recorder* dated 14 June 1844. After the first year, the paper's revenues were sufficient to pay expenses, but there were some who felt that in order for it to be a truly denominational paper, the ownership and management ought to involve a broader denominational representation. In 1848, the Eastern Association proposed a permanent publishing organization to meet the growing needs of the denomination. They called for a convention of delegates from the other associations to meet with their delegates "to mature a plan for a Seventh-day Baptist Publishing Establishment."[13]

By May 1849, the Seventh Day Baptist Publishing Society organized, and the responsibility for the Sabbath Recorder transferred to that body. Membership in the society was granted to anyone contributing $5, whereas any contribution of $25 would make one an Honorary Director with the privilege of participating in the deliberations of the Publishing Society board. George B. Utter continued as editor until he retired in 1857. Then, for a time, the *Recorder* operated through a committee appointed by the board.

Financial difficulties, caused by subscriber delinquency and the wartime economy, led to the Publishing Society's decision in 1862 to return the paper with its assets and liabilities to George Utter and his publishing house in Westerly, Rhode Island. Utter continued as editor, publisher, and proprietor until June 1872, which amounted to twenty-five years of service as editor. The Publishing Society continued to exist until 1866, but during its last three years, the only action it reported was the election of officers.

When the American Sabbath Tract Society established a new publishing house at Alfred, New York, in 1872, the *Sabbath Recorder* came under its auspices. In 1895, the publishing house relocated to Plainfield,

---

[13] Eastern Association Minutes (May 1848) 12.

New Jersey, to place it nearer the location of the Tract Society in New York City. For over eighty years, the *Sabbath Recorder* was published in Plainfield by the Tract Society. In 1982, when the denominational offices were moved to the Seventh Day Baptist Center in Janesville, Wisconsin, the production offices were moved to Southern Wisconsin. The editing and management remained with the Tract Society until that body merged with the General Conference in 1986.

Although the *Sabbath Recorder* faced many problems in a highly competitive publishing field with ever-changing technology, one can hardly overemphasize its importance to the expanding mission of Seventh Day Baptists both at home and abroad. For many families in the nineteenth century, the weekly *Recorder* was their primary source for national and international news. Hundreds of articles were devoted to such issues as the emancipation of slaves, temperance, and both home and foreign missions. The century-long China Mission depended on reports in the *Recorder* for its success. Increasingly the publication became the international voice of Seventh Day Baptists. A testament to its influence was, for example, the fact that James Begg of Scotland, whom the publication listed as a British correspondent for more than 20 years, contributed over 100 articles on the Sabbath in the British Isles and other parts of Europe.

Sabbath Reform Periodicals

During the last two decades of the nineteenth century, the reform movement spawned several periodicals devoted to reformation in two major areas: the Sabbath and temperance. The most important reform periodical was the *Outlook,* which began publication in April 1882. It took the name *Outlook and Sabbath Quarterly* in 1884 as its content became more directly related to the Sabbath debate. It was aimed particularly at reaching the clergy and other leaders who reflected the theological thought of the day. Men such as A. H. Lewis believed that once these leaders were convinced of the Sabbath, the concept would be widely accepted. At the Tract Society annual meeting in 1885, W. C. Daland, who later would become president of Milton College, referred to the *Outlook* as having called his attention to the Sabbath question.[14] At the time, he was a Baptist student at Union Theological Seminary. Fifty-five thousand copies of the *Outlook* were regularly sent to clergy in the United States and Canada, and one special 1889 issue, which contained

---

[14] American Sabbath Tract Society, Conference Minutes, *SDB Yearbook* (1885) 73.

information concerning the Blair Sunday Rest Bill proposed by Congress, was sent to 65,000 lawyers in addition to the clergy.[15]

During this same period, beginning in August 1885, a companion paper, the *Light of Home*, was published for circulation among the laity. The first year, 115,000 copies per month were sent out. In 1886, only 5,000 were issued, about half to Seventh Day Baptist homes. The following year, members of the Women's Christian Temperance Union provided the names of more than 40,000 Christian women to whom the magazine was sent, bringing the circulation to about 50,000. The final issue was published in November 1889, when Lewis's changing responsibilities led to it's demise.

In 1893, a new weekly publication called the *Evangel and Sabbath Outlook* combined features of the former *Outlook* and the *Light of Home*. In the first issue, A. H. Lewis commented that the work of research should give place to the "practical relations of Sabbath Reform to individual Christian life, to Christianity in general, and the cause of Protestantism in particular."[16] When Lewis became corresponding secretary of the American Sabbath Tract Society, he found that the duties of that office, with expanded work in other areas of Sabbath promotion, made it impossible to continue the publication of the *Evangel*. Publication ceased with the 17 June 1897 issue, and much of the material was later incorporated into the *Sabbath Recorder*.

Historical Periodicals

Two periodicals published in the last half of the nineteenth century have been of particular value to the student of history. The *Seventh Day Baptist Memorial* and the *Seventh Day Baptist Quarterly* gathered and reported on the distant and recent history of Seventh Day Baptists and are still valuable resources today.

The Seventh Day Baptist Memorial—At the 1852 triennial session of the General Conference, the Business Committee reported that they found themselves "embarrassed for the want of a clear knowledge of the powers, objects, and purposes of this organization." They recommended that a committee collect all of the conference documents and submit them to the Publishing Society "that through this channel we may secure a reliable history of the rise, progress, and objects of the Conference."[17]

---

[15] "What Are We Doing?" *Sabbath Recorder* 45/10 (7 Mar 1889): 152.
[16] "The Evangel and Sabbath Outlook," *Evangel and Sabbath Outlook* 1/1 (1 Jun 1893): 1.
[17] Report of the Business Committee, Conference Minutes, *SDB Yearbook* (1852) 7-8.

Lucius Crandall, Walter B. Gillette, and Thomas B. Stillman undertook the task of collecting and editing material that resulted in the publication of a quarterly titled the *Seventh Day Baptist Memorial.*

The historical quarterly existed for only three years (1852–1854), but the biographical sketches of the denomination's early leaders and the histories of its early churches provided a valuable historical resource for later generations. The editors made a plea for members to preserve records and old papers. "We are grieved, to understand that a few years since, in one of the churches, many old papers were destroyed because they were very old, and not likely to be used again. Is it any wonder that our archives are so bare of matter relating to the past?"[18] This concern stimulated interest that led to the formation of the Historical Committee as a standing body of the General Conference.

The Seventh Day Baptist Quarterly—Thirty years later, the Tract Society made another effort to preserve biographical and historical material. In 1884, the *Seventh Day Baptist Quarterly* was published under the editorship of W. C. Whitford, the president of Milton College. It was discontinued after the first year because of a lack of financial support.[19] President Whitford continued collecting material in the hopes of publishing a popular history of the denomination. His death in 1902 prevented that project's fulfillment.

Foreign Language Publications

The American Sabbath Tract Society became involved, either directly or indirectly, in the publication of several Sabbath periodicals for foreign use. Among these were the following: (1) *De Boodschapper (The Messenger in the Service of the Lord Jesus)* was published in Holland from 1876 to 1906 by Bro. Velthuysen. When he became a Sabbathkeeper in 1877, he lost most of his subscribers, so Seventh Day Baptists in America assisted in the periodical's publication.[20]

(2) The *Evangelii Harold (Gospel Messenger)* was a monthly paper printed in Swedish for use among Swedish immigrants in America. It was published by the American Sabbath Tract Society and printed in Chicago at a Swedish printing office during the 1880s and 1890s.[21]

---

[18] L. Crandall, T. B. Stillman and W. B. Gillett, "History of the Seventh-day Baptist General Conference," *SDB Memorial* 3/4 (Oct 1854): 192.

[19] "Catalogue," *Seventh Day Baptists in Europe and America,* 2:1337.

[20] Ibid., 2:1338.

[21] Ibid., 2:1337.

(3) *Eduth le Israel (Witness to Israel)* was published by the Tract Society in Hebrew for about two years from 1888 to 1890.[22] This was in addition to *The Peculiar People*, which was published in England from 1888 to 1898 for Sabbathkeeping Christian Jews.

TRACTS AND PAMPHLETS

The early Seventh Day Baptists in England used printing as a major component of their witness, but in America this medium was little used until about the third decade of the nineteenth century. Unlike their earlier English brethren, Americans were much freer to preach whatever or wherever they desired. They relied more heavily on the migrations of Seventh Day Baptists and traveling missionaries to spread their doctrines. Furthermore, the early mission effort in America was largely directed toward strengthening the scattered members of the fellowship, which could best be accomplished with personal contacts through visiting ministers and periodicals. The wholesale distribution of tracts was rarely used in early evangelism.

In 1825, several Protestant denominations joined together in New York City to organize the American Tract Society. It recognized tracts as the most effective means of evangelism next to the Bible and the living ministry. The short, plain, striking, and entertaining tracts could be read at leisure and thus were particularly adapted to the poor. The laity as well as the clergy could distribute them and travelers could leave them in inns, trains, or on shipboard. A tract of ten pages could be produced at a cost of a single cent.[23]

The colporteur system, which relied on traveling peddlers to distribute Bibles and religious literature, was endorsed by the Tract Society. Sometimes these tracts were sold and sometimes they were given away. This system, which had been used in the mission fields, was adaptable to the frontier. [24] Seventh Day Baptists, as they expanded into this frontier, saw the distribution of tracts as a means of spreading their

---

[22] Ibid., 2:1338.

[23] "Address of the Executive Committee," in *The American Tract Society Documents, 1824–1925* (New York: Arno Press, 1972) 3, 4-6, quoted in Edwin S. Gaustad, ed., "American Tract Society (1825) and Colporteur System," *A Documentary of History of Religion in America to the Civil War*, A Documentary of History of Religion in America, 2 vols. (Grand Rapids MI: William B. Eerdmans Publishing Company, 1982) 1:332-33.

[24] "American Colporteur System," in *The American Tract Society Documents, 1824–1925*, quoted in Gaustad, ed., "American Tract Society (1825) and Colporteur System," A Documentary of History of Religion, 1:334.

religious convictions throughout the American frontier, as well as among their own churches and neighbors.

Seventh Day Baptist General Tract Society

The General Conference made efforts in tract publication and distribution after it adjourned its 1831 session. While the members were still present, a resolution was approved and printed with the minutes of that session recommending that individual churches tract societies and encourage the publishing and circulation of tracts. This "unofficial action" recommended that these societies become auxiliary to a General Tract Executive Committee, which the conference would appoint annually.[25]

As a result, the Seventh Day Baptist General Tract Society, which also went by the name American Seventh Day Baptist Tract Society, was organized to publish tracts and other written materials. The first few reports were discouraging due to a "want of original Tracts: but one only having been presented, which was deemed proper to publish."[26] In 1838, it was recognized that if original tracts were not presented it would be cheaper to purchase tracts from the American Tract Society.[27]

New York City Sabbath Tract Society

To fill the void caused by the General Tract Society's ineffectiveness, a local society organized in 1842 as the New York City Sabbath Tract Society. Although it lasted only about three years, the society's publication of the *Sabbath Vindicator* provided a platform to discuss the Sabbath[28] and helped to sharpen the interest of the editor, George B. Utter, in work he was to pursue for the rest of his life. The society's collection of Sabbath publications, which it obtained by sending Utter to England, included such early writers as Theophilus Brabourne, Francis Bampfield, and the Stennetts. Some of these early books from England were republished for distribution in America. The collection eventually became the nucleus for the Historical Society's library.

---

[25] Appended to Conference Minutes, *SDB Yearbook* (1831) 6-7.

[26] American Seventh-day Baptist Tract Society Minutes, Conference Minutes, *SDB Yearbook* (1837) 21-22.

[27] Tract Society Minutes, Conference Minutes, *SDB Yearbook* (1838) 28-29.

[28] Arthur L. Titsworth, "The American Sabbath Tract Society," *SDBs in Europe and America*, 1:431.

General Conference Acts in Tract Promotion

In 1841, the General Conference explored cooperation with the American Tract Society on the same terms as other denominations.[29] The agent of that society presented a plan for future operations and called for contributions to assist in carrying it out. The plan included the publication and circulation of tracts bearing exclusively on the subject of the Sabbath. While the proposal held some possibilities, the question was raised as to whether Seventh Day Baptists should rely on others to do what was essentially their own responsibility.[30]

In 1842, the General Conference organized the Missionary Society for the purpose of carrying out "the various benevolent enterprises of the denomination with the greatest possible efficiency"[31]; this action led to the organization of a membership society for tracts along similar lines. Initially the society was called the General Sabbath Tract Society,[32] but in 1844 the organization was referred to as the American Sabbath Tract Society.[33]

The American Sabbath Tract Society

The decade of the 1840s was a time of considerable change in America that affected the tract ministry. The concept of "manifest destiny," connected with the Texas rebellion in 1835 and the Mexican War, brought many people to believe in America's inevitable expansion from shore to shore. People began to see new opportunities for the spread of the gospel. Presbyterians Marcus and Narcissa Whitman had paved the way to extend missions to the coast in 1837. The first Seventh Day Baptist Church in the Wisconsin Territory was established in Milton in 1840, and from this center other churches sprang up in the West.

This decade was also a time for new ideas and diverse religious doctrines to come to the surface. The controversy over Joseph Smith and the Mormons reached its peak in 1844 with Smith's martyrdom. The following year, Brigham Young led the trek to Utah. Spiritualism became a fashionable cult with the visions of Margaret Fox in 1847. The teaching

[29] Report of the Committee on State of Religion, Conference Minutes, *SDB Yearbook* (1841) 19.

[30] James Bailey, "Sabbath Tracts—Our Obligation," *SDB Register* 3/17 (22 Jun 1842): 1.

[31] Conference Minutes, *SDB Yearbook* (1842) 17. See also Appendix 1, *SDB Yearbook* (1842) 21-24.

[32] Minutes of the Tract Society, Conference Minutes, *SDB Yearbook* (1843) 16-17.

[33] American Sabbath Tract Society Minutes, Conference Minutes, *SDB Yearbook* (1844) 11, 16.

of William Miller concerning the second coming expected in 1844 gave rise to the Millerite movement. In 1845, Rachel Oakes Preston, a member of the Verona, New York, Seventh Day Baptist Church, brought the Sabbath doctrine to those who later were known as Seventh-day Adventists.

From its organization in 1843 to the establishment of a denominational publishing house at Alfred, New York, in 1872, most of the Seventh Day Baptist General Conference's publishing and printing was done by private enterprise. Texts were distributed through churches or agents and colporteurs. Some of the agents were hired, while others relied on commissions to supplement other income. As early as 1852, bound volumes of tracts and periodicals were placed in public libraries and the libraries of colleges and theological schools. It was hoped that, through a wide circulation of Sabbath claims, many who were already Christians would become Seventh Day Baptists.

The date 1872 marked not only a change in tract publishing, but also a shift in the method of distribution.[34] The annual meeting of the Tract Society in 1877 recognized from past experience that sending lecturers out "to spread the distinctive truth was expensive in proportion to results"; instead, the society recommended that in the future Seventh Day Baptists should go out to evangelize "not one part, but the whole."[35] The following year saw the beginning of evangelistic crusades housed in large tents. One or two preachers, often accompanied by singers, provided the evangelistic messages. The use of quartets—male, female, or mixed—in these evangelistic outreaches continued into the twentieth century.

The idea of going to the unchurched with a basic gospel ministry was projected, but Sabbath convictions continued to dominate the content of the preaching. The ones who most often responded were those who already had a church home. Nonetheless, during this second period there did appear to be an increase in the printing and distribution of general salvation tracts.

Publishing House Choices

An important chapter in the work of the American Sabbath Tract Society centered on two questions: whether the society should undertake its own printing and, if so, where it should do it. A special committee,

[34] Titsworth, "American Sabbath Tract Society," *SDBs in Europe and America*, 1:435-36.
[35] American Sabbath Tract Society Minutes, Conference Minutes, *SDB Yearbook* (1877) 2.

appointed in 1870 to consider the potential costs of such a venture, reported a marked increase that year of Seventh Day Baptists' interest in the question of Sabbath Reform among non-Sabbathkeepers, but as a whole the denomination was not taking advantage of this potential audience. "The most dominant and rapidly increasing denominations in our country are those which early matured and endowed their publishing interests," they reported. They cited the Methodist Book Concern and the American Baptist Publication Society as examples of publishing houses that were not only self-supporting but made a profit as well. During a relatively short time, the Seventh-day Adventists had grown from a few hundred to many thousands "in no small degree by the efficiency of their Publishing Association." By contrast, the American Sabbath Tract Society's committee reported their shame at the feeble enterprises undertaken by Seventh Day Baptists, who, except for the exclusive property of individuals, did not own "a penny's worth of property in the publishing establishment."[36]

The articles of the *Sabbath Recorder* during that year showed considerable difference of opinion as to whether or not the denomination should have its own publishing house. Arguments against it ranged from previous failures to the ethical question of whether a church should engage in competition with private enterprise. Questions were even raised as to whether it were possible to find a publisher who could fully represent Seventh Day Baptists or who could publish "just what and only what the whole denomination believes."[37] Nonetheless, during the year, efforts were successfully made to raise money to purchase a facility and equipment.

Arguments for the publishing house's location at Alfred, New York, included cheaper rent and low cost of living, a more centralized location for an expanding audience, nearness to a community that was predominantly made up of Sabbathkeepers, and proximity to the theological department of Alfred University. Plainfield, New Jersey, on the other hand, was nearer the center of news by virtue of being on the eastern seaboard and closer to the urban centers; nearer the sources that supplied printing materials, especially paper; and closer to the office of the American Sabbath Tract Society.[38] In 1872, the committee to whom

---

[36] American Sabbath Tract Society Minutes, Conference Minutes, *SDB Yearbook* (1870) 28.

[37] "Denominational Publishing," *Sabbath Recorder* 27/45 (2 Nov 1871): 178.

[38] "Report on Publishing," *Sabbath Recorder* 26/49 (1 Dec 1870): 194.

the question of location was referred decided on Alfred and accepted the offer of a rent-free building provided by the citizens of the vicinity.[39]

For about twenty years, the American Sabbath Tract Society published at Alfred, but not without lamenting "the difficulties and inconvenience of carrying on the work of the Society with the Board located four hundred miles from the printing office." [40] By 1890, the society resolved that the publishing house ought to relocate, and that the issue be brought before the Denominational Council expected to meet that October in Chicago.[41] At that 1890 Chicago council, the committee appointed to consider the matter advised that the society move the publishing house "to some great commercial center, conveniently located for our denomination, as soon as it can be done without serious embarrassment, or loss to the interests involved."[42]

Both the Chicago and New York City areas were considered as possible sites for the publishing house's relocation. Those favoring Chicago pointed out that the city was the denomination's geographical center, was more easily accessible from both east and west, and was a growing religious center, having become home to several seminaries along with the Woman's Christian Temperance Union (WCTU) headquarters. Real estate was comparatively cheap and living costs lower than in the East. Chicago was also considered a more promising field for spreading the Sabbath message, since the area was in a more formative state, public opinion was less conservative, and new ideas received a more respectful hearing.[43]

On the other hand, New York as the nation's literary and religious center had no equal; its libraries were the best; it was the center of the publishing industry and the center of communication with Europe. Geographically, it was central to the longer-established congregations in the conference and nearer the office of the Tract Society's Executive Board.

The 1891 meeting of the American Sabbath Tract Society wrestled at length with the question of relocation. Arguments ranged all along the gamut; one side argued that to locate in the denomination's geographic

---

[39] American Sabbath Tract Society Minutes, Conference Minutes, *SDB Yearbook* (1872) 36.

[40] "Location of the Board," American Sabbath Tract Society Minutes (1885) 105.

[41] American Sabbath Tract Society Minutes, Conference Minutes, *SDB Yearbook* (1890) 6.

[42] *Proceedings of the Seventh-Day Baptist Council, Held at Chicago, Ill., Oct. 22–29, 1890* (N.p.: n.d.) 69.

[43] "Report Concerning Chicago," American Sabbath Tract Society Minutes, Conference Minutes, *SDB Yearbook* (1891) 20-21.

center was impractical, for "by taking China into consideration, such a center would be in the Pacific Ocean"; the other side argued that the matter should not be decided by a few ministers but should be left in the hands "of business men who are clear headed and who have for years managed its affairs and who know best regarding both the time and the place." In the end, the Executive Board voted "to move the Publishing House from Alfred to the city of New York as soon as it can be done in accordance with the best interests of the Society."[44]

In 1892, an office at 100 Bible House in New York City opened for use as an editorial room and tract depository; a second depository for tracts and publications opened in Chicago. It was not until 1894 that the decision was made by the Tract Society and General Conference to move the publishing business to Plainfield, New Jersey (close to New York City). Once the choice was made, the move was effected within months. In January 1895, ten years after the first action to place the board and the publishing house in a single location was proposed, publication began in the Babcock Building in Plainfield.[45]

LESSON MATERIALS

Most church histories list the beginning of the church school movement with the work of Robert Raikes of England, who in 1780 established a reading and catechism school for the "ignorant and depraved children" of his town. Many of these children had to work all week, and thus Sunday was the only day they had time for any kind of education.[46] Yet, forty years prior to Raikes, Ludwig Hocker of the German Seventh Day Baptists at Ephrata, Pennsylvania, had established a Sabbath school for the religious education of the town's children.[47] The presence of Sabbath schools generated a need for instruction materials.

---

[44] American Sabbath Tract Society Minutes, Conference Minutes, *SDB Yearbook* (1891) 5-9.

[45] American Sabbath Tract Society Minutes, Conference Minutes, *SDB Yearbook* (1895) 196.

[46] Robert Torbet, *A History of the Baptists*, 3rd ed. (1950; repr., Valley Forge PA: Judson Press, 1963) 121-22.

[47] Julius Friedrich Sachse, *The German Sectarians of Pennsylvania, 1742–1800: A Critical History of the Ephrata Cloister and the Dunkers* (Philadelphia: n.p., 1900) 297.

Question-and-Answer Lessons

The earliest lesson material designed specifically for use in the Sabbath school involved a series of questions and answers. In 1761, Rev. Jonathan Dunham of the Seventh Day Baptist Church in Piscataway, New Jersey, published *A Brief Instruction in the Principles of the Christian Religion*, which contained 116 questions with scriptural answers for use by both adults and children. While no original copy is known to remain in existence, a handscript copy was made in 1849 by W. B. Gillette.[48] A similar publication was used in 1814 by the Seventh Day Baptist Church in Shiloh, New Jersey. The seventy questions of the lesson were answered with Bible verses and references to related passages. An appendix contained thirty-nine questions on the Ten Commandments. The first question on each asked what the commandment stated. The rest of the questions regarded what the commandment required and what it prohibited.[49]

The first reference to the General Conference's participation in the production of lesson aids appeared in 1836, when it was reported to have appointed a committee "to compile a volume of questions of convenient size, embracing the prominent historical facts, doctrines and duties contained in the New Testament for the use of Sabbath Schools and Bible Classes in our connection."[50] The following year, a 206-page book designed for Sabbath school and Bible school use was printed by the Tract Society under the title, *A Series of Questions on the Historical Parts of the New Testament; Embracing the Gospels of Matthew, Mark, Luke and John and the Acts of the Apostles.* Limitation to a convenient size and concern that abridgement would make the work too superficial precluded the inclusion of the whole New Testament.[51] This work did not include the answers, but since the questions followed the biblical sequence, the answers could easily be found.

---

[48] Ira Lee Cottrell, "The Sabbath School Board," *SDBs in Europe and America*, 1:272.

[49] *A Brief Summary of the Principles of the Christian Religion, Expounded by Way of Questions, with Answers in the Words of the Sacred Scriptures; with an Appendix, Containing an Exposition of the Ten Commandments, for the Instruction of Youth,* bound with *Sabbatarian Tracts* (Plainfield NJ: American Sabbath Tract Society, n.d.) BV125.A4, SDB Historical Society Library.

[50] Conference Minutes, *SDB Yearbook* (1836) 12.

[51] Preface, *A Series of Questions on the Historical Parts of the New Testament; Embracing the Gospels of Matthew, Mark, Luke and John, and the Acts of the Apostles for Use of Sabbath Schools and Bible Classes* (DeRuyter NY: n.p., 1837) iii-iv.

Sabbath School Papers and Lessons

The first Sabbath School periodical was the *Sabbath School Visitor* published by the board of the Seventh Day Baptist Publishing Society from 1851 to 1860. With a circulation of 1,500, it was largely self-sustaining. It was succeeded by a paper known simply as the *Sabbath School Paper*, which circulated from 1863 to 1864. Both of these publications were largely the work of editor George B. Utter.

The *Sabbath School Gem* was an independent publication that received some endorsement from the General Conference. It was published by Rev. J. E. N. Backus and his wife from 1861 to 1862 and later from 1868 to 1874. It was published and printed in central New York, where Backus was a pastor; he later moved to Albion, Wisconsin, when he became pastor of the town's church.[52]

The Sabbath School Department

By 1872, a Sabbath School Department was established as a part of the General Conference.[53] The following year, the department reported that it had held several Teachers' Institutes and recommended publishing a monthly *Sabbath School Journal* "devoted to analysis, explanation and illustrations of the International Lessons." The department proposed that the journal would contain special lessons of denominational interest so that "all our Sabbath School work can be made to bear a very important part in our distinctive mission as Seventh Day Baptists."[54]

The Sabbath School Journal

The first edition of the *Journal* appeared in January 1874, accompanied by lesson papers for students. Circulation reached 625 at the regular price of $1.25, with 4,500 lesson papers distributed among Seventh Day Baptists at no charge. The *Journal* did not lack merit and scholarship, but the subscriber field was too limited to meet expenses and so it was discontinued after the first year. Some of the material was incorporated into the *Sabbath Recorder* from 1875 to 1910, after which the *Recorder* only included the list of study topics and scriptural selections.

---

[52] Stephen Burdick, "Seventh-day Baptist Publications," in *Jubilee Papers* (Westerly RI: Board of Managers of SDB Missionary Society, 1892) 107-108.
[53] Conference Minutes, *SDB Yearbook* (1872) 7.
[54] Conference Minutes, *SDB Yearbook* (1873) 9-12.

Lesson Leaves were printed by the Recorder Press and distributed at a cost of 75 cents per hundred per month, including postage.[55] A report by the press to the General Conference in 1880 indicated concern that the *Leaves* more helpful in biblical study and "less of a pony for both teacher and scholar to ride in class." The report also expressed concern that printed material was merely a substitute for the Bible and discouraged original thought; as a result, the scriptural text was omitted in subsequent editions of both the *Leaves* and the *Recorder*.[56]

In 1877, the Tract Society agreed to publish a monthly circular known as the *Bible Scholar*, provided there was a guarantee against any financial loss and the editing was provided outside the society. A change of pastorate for the editor and the publication's inability to fully support itself caused its discontinuance after just two years. In 1878, the Sabbath School Executive Committee reported, "In the matter of the *Bible Scholar* we can only say that as that is a private enterprise it is not in the province of this Board, or of the Conference, to dictate as to its management."[57]

This relationship between the General Conference's Sabbath School Department and the Tract Society in connection with the continued publication of Sabbath School materials illustrates a problem that has persisted for over a century. The Sabbath School Department saw the need for materials but had no way to produce them. The Tract Society had the physical facility to print material, but could do so if revenues kept pace with expenditures. This difficulty of resolving this dilemma was compounded by the numbers factor; there simply was not a large enough market among Seventh Day Baptists to make publication cost-effective. The money problem became even more pronounced in dealing with Sabbath school children's aids. While the total number of adults in the potential market might be numbered in terms of a few thousand, the number of children in any age bracket was limited to a few hundred.

Children's Sabbath School Lessons

In 1880, the Tract Society resolved that "in view of the pressing need of our children," its Executive Board should assume responsibility for publishing a children's paper, to which the board agreed provided that

---

[55] "Sabbath-School Journal," *Sabbath Recorder* 45/32 (8 Aug 1889): 502.
[56] Conference Minutes, *SDB Yearbook* (1880) 4.
[57] Conference Minutes, *SDB Yearbook* (1878) 20.

the Sabbath School Board would do the editing. The Sabbath School Board, located in the New York City area, felt that it would be impossible to edit satisfactorily at a distance of 400 miles from the publishing house at Alfred and suggested that the printing be done locally. Reluctantly, the Tract Society Executive Board agreed to contribute to the cost of printing locally, but the work was not to bear the publishing house's imprint. The Sabbath School Board, fearing that the paper thus published would appear hostile to the denominational publishing house, decided that the decision should be made by the General Conference.[58]

Conference discussions motivated Mr. and Mrs. Edwin Bliss to donate the proceeds of certain oil property they owned to support a weekly Sabbath School paper. On 2 March 1882, the first edition of *Our Sabbath Visitor* appeared under the auspices of the Sabbath School Board, with George Babcock and Miss E. Lua Clarke as editors. Discussions continued over the involvement of the Sabbath School Board and the Tract Society in the publishing. When publishing and printing costs exceeded income from the Bliss endowment and subscription revenues, the board proposed to publish the paper on a biweekly schedule; however, the Blisses objected, proposing instead that if the denomination would pay the $600 indebtedness, they would underwrite the entire net expense.[59]

In 1902, the Sabbath School Board purchased the *Sabbath Visitor* from the Blisses' private ownership. The board provided the editorial work and the Tract Society published the paper and assumed financial responsibility. Economic factors led to the project's suspension in 1923, when a children's page in the *Recorder* was instituted to partially replace it.[60] In 1948, the Board of Christian Education again adopted the name *Sabbath Visitor* for its children's paper.[61]

The Helping Hand

The most successful educational publication over the years of the denomination's history has been the *Helping Hand*. In 1885, A. E. Main offered "to conduct a quarterly" in response to the demand for more

---

[58] Conference Minutes, *SDB Yearbook* (1881) 19.

[59] Conference Minutes, *SDB Yearbook* (1885) 24.

[60] "Publications," *Sabbath School Board Report*, Conference Minutes, *SDB Yearbook* (1923) 301.

[61] "Committee on Church Schools," *Report of Christian Education, Document D*, *SDB Yearbook* (1948) 198.

useful material for adult Sabbath school lessons. Three issues were published that year.[62] At first, the quarterly was almost completely a production of the Tract Society, but in 1893 the publication's management and support were placed in the hands of the Sabbath School Board.[63] Two years later, the board agreed to furnish the writing and editing while the Tract Society continued to manage the project's financial and mechanical components.[64] This shared arrangement between the Tract Society and the Sabbath School Board and its successor, the Board of Christian Education, has continued to the present. Part of the time volunteers provided the editing and writing, but as the volunteers' responsibilities grew, the Tract Society began to compensate them.

BOOKS

Most of the books printed by Seventh Day Baptists have been in the categories of (1) history, (2) biography and journals, (3) Sabbath philosophy, and (4) hymns. Some of those now classified as books first appeared as articles published in periodical form and were later compiled into single volumes. In addition, a number of books written by English Sabbathkeepers were reprinted in America during the nineteenth century.

Historical Works

The earliest historical book printed under the auspices of the General Conference was the one Henry Clarke wrote and published in 1811. Its full title reveals its content: *A History of the Sabbatarians or Seventh Day Baptists In America, Containing Their Rise and Progress to the Year 1811, With Their Leaders' Names, and Their Distinguishing Tenets, etc.* This work served both as a record of the early history of American Seventh Day Baptists and as a source for doctrinal study.[65]

In 1851, Mrs. Tamar Davis wrote and independently published a *History of Sabbatarian Churches*. This book did not have wide circulation, for it contained too many inaccuracies and unsupported suppositions.

[62] "The Helping Hand," American Sabbath Tract Society Minutes, Conference Minutes, *SDB Yearbook* (1885) 87.

[63] "The Helping Hand," American Sabbath Tract Society Minutes, Conference Minutes, *SDB Yearbook* (1893) 239.

[64] "The Helping Hand," American Sabbath Tract Society Minutes, Conference Minutes, *SDB Yearbook* (1895) 22.

[65] See bibliography for information on books listed in this section.

Shortly after its publication, a note in the *Sabbath Recorder* called it "a worthless production" and added, "We hope no one will receive it as a correct picture of the Seventh Day Baptists denomination."[66]

Of more historic value were the following texts: James Bailey's *The History of the Seventh Day Baptist General Conference*, published in 1866; *The Proceedings of the Seventh Day Baptist Council*, chronicling the events of the 1890 Chicago Council; and the *Jubilee Papers*, a collection the Missionary Society published in 1892 to commemorate its fiftieth anniversary and the centennial of the William Carey foreign mission movement.

The most important historical work covering the nineteenth century grew out of the 1902 centennial celebration of the General Conference's organization. *Seventh Day Baptists in Europe and America, Volumes I and II*, edited by Corliss F. Randolph, was a publication of 1,500 pages covering nearly every aspect of denominational history and activity. Over two dozen people collaborated in the writing of its many sections. A third volume was published in 1972, under the editorship of Rev. Albert N. Rogers, to update the record.

Also appearing in the first decade of the twentieth century but covering nineteenth-century history was *A History of Seventh Day Baptists in West Virginia* by Corliss F. Randolph. Its historic value is not limited to West Virginia, for it contains the account of the Shrewsbury Church, including its migration through Pennsylvania to become the New Salem Church in western Virginia and information concerning families who migrated further west.

Biographies and Journals

James L. Scott, who was mentioned in the previous chapter, was but one of a number of pastors who recorded visits to frontier settlements during extended missionary tours. These accounts give testimony not only to these individuals' own courage and dedication, but also to the eagerness of many pioneers to hear the gospel and be supported by the more established churches. Among those whose autobiographical sketches and journals were printed in book form were James Ball Davis, Samuel D. Davis, and Ethan Lanphere. The list would be considerably greater if all who recorded these missionary tours had published them in book form. Reports of others, such as those of Amos R. Wells, have been preserved in various denominational periodicals of the time.

---

[66] *Sabbath Recorder* 7/51 (Jun 1851): 202.

Sometimes family members or close friends were responsible for publishing biographical materials. James Bailey edited the *Biographical Sketches of Elder Eli S. Bailey* in 1871. Charles Burdick was responsible for editing the *Autobiography of Rev. Alexander Campbell* in 1883. The wife of Jonathan Allen, president of Alfred University, edited and compiled the *Life and Sermons of Jonathan Allen* in 1894, and Edwin Lewis compiled a related work, *Allen of Alfred*, in 1934. The Tract Society published Theodore Gardiner's *Biographical Sketch of Abram Herbert Lewis* in 1909.

Sabbath Philosophy and History

The earliest and most abundant denominational books published in both England and America dealt with the distinctive doctrine of the Sabbath. Books by Edward Stennett and Robert Burnside were republished in America. *A Discussion of the Original Institution, Perpetuity and Change of the Weekly Sabbath* was written by William B. Maxson and William Parkinson in 1836. In 1888 James Bailey published a *Sabbath Commentary*, a scriptural exegesis of all the passages in the Bible that relate to the Sabbath doctrine.

The most prolific writer of Sabbath texts was Rev. Abram H. Lewis. His book *The Sabbath and Sunday,* which appeared in 1870, was later enlarged to three volumes with descriptive titles: *Biblical Teachings Concerning the Sabbath and Sunday* (1888); *Critical History of the Sabbath and Sunday in the Christian Church* (1903); and *A Critical History of Sunday Legislation from A.D. 321 to 1888* (1888).

Later books by A. H. Lewis, published in the last decade of the nineteenth century, included the following: *Paganism Surviving in Christianity* (1892); *The Catholicization of Protestantism on the Sabbath Question, or Sunday Observance Non-Protestant* (1897); *Studies in Sabbath Reform* (1898); *Swift Decadence of Sunday; What Next?* (1899); *and Letters to Young Preachers and their Hearers* (1900).

The most significant of A. H. Lewis' writings was *Spiritual Sabbathism*, edited after his death by his son E. H. Lewis and published by the American Sabbath Tract Society in 1910. It is still a primary resource in the Sabbath Theology course for Seventh Day Baptist ministers.

Hymn and Music Books

Seventh Day Baptists have traditionally chosen music as an expression of worship and praise. The Stennetts in England were hymn writers, and Seventh Day Baptists' interest continued in America, where music was from early days a major component of worship. As mentioned in Chapter 11, the first denominational collection of hymns, *Psalms and Hymns From the Most Approved Authors*, appeared in 1826 and contained some 587 hymns. In 1846, in response to a request from the Eastern Association for a new hymnbook, the General Conference appointed a committee to prepare such a book, with the provision that the conference "does not assume any responsibility, but promises to use its influence to procure for the book as extensive circulation as possible." The hymnbook, *Christian Psalmody* published by George Utter, became the most widely used hymnbook among Seventh Day Baptist churches. The first edition appeared in 1847, with five subsequent editions emerging during the next three decades. In its final edition, *Christian Psalmody* contained the words for over a thousand hymns. It gave way in 1879 to the *Seventh Day Baptist Praise Book*, which contained both the words and the music for the included hymns.[67]

In 1855, Lucius Crandall compiled a collection of Seventh Day Baptist songs and selected other music for use in the Sabbath schools and other gatherings. Jairus Stillman, professor of music at Hopkinton Academy, Alfred University, and Milton College, was associate author of a songbook called *The Cluster* and another for Sabbath schools called *Good Will*. He also compiled a collection known as *Anthem Treasures*.

SUMMARY

Throughout the nineteenth century, Seventh Day Baptists chose to use the power of the press to spread the gospel and their distinctive beliefs. The printed word had many advantages over the spoken word. It went where few individuals were able or willing to go. It expanded the audience of those God had called to minister and enabled many volunteer writers to utilize their talents and gifts.

The printed word served to unite the people in a common cause and to maintain a sense of brotherhood among a widely scattered and diverse people. It provided a means of communication with those outside the family of Seventh Day Baptists, thus enlarging the fellowship. This period of increased publication was the period of greatest denominational growth. The publication of periodicals, tracts, pamphlets, lesson materials, and books spans time and memory. It

---

[67] Preface, *The Seventh Day Baptist Praise Book* (Westerly RI: George B. Utter, 1879) 3-5.

makes possible a more accurate study and deeper appreciation of the past, giving insight for the present and hope for the future.

15

EDUCATIONAL PURSUITS OF SEVENTH DAY BAPTISTS

Seventh Day Baptists have always held education as essential in order for its members to properly interpret facts, events, and ideas. Along with other churches in the Free Church tradition, they have held that an enlightened conscience takes precedence over authoritarian indoctrination. Reliance on biblical interpretation rather than ecclesiastical decree requires the ability to read and write and the ability to think, reason, and understand relationships.

Legacy of Educated Leaders

In England during the seventeenth century, men such as James Ockford, William Saller, and Henry Jessey began to write and appeal to reason in defending the Sabbath as a part of "the commandments of God and the faith of Jesus." Leaders such as Dr. Peter Chamberlen and the Stennetts were well educated, and they passed their enlightened legacy on to others.

In America during these same years, men and women such as Samuel and Tacy Hubbard moved several times to find a place where they could practice the beliefs that stemmed from their study of the Scriptures. The first pastor of the Newport Seventh Day Baptist Church, William Hiscox, was well recognized as a man of outstanding ability and knowledge. The second pastor, William Gibson, was educated in England before coming to America. Others from that church were prominent in the educational and cultural pursuits of the colony. Henry Collins completed his education in England and, upon his return, made such a contribution to the fine arts that he was called "the Lorenzo de Medici of the Colonies."[1]

Cooperation in Higher Education

Samuel Ward, while Governor of Rhode Island, was involved in 1762 in the founding of Rhode Island College, later renamed Brown

---

[1] L. A. Platts, "Seventh-Day Baptists in America Previous to 1802," *Seventh Day Baptists in Europe and America*, 3 vols., ed. C. F. Randolph (Plainfield NJ: SDB General Conference, 1910) 1:144. See also "Henry Collins," *SDB Memorial* 3/4 (Oct 1854): 154.

University. He signed the petition for its charter and was one of the college's original trustees.[2] Others such as Dr. Joshua Babcock,[3] Col. Job Bennett,[4] John Tanner, and Rev. Joshua Clarke also served as trustees at Brown.[5] Among the Seventh Day Baptist graduates were Governor Ward's son, Col. Samuel Ward, Chaplain Ebenezer David, and Rev. Solomon Carpenter, one of the first Seventh Day Baptist missionaries to China.[6]

The Rise of Educational Societies

As people migrated west, opportunities for education were not readily available, but they still held the desire to learn. Alexander Campbell recalled that when he was considering joining the Seventh Day Baptists, his former pastor tried to dissuade him by pointing out that Seventh Day Baptists did not have a single school where he could complete his education. Campbell resolved that "should his lot be cast among those illiterate people, with God's help he would do all in his power to remove that reproach from that people."[7]

Pioneers in Higher Education

Alexander Campbell was instrumental in helping found DeRuyter Institute in 1837. Located in a small village in central New York State, DeRuyter was one of the first of several such schools initiated by Seventh Day Baptist that preceded public school education in towns where they had settled. For several years prior to the institute's opening, Campbell devoted much of his time and energy to raising money to establish a school. In the process of promoting his educational cause, he visited many churches. The pages of the *Protestant Sentinel* and the *Seventh Day Baptist Register* focused the denomination's attention on the need for an educated clergy. In 1833, an article in the *Sentinel* called for a

---

[2] Charles H. Denison and John Ward, *Governor Samuel Ward of Rhode Island, 1725–1776* (Plainfield NJ: SDB General Conference, 1907) 70.

[3] William G. McLoughlan, ed., *The Diary of Isaac Backus* (Providence: Brown University Press, 1979) 606 note.

[4] David Weston, in Isaac Backus, *A History of New England with Particular Reference to the Denomination of Christians Called Baptists*, 3 vols. (Newtown MA.: Backus Historical Society, 1871) 2:348-49, note.

[5] William L. Burdick, "The Eastern Association," *SDBs in Europe and America*, 2:609, 635.

[6] W. C. Whitford, "Education Among the Seventh Day Baptists," in *Jubilee Papers* (Westerly RI: Board of Managers of the SDB Missionary Society, 1892) 92-93.

[7] Alexander Campbell, *Autobiography of Rev. Alexander Campbell*, ed. C. A. Burdick (Watertown NY: Post Printing House, 1883) 18-19.

denominational institution "for the education of such as God shall call and ordain to be ministers of the cross of Christ."[8] Those who opposed this idea argued that the denomination was too small to sustain a school, that missionary institutions needed more assistance, and that local ministers were not well supported (thus, resources were already stretched too thin). One writer urged the denomination to "be content to learn in the school of Christ until he enlarge our numbers and give us the ability to be like others."[9]

Because of this dialogue, in 1834 the General Conference recommended that the denomination form an Education Society to raise funds to assist in educating young men who gave evidence of a call to the ministry.[10] Three months later, the editor of the *Protestant Sentinel* suggested a plan whereby women might become involved in the fundraising effort. "Females are naturally endowed with capacities to aid essentially the cause of benevolence," he wrote. "When they take hold of an object with union and interest they will most generally succeed. Let them now take hold upon the education of the ministry, and they will have an object worthy of their labors, and which will pay them for their care."[11]

The first report of the American Seventh Day Baptist Education Society, which appeared in 1837, clearly showed that much of its resources were contributed by "Female Education Societies" or "Female Mite Societies" within local churches. Financial aid was given that year to Bethuel C. Church and William C. Kenyon.[12] Both Church and Kenyon returned that investment with significant contributions to Seventh Day Baptist education.

Bethuel C. Church was recruited to establish a select school (a private school) at Alfred, New York. In 1836, he began teaching a class for about three dozen students recruited from the area. One of those first students was Jonathan Allen, who paid his tuition by cutting and hauling 6 cords of 4-foot wood.[13] Allen later went on to serve for twenty-five years (1867–1895) as president of that school, which by then had

---

[8] "A Suggestion," *Protestant Sentinel* 4/47 (5 Mar 1834): 186.
[9] Letter to editor, *Protestant Sentinel* 52 (11 Jun 1834): 22.
[10] Conference Minutes, *SDB Yearbook* (1834) 8-9.
[11] "Education," *Protestant Sentinel* 5/27 (3 Dec 1834): 418.
[12] American SDB Education Society Minutes, Conference Minutes, *SDB Yearbook* (1837) 18-19.
[13] E. H. Lewis, biographical sketch in *Allen of Alfred*, ed. E. H. Lewis (Milton WI: Davis-Greene Corp. Press, 1932) 17-18.

grown to become Alfred University. In 1844 Bethuel Church served as the first principal at Milton Academy, later to become Milton College, in Wisconsin Territory.

While William C. Kenyon was a student at Union College in Schenectady, New York, he was contacted to assume the principalship at DeRuyter Institute; however, the Board of Trustees rejected him because his handwriting was not pleasing to some of its members.[14] Subsequently, in 1839, he went to Alfred, where he became an efficient leader and teacher. He was principal when Alfred was incorporated as an academy in 1843 and became its first president when it was chartered as a university in 1857. For twenty-nine years, Kenyon provided educational leadership at Alfred.

A few others received support, but in 1838 the last report to the General Conference of this first denominational Education Society showed difficulty in meeting the requests of applicants. Education Societies were not listed in the resolution passed in 1840 by the conference, which resolved that "Sabbath Schools, Missionary Societies, Bible Classes, and Monthly Concerts be considered as institutions of the church, and recorded as such in the minutes."[15] General Conference support for a unified Educational Society seemed to have waned.

Seventh Day Baptist Education Society

In 1849, the General Conference appointed an Educational Committee to secure funds "and take such other measures for the establishment of a College and Theological Seminary as they may deem proper, with exception of locating the institution."[16] That same conference encouraged young men preparing to enter the ministry to pursue a regular collegiate course of instruction prior to ordination; likewise it recognized the responsibility of churches to aid ministry students by helping fund their studies.[17]

In 1855, the Education Committee appointed Jonathan Allen as a general agent to visit the entire denomination to solicit money and support. His report indicated problems that stood in the way of complete success. He observed that the "leading and controlling minds of the denomination had not, as a general thing, committed themselves,

[14] Leander Elliott Livermore, "Extinct Schools," *SDBs in Europe and America*, 1:570.
[15] Reports from the Churches and Associations, Conference Minutes, *SDB Yearbook* (1840) 13.
[16] Conference Minutes, *SDB Yearbook* (1849) 8.
[17] Conference Minutes, *SDB Yearbook* (1849) 9.

publicly and decisively to the measure." The greatest difficulty was "the financial embarrassment resting on all departments of business and the question of location being undetermined." In addition, no adequate plan was developed for support of the agent, so he had to return to his "accustomed pursuit" for support. He had obtained subscriptions of $20,000 at a personal expense of $250 for which he received $1.00.[18]

The location for a school was decided in 1855, when a vote from the churches of the General Conference showed 690 out of 769 delegates favoring Alfred, New York. Plainfield, New Jersey, which had received 51 votes, was a distant second. (Only 19 churches sent votes, and of these a dozen were from the Alfred area.) The General Conference later corroborated the decision on the basis of merit, citing such reasons as the availability of facilities and personnel in Alfred, the city's low living costs, and its healthy climate, adding that "being a retired and rural district, it is favorable both to study and morals."[19]

A Seminary Located at Alfred

In 1855, the Education Committee called a convention to organize a new society for the education of ministers. The proposed constitution provided the structure and much of the philosophy of the Education Society for the succeeding 85 years, until it merged in 1940 into the Board of Christian Education. Its object was the "promotion of Education in such a manner as shall tend to the ultimate founding of a full endowment of a Denominational College and Theological Seminary." It provided for both annual and life membership on the basis of donations and specified that professors in the theological seminary and three-fourths of the institution's trustees ought, at all times, to be Seventh Day Baptists. The constitution also stated that tuition in the theological department would be free.[20]

A curriculum of study was developed for both a three-year Academic Department (roughly equivalent to a high school education) and a four-year Collegiate Department divided into three divisions: the classical course, the scientific course, and a ladies' course that contained many of the same classes found in the other areas of study. Rather than granting a bachelor's degree to women, Alfred originated the "laureate"

---

[18] Conference Minutes, *SDB Yearbook* (1855) 8-9.
[19] Report of the Committee on College Location, Education Society Minutes, *SDB Yearbook* (1856) 7-8.
[20] "Organization of the Society," Education Society Minutes, *SDB Yearbook* (1856) 5-6.

degree, which it continued to give for twenty-four years before it was dropped at the women's request (other options were available for degree programs at that time).[21] There was no theological course at this initial stage, although the Education Society stated in its minutes that the study of Greek was offered in both the Academic and Collegiate departments, adding in a footnote: "All students in Greek will be required to read the Greek Testament once each week through the Junior and Senior Years." The Collegiate Department offered courses in Hebrew Grammar, Hebrew Bible, Greek Testament, and Ecclesiastical History, plus it offered Natural Theology to women.[22]

The prospect for establishing a theological seminary prompted the academy's Board of Trustees to apply for a university charter from the State of New York. Jonathan Allen was appointed to lobby for the necessary legislation. For over two years he met with opposition, but finally in March 1857 the bill was signed by the governor and Alfred became a recognized University.[23]

Securing a charter did not create a theological department; that was several years in the future. In 1858, Jonathan Allen was appointed Professor of Theology, but since he had never served in the pastorate, he declined to serve unless a Professor of Practical Theology be appointed. Financial problems in both the university and the country did not allow the hiring of an additional professor.[24] Finally, in 1862, Allen was reaffirmed and his church was asked to ordain him as a minister of the gospel.[25] Allen began offering courses in theology as a part of the collegiate program. In 1865, the pastor of the Alfred church, Rev. N. V. Hull, consented to teach a course in Pastoral Theology, which he continued to do for thirteen years. With the death of President W. C. Kenyon in 1867, Jonathan Allen assumed the presidency of Alfred University, which made it necessary to recruit other instructors for the department.

One of those recruited was Rev. Thomas R. Williams, who had served for seven years as principal of the Albion Academy in Wisconsin. His education included degrees from Alfred and Brown Universities and Union and Princeton Theological Seminaries. For nearly a quarter of a

---

[21] J. Nelson Norwood, *Fiat Lux, The Story of Alfred University* (Alfred NY: Alfred University Press, 1957) 44.

[22] Curriculum of Study, Education Society Minutes, *SDB Yearbook* (1856) 11-12, note b.

[23] Education Society Minutes, *SDB Yearbook* (1857) 9-10.

[24] Education Society Minutes, *SDB Yearbook* (1862) 6.

[25] Ibid., 2.

century he was on the faculty of the theological department of Alfred, taking time out to serve as acting president of Milton College from 1880 to 1882. In 1871, the theological department became a separate school within the university with power to grant what was then a graduate-level degree, the Bachelor of Divinity. In 1874 the first graduating class included David Davis, later a missionary to China; John Huffman, a future founder of Salem College in West Virginia; and Theodore Gardiner, Salem's president from 1893 to 1906 and later longtime editor of the *Sabbath Recorder*.

The Alfred University School of Theology continued as the primary institution for the training of Seventh Day Baptist ministers for nearly a century until 1963, when requirements for academic accreditation in terms of student population and the number and degrees held by faculty forced it to close. The following year, the General Conference created a Center on Ministry to offer financial support and supplemental training for Seventh Day Baptist students attending other seminaries. Thus, for a century and a half, the denomination has maintained its underlying commitment to a well-educated ministry and the responsibility of its members and churches to provide this education at minimal cost to individual students.

Alfred University and Seventh Day Baptists

Around the turn of the century, Alfred University's relationship to Seventh Day Baptists changed. J. Nelson Norwood, in his history of Alfred University, described the difficult tenure of President Boothe C. Davis, a Seventh Day Baptist minister who became president of the university in 1895 and served until 1933. Increased support for buildings, faculty salaries, and endowments were necessary for Alfred to compete with other institutions of higher education. Resources from within the denomination were not forthcoming. Moreover, the potential for Seventh Day Baptist students attending Alfred had been cut by the rise of two newer colleges, Milton in Wisconsin and Salem in West Virginia. All three schools looked to the same small denomination for support and students.

In an address before the General Conference in 1898, President Davis expressed his belief that the denomination could not support three colleges; instead, he suggested that Alfred be designated its leading institution and be adequately equipped for specialized training, while Milton and Salem become tributary or junior colleges. This address delivered at Milton Junction, within a mile of Milton College, did not meet with acceptance. In 1915, some of the same thoughts were expressed in an article prepared for publication in the *Sabbath Recorder*, but the article was withdrawn at the request of President Daland of Milton College.[26]

President Davis felt that Alfred University, in order to survive, must supplement church support with other sources, including support from philanthropic foundations and public funds. The presence of high-grade pottery clay in the area and the proximity of the Caledon Terra Cotta Company plant in Alfred suggested the possibility of a school of clayworks and ceramics. In 1900, the State of New York established a College of Ceramics at Alfred. This portion of the university soon earned a reputation as a leader in the field of ceramics and attracted students from throughout the world. Later, a State School of Agriculture was also established at Alfred. The university continued to recruit its presidents from among Seventh Day Baptists until 1945, but the control of the school gradually went to others as its board of directors was slowly devoid of Seventh Day Baptists. That decline, combined with becoming a publicly funded university, led to the school's being controlled by groups other than Seventh Day Baptists.[27]

AFFILIATED ACADEMIES AND COLLEGES

The Education Society in 1860 reaffirmed the basic commitment of Seventh Day Baptists to education. This included the "right, duty and privilege of woman to avail herself of those opportunities to secure her intellectual equality with man which the present age so abundantly affords." The society also stated that "the surest way by which we, as a denomination, may expect to succeed is through such a moral and intellectual development as will command the respect of those around us."[28] Such commitments were responsible for the establishment of several other schools in addition to the one at Alfred. DeRuyter in New York; Milton and Albion in Wisconsin; and Salem in West Virginia have all made outstanding contributions to the education of the public in general and to Seventh Day Baptists in particular.

---

[26] Boothe C. Davis, *Memoirs of Boothe C. Davis and Estelle Hoffman Davis* (1937), transcript, LD131.A317, pp. 88-90, 294-30, SDB Hist. Soc. Lib.

[27] Norwood, *Fiat Lux*, 111-12.

[28] Education Society Minutes, *SDB Yearbook* (1860) 4.

DeRuyter Institute in New York

DeRuyter Institute was founded about the same time as the select school at Alfred. Alexander Campbell, pastor at DeRuyter in 1835 shortly before the school at DeRuyter was established, recalled that "it frequently came to his ears that some of our young men of much promise were drifting away from us because the advantages they sought could not be obtained from us."[29] Feeling the time was right to act on the same determination he had felt when he became a Seventh Day Baptist, he resolved to remove the public's reproach of what they perceived as Seventh Day Baptists "being an uneducated people."

Aided by several close colleagues, Campbell began the task of raising money to build an educational institution chiefly among Seventh Day Baptists. A four-story stone building, 80 feet by 90 feet, was completed in 1836, and the first classes commenced in 1837. Throughout its nearly forty years of existence, the institute was hampered by financial difficulties. Yet, in spite of many difficulties, DeRuyter Institute provided quality education for many students in those years before the public school system brought education to the public at large. In 1874, the building was sold to the public school district due to the ongoing financial difficulties and the presence of public schools in the area.

During those forty years, DeRuyter exerted tremendous influence on the denomination through its network of educated leaders. Students who entered the ministry included such noteworthy individuals as James Bailey, Thomas R. Williams, Charles Burdick, and David Davis. Seventh Day Baptist publishing interests were greatly influenced by those living in DeRuyter's shadow. For a time, the *Protestant Sentinel* was published within the walls of the institute while the remaining structure was being built. Graduates such as George Babcock, an inventor and manufacturer of printing presses and steam engines, made their mark in industry, enabling them to make contributions during their lifetime and leave endowments for the denomination's continuing work.[30]

Perhaps the greatest contribution of DeRuyter Institute was that it extensively and effectively championed higher learning. Even financial difficulty served to promote education, as it forced leaders to travel widely to encourage education among Seventh Day Baptists and expand the institute's student base. Several of those recruited to teach at DeRuyter went on to become leaders in other schools. One of its most

---

[29] Campbell, *Autobiography*, 65.
[30] Livermore, "Extinct Schools," *Seventh Day Baptists in Europe and America*, 1:567-73.

noted students was William C. Whitford, who for over forty years guided the destiny of Milton College.

Milton College in Wisconsin

Like Alfred, Milton College began as a select school for the immediate benefit of the local residents. Joseph Goodrich was the prime mover in establishing a school in that section of Wisconsin Territory. In summer 1838, accompanied by Henry Crandall and James Pierce, Goodrich left Alfred and journeyed to southern Wisconsin in search of suitable land for settlement. Both Crandall and Goodrich returned to Alfred to pack up their families and move. The Crandalls arrived that fall while the Goodrich family waited until winter, arriving in March 1839 at what was then Prairie DuLac, later named Milton.

According to later reminiscence in her diary, Nancy Goodrich was reluctant to make the move. She asked Joseph to consider what it meant to leave a pleasant community and the privileges of church and school. Joseph is reported to have said, "Would it be impossible to have schools and churches in the new land? Assuredly it would be unwise to deny our children the right to learn and grow up in the atmosphere of religion. Would it not be a service that we could render to this new community if we could take these into the new land?"[31]

True to his word, he helped establish both church and school in the community. The church was formally organized in November 1840 and the school in 1844. For the school's first few years, Joseph Goodrich had sole management and paid all expenses beyond any tuition proceeds. He persuaded Bethuel Church, Alfred's first teacher, to come to Milton in a similar capacity. In 1848, the legislature of Wisconsin Territory incorporated the school as DuLac Academy.

The old building that Joseph Goodrich had built to house a school and that the community for a time had used as the church meetinghouse fell beyond repair in 1853, but the school continued in private homes until a new building, Main Hall, opened in 1855. Two years later, the school erected another building bearing the name Goodrich Hall. The attendance in 1856 reached 212, and three women graduated from the teacher's course, the first of many teachers to be educated at Milton. During the next decade, Milton Academy progressed to the point that in 1867 the legislature granted it a college charter.

---

[31] Centennial Drama of Milton SDB Church (1940), MS 1983.46.3.2, p. 1, SDB Hist. Soc. Lib.

Although it never officially declared itself a Seventh Day Baptist College, Milton's connections with Seventh Day Baptists were strong. It was founded by individuals who were Seventh Day Baptists. Most of its early faculty belonged to that denomination. In 1858, the trustees asked the pastor of the Milton church, Rev. William C. Whitford, to assume charge as principal for the fall term. He completed the school year, and at the end of that year resigned as pastor of the church to become the school's principal. When the academy became a college he was elected as its president, a post he held for over forty years.[32]

In 1867, Milton College began to make annual reports to the General Conference. It received contributions from individual benevolences and participated in denominational emphases in the support of education. Many of its students came from Seventh Day Baptist churches, including several from the mission in China. Until 1954, all of its presidents were Seventh Day Baptists, most of whom were drawn from the ranks of the ministry.

Milton College gave to the denomination far more than it received. Well over fifty Seventh Day Baptist ministers claim Milton College as their alma mater. Though it was not a sectarian school, the number of teachers who have gone from its halls into Seventh Day Baptist communities is much larger. Its campus, along with the church, hosted sessions of the General Conference fifteen times. Only Hopkinton, which hosted sessions seventeen times (mostly during the early years when the conference was on a three-year rotation), and sister colleges of Alfred and Salem, with sixteen sessions each, exceed that number.

In 1982, Milton College was forced to close due to economic pressure and overdependence on federally subsidized loans and grants. In its effort to compete for students, it lost some of its distinctive qualities as a private liberal arts college with a religious heritage.

Albion Academy in Wisconsin

Closely related to Milton College was an academy located 15 miles to the northwest in the Seventh Day Baptist community of Albion. In 1852, the Committee on Education of the North Western Association recognized that the school at Milton was "laboring under great embarrassment for want of adequate room and other facilities." The committee was of the opinion that the present accommodations and facilities were inadequate for the denomination's needs. After

---

[32] Edwin Shaw, "History of Milton College," *SDBs in Europe and America*, 1:529-32.

considerable discussion, a Board of Education was appointed consisting of two members from each of the five Seventh Day Baptist churches in the state: Albion, Berlin, Christiana, Milton, and Walworth. The following year, a 3-story brick building, 36 by 48 feet, was under construction and a charter was granted by the state "under which a Board of Trustees has been constituted with the design of being directed by the Association in the great and vitally important operations of the Institution."[33]

The competition between Milton and Albion for both students and support appears to have been beneficial for both schools. In 1854, the Committee on Education reported that it was "gratified and encouraged to see a wide spread and growing interest in general education." A new building was under construction at Milton, and the building at Albion was nearly ready for classes to begin under the superintendency of Thomas R. Williams, a graduate of DeRuyter Institute who later went on to direct the School of Theology at Alfred.[34]

The Albion Academy lasted forty years, until the trustees voted in 1894 that it would not be wise to continue as a denominational school. The property was sold to a private individual, who ran it for about seven years then sold it to the Norwegian Lutherans, who operated it until 1918. One of its buildings was preserved as a museum until it was destroyed by arson in 1965. A replica built on the site continues as a museum. When the Wisconsin State Historical Society published a series of Badger History booklets in the 1970s, they chose the Albion Academy to represent the early coeducational schools in the state.

Like its sister school at Milton, Albion contributed to the denomination in training teachers and ministerial students. The principal during the 1880s, Rev. Sanford L. Maxson, left Albion in 1889 to become the president of the newly created college in Salem, West Virginia.

Salem College in West Virginia

The heritage of education accompanied the first Seventh Day Baptist settlers among the hills of western Virginia, but their opportunity was restricted. Travel was difficult and few could afford the luxury of going to Alfred or Milton for education. Early in the 1850s, the General Conference sent Rev. Azor Estee to western Virginia as a missionary, but

---

[33] Report of the Board of Education, Minutes of Northwestern Association (1853) 12.

[34] Report of the Committee on Education, Minutes of Northwestern Association (1854) 10.

his true calling proved to be promoting education. In 1852, three men in West Union were moved by his enthusiasm to open a school in West Union (West Union Academy) that was incorporated by the State General Assembly. Difficulty in securing teachers and economic concerns caused the school to close after about three years.

In 1870, Charles A. Burdick, who had attended school at Albion, DeRuyter, and Alfred, came to Salem as a general missionary. Sensing the area's need for education, he opened a select school that operated for two terms. In 1886, the Methodist Episcopal General Conference of West Virginia sent a committee to Salem with a plan to build a seminary there. By a slim margin, the decision was made by the committee to build in Buckhannon instead, which led Seventh Day Baptists to conclude that the time was right to build their own school in Salem.[35]

The South-Eastern Association took the initiative to promote an academy and college. It appointed a committee in 1887 to canvass the area and take the necessary steps to establish a school. The committee confirmed that the time was right, that Salem was the proper location, and that steps should be taken to raise money, secure land, and begin building. The General Conference took note "with approval" of the recommendations but offered only moral support.[36]

The initial capital for the founding of the college was raised by the sale of stock to thirteen men, who became the incorporators and to whom the state issued the charter on 28 December 1888. Although the charter was issued to a corporation under the name Salem Academy, it specified that the academy was subject to the regulations of the Seventh Day Baptist Education Society. The charter also carried the provision that the academy become a college "as soon as the financial conditions and circumstances will warrant." The change from academy to college took place in 1890.[37]

The first classes were held in the Seventh Day Baptist Church in spring 1889, with Rev. John L. Huffman acting as principal until Sanford L. Maxson was able to leave Albion to head the school. Maxson retired in 1892 and was replaced by Rev. Theodore L. Gardiner, who served for fourteen years before returning to the pastorate in 1906. For over eighty

---

[35] Minutes of South-eastern Association (1887), repr. in Corliss Fitz Randolph, *A History of the Seventh Day Baptists in West Virginia* (Plainfield NJ: American Sabbath Tract Society, 1905) 369-70.

[36] Education Society Minutes, *SDB Yearbook* (1888) 4.

[37] Randolph, *History of SDBs in West Virginia*, 371-72.

years, the presidents of Salem College and many of the faculty and trustees were Seventh Day Baptists.

In the college's centennial year of 1988, the General Conference met on Salem's campus. Tribute was given to forty-one pastors and other key denominational leaders who had graduated from that institution. There has been a close relationship with Seventh Day Baptists throughout Salem's hundred years, even though the college has remained independent and nonsectarian.

In July 1989, Salem College announced that it had joined with Teikyo University of Japan to establish a unique venture in international education. As Salem-Teikyo University, the joint venture retained its private status on a more stable economic base as it expanded to include a strong intercultural and international dimension.[38] However, in 2000 this alliance was terminated and the name was changed to Salem International University. Through these changes, the college continues to draw students who wish to receive an education near a Sabbathkeeping church.

Other Seventh Day Baptist Educational Institutions

Alfred University, DeRuyter Institute, Milton College, Albion Academy, and Salem College have been cited as examples of Seventh Day Baptist educational institutes because of their unique relationships with Seventh Day Baptists and the relationship the institutions had with each other. There were other schools that also contributed to the denomination's educational emphasis. Most of these schools served their communities until the public school system was established. Among these academies were the following: Brookfield (1841–1876) and Petersburg (1857–1859) in New York; Shiloh (1848–1882) and New Market (1854–1861) in New Jersey; Farmington (1849–1852) and West Hallock (1857) in Illinois; Walworth (1857–1881) in Wisconsin; Hopkinton (1857–1869) in Rhode Island; and West Union (1857) in West Virginia. Others were located for short periods in places where church members demonstrated their concern for the education of their young people.[39]

---

[38] See "Salem College News Release," 28 Jul 1989, e-file 1, folder 39. Compare "How About Salem-Teikyo University?" *Sabbath Recorder* 211/9 (Sep 1989) 10.
[39] Livermore, "Extinct Schools," *SDBs in Europe and America*, 1:559-73.

Fouke Missionary School and Academy in Arkansas

During the early years of the twentieth century, the Fouke Academy in Arkansas continued the legacy of Seventh Day Baptist education in the American South. The first denominational school in the Southwestern Association was Bampfield Academy, which began operation in 1891 but lasted only a few years before it gave way to the public school system of Arkansas.

In 1898, Rev. Gideon Henry Fitz Randolph became the association's general missionary under the direction of the Missionary Board; he held this position for over seventeen years. He observed that the children in Arkansas were not receiving a sound education in the public school system. His wife Lucy reported to the women in attendance at conference sessions in 1908 that "many children did not get even one month's schooling during the entire year.... Morals and corrective discipline are seldom a matter of consideration in these schools, and the child is in peril of soul, body and mind."[40]

Pastor Randolph saw both the need and the opportunity for Seventh Day Baptists to establish a mission school at Fouke. In 1899, Elizabeth Fisher from New Jersey began working toward this end by meeting the residents, further assessing their needs, and recruiting students. Classes began in 1901 and continued for over a quarter of a century. In 1916, the school became an academy while retaining its missionary concept. The school received help from the Missionary Board and such other denominational sources as the Woman's Board and the Young People's Society. Most of its faculty were volunteers giving dedicated service with minimal financial support.

The school was primarily established for the Seventh Day Baptist community, but it served others who felt their children could gain a better education there. In 1948, J. W. Ramsey, the Superintendent of Schools in Fort Smith, Arkansas, recalled that even though his family members were Baptists, his mother sent her children to the Seventh Day Baptist school because the public school in the community was substandard. Some forty years after he left the school, he considered his attendance the turning point in his life, recalling that the school was "an oasis in a desert, and rendered unusually effective service to every one

---

[40] Mrs. G. H. Lucy F. Randolph, "The South West and Its Needs," in *A History of the Seventh Day Baptist Mission School at Fouke, Arkansas,* ed. Elizabeth Fisher Davis, 1954, transcript, BX6394.A7D3, n.p., SDB Hist. Soc. Lib.

whom it reached. I regard Rev. Fitz Randolph as a real missionary and a disciple of the teachings of the Savior. I shall always be grateful to him for the opportunity that I had coming under his influence in my life."[41]

In 1927, the school relinquished its function to the public school system, which, partly through the influence of the academy, raised its level of instruction. The school was reopened briefly as a private school in 1981 but closed in 1985 due to the death of Dr. Floyd Goodson, then pastor of the Fouke church.

SUPPORT FOR EDUCATION

A common thread running through the denomination's educational history has been the lack of a strong financial base to support the high-quality education Seventh Day Baptists desired. Many of the leading educators had to spend much of their time and energy to solicit support. Some associations contributed limited resources, but few were in position to offer any substantial financial backing. The General Conference, as a voluntary association of churches, has never had the means to give more than moral support. The Education Society made efforts through local societies to provide some assistance, but much of this went primarily to individual students.

Recognition of this need gave rise to the Memorial Fund, one of the denomination's most significant agencies over the past century. The fund did not solve all financial problems, but it has provided a means of denomination-wide support for education and other benevolences through various investments and bequests.

The Memorial Fund

As the year 1871 approached, attention was drawn to a celebration to mark the 200th anniversary of the first Seventh Day Baptist church in America. Through the pages of the *Sabbath Recorder*, Milton College president W. C. Whitford suggested that an appropriate memorial might be the establishment of a permanent endowment to be used to further the cause of education.[42]

Jonathan Allen of Alfred responded with the specific recommendation for setting up a fund of $100,000 without further debate on the topic, a time when "all criticism, fault finding about every one

---

[41] J. W. Ramsey, "The S.D.B. Mission School: Fouke, Arkansas" (25 Aug 1948), in Davis, *History of Mission School at Fouke.*

[42] "Our Bicentennial," *Sabbath Recorder* 27/50 (7 Dec 1871): 2.

and every thing be laid aside. Let no more of it appear in the *Recorder*, or in our public gatherings, till the whole sum be raised."[43] During the early months of 1872, no less than twenty articles appeared in the *Sabbath Recorder* in support of the idea. One writer suggested that $200,000 would be more in keeping with the bicentennial. Others suggested that additional money might be raised for other benevolences.

In June 1872, the Eastern Association formally proposed the establishment of the Memorial Fund and forwarded the proposal to the delegates of other associations and to the session of the General Conference. The plan was unanimously approved, and the fund became a reality. Over half of the goal was reached through individual contributions during the first year, with three-fourths of the contributions designated to specific educational institutions and the rest given to the Bicentennial Fund. Alfred University and the school's Theological Department received the largest endowments, but Milton College, Albion Academy, DeRuyter Institute, Shiloh Academy, and Walworth Academy also benefited. Some of the funds were simply earmarked "to aid young men preparing for the ministry."[44]

Endowments made for the benefit of the Missionary and Tract Societies established the precedent for the Memorial Fund to become an investment agency for much of the denomination. Even though other agencies within the denomination were organized along the societal principle, the Memorial Fund trustees continue to be elected by the General Conference and have always been directly responsible to the conference for administering the funds in direct accord with donors' expressed wishes.

Despite the many challenges faced by Seventh Day Baptists in establishing and maintaining schools, it is clear that education has been central to their mission for generations. These educational pursuits have taken many forms, but all sought to train people who were able to clearly understand the claims of Scripture on their lives as well as making Jesus known in the academy. Growing financial and cultural pressures ultimately severed the explicit connections between Seventh Day Baptists and the institutions they founded that still survive. However, through supporting individual Seventh Day Baptist students,

---

[43] "Memorial Fund," *Sabbath Recorder* 27/52 (21 Dec 1871): 2.
[44] Report of the Memorial Board Treasurer, Conference Minutes, *SDB Yearbook* (1873) 19.

the educational concerns so central to them are still championed. Seventh Day Baptists remain a people committed to educational excellence.

16

GENERAL CONFERENCE SPECIAL INTEREST AGENCIES

The missions, the publishing activities, and the educational work undertaken by Seventh Day Baptists during the nineteenth century was carried out through a societal form of organization in which the General Conference, in its "advisory capacity," provided direction and support. Three other related agencies were organized during the nineteenth century as integral parts of the General Conference: (1) the Woman's Board founded in 1884; (2) the Young People's Committee organized in 1889; and (3) the Historical Committee first established in 1863. The Woman's Board continues to function as a part of the General Conference; the Young People's Committee merged with the Sabbath School Board and the Education Society into the Board of Christian Education in 1940; and the Historical Committee was incorporated in 1916 into the Historical Society.

THE LEADERSHIP ROLE OF WOMEN

From the first Sabbath convert in America to missionaries, ministers, and General Conference presidents, women have played a vital role in Seventh Day Baptist life. Colonial trailblazer Tacy Hubbard "took up the keeping of the Lord's holy 7th day Sabbath the 10 day March 1665" and was followed by her husband and other members of her family. [1] Countless other women exerted tremendous influence as wives and mothers. For example, the Bowen women from Swansea, Massachusetts, played an important role in influencing their husbands in the settlements in South Jersey.[2] Hannah Lanphere Hull played a strong role in the conversion of her husband Elder Richard Hull. She taught him to read and write so that he became a student of the Bible and an effective evangelist and pastor. Four of their sons—Oliver, Varnum, Nathan, and Hamilton—became prominent pastors, while a daughter,

---

[1] Samuel Hubbard, *Register of Mr. Samuel Hubbard* (transcription of excerpts with notes by Isaac Backus), ca. 1775, Isaac Backus Papers, MSS 273, B1, F27, p. 1, Rhode Island Historical Society. See also MS 194x.6, p. 1, Hist. Soc. Lib.

[2] John H. Bonham, "Three Girls of Swansea," *Sabbath Recorder* 108/1 (6 Jan 1930): 28-29.

Martha, also filled the pulpit on occasion.[3] Many women became teachers whose influence on their students is immeasurable in the history of the church and the larger society.

Much of the China mission's success owed to the dedicated work of Lucy Carpenter and Olive Wardner, who had both taught school before accompanying their husbands onto the mission field. It was their correspondence with those in America that sparked much of the interest in foreign missions. The medical work provided by Dr. Ella Swinney, Dr. Rosa Palmborg, Dr. Grace Crandall, Miriam Shaw, and Sarah Becker, along with the educational work of Susie Burdick and the Wests, gave added impetus to womens' roles in missions.

For over a hundred years, Seventh Day Baptists have accepted women for ordination into the gospel ministry. Rev. "Perie" (Experience Randolph) Burdick, who was ordained to the ministry in 1885, was the first of a number to enter the active ministry of Seventh Day Baptist churches. Since 1964 and into the twenty-first century, eight women have served as General Conference presidents; one of these, Doris Fetherston, served as executive secretary from 1956 until 1961.

Seventh Day Baptist women have fulfilled leadership roles in advance of that found in many other churches. Yet, for many years they have been best remembered for their supportive contributions. The familiar term "Ladies Aid Society" was an apt description of womens' perceived function. They provided aid in terms of both moral and financial support for many of the programs that relied on voluntary contributions for their success.

Local Women's Societies

The beginning of the nineteenth century saw the origins of women's societies within the local churches. In 1800, a member of the Massachusetts Missionary Society, Mary Webb, felt a burden for missions. She founded the Boston Female Society for Missionary Purposes, which initially included both Baptists and Congregationalists. Not content to work only within her own state, Mary Webb organized a network of societies and women's missionary groups from Maine to Georgia. Many of these voluntary societies were organized along single purpose lines, some for a local mission, some for a specific foreign mission, although there were others that supported missions in general.

---

[3] "Elder Richard Hull," *Sabbath Recorder* 45/2 (10 Jan 1889): 5-6. See also "William Satterlee," *SDB Memorial* 1/4 (Oct 1852): 170.

William Brackney viewed this organizing principle as "a unique type of denominational advance which brought an integrated system to a voluntary, disintegrated and often competitive church structure."[4]

Seventh Day Baptist women established missionary societies about this same time. The report of the Seventh Day Baptist General Board of Missions in 1826 included contributions from the Brookfield (New York) Female Missionary Society and the Shiloh (New Jersey) Female Mite Society. The circular letter from the General Conference called upon women to "plead with all their souls for the conversion of the apostate race." "If every intelligent, pious and benevolent female would engage, heart and hand, in this excellent work, great would be the success. Their influence would be felt not only in all the churches, but throughout the world."[5]

Other references show the reliance of missions and missionaries on the support women provided through local societies. Women's contributions were not limited to money. Many of the home missionaries reported gifts of handknitted gloves, scarves, and even homespun shirts and other articles of clothing. Women were involved in tract distribution and publishing activities. Much of the impetus for the Education Society came from the women's societies.

During the nineteenth century, women were actively involved in social reform. In the first half of the century, they were strong in their opposition to slavery and worked for its abolition. Throughout the entire century and well into the twentieth, women were at the forefront of the fight against alcohol and tobacco. Through such organizations as the Women's Christian Temperance Union (WCTU), they kept this issue constantly before the public.

Delegate Status of Women

In spite of this behind-the-scenes activity and influence, decades passed before women were included in the official business of either church or denomination. Women were first listed among the delegates to the General Conference at the fifty-second session held in 1866. At that time, ten women's names appeared in the list of official delegates, but only one name was mentioned in the minutes. During that session, Mrs. E. Lyon of the New York City Church was appointed to a committee to take into consideration "the whole subject of aiding the Freedmen,

---

[4] William Henry Brackney, *The Baptists* (New York: Greenwood Press, 1986) 76.
[5] Conference Minutes, *SDB Yearbook* (1826) 7, 9.

especially in the way of teaching."[6] One could hardly picture Ann Lyon as being silent on that subject, for she had spent much of her life working among Brooklyn's poor and on behalf of Civil War soldiers, first at a hospital in Washington and then directly on the battlefield.[7]

The catalyst of that 1866 session to include these women might have been an item presented by the Committee on Resolutions that "Resolved that all the members of a church have an equal right to participate in all business and disciplinary transactions." The names of eight people, including Mrs. E. Lyon, were listed as having addressed the issue.[8] It is possible that after the adoption of this motion, the names of the women who were attending with their husbands were added to the list of delegates, but for the next few years, when delegates were designated by churches, only three or four women were so listed. During the next decade, the list of delegates often included the phrase "and wife" after the husband's name. For close to twenty more years, few women's names were mentioned in connection with appointments to committees or conference discussions.

THE WOMAN'S BOARD IS ORGANIZED

At the 1884 session of the conference, during an informal meeting, the women present asked permission to organize a Woman's Board of the General Conference. The plan presented by Mary C. Bailey of Milton, Wisconsin, called for the General Conference to appoint an Executive Board for the new Women's Board at the same time and manner as other boards were appointed. The new board would include the normal officers plus one vice president from each of the associations embraced in the conference. Its duties would still viewed as supportive rather than creative, with their duty to be "to raise funds for our various denominational enterprises, and to enlist the women of the denomination in these enterprises, in such ways and by such means as may seem to them practical and best, provided they do not involve this Conference in financial responsibility."[9]

---

[6] Conference Minutes, *SDB Yearbook* (1866). Compare pp. 4, 8, 9, 15 of same source.

[7] Corliss Randolph Fitz, *A Century's Progress: An Historical Sketch of the First SDB Church of New York City* (Plainfield NJ: Recorder Press, 1948) 75-76. A chapter titled "Some Outstanding Characters" lists eleven notable participants (in the 1866 session?), four of whom are women. Along with Ann Lyon, the chapter includes Mrs. Henrietta Babcock, Dr. Pheobe Waite, and Miss L. Adele Rogers.

[8] Conference Minutes, *SDB Yearbook* (1866) 4, 9.

[9] Conference Minutes, *SDB Yearbook* (1884) 12-13.

The Woman's Board was appointed with principal officers located in the Alfred, New York, area. The following year, the board's report consisted of rather detailed accounting from each of the associations and churches within them. The Executive Board reported of its progress that "while many have entered heartily, and at once, others have felt disposed to wait and see whether any definite good would be accomplished through it, any results attained which would not be as fully reached without it." Board members also reported that some were opposed to the reporting itself, for it was too much like boasting. They cited the biblical passage that "the left hand should not know what the right hand doeth." Still others felt the report was misleading, for the report did not reveal how much women were really contributing since many gave directly through envelope subscriptions and regular giving to the church.[10]

After two years in Alfred, the board was moved to Milton, for it was recognized that Mary Bailey, Milton resident and the daughter of Rev. James Bailey, was the ruling spirit of the movement. She became the corresponding secretary and spent much of her time and energy during the next few years promoting women's work in the denomination. She died in 1893 at the age of forty-six, but in those few years she set the course for women's continued work in the denomination.

The Woman's Board Serves in Missions and Education

The interest in missions that gave rise to the Woman's Board found added meaning under Mary Bailey's leadership. In 1886, the Woman's Board reported that its goal was to raise a sum sufficient to pay Dr. Ella Swinney's salary. Dr. Swinney's letters revealed how much encouragement the support gave to those serving in China.[11] Dr. Rosa Palmborg, who served in China as a medical missionary for over forty years (1894–1937), came under the influence of Mary Bailey while studying at Milton College. Another of Bailey's missionary friends was Susie Burdick of Alfred, who accepted the call to supervise a girls' school in Shanghai. A carefully defined agreement was worked out between the Missionary Board and the Woman's Board concerning the boards' mutual obligations in sending out missionaries; the former made the appointment and employed Miss Burdick, while the women of the

---

[10] Conference Minutes, *SDB Yearbook* (1885) 10-15.
[11] Report of the Woman's Executive Board, Conference Minutes, *SDB Yearbook* (1886) 8.

denomination, through the Woman's Board, assumed the responsibility for her support.

For forty-three years, the Woman's Board leadership remained in Milton and continued its support of both foreign and home missions. They helped support evangelistic teams including women's quartets and field evangelists. In more recent years, the Summer Christian Service Corps (SCSC) program has been a project that has carried on some of the same work of earlier years. Their commitment to education helped support the Fouke Academy and encouraged young women to seek higher education. During one academic term, sixteen young women whom President Whitford considered among the very best students were assisted by the Woman's Board in attending Milton College.[12]

In 1929, the Woman's Board moved to the Salem, West Virginia, area for a period of twenty-two years. In 1940, it changed its name to Women's Society of the Seventh Day Baptist General Conference, and all women who were members of a recognized Seventh Day Baptist Church were considered, by virtue of that membership, members of the society. The society elected a board of directors annually to guide the organization's work.[13]

In 1951, the society began a rotation plan whereby women from different geographic areas took on the leadership commitment for a ten-year span each. During the 1950s, the Michigan churches at Battle Creek and White Cloud were responsible for leadership. The society moved back to Southern Wisconsin during the 1960s, relocated to Colorado for the 1970s, and then transferred to Southern California for the decade of the 1980s. South Jersey women, centered at Shiloh and Marlboro, served through the closing decade of the twentieth century and passed the mantel on to Florida women in 2000.

YOUNG PEOPLE'S WORK

Theodore L. Gardiner, in a series of *Recorder* articles on student evangelism in the 1870s, wrote that much of the denomination's early youth work was volunteer work that had never been reported to any denominational board and thus was never recorded.[14] There was only an occasional mention of the spiritual life of young people and almost

---

[12] Emma Tefft Platts, "The Woman's Board," *Seventh Day Baptists in Europe and America*, 3 vols., ed. C. F. Randolph (Plainfield NJ: SDB General Conference, 1910) 1:255.

[13] Conference Minutes, *SDB Yearbook* (1940) 57

[14] Theodore L. Gardiner, "Student Evangelism in the Early Seventies," *Sabbath Recorder* 56/10 (5 Mar 1900): 152.

nothing of their activities. Yet, during the 1870s and extending through the next few decades, a spiritual revival among young people coincided with one of the most active periods in denominational history.

Student evangelistic work grew out of a revival among the students at Alfred University in 1868. An outpouring of the Spirit broke out in student meetings held in the "bell room" and inspired spontaneous prayer meetings often held in dormitory rooms. President Jonathan Allen often met with the students and channeled their religious fervor into evangelistic work as they visited neighboring communities with the gospel. This revival signaled the beginning of the evangelistic quartet movement among both men and women, which accounted for the establishment of a number of churches.

The Excel Band

One of the first organizations within the denomination specifically intended for young people was founded in 1882 by George H. Babcock, who is best known for philanthropic works made possible through endowments started by him and held by the Memorial Board. While superintendent of the Sabbath school at Plainfield, New Jersey, he established the Excel Band for youth as a part of the sabbath School. The first issue of *Our Sabbath Visitor* for March 1882 called the Excel Band "a Temperance Society, an Anti-Vulgarity Society, an Anti-Tobacco Society, an Anti-Swearing Society, a Society for the Prevention of Cruelty to Animals, a Helping-Hand Society, a Truth-Telling Society and a Mutual Aid Society, all in one organization."[15] The article gave encouragement for the establishment of similar "bands" throughout the denomination. Subsequent columns carried news of these groups for the next three years. The last column appeared on 1 October 1885.

Christian Endeavor

The Excel Band was replaced in many churches by the popular interdenominational organization known as the Young People's Society of Christian Endeavor. CE, as it was often called, was founded in a Congregational Church in Portland, Maine, by Francis Clark in 1881. The society's purpose was to train young people in the duties of church membership and the activities of a Christian life. Its principles included an open confession of Christ, individual responsibility, the cultivation of

---

[15] "The Excel Band," *Our Sabbath Visitor* 1/1 (2 Mar 1882): 3.

private devotional life, loyalty to the local church, and fellowship with its people.[16]

The first Seventh Day Baptist Youth Rally on record was held in Plainfield, New Jersey, in 1892; its organizers planned the event to coincide with the International Convention of the Young People's Society of Christian Endeavor in nearby New York City, which attracted a number of denominational delegates.[17] Some questions were raised by Seventh Day Baptists at the time concerning their relationship with the Christian Endeavor Union, for Seventh Day Baptists were not recognized on the official program. Dr. A. H. Lewis called this to the attention of the Christian Endeavor's founder-president, Dr. Clark, and Clark responded that the omission was intentional. The reasons Clark gave were that Seventh Day Baptists had refused to sign the petition to have the World's Fair closed on Sunday, and that their position on the question of the Sabbath was directly opposed to the society's efforts to promote better Sunday observance. It was decided that participating in the Union was important enough to overlook the intentional omission, and Christian Endeavor became the recognized form of organization for young people throughout the denomination.[18]

The report of the Sabbath School Board in 1885 indicated an increasing interest in missions work among young people.[19] At the General Conference in 1887, O. U. Whitford led a discussion on the topic "Our young people—how train them in religious and denominational work."[20] The following year, Whitford presented a paper on the CE movement. It was at this time that sessions of conference were changed from September to August so as not to conflict with the school calendar and allow young people to attend.[21]

For many young people, Christian Endeavor, with its many unions on local, district, state, national, and international levels, provided areas of service and fellowship not available within a denomination so widely

---

[16] "Father Endeavor Clark," *Sabbath Recorder* 102/24 (13 Jun 1927): 753-55. See also Agnes Babcock, "The Young People's Permanent Committee," *SDBs in Europe and America*, 1:262-63.

[17] Report of the Young People's Permanent Committee, Appendix I, Conference Minutes, *SDB Yearbook* (1892) 49-50.

[18] A. H. Lewis, *Sabbath Recorder* 48/46 (17 Nov 1892): 732-33. See also Agnes Babcock, "The Young People's Permanent Committee," *SDBs in Europe and America*, 1:265.

[19] Report of Sabbath School Board, Conference Minutes, *SDB Yearbook* (1885) 8.

[20] Conference Minutes, *SDB Yearbook* (1887) 17.

[21] Agnes Babcock, "The Young People's Permanent Committee," *SDBs in Europe and America*, 1:265.

scattered as the Seventh Day Baptists. In addition, the organization offered societies adapted to all ages and grade levels, from juniors to adults. These CE groups continued among Seventh Day Baptists well into the twentieth century and provided an identity for young people that earlier generations lacked. It provided them with experience in the work of societies that led to greater participation in the denomination. For about forty years (1892–1932), a regular feature in the *Recorder* was the Christian Endeavor page.

The Young People's Board

At the 1888 General Conference session, a resolution was brought to the floor by a committee "appointed by the young people of the Conference in mass-meeting assembled." The young people stated that the time had come for "united action by the young people of the denomination in denominational work." They asked that the General Conference appoint a committee to develop a method for accomplishing that end.[22] The following year, that committee reported its plan to establish the Young People's Board, initially called the Permanent Committee on Young People's Work. The organization was set up on an associational level with three members from one association to serve as officers and one member-at-large to represent each of the other associations. The committee requested that a time be set apart during sessions of the General Conference so that each association could discuss subjects concerning young people's work in the churches and denomination.[23] The ages of the first officers ranged from twenty for the secretary to twenty-nine for the president and from twenty-three to thirty-eight for the associational secretaries. It appears that at this time many leaders felt that to effectively work with youth, maturity and experience were more important than being a teenager.

The first report of the Young People's Permanent Committee revealed the scope of its members' work, which ranged from supporting Susie Burdick on the mission field in China to such evangelistic work as the establishment of CE groups in the churches on the home field. One great need committee members expressed was to find a special work that would provide a common ground on which young people could unite. Suggestions included assistance to small churches, support of home field

---

[22] Conference Minutes, *SDB Yearbook* (1888) 27-28.
[23] Report of the Young People's Committee, Conference Minutes, *SDB Yearbook* (1889) 7.

missionaries, and distribution of tracts. Their final statement revealed their commitment to the denomination: "May we not also make the regular work of the denomination and of our churches *our own*, and strive earnestly to do all in our power along these lines that the coming year may be filled up with loyal endeavor among our young people for Christ and the church."[24]

In 1891, the report to the General Conference showed continued growth with forty-five Young People's Societies reporting an aggregate membership of 2,000, an average attendance at prayer meetings of 27, and 161 conversions. Their major project for the year was the support of Rev. J. L. Huffman as a missionary evangelist in the Southeastern Association. Huffman was employed by the Missionary Society, which paid his travel and expenses, while the Young People's Board assumed responsibility for his salary. The board proposed similar work for another year, possibly in underwriting something that the Tract Board might designate, such as tract depository work in New York and Chicago through contributions, distribution, and the securing of mailing lists.[25]

In 1892, the officers of the Young People's Permanent Committee were appointed from the Northwestern Association centered at Milton, Wisconsin. The emphasis shifted from the support of one missionary evangelist in the field to the support of student evangelistic teams during vacation periods. In 1892, six students at Morgan Park Seminary in Illinois spent their summer vacation performing evangelistic work. Each of those six—L. C. Randolph, George B. Shaw, T. J. Van Horn, Frank Peterson, D. B. Coon, and W. D. Burdick—was later ordained and gave years of devoted leadership to the denomination. This evangelistic team was underwritten by a private individual rather than receiving the direct support of the Young People's Committee, but it provided a pattern for further dedicated service among the denomination's young people. The following year, fifteen young people were sent out as evangelists and more could have been sent if money had been available. This work was later taken up by the Missionary Board, so that by 1900, nine quartets

---

[24] Report of the Young People's Permanent Committee, Appendix H, Conference Minutes, *SDB Yearbook* (1890) 50-51; emphasis original.

[25] Report of the Young People's Permanent Committee, Appendix I, Conference Minutes, *SDB Yearbook* (1891) 64-66.

composed of students from Alfred University and Milton and Salem Colleges were sent out to minister.[26]

In 1894, an added project in support of missions pledged to provide half of the salary for Dr. Rosa Palmborg in China. Much effort went into the organization of Junior CE Societies among the churches during this period. The middle of the decade of the 1890s showed the largest total membership at about 2,577, with nearly 2,000 members listed as active in the senior societies and 263 in the junior division. Over 1,000 of this total were in the Northwestern Association, with the 114 members at Milton the largest single society.[27]

Some of the membership statistics may include those whose youth status could be questioned. Rev. H. C. Van Horn is quoted as having stated that one of the problems with the Christian Endeavor Societies of his time was "the presence of too many bald heads." Some who grew up in CE did not let go of their leadership role when they grew older. As a consequence, they deprived the younger members of a chance to build a society with which they could closely relate.[28] On the other hand, in many smaller churches, the only way that a CE could exist was to include older members. In an age that stressed intergenerational activities, the wide range of ages represented in the CE had some advantages; for one thing, the young learned from the old.

In 1904, the name Young People's Board had replaced the name Permanent Committee, but the organization's work continued in similar fashion. It continued the support of foreign missions, took an active role in the support of Fouke Academy, and in time added such other programs as summer youth camps. In 1940, the Young People's Board merged with the Education Society and the Sabbath School Board to form the Board of Christian Education.

THE HISTORICAL SOCIETY

One of the first official acts of the General Conference was to encourage the publication in 1811 of Henry Clarke's book *A History of the Sabbatarians or Seventh day Baptists in America*. During the next fifty years records were kept by the local churches and the General Conference, but there was little attempt to organize them or communicate their history in

---

[26] Babcock, "Young People's Permanent Committee," *SDBs in Europe and America*, 1:266-68.

[27] Young People's Permanent Committee Report, Conference Minutes, *SDB Yearbook* (1895) 40-41.

[28] Heard from H. C. Van Horn, unknown date and place.

any meaningful way. In 1863, the General Conference took two particular actions to establish its Historical Board. The first of these commissioned a written history of the General Conference. The second established a standing committee dedicated to historical matters.

James Bailey Publishes a Conference History

The Committee on Essays in 1863 asked James Bailey to prepare and present a history of the General Conference from its beginning to the present time.[29] Bailey began collecting materials and discovered, between forgotten writings and memories, much previously unpublished information. He recorded, "I commenced arranging and writing. A desire to rescue from forgetfulness much that had almost passed away, led me on till the work had assumed unpremeditated dimensions."[30] The General Conference encouraged the publication of this history but postponed action for a time since "the expense of printing the essay was about twice as much as before the war." After a short delay, they recommended that Elder Bailey have it published and that members of the churches buy copies.

Historical Board Established

The second action of the 1863 conference was the resolution that "a committee of five be appointed to take into consideration the propriety of organizing a Seventh Day Baptist Historical Society." That committee recommended the appointment of a Historical Board of four persons, one from each association. Arrangements were made with Alfred University for the housing and care of all documents collected. Later, members of Alfred's Theological Department faculty comprised the board.[31]

In 1866, the board reported holdings that became the foundation of the Historical Society's collection. The most significant documents listed were:

(1) A Cranmer's New Testament printed in 1549. (This is believed to be the testament hidden by Samuel Hubbard's grandfather "in

---

[29] Conference Minutes, *SDB Yearbook* (1863) 6.

[30] James Bailey, preface, *History of the Seventh-day Baptist General Conference: From Its Origin, September, 1802, to Its Fifty-third Session, September, 1865*, ed. Bailey (Toledo OH: S. Bailey & Co., 1866) iii-iv.

[31] Conference Minutes, *SDB Yearbook* (1865) 8.

the bed straw during the reign of Queen Mary lest it be burned."
It is the same testament that was stolen from the Historical
Society museum in Plainfield, New Jersey, in 1981 and returned
for a $500 ransom);

(2) A nearly complete set of the *Protestant Sentinel*, the *Seventh Day
Baptist Register*, and the *Sabbath Recorder*;

(3) Manuscript minutes of General Conference sessions for the years
1803 to 1806 and a bound copy of the minutes from 1808 to 1838;

(4) Histories of the Piscataway and Plainfield (New Jersey)
churches;

(5) Bailey's *History of General Conference*; and

(6) Miscellaneous collection of sermons, letters, journals, abstracts,
and essays running back 150 years from both England and the
United States.[32]

Reports of the Committee on Denominational History regularly
contained the plea for collection and preservation of historic material.
The committee requested more biographical information, particularly
concerning deceased pastors and other leaders, and records or
reminiscences from some of the older pastors. Some of these they
intended to include in the *Seventh Day Baptist Quarterly*, which was
designed for that purpose. Each church was asked to take advantage of
anniversaries to present its history.

During the next decade, the pages of the *Sabbath Recorder* were used
to communicate history and to give special mention of the importance of
the *Jubilee Papers*, a publication of the Missionary Society in 1892 that
contained articles on subjects of historical interest to the denomination.
A historical exhibit at the Chicago World's Fair was also given at the
direction of the committee in 1893.

Seventh Day Baptists in Europe and America

In 1881, the Committee on Denominational History reported that "a
manifest need of the denomination is a concise but complete history of
its rise, progress, and present condition."[33] This need was expressed in
subsequent reports until, in 1897, the committee was able to report that a
popular history was being prepared by President Wm. C. Whitford of

---

[32] Conference Minutes, *SDB Yearbook* (1866) 6-7.
[33] Report of the Committee on Denominational History, Conference Minutes, *SDB Yearbook* (1881) 13-14.

Milton College, who also served as the committee's chairman. Over the course of four years, progress reports were made indicating that it was taking longer than anticipated due to the amount of research needed and other pressing duties. Upon Chairman Whitford's death in 1902, the committee reported that "he had collected much data and valuable material concerning Seventh Day Baptists, but much of it would be difficult for another to fully use." They recommended that "someone well acquainted with Seventh Day Baptist history be found to carry on the work left incomplete."[34]

About this time, interest in the publication of historical material shifted to the General Conference's centennial celebration. A special committee was appointed to arrange for the 100th anniversary celebration during sessions at Hopkinton, Rhode Island, in 1902. That committee reported that a series of historical papers was to be given by a variety of authors and later bound for distribution. These papers resulted in the 1910 publication of the massive 2-volume, 1,500-page work titled *Seventh Day Baptists in Europe and America*, edited by Corliss F. Randolph. The third volume, which covered the years 1900 to 1955, was written by Historian Albert N. Rogers and published in 1972 by the Historical Society.

Sources of Information and Ideas

The Committee on Denominational History did not confine its interests and activities to the past. It made several recommendations to the General Conference that grew out of its historical perspective. For example, in 1910 the committee became aware that, according to New Jersey law, the property of any Baptist church in the state that closed its doors would be placed under the control of the General Baptist Missionary Society. Action was taken to change that law so that property would instead go to the Seventh Day Baptist Missionary Society. This investigation was called to the attention of churches in other states that similarly might face loss of property.[35] It has continued to be a function of the Historical Society to bring before the people ideas that have relevance for the present and the future.

---

[34] Report of the Committee on Denominational History, Conference Minutes, *SDB Yearbook* (1902) 29.

[35] Report of the Committee on Denominational History, Conference Minutes, *SDB Yearbook* (1910) 29ff.

The Historical Society Incorporates

From its beginning in about 1863 until 1916, the Committee on Denominational History was a part of the General Conference. Its members were appointed by and answered to the conference. It relied almost completely on volunteers to acquire and preserve historic materials. The General Conference made few, if any, appropriations to support the committee's work.

Around 1916, a valuable collection of manuscripts, books, and artifacts known as the Sachse Ephrata Collection became available to the Historical Committee. Over a period of thirty years, Dr. Julius F. Sachse of Philadelphia had devoted much of his time researching and writing about the German Pietistic movement in Pennsylvania, including the cloisters of German Seventh Day Baptists at Ephrata. Sachse expressed the wish that his collection be kept intact and remain in the possession of Seventh Day Baptists. He even contributed one-third of the cost for this collection, which was valued at many times the $1,500 asking price. In order for the society to purchase and gain clear title of the collection, it was necessary for the Historical Committee to incorporate in the State of New Jersey. On 28 June 1916, a charter was granted to the Seventh Day Baptist Historical Society.[36]

The organization of this Historical Society as a separate corporation changed its relationship to the General Conference, but not its work or service to the denomination. Many members of the Committee on Denominational History were active in the new Society. The chairman of the committee, Corliss F. Randolph, became president of the Historical Society, a post he held from 1916 to 1954. The Committee on Denominational History continued to be a part of the General Conference and served as the agency through which the society made its report to conference until 1929.

The new Society established its office, museum, and library in the denominational building in Plainfield, New Jersey, eventually moving most of its holdings from Alfred. Under Randolph's leadership, the collection greatly expanded. In 1982, when the General Conference offices were moved to Janesville, Wisconsin, the Historical Society was incorporated in that state, and its library, archives, and offices were moved to the new Seventh Day Baptist Center. At that time, most of the Sachse Ephrata collection was placed on permanent loan with the

---

[36] Conference Minutes, *SDB Yearbook* (1917) 34-36.

Pennsylvania Historical Commission so that it could be housed in the Sate Archives in Harrisburg, where it could be kept safe and made accessible to those researching history in the Ephrata area.

17

A TIME FOR CHOOSING DIRECTIONS

For Seventh Day Baptists, the nineteenth century may not have been a period marked by a wandering in the wilderness, but it most certainly was a period of development as a people. With great expectations, the denomination now faced uncharted areas of thought and action that were as challenging as the land of Canaan was to Joshua.

The same basic choices offered by Joshua were being presented to many Christians at the close of the nineteenth century. The twenty-fourth chapter of Joshua recalled the history of God's dealings with the people, beginning with the heritage of Abraham, Isaac, and Jacob and ending with their present opportunity to "choose this day whom you will serve." The people of the nineteenth century were not tempted to serve any pagan gods of their forefathers, but they were tempted to prefer the comfortable security of a known past as opposed to the uncertainty of an unknown future. They also faced the temptation for an easy accommodation to the "gods of the Amorites in whose land you dwell," that is, to a weakening of faith by accepting the secularism of the society around them.

THE FRONTIER EXPANSION

A previous work by this writer, *A Free People in Search of A Free Land*, documents the growth of Seventh Day Baptists in America to their highest numerical strength at the very time the frontiers of settlement were closing. In 1893, American historian Frederick Jackson Turner advanced his "frontier thesis" as a means of explaining the distinctive features of American civilization. The existence of an area of free land and the westward migration, with its attendant adaptation to the new environment and the sloughing off of "cultural baggage," characterized much of the nineteenth century. The US Census of 1890 revealed that there were no habitable regions with less than two to six persons per square mile. This, by Turner's definition, marked the closing of the frontier.[1]

---

[1] Frederick Jackson Turner, *The Frontier in American History* (1920; repr., New York: Holt, 1947).

A student of Turner, Ray Allen Billington, described the frontier as being both a place and a process. The low man-to-land ratio and the wealth of untapped resources gave the opportunity for individuals to advance themselves economically and socially. The frontier was a process through which individuals and their institutions were altered by contact with a social environment that provided unique opportunities for self-advancement.[2]

Seventh Day Baptists were directly affected by both the geographic movements and the social processes of this frontier. From about 1,200 members spread across 8 churches in 4 Atlantic states at the beginning of the nineteenth century, Seventh Day Baptists saw an increase to 9,096 members in 116 churches located in 23 states.[3] In addition, Seventh Day Baptists established over 80 other churches during the century that did not last into the twentieth century. Many of these were born and died as the direct result of geographic migrations into the frontier as people sought the economic value of cheap land and the social value of living in a colony where others were also keeping the Sabbath.

The frontier affected the social and religious processes of the denomination. The frontier stimulated mission activity. The expansion brought the realization that Christ's "Great Commission" to "go and make disciples, to baptize, and to teach the observance of his commandments" involved the Seventh Day Baptists in missions that could best be done cooperatively. The General Conference itself was organized for this purpose, and local, regional, and denominational societies formed to involve the people in missions. During the first half of the century, traveling ministers were sent out to visit scattered families and churches. Similar work was carried out in the latter half of the century by home missionaries and quartets of young people.

In addition, there were societies for specific missions, such as the mission to the Jews. The China mission began as a preaching mission but expanded to include medical service and educational and vocational training. The centennial report of the General Conference in 1902 listed churches in China, England, Germany, Denmark, Holland, the Gold Coast, and Nyasaland (now Malawi).

The need for communication expanded greatly as the frontier widened. The early periodicals—the *Missionary Magazine*, the *Protestant*

---

[2] Ray Allen Billington, *The American Frontier Thesis: Attack and Defense* (Washington DC: American Historical Association, 1971) 19.

[3] Statistics appended to Conference Minutes, *SDB Yearbook* (1902) no page.

Sentinel, and the *Sabbath Recorder*—began as house organs but expanded to become family newspapers and evangelical tracts to reach the unchurched. During the final quarter of the century, there was a shift toward Sabbath Reform in the publication effort, whereby some periodicals were written for intellectuals while others were written for use in the home.

Educational efforts were likewise affected by the frontier, where the earliest schools were established to provide what later became the responsibility of the state. Academies and colleges were established so that Seventh Day Baptist young people would have the advantages of higher education. Many of these efforts were related to the desire for a trained ministry. As a result of efforts in missions, communications, and education, roles for both women and young people was clarified.

Thus, by the close of the nineteenth century, there existed a people with a distinct mission who were educated beyond the average, who envisioned a purpose, and who looked with anticipation to the future. Yet the conditions of the time were rapidly changing. The possibility of moving west, which Turner called a safety valve to relieve the pressures of urbanization, no longer existed. So these people were forced to find other ways to fulfill their perceived mission.

The scientific and industrial ages, which had direct bearing on the thought and actions of all people, posed a particular challenge to Seventh Day Baptists due to increased urbanization and cultural change. Thus, in the 1890 session of the General Conference, the conference president appointed a committee to arrange for a denominational council "to consider and report upon all important questions pertaining to our present and future work, and our denominational status and duty."[4] This council met in Chicago in October of that year.

THE CHICAGO COUNCIL

Two delegates from each church were invited to the Chicago Council. In addition, four delegates from the General Conference (two at large and one each from the Woman's Board and the Young People's Committee), two from each of the three societies (Missionary, Tract, and Education), and two from the Memorial Board were invited to attend.

---

[4] Conference Minutes, *SDB Yearbook* (1890) 8.

Close to 100 official delegates were listed in attendance, about half of them ministers. Only two women were listed as official delegates.[5]

Fourteen committees were appointed to evaluate different aspects of denominational life ranging from the work of the societies and agencies to Sabbath Reform and questions of denominational polity. From the perspective of history, this council prompted four significant results, although they were not fully realized at the time.

A Creative Process

First, the very process of meeting was important, for it brought together the key denominational leaders in what later generations might call a "think tank" or "brain trust." Management by objective was a method more commonly used in industry than in the churches of that era. The annual sessions of the General Conference did not allow time nor the balanced representation needed for creative planning.

Review and Projection of Programs

Second, the council provided a more objective assessment of the work of the societies. For example, the Committee on Missionary Interests affirmed the work of foreign missions in China but urged greater efforts in home mission fields, particularly in the American West and South. In noting the shift of population in these directions, the committee concluded that these "newer parts of the country are places above all other places for planting seeds, laying foundations, shaping thought, fixing beliefs and determining the future direction of many and great moral forces."[6] The rural frontier mentality continued to dominate much of the committee's thinking. Only in passing was urbanization considered with the question, "If there be truth in the saying that God made the country, but man made the city, why may not even we have a hand in winning the cities also for God?"[7]

The Committee on Publishing Interests identified the target areas for each of the periodicals and noted that the content was modified by whether it was (1) financially self-supporting or (2) supported largely by contributions from the people of the denomination. For example, the committee asserted that the *Sabbath Recorder* must be readable and

---

[5] *Proceedings of the Seventh-Day Baptist Council, Held at Chicago, Ill., Oct. 22–29, 1890* (N.p.: n.d.) 19-21.

[6] *Proceedings of the SDB Council, Chicago*, 58.

[7] Ibid., 57.

attractive and have value as a religious newspaper rather than just a denominational paper. It should appeal to those "not particularly alive to our peculiar denominational interests" so that they would be willing to pay for it.[8]

The Committee on Education reaffirmed the commitment to higher education as essential for the age, particularly among future ministers "who are prepared, by thorough and liberal culture, to stand on the highest planes of intellectual and scholastic attainments as well as by deep convictions and spiritual training in profound sympathy with our denominational life and work." Committee members were persuaded that the best places for young people to get this preparation was within denominational schools, and urged the conference and its constituent members to support these schools.[9]

The Committee on the Woman's Board reflected the attitude of the times, making little recommendation beyond the committee's traditional role of advancing the interests of the Missionary and Tract Societies.[10] The Committee on Young People's Work recognized that the future of the denomination would soon rest with them. They placed high priority on the promotion of personal growth and urged support of missions and evangelism through churches and denominational agencies. They reported that it was "advisable for our young people to unite in the support of some missionary enterprise which they could call their own," and suggested that a young man be employed by the Missionary Board, supported by the youth, and placed on the home field in associations and local societies unifying them in denominational work.[11]

Church and Denominational Polity

Third, the Committee on Church and Denominational Polity faced the continuing dilemma that existed between the societal and associational principles of organization and urged that each of the societies enter into closer relations with the General Conference by establishing two classes of membership: (1) life members or others who contribute directly, and (2) those who are members because of membership in a church of the General Conference.

---

[8] Ibid., 62-64.
[9] Ibid., 64-65.
[10] Ibid., 66.
[11] Ibid., 66-68.

This committee also recommended that: (1) ordination of ministers be a responsibility of the association; (2) unworthy ministers be deposed by an authority similar to that by which they were ordained; (3) the Bible and Exposé of Faith as adopted by the General Conference be the basis for examination for ordination; (4) official recognition be extended to ministers coming from other denominations by an authority like that by which we ordain or depose ministers; (5) pastors be called for an indefinite period rather than on a year-to-year basis; and (6) the office of deacon be exalted and made more prominent and efficient in the spiritual culture and government of local churches.[12]

Sabbath Reform and Propagation

An underlying consideration of the Chicago Council was Sabbath Reform and promotion. A. H. Lewis, who had proposed the council, partially to address this need, had a deep conviction that he later revealed in his book *Swift Decadence of Sunday. What Next?*[13] The Committee on Sabbath Reform recognized that the Sunday of the Puritans was fast disappearing and was not likely to be reestablished in the culture of the times, making the passing of Sunday laws ineffective. The solution to no-Sabbathism, they believed, was the observance of the Sabbath, which was commanded by God. "We have a great work before us and this work will not be done unless it be done by Sabbath-observers." They cautioned that if Christian people in general could not be brought to the observance of the seventh-day Sabbath, then the coming generations of the denomination's own people would be swept away in the "overwhelming tide of no-Sabbathism, so that the work of saving our own people to the Sabbath largely depends upon success in bringing other Christians to its observance."[14]

Summary Report

The voluntary nature of the Chicago Council precluded any concrete action or program. It had no authority or control over resources. Its role was strictly advisory. Yet, it did focus attention on both the strengths and the weaknesses of the denomination. The cautious optimism of its reports was based on a view of the past and a hope for

---

[12] Ibid., 54-55.

[13] Compare Abram Herbert Lewis, *Swift Decadence of Sunday; What Next?* (Plainfield NJ: American Sabbath Tract Society, 1899).

[14] *Proceedings of the SDB Council, Chicago*, 60-61.

the future. The report of the Committee on Our Denominational Future called for continuing faith and unity, overcoming the present indifference and disloyalty of church members, and remaining a progressive people. The report cautioned against any expectation of a large rush of incoming members and urged patience in the anticipation of final success. The committee expressed the consciousness that Seventh Day Baptists were on the Lord's side, that one plants and another waters but God gives the increase; that the Sabbath was supported by biblical truth; and that God always blesses his truth and its supporters. It concluded its report with the statement, "Our people must not lose faith, else God will honor others with his final triumph."[15]

This council may not have done all that some had hoped it would do, but it was followed by one of the most productive periods in the denomination's history. In a sense it forced many people to make the decision Joshua put to the children of Israel: "Choose ye this day whom ye shall serve."

---

[15] Ibid., 51-52.

PART V: SEVENTH DAY BAPTISTS IN 20TH CENTURY

PART V TIMELINE:

Date/ Lifespan	Event / Person
1890	Chicago Council
1892	*Jubilee Papers*
1898	Nyasaland (Malawi) Africa mission
1898	Gold Coast of Africa mission
1899	Sabbath Evangelizing & Industrial Association
1900	A.H. Lewis' *Letters to Young Preachers*
1900	Ecumenical Conference on Foreign Missions
1901-1933	A.E. Main is dean of Alfred School of Theology, NY
1902	Centennial of General Conference
1905	Baptist World Alliance formed
1905	SDB Advisory Board formed
1906	South African witness begins
1907	Rauschenbusch's *Christianity and the Social Crisis*
1908	Federal Council of Churches founded
1909	SDB General Conference's Executive Committee enlarged
1910	*Seventh Day Baptists in Europe & America*
1910	*Spiritual Sabbathism*
1914-1918	World War I
1914	Committee on Denominational Activity
1915	Guyana mission
1915	Forward Movement begins
1916	SDB Historical Society formed
1916	Commission of SDB General Conference formed
1917	U.S. enters World War I
1919	New Forward Movement begins
1920	SDB Denominational Budget
1920	SDB Publishing House project begins in Plainfield, NJ
1923	Baptist Bible Union

1923	SDBs in Jamaica
1924	Onward Movement begins
1925	*State of Tennessee v. Scopes*
1925	SDB Bible Defense League formed
1925-1929	*The Exponent*
1927	World Conference on Faith and Order, Lausanne, Switzerland
1929	"Black Friday" begins the "Great Depression"
1929-1931	"The Fundamentalist Page" published in *The Sabbath Recorder*
1929	Completion of SDB Denominational Building in Plainfield, NJ
1932	SDBs in Germany
1933-1952	A.J.C. Bond is Dean of Alfred School of Theology, NY
1935	SDB General Conference join Baptist World Alliance
1937	SDB *Statement of Belief*
1938	Utrecht Conference (drafts constitution for World Council of Churches)
1938	SDB General Conference incorporates
1939-1945	World War II
1940	SDB Board of Christian Education formed
1940	SDBs in New Zealand
1940	"Five-Year Plan"
1941	United States enters World War II
1945	Second Century Fund
1947	Nyasaland (Malawi) mission reestablished
1948	1st Assembly of the World Council of Churches, Amsterdam, The Netherlands
1950	National Council of Churches formed
1950	China closed to Western Missions/ close of SDB missions in China
1950	SDBs in Brazil and India
1952-1963	Albert Rogers is Dean of Alfred School of Theology

1953-1955	A. Burdett Crofoot is Executive Secretary of General Conference
1954	*Brown v. Board of Education of Topeka*
1956-1961	Doris Fetherston is Executive Secretary of General Conference
1956	Our World Mission
1959-1964	Program for Advance
1961-1964	Harley Bond is Executive Secretary of General Conference
1961	US Supreme Court upholds Sunday Laws
1962	SDBs in Poland
1963	SDB General Conference's Christian Social Action Committee formed
1963	Alfred School of Theology closes
1963	SDBs join Baptist Joint Committee on Public Affairs (now Baptist Joint Committee for Religious Liberty)
1964	Civil Rights Act
1964	Summer Christian Service Corps (SCSC) program begins
1965	SDBs in Burma
1965-1975	Alton Wheeler is Executive Secretary of the General Conference
1965	SDB World Federation is founded
1965	Study of SDB General Conference Structure commissioned
1965	Facing Frontiers with Faith
1965	SDBs in Mexico
1966	SDB General Conference joins North American Baptist Fellowship (NABF)
1973	SDB General Conference withdraws from National Council of Churches
1973	Abortion legalized
1975	SDBs in Australia and Philippines
1975-1981	K. Duane Hurley is Executive Secretary of the General Conference

1975	Commitment to Growth
1976	SDB General Conference withdraws from World Council of Churches
1976	Harold Lindsell's article "Consider the Case for Quiet Saturdays" is published in *Christianity Today*
1978	General Council is instituted
1980	Decade of Discipleship
1981-1990	Dale Thorngate is Executive Secretary of the General Conference
1981-1982	SDB General Conference offices move to SDB Center in Janesville, WI
1987	New SDB *Statement of Belief*
1990	MORE 2000
1990-2000	Calvin Babcock is acting Executive Secretary and General Services Administrator for the General Conference
2000-2005	Lewis H. V. May is Executive Secretary of the General Conference
2005-	Robert A. Appel is Executive Secretary of the General Conference
2009	SDBs in Burundi, Kenya, and Zambia

18

ENTERING THE NEW CENTURY

In 1900 A. H. Lewis wrote *Letters to Young Preachers,* which concluded with a prophetic look into the first fifty years of the coming century. He predicted four characteristics of the first half century that later would prove remarkably true.

First, he saw the period as being dominated by an intensely commercial and world-loving spirit. He recognized the impact of plans to build a canal linking the Atlantic Ocean with the Pacific. He envisioned that the new frontier of Alaska and other acquired territories would beckon young men of a new generation; that changes in Japan, Russia, and China would affect this commercial age; and that Africa would provide rich fields of commercial enterprise. In this context, Lewis advised young preachers that many of these influences would "turn men away from religious living and endanger some of the best interests of society and the church."[1]

Second, Lewis foresaw that the political life of the age would involve ethics. Some of the great reforms of nineteenth-century government, he predicted, would be intensified and "the church through its leaders must take a more prominent place than before in defending the right, condemning the wrong, pleading the cause of the weak, and turning aside evil influences which thrive in all great political contests."[2]

Third, Lewis noted that in a scientific age, periods of great intellectual activity were likely to be unfavorable to the growth of spiritual religion. He saw danger in the scientific investigation that threatened the conservative elements of religion. To the young theologians he advised that in such a period they "must be conservative without bigotry, broad-minded without recklessness, and able to save men from that indifference to religion that comes from intellectual greatness and scientific research." He foresaw changes from which they would "learn that it is a part of God's plan that much which is traditional in religious life or imperfect in our understanding of the plans and purposes of God, must yield to the unfolding of greater knowledge in

---

[1] Abram Herbert Lewis, *Letters to Young Preachers and Their Hearers* (Plainfield NJ: American Sabbath Tract Society, 1900) 222.
[2] Ibid., 223.

the on-going history of the world." Therefore, these young preachers "must be well-informed not only in matters pertaining to religion, but in matters touching all these practical questions."[3]

The fourth characteristic of the twentieth century that greatly concerned Lewis was the "Sabbathless age" that had come on society. The attitude of much of the church to Puritan Sunday had caused a drifting away from any concern over sacred time. He saw a particular threat to Seventh Day Baptists in the attitudes of those who might acknowledge the spiritual bravery of Sabbathkeepers in trying to stem the tide of secularism, but who would pity their folly and laugh at what others called their impracticability. This threat could be met only by attaining larger views concerning the meaning of the Sabbath and deeper convictions of its importance than previous generations had held. "You cannot succeed in the next century as Seventh-day Baptists without giving careful and constant attention to the reason why you are such. When the world says it is folly to be a Seventh-day Baptist you must be able to show that it is wisdom."[4]

Each of these characteristics Lewis observed had its effect on Seventh Day Baptists throughout the twentieth century. The remainder of this volume is dedicated to exploring these effects.

The *commercial spirit* of the age is seen in the continuing attempt to apply principles from the business world to the denomination's organization (that is, the corporate entity's organizational traits), finances, and structure (that is, the relationships between the constituent entities that compose the conference with the conference as a corporate entity).

The *world-loving* spirit caused a shift from colonialism in the secular world and a parallel shift toward indigenous or self-sustaining missions. The ultimate expression of this spirit was the formation of the World Federation of Seventh Day Baptist Conferences.

The *political life* of the age, which brought the vote to women, also brought the realization that the common people could and should take more active roles in affairs of government. The application of the social gospel carried implications that at times caused serious differences over the relationship between the individual and the corporate responsibilities of Christians and their churches.

---

[3] Ibid., 224.
[4] Ibid., 226.

The *scientific age* stimulated deep theological struggles that threatened to divide the denomination. This division was seen most sharply in the fundamentalist-modernist debate that affected biblical interpretation, support of schools, and training of ministers.

The *Sabbathless age* continued to bring both problems and opportunities to later generations. The close identification of the Sabbath with rural lifestyle during the first half of the century delayed the denomination from coming to grips with a rapidly expanding urban population.

It is to some of these specific areas that attention is now turned. The following chapter will illustrate the choices Seventh Day Baptists made during the twentieth century and how these decision shaped the modern denomination.

19

DENOMINATIONAL ORGANIZATION
IN A COMMERCIAL AGE

At the turn of the century, several of the denomination's leading men were also leaders in business and industry. Men such as George Babcock, Charles Potter, J. F. Hubbard, and Charles Chipman were well-known and highly respected persons in metropolitan New York's business, industry, and public service sectors. Successful executives from other places also contributed much to the denomination's leadership at the turn of the century.

DENOMINATIONAL ECONOMY

The president of the General Conference in 1890 was Henry D. Babcock, president of the Babcock Manufacturing Company, which made farm equipment in Leonardsville, New York. Babcock was described as having a "genius for organization and promotion."[1] He attempted to bring some of this genius for organization to the General Conference. In his address titled "Denominational Economy," he pointed out several areas in which the denomination did not practice economy. First, there was a need for uniformity in denominational work. Individuality had some advantages, but it had one great disadvantage, and that was *waste*. Babcock argued that a great deal of effort was wasted because the denomination lacked a standardized system. Individual members and pastors, churches and associations, as well as members and officers of the boards "must all take a broader view of the work as a whole and unite upon that which is for the best interest of the whole denomination, as well as upon that which will advance the cause in each locality, or in each line of work."[2]

A second weakness Babcock noted was lack of centralization in executive functions, where he saw considerable tendency toward divisiveness and separation. "The division and almost endless sub-division of the executive function is wasteful. In every well ordered

---

[1] Obituary—Henry Dwight Babcock, *Sabbath Recorder* 97/19 (10 Nov 1924): 602, 606.

[2] Henry D. Babcock, "President's Address," Appendix A, Conference Minutes, *SDB Yearbook* (1890) 17-18.

business establishment or factory the division of labor is carried out to the farthest limit, but no successful business was ever prosecuted where there was a division of the executive function."[3]

A third weakness he identified involved change. Babcock noted that in any successful business, "when one line of policy is followed for a fair length of time, and found to fail, or to be attended with more loss than gain, or where the gain is not commensurate with the amount of money and energy expended, the line of policy should be changed for one better adapted to secure the end desired."[4]

Throughout the twentieth century, those who had been successful in business but who felt frustration in denominational life spent much effort trying to effect some measure of the efficiency and economy they envisioned. By the century's end, they had found some success, but a robust discussion about the value and appropriateness of such efforts remained.

A Call for Readjustment

The General Conference session in 1902 is best remembered for its centennial celebration, yet, in the midst of reminiscence of the past, the conference's actions looked to the future. A Pre-Conference Council of representatives from General Conference, the denominational societies, boards, and institutions of learning called for an adjustment of denominational organization, more women on the boards, and an increased unity and strength in denominational life and action.[5] An Advisory Council was called to report the means and methods required to unify and strengthen denominational interests and work.[6]

The Alfred Council

The Alfred Council met in Alfred, New York, in December 1902 with goals that were reminiscent of the 1890 Chicago Council. The council drew representatives from among those most directly charged with implementing denominational programs rather than from individual churches.

The council began with a premise of unity based on common ancestry, traditions, interests, and hopes for the present and the future,

---

[3] Ibid., 18-19.
[4] Ibid., 19.
[5] Conference Minutes, *SDB Yearbook* (1902) 7.
[6] Ibid., 47.

but it implied a certain disunity in practice. "We need a close-knit organization, whether actual or virtual, to plan our denominational work, and to apportion it and carry it to success," the council reported.[7]

Out of that council came the conclusion that "a closer union of denominational organization should be accomplished by some form of merging or federating all our denominational lines of work, provided legal obstacles can be overcome." After consultation with a number of lawyers, committee members concluded that (1) the societies can be "fully and completely merged without risk to their funds or officers"; (2) this cannot be done by the societies themselves, but by a decree of a court of competent jurisdiction on petition from the societies; (3) the societies can legally include in their membership all the regular conference delegates and they can therefore elect the officers of the societies; but (4) the annual meetings of the societies for election of officers are illegal outside the state where they are incorporated.[8]

At the conference session of 1903, hopes were high that the difficulties could be overcome. Theodore L. Gardiner outlined the historical growth of the General Conference and the societies and lamented that among them all there was not one that could be called the representative head of the Seventh Day Baptist denomination. "For forty years the question of simpler organization has been knocking at our doors," he said, adding, "The spirit of re-adjustment is in the air. Hundreds feel today that it will not down at our bidding. It has undoubtedly come to stay; and we might as well meet and settle it now, as to postpone action to some future time."[9] Yet, the separate reports of the Missionary Society, the Education Society, and the Tract Society indicated obstacles that led to the conclusion adopted by the conference "that while the merging of the three denominational Societies with the General Conference would be legally possible, to attempt such merging is not advisable or practicable."[10]

Changes were made that more clearly defined the powers of the officers, made members of the societies members of the General Conference by virtue of such membership, and specified the ways in which the societies should report to the conference. A nine-member Executive Committee was created, composed of the president, the

---

[7] Report of the Advisory Council, Conference Minutes, *SDB Yearbook* (1903) 28.

[8] Report of the Advisory Board, Conference Minutes, *SDB Yearbook* (1903) 31.

[9] Theodore Gardiner, "President's Address," Conference Minutes, *SDB Yearbook* (1903) 4-5.

[10] Conference Minutes, *SDB Yearbook* (1903) 39.

recording and corresponding secretaries of the conference, and six other members elected by the conference for three-year staggered terms.[11] The following year, Boothe C. Davis commented that the choices made the preceding year for the first time made "the form of Conference conform to the spirit of unity which has wearily won its way through centuries of our denominational life."[12]

Continued Concern over Organization

Still, concern remained over the perceived inefficiency of the General Conference's organization. The fact that denominational growth had reached a plateau and then had begun to decline caused many to look critically at the organizational structure as a possible reason for lack of growth. Most Seventh Day Baptists recognized that lack of individual conviction and spirituality was a root cause of the problem, yet many felt that with proper organization and more unified leadership the Spirit of God would work more fully.

The conference session of 1904 revealed the denomination's? depth of feeling concerning lack of unity of operation. The president, Dr. George W. Post, called for Seventh Day Baptists to keep up with the rapidly changing times. He spoke of a weakness whereby "our branches of work are well conducted, but too independent of each other, so that from lack of mutual knowledge there results, not willingly, but unavoidably, a little rivalry, a little friction, a little captious criticism."[13] A. H. Lewis called for greater leadership from the pastors, saying, "Our church polity is so simple that we lose organic power, as do all who follow an extreme congregational organization in the matter of leadership."[14] As advertising executive Charles B. Hull pointed out, what is everybody's business is often nobody's business. "If you want counsel and advice, have a large committee," he said, "but if you want something done, have a committee of one.... Re-organization without the central idea of someone to do something is a hollow mockery and will be a failure. But re-organization, if it is an organization standing loyally

---

[11] Ibid., 39.

[12] Boothe C. Davis, "Our Denomination, Its Aims and Its Resources," Conference Minutes, *SDB Yearbook* (1904) 11.

[13] Geo. W. Post, President's Address," Conference Minutes, *SDB Yearbook* (1904) 6.

[14] A. H. Lewis, "Christian Leadership or Christ Our Leader," Conference Minutes, *SDB Yearbook* (1904) 62.

back of a chosen leader, may lead us out into a new and promised land."[15]

ADVISORY BOARD ESTABLISHED

George Post called for the conference president to have a group of men living near him with whom he could consult without delay on matters requiring quick decision. He asked for an advisory board that would be an effective force "and not a purely complimentary appointment."[16] From this request came a General Advisory Board of eleven members, six ministers, and five laypersons, including the conference president as chairman. Two of the elected members were to be from the same general area as the chairman; together these three would constitute an executive committee. On matters of denominational interest that required prompt action, the Advisory Board was authorized to initiate steps between meetings of the conference. However, at the earliest practicable time the Advisory Board was to turn the matter over to the conference board or agency, under whose jurisdiction it naturally fell. This board was to have "the prerogative of an advisory board in its relation to other boards, to our schools, to the Conference, associations, churches and people, either by request or itself taking the initiative, always having the view of the promotion of all possible unity, strength and efficiency."[17]

One year later, the General Conference, "in order to confine the functions of the Advisory Board clearly within the constitution of Conference," removed any initiatory powers from the Advisory Board. Thus, in matters involving interrelationship of boards, agencies, associations, and schools, or cases involving ministers or serious church difficulties, the Advisory Board had no authority.[18]

For several years, the General Conference operated with an organizational structure that consisted of a president, six nonfunctioning vice presidents representing the six associations, a recording and a corresponding secretary, a treasurer, an Executive Committee, and an Advisory Board of six ministers and five laypersons, including the president and two others that constituted an Executive Committee

[15] Charles B. Hull, "Systematic Leadership," Conference Minutes, *SDB Yearbook* (1904) 98-106.

[16] George W. Post, "President's Address," Conference Minutes, *SDB Yearbook* (1905) 8.

[17] "Report of the Executive Committee," Conference Minutes, *SDB Yearbook* (1905) 12.

[18] Report of the Special Committee to Revise Phraseology of Articles Setting Up Advisory Board, Conference Minutes, *SDB Yearbook* (1906) 109-10.

within the Advisory Board. It is little wonder that A. E. Main, in his 1907 president's address, stated that "the duties of the Board and of the Executive Committee are somewhat confused." He suggested that a special committee be appointed to investigate this matter and that action by the Advisory Board be suspended until their report could be received and acted on.[19] A year later, the Committee of Fifteen, as it was called, concluded that the Advisory Board was not needed.[20]

The Executive Committee Enlarged

In 1909, two recommendations were made by Wardner Williams to give a greater role to General Conference. The Executive Committee was expanded to include all the former conference presidents and the presidents of the Missionary, Tract, and Education Societies.[21] This first recommendation was adopted, which increased the Executive Committee by twenty-seven members (for an approximate total of forty-two members). The appointment of the past presidents and the presidents of the three societies continued until 1921, when changes to the constitution omitted these from the list of officers.[22]

The second recommendation called for the president to give his full time to the work of the denomination and receive a salary. There was a recognition of the need for one person to be able to attend board meetings and communicate on a personal basis with the churches, but the proposal for employment was not adopted.[23] The revised 1921 constitution listed the visiting of the denomination's churches as a duty as well as a privilege of the president, but the presidency has never been an employed position.[24]

In 1913, the Tract and the Missionary Societies established a joint committee to promote work in which both were concerned. They proposed the hiring of a General Denominational Secretary who could "plan, speak and write in the interests of all the work committed to us as Seventh Day Baptists."[25] When the plan was submitted to the churches for approval, thirty-three responded. Only nine churches favored the

[19] A. E. Main, "President's Address," Conference Minutes, *SDB Yearbook* (1907) 13.
[20] Report of Committee of Fifteen, Conference Minutes, *SDB Yearbook* (1908) 98.
[21] Report of the Committee to Consider Recommendations of Wardner Williams to the General Conference, Conference Minutes, *SDB Yearbook* (1909) 92.
[22] Constitution, Conference Minutes, *SDB Yearbook* (1921) 81.
[23] Conference Minutes, *SDB Yearbook* (1909) 92.
[24] Constitution, Conference Minutes, *SDB Yearbook* (1921) 82.
[25] Conference Minutes, *SDB Yearbook* (1913) 117, 128-29.

plan; six flatly rejected it; one favored a central advisory committee without authority to employ a joint secretary; one favored postponement for two years; three favored a plan of unification; and thirteen indicated satisfaction with the way things were. The action therefore was to "adhere to the present plan until the people are more nearly unanimously in favor of a change."[26]

COMMISSION ESTABLISHED

Boothe C. Davis, the president of General Conference in 1912, made efficiency a major emphasis in his presidential address. Applying the mechanical engineer's definition of efficiency, "the ratio of useful work to the energy expended," to the denomination, he found it lacking in many places.[27] Three significant actions were prompted by his address. First was a proposal to include the vice president and treasurer as ex officio members of the Executive Committee.[28] A second proposal was the creation of a Committee on Denominational Activities, which was composed of seven members, one each representing six boards and one who, as far as possible, acted as an all-around denominational worker and committee chairman. The Committee on Denominational Activity was designed to sift the reports of the boards and agencies and bring significant recommendations to the General Conference, acting as a committee of the whole.[29] Much of the General Conference's action for the next decade came through this committee, which served a function similar to the Reference and Counsel Committees of later years.

Boothe's third recommendation was to establish a Commission of the Executive Committee.[30] The first commission included the president, the vice-president, the recording secretary, the treasurer of the General Conference, and five former presidents.[31] By 1916, the Commission of the Executive Committee was largely composed of ex officio members, including the presidents of the Missionary and the Tract Societies. One

---

[26] Report of the Commission, Conference Minutes, *SDB Yearbook* (1914) 8.

[27] Boothe C. Davis, "President's Address," Conference Minutes, *SDB Yearbook* (1912) 5, 8.

[28] Proposed Amendment, Conference Minutes, *SDB Yearbook* (1912) 108. It is uncertain whether the proposal was enacted during the 1913 conference session, but the treasurer's name does appear in the list of Executive Committee members.

[29] Report of the Executive Committee and Boothe C. Davis, "President's Address," Conference Minutes, *SDB Yearbook* (1912) 7, 18.

[30] Report of the Committee on Denominational Activities, Conference Minutes, *SDB Yearbook* (1912) 43.

[31] Conference Minutes, *SDB Yearbook* (1913) 132.

year later, a committee to consider the president's address recognized the limitations posed by the congregational or democratic polity of Seventh Day Baptist churches and the denomination as a whole. The committee suggested that "the road to effective administration lies in the processes of gradual adjustment and evolution, rather than in radical effort to overturn the polity, methods and traditions that are the rich heritage of the denomination through three centuries of illustrious leadership, consecration and devotion to truth."[32]

After the commission studied these challenges, it suggested in 1918 several changes to the commission's composition and operation. Through mandates, membership was made more geographically diverse. Provisions were made for meetings at least two or three times a year at some central point, with the General Conference paying the expenses. Members were elected for three-year staggered terms. The president was to be selected from among the commission members. An executive secretary, who would serve without salary, was to be appointed. He would, however, be provided with an expense fund, including the hiring of a stenographer.[33]

The recommendation for selecting an executive secretary and electing the president from among the current members of the commission was not adopted. Instead, the General Conference requested that the joint secretary of the Missionary Society and the Tract Society be the secretary of the commission, provided the two societies concurred.[34] In 1919, the commission was authorized to hire a "New Forward Movement" director for a major financial campaign.[35] This position was later filled by a fulltime general secretary of the "Onward Movement," with a considerable portion of his time to be "given up to the spiritual welfare of our people, and the balance of his time and energy employed in raising the money necessary for carrying on our denominational activities."[36] This position was discontinued in 1929, although some of the duties were assumed by the Missionary Board Secretary. It was thirty

---

[32] Conference Minutes, *SDB Yearbook* (1917) 72.

[33] Report of the Commission, Conference Minutes, *SDB Yearbook* (1918) 9-10.

[34] Report of the Committee on Denominational Activities, Conference Minutes, *SDB Yearbook* (1918) 62.

[35] Conference Minutes, *SDB Yearbook* (1919) 59. Walter Ingham was employed in this capacity in 1920.

[36] Report of the General Secretary, Conference Minutes, *SDB Yearbook* (1929) 62.

years before the General Conference employed a denominational administrator.[37]

Changes in the Commission

In 1920, the Executive Committee was replaced by the nine-member Commission.[38] For the next decade, this commission functioned without change in format. Events surrounding the stock market crash of 1929 and the accompanying depression forced the denomination to look for ways of increasing the efficiency of its work by decreasing the overhead expenses. Over the next decade, several changes were made in the Commission's composition. In 1938, a Council Committee on Denominational Administration recommended that the Commission be reduced to six members, including pastors and laymen. One of these six also served as the president of the General Conference.[39] Although the societies and boards were omitted from membership, they were expected to be available for consultation. This six-member commission was the basic administrative body of the General Conference "between sessions" for forty years until 1978, when it was replaced by the General Council. To provide a year's advance preparation for the conference presidency, the first vice president was designated as president-elect in 1953 and joined those elected to the Commission.[40] Attempts were made to elect the other members from different associations, thereby maintaining a balance between pastoral and lay representation. For many years, the presidency alternated between pastors and laity.

Executive Secretary Employed

In 1951, the General Conference voted to hire an executive secretary "to provide administrative leadership in program planning, activating the program through inter-agency coordination, and budget promotion."[41] Nearly two years later, in May 1953, A. Burdett Crofoot was hired and served until his untimely death from a heart attack in 1955. He was succeeded by Doris Fetherston (1956–1961), Harley Bond

---

[37] Conference Minutes, *SDB Yearbook* (1951) 39-40.

[38] Report of the Commission of Executive Committee, Conference Minutes, *SDB Yearbook* (1920) 61. Compare Conference Minutes, SDB Yearbook (1921) 61, 81.

[39] Report of the Council Committee on Administration, Conference Minutes, *SDB Yearbook* (1938) 69.

[40] Conference Minutes, *SDB Yearbook* (1953) 48.

[41] Report of the Commission, Conference Minutes, *SDB Yearbook* (1951) 33, 39.

(1961–1964), Alton Wheeler (1965–1975), K. Duane Hurley (1975–1981), and Dale Thorngate (1981–1990).

The nature of the office of executive secretary varied with each person holding the position. In 1965, "in keeping with the scope of purpose, function, and duties" of the office, the title was changed to general secretary.[42] Ten years later, the name reverted to executive secretary. Such changes indicate the continuing difficulty in defining the function of an administrative position within an organization that remained basically advisory. The fundamental questions of authority within congregational polity remained.

In 1990, the General Conference hired a general services administrator to supervise the management of the Seventh Day Baptist Center at Janesville and assume part of the responsibilities previously designated to the executive secretary. Calvin Babcock, who had served as president of General Conference and part of two terms on the General Council, accepted the position. In 1991 he was appointed acting executive secretary, thus combining the two positions.

In 2000, Lewis H. V. May was selected to serve as executive secretary on a part-time basis, while the general services administrator continued to manage the Center at Janesville. This arrangement lasted until 2004, when the conference hired Robert A. Appel to serve in the role full time. In 2005, the title of the position was changed to executive director. At that time, the duties of the general services administrator were split between the executive director and the financial director of the General Conference.

GENERAL COUNCIL IS FORMED

In 1965, the Southeastern Association recommended to the General Conference that something be done immediately "to bring the action of the boards and agencies into harmony with the expressed wishes of the delegates of the churches in Conference assembled." The General Conference called on the churches and the associations to study the need for reorganization and possible plans to meet the need.[43] During that year, a series of four studies was prepared and distributed to the churches.

Out of this study came an appreciation of the paradox between Baptist principle and Baptist organization. One of the study's statements

---

[42] Conference Minutes, *SDB Yearbook* (1965) 67-68.
[43] Conference Minutes, *SDB Yearbook* (1965) 64.

recognized that although Baptists have always believed in religious liberty, this liberty is not the basis of Baptist church life, nor can it be a unifying principle. Religious liberty means the right of each person to be free in forming his or her own religious associations, but having chosen his affiliation, liberty is limited by the general position of the body with which the individual unites. The unifying tie is not liberty but the agreement that constitutes the reason for the organization's existence.[44]

Ten years later, the Ministers' Conference of 1975 provided the stimulus for one more denominational self-study. This study initiated steps that led to the formation of a General Council three years later. An ad hoc committee representing a cross-section of denominational personnel recommended the formation of a five-member task force to study and report specific changes to increase efficiency and effectiveness.[45] After research, consultation, and input from individuals, churches, and societies, the task force reported six areas of concern: (1) structure; (2) accounting procedures; (3) the interrelationships of boards, agencies and the General Conference; (4) the need for continuing study of these matters by the conference; (5) the location of headquarters; and (6) lack of leadership and negative attitudes.[46]

Although action was taken to establish a General Board to replace the Commission, the details of the new board's organization were referred to an ad hoc committee consisting of three members of the task force, three from the commission, and three from the societies affected by any structural change. This committee's study reflected a surge of optimism growing out of a "Commitment to Growth" program the denomination undertook in consultation with John Wimber and the Fuller Evangelistic Association. Beginning with the denomination's purpose "To win people to Christ and nurture them in love and service," the committee considered the concept of "Full-Circle Administration." This committee assumed nothing, and purported to suggest an organization based only on the needs of the times.

The committee deemed three departments necessary—a Department of Extension, a Department of Nurture, and a Department of Supportive Services—all linked together by some form of administrative office. Immediately questions arose when projections were made to fit

[44] "Seventh Day Baptist Structure Study," in Commission's Study Guide, *General Conference Task Force Notebook* IV (Feb 1966), transcript, MS 1990.3, p. 3, SDB Hist. Soc. Lib.

[45] Report of Commission, Conference Minutes, *SDB Yearbook* (1975) 64.

[46] Report of Task Force, Conference Minutes, *SDB Yearbook* (1976) 59-60.

the existing agencies and ministries of the conference into this "full circle." The various boards and agencies already in existence were carrying out these missions under independent charters and legally designated bequests and funding. To complicate matters further, the functions of several agencies were not confined to extension, nurture, or supportive services. In addition, the longstanding legal polity of the General Conference, which limited it to an advisory role, did not lend itself to "full circle" administration. The conference eventually voted down the proposal in 1979.

However, some of the proposal's basic concepts were implemented in 1978 with the establishment of the General Council to replace the Commission. This new body in essence retained the at-large concept of six elected members, including the president and president-elect, and added the employed executives of the major boards and agencies and the president of the Women's Board. The president of the Memorial Board was added later. The executive secretary held a nonvoting ex officio position until conferred with a vote in 2005. The at-large members became an Executive Committee in matters of personnel, whereas the representatives of boards and agencies who previously had formed the Planning Committee became the Coordinating Leadership Team chaired by the executive secretary for program and budget recommendations to the General Council.[47]

The millennium brought a time to reflect on the General Conference's many organizational and structural efforts. It is clear that Seventh Day Baptists have had an ongoing discussion about the value and appropriateness of importing cultural organizational paradigms into the life of the General Conference. Despite this discussion, Seventh Day Baptists have taken steps to amend their organizations to respond to specific needs and redress known inefficiencies. With times and needs continuing to change, Seventh Day Baptists will likely face continued structural and organizational challenges, but their history of thoughtfully and passionately considering such matters bodes well for their future.

---

[47] Report of the Committee on Reference and Counsel, Conference Minutes, *SDB Yearbook* (1978) 65-66.

20

CHOOSING GOALS IN THE TWENTIETH CENTURY

During the twentieth century, Seventh Day Baptists applied some of the same principles of business that prompted efforts at reorganization to the denomination's program development. The setting of specific goals was a principle designed to bring efficiency and unity to the mission of the church. Three specific areas of focus were budgeting, program development, and the establishment of an office center.

CHOOSING GOALS IN FINANCES

The Chicago Council of 1890 recommended that systems of weekly envelopes for offerings and tithing be used in the churches and "that a standing committee on Systematic Benevolence be appointed by the General Conference to promote its advancement."[1] It was not until after the Alfred Council of 1902 that the proposals were implemented.

Board of Systematic Benevolence

The Alfred Council recommended four specific actions: (1) the establishment by the General Conference of a Board of Systematic Benevolence to devise ways and means of raising funds for benevolent purpose, (2) the preparation of an annual budget of expenses, (3) the use of the pledge and envelope system, and (4) the appointment of a financial agent for the denomination as a whole.

The Board of Systematic Benevolence was elected[2] and for close to twenty years it worked in an advisory capacity to implement some of the Alfred Council's other suggestions. Weekly envelopes were printed and distributed to churches. In 1905 the board, later called the Board of Systematic Finance, compiled an annual budget by adding together the expenses of all the boards.[3] The recommendation to hire a financial agent was not implemented because one of the boards refused to support the idea.[4]

---

[1] Report on Financial Matters, *Proceedings of the Seventh-Day Baptist Council, Held at Chicago, Ill., Oct. 22–29* (N.p.: n.d.) 56-57.

[2] Conference Minutes, *SDB Yearbook* (1903) 39-41.

[3] Report of the Board of Systematic Benevolence, *SDB Yearbook* (1905) 59.

[4] Conference Minutes, *SDB Yearbook* (1906) 80.

For several years, the Board of Systematic Finances attempted to establish a working budget by asking the four major societies to prepare itemized statements showing proposed expenditures and income expected from permanent funds or other sources. The contributions from individuals and churches necessary to carry out the proposed work could be determined from this data.[5] It was not until 1913 that the plan was fully implemented and the budget was apportioned among churches according to membership. The budgets, as thus circulated, remained a compilation of individual budgets with all contributions made directly to each board or agency.[6]

A United Program Leads toward a United Budget

With the development of the Forward Movement in 1915, including the establishment of a director for it, came a greater sense of total mission. By 1920, churches and individuals had found it convenient to remit all funds for denominational work to one central point for distribution to the causes represented in the budget. The Commission recommended the appointment of a treasurer to receive and distribute any such funds sent for the denominational budget "in such manner as may be directed by the Commission of the Executive Committee and according to the wish of the donors."[7] The Board of Finance was dissolved, since its duties had largely been delegated to Commission.[8] The establishment of a denominational treasurer and the linking of the finances to the Commission were steps in the development of a unified budget, yet true unity did not come easily, particularly at times when the projected budget was not raised.

Such was the situation in 1921, when only about 73 percent of the budget was raised. It was recommended that each agency reduce its budget by 25 percent. At the same time, there was a strong movement for the Tract Society to hire a fulltime person to work in Sabbath Reform and Promotion. A lengthy debate ensued between those who felt that this was a priority item and others (like D. Burdett Coon) who argued that even though they believed thoroughly in Sabbath reform they felt

---

[5] Conference Minutes, *SDB Yearbook* (1910) 40-41.

[6] Report of the Board of Finances, Conference Minutes, *SDB Yearbook* (1913) 118-21.

[7] Report of the Commission of Executive Committee, Conference Minutes, *SDB Yearbook* (1920) 60.

[8] Report of the Commission, Conference Minutes, *SDB Yearbook* (1920) 61.

that, to be consistent, they could not say to some, "Keep down to 75 percent of the budget, and yet allow others to take on new work."[9]

This particular issue was finally resolved by adding the task of Sabbath reform work to the job of the Forward Movement director.[10] However, the question of separate appeals for extra-budgetary items remained. For example, in 1922, the General Conference recognized that even though the three colleges (Alfred, Milton, and Salem) received support from the denominational budget, their needs greatly exceeded the amount the conference allocated. Therefore, they were granted the "liberty to make general appeals to the denomination in such manner as the management of the respective colleges and the Commission may approve."[11] Other special ministry projects through the years have been given license to directly appeal to individual Seventh Day Baptists with the recognition that such appeals can be an effective means of supporting ministry beyond the budget.

Our World Mission

For thirty years, the denominational budget was called Our World Mission. The name was adopted to indicate that one's giving was not just toward a budget, but was a part of the total program of the church.[12] Because the term *mission* often had a limited meaning, the General Council recommended in 1987 that instead the General Conference use the name Partnership In Ministry. A conference committee reported, "While we agreed with the need to stress to churches and individuals that we are partners in ministry, it would be more clear to refer to the budget as the denominational budget."[13]

The Power of the Purse

In any organization that relies on voluntary contributions for support, the relationship between budget and program is close. The "power of the purse," through the giving or withholding of funds, has often been the determining factor in the execution of any proposed action. Many people feel that financial involvement is the only direct

---

[9] Conference Minutes, *SDB Yearbook* (1921) 44, 50-51.

[10] Conference Minutes, *SDB Yearbook* (1922) 89.

[11] Report of the Commission, Conference Minutes, *SDB Yearbook* (1922) 89.

[12] Report of the Committee on Reference and Counsel, Conference Minutes, *SDB Yearbook* (1956) 45.

[13] Report of the Committee on Reference and Counsel, Conference Minutes, *SDB Yearbook* (1987) A70.

way they can participate in the decision-making of the organization. At times even the conference has used the budgeting power to extend its advisory role in relation to the societies.

A unified budget has been a means of overcoming a lack of organizational unity. The process of budget preparation by the General Council, which includes the executives of those agencies sharing in the unified budget, has worked toward achieving the "full circle ministry" that was rejected organizationally. When those who are largely responsible for program work meet with representatives of the General Conference as a whole to consider priorities for expenditures, the process can bring a new sense of unity that was sometimes lacking when each board or agency presented its needs independent of any total denominational strategy of operation and mission.

SETTING PROGRAM GOALS

Through much of its first century, the activities of the General Conference were the collective activities of individual churches, associations, and societies. A great deal of cooperation existed among these separate entities, as all sought many of the same ultimate goals. Programs at each session of the conference were generally arranged by either the president or some form of an executive committee; thus the emphasis varied from year to year according to the personnel and the specific requests of boards and agencies.

The second century of General Conference history is marked by a series of denomination-wide programs that often resulted from some of the efforts to bring organizational unity amidst structural diversity. One of the first such programs arose in the midst of World War I, as Seventh Day Baptists proposed a three-year united program known as the Forward Movement.

Forward Movement Plan Adopted

The report of the Missionary Society to the 1915 session of the General Conference ended with the plea that the denomination had to decide whether to take the role of *conformer* or *reformer*, pointing out that "Hitherto we have led in every forward movement to elevate men to sane and useful living. Of late, the emphasis has been placed not on reform, but on conforming to popular ideals and standards."[14] From this

---

[14] Missionary Society Minutes, Conference Minutes, *SDB Yearbook* (1915) 177.

report came a proposal to launch an aggressive three-year program called the Forward Movement.

The Young People's Board in 1913 had introduced a pamphlet outlining a means to measure the effectiveness of a program. This plan, as adopted by the General Conference, called for specific measurable goals the denomination should reach by 1919. Some of the goals called for the addition of 500 converted people annually, a similar increase in Sabbath school membership, and 200 new members of the Christian Endeavor societies. Each of the boards and agencies was asked to cooperate fully and to send representatives to member churches to promote this Forward Movement.[15]

The following year showed encouraging reports of 114 new church members, a net gain of 300 pupils to the Sabbath schools reporting, and 145 new members to the 34 Christian Endeavor societies that responded. Thus, it was voted to continue the program with increased target goals recommended by the Young People's Board.[16] In 1918, the report of the Committee on Denominational Activity recommended that commission "formulate and set before the denomination a new Forward Movement plan."[17]

New Forward Movement

In 1919, a five-year New Forward Movement was designed "to marshall all the spiritual and material forces available in a united and effective way to carry on the work of God on earth." Specifics of this program included a five-year budget amounting to about a half-million dollars to cover both home and foreign missions, ministerial education and retirement, and increases in other denominational programs through the agencies. In order to properly carry out the program, it was deemed necessary to employ a fulltime director for the New Forward Movement.[18]

Walton H. Ingham, an insurance agent from Fort Wayne, Indiana, served as director for the first year. It was hoped that a businessman rather than a pastor might serve as an example to inspire other

---

[15] Report of the Sectional Committee on Missionary Work, Conference Minutes, *SDB Yearbook* (1915) 78-79.

[16] Report of the Committee on Denominational Activities, Conference Minutes, *SDB Yearbook* (1916) 51.

[17] Report of the Committee on Denominational Activities, Conference Minutes, *SDB Yearbook* (1918) 64.

[18] Report of the Commission, Conference Minutes, *SDB Yearbook* (1919) 53-60.

businessmen in each church to render like services.[19] Weekly columns in the *Sabbath Recorder* and the listing of a roll of honor for churches meeting their quota spurred initial success. However, the economic depression of the postwar years had its effect on giving, so that when only 75 percent of the projected funds were raised, the boards and agencies that programmed on the basis of expected income found themselves with deficits.

. Rev. Ahva J. C. Bond was hired as the program's second director, splitting his time with the Tract Society in Sabbath promotion. His work during his four-year term as director showed better correlation of denominational activities, a spiritual awakening, and an untiring effort to raise the funds called for in the budget.[20] Statistics for this period showed considerable financial gain[21] but little improvement in church growth. Total membership dropped by about 600, while Sabbath school enrollment and Christian Endeavor Society membership remained about the same.[22] Nonetheless, in 1924 the Commission expressed its firm belief that the program was fully justified and warranted a continuance in a new program to be known as the Seventh Day Baptist Onward Movement.[23]

Onward Movement

The Onward Movement adopted in 1924 proposed the hiring of a general secretary with duties similar to that of the prior New Forward Movement director. A job description called for responsibility in raising the denominational budget, visiting associations and churches, assisting pastors, and such other work as the Commission might direct. The ideal candidate was to "labor with freedom and initiative, under the direction of Commission," while his relation to the denominational boards was that of "counselor and coordinator."[24]

Willard D. Burdick, who had previously served as evangelist for both the Missionary and Tract Societies, was chosen as the general secretary. After four years, he resigned to return to the pastorate. His

---

[19] Report of the Commission, Conference Minutes, *SDB Yearbook* (1920) 63.
[20] Report of the Commission, Conference Minutes, *SDB Yearbook* (1924) 108.
[21] Ibid.
[22] The statistics from the *SDB Yearbook* (1919 and 1924) show changes in membership from 8,475 to 7,873 for church members, 4,516 to 4,521 for Sabbath school attendance, and 662 to 639 for Christian Endeavor Society membership.
[23] Report of the Commission, Conference Minutes, *SDB Yearbook* (1924) 100-101.
[24] Ibid., 102.

concluding remarks noted that the year 1929 was a banner year in giving for the Onward Movement Budget and special ministries off the official budget, but he cautioned that Seventh Day Baptists were "near the point of supporting specials to the detriment of the long established lines of work upon which the very life of the denomination depends."[25] Instead of hiring a new director for the Onward Movement, the General Conference assigned the duties of the general secretary to two committees, one to promote the financial program and the other to promote the spiritual program.[26]

The name Onward Movement continued in financial reports until 1933, when it was recommended that the budget be designated as the Denominational Budget.[27] It was not until the beginning of the next decade that a new overall plan was projected for coordinated effort along several lines. In his president's address in 1940, Dr. Ben Crandall proposed a "Five-Year Plan" for increasing the enrollment and attendance in church, Sabbath school, and young people's groups and for providing for these entities' support.

Five-Year Plan

The Five Year Plan, as adopted by Conference, was oriented toward the local church. It set broad general goals and placed the responsibility on the laity as well as the clergy. Little mention was made of the role of boards and agencies other than the placing of the *Sabbath Recorder* in every Seventh Day Baptist home and the use of materials recommended by the Board of Christian Education.[28] The Commission appointed Dr. Crandall to assign parts of the Five-Year Plan to appropriate agencies and to follow up on their activities in response to the assignment.[29] The responsibility for developing the Five-Year plan was eventually placed with the Board of Christian Education.[30] In 1942, the Five-Year Plan was dropped and the denomination participated in the interdenominational

---

[25] Report of the General Secretary, Conference Minutes, *SDB Yearbook* (1929) 61.

[26] Report of the Commission, Conference Minutes, *SDB Yearbook* (1929) 64.

[27] Report of the Commission, Conference Minutes, *SDB Yearbook* (1933) 51.

[28] Report of the Commission, Conference Minutes, *SDB Yearbook* (1940) 39-40.

[29] Report of the Commission, Conference Minutes, *SDB Yearbook* (1941) 24.

[30] Report of the Section on the Five-Year Plan, Conference Minutes, *SDB Yearbook* (1941) 31.

United Christian Advance Movement, which was producing a wealth of valuable material.[31]

American involvement in World War II with its demands on personnel, finances, and restrictions on travel limited the scope of the Five-Year Plan and its successor program. No sessions of the General Conference were held in 1943 and 1945. However, the Commission met in these years and in 1945 recommended a united effort outside the budget for mission reconstruction and expansion. Since funds were to be raised before the 100th anniversary of the opening of the China mission, the program was called the Second Century Fund.[32]

Second Century Fund

The Second Century Fund was administered by the Missionary Board, with 35 percent of the funds designated for rebuilding the China mission. Other sums were used on the home field in such programs as Efficiency for Evangelism; this program involved cooperative planning for two-week-long evangelistic programs in local communities using visiting pastors as part of a long-range program to expand lay evangelism, stewardship, and missionary knowledge and to establish new churches.[33] As a part of the Second Century Fund, a pilot project under the auspices of the Missionary Board was the establishment of a new church in an urban area in Indianapolis.

Our World Mission

To express a broader concept of mission, the General Conference used the name Our World Mission beginning in 1956. A basic seven-step Program for Extension and Growth was adopted. Although none of the steps were new, the program spelled out in detail the channels through which individuals or churches might receive help. These channels included the newly created post of executive secretary, the denominational boards and agencies, the associations, and the local churches. The General Conference also recognized fellowships as groups of believers who gathered regularly for worship but did not yet constitute a formal congregation.[34]

---

[31] Report of the Section on the Five-Year Plan and Denominational Finance, Conference Minutes, *SDB Yearbook* (1942) 26.

[32] Report of the Commission, Conference Minutes, *SDB Yearbook* (1945) 9-10.

[33] Report of the Missionary Society, Conference Minutes, *SDB Yearbook* (1947) 126-27.

[34] Report of the Commission, Conference Minutes, *SDB Yearbook* (1956) 54-56.

In 1959, in an effort to mobilize the denomination for growth, Seventh Day Baptists adapted materials from the Lay Development Program of the American Baptist Convention. The ABC developed these materials for their Jubilee Advance.

Program for Advance

The Program for Advance adopted by the General Conference included a chart of activities and specific goals for the conference and all related agencies for a five-year period. The first two conference years (1959–1960 and 1960–1961) were designated as Mission to the Local Church. The next year (1961–1962) was titled the Mission to the Unchurched, followed by Missions to the Social Frontiers (1962–1963) and Mission to the World (1963–1964). Major activities and goals for those first two years included a lay-development program, a study of Seventh Day Baptist beliefs, a geographical survey of churches assets including leadership potential and numbers, a personal spiritual inventory, new fellowships and churches, a full-time field evangelist, a home missions secretary, and a youth field worker.

The planning and supervision of the program was left in the hands of the Commission and the Planning Committee (made up of conference and board executives). Each board and agency was asked to promote the program by using its available resources of money, materials, and personnel.[35] The Board of Christian Education, for example, responded by preparing a special issue of the *Helping Hand* quarterly devoted to an in-depth scriptural and historical study of the Statement of Belief.[36] The Committee on Christian Social Action provided study materials and statements of positions generally held in such matters as church-state relations, race relations, and other social issues.[37] This committee also recommended a special social concerns issue of the *Helping Hand* that appeared in 1966.

Growing out of emphases on missions to the unchurched and the social frontiers, the Women's Society in 1964 recruited a team of four young people to give dedicated service in what became the Summer Christian Service Corps (SCSC).[38] This SCSC program has continued for over four decades to provide leadership training and service among the

---

[35] Report of the Commission, Conference Minutes, *SDB Yearbook* (1959) 46, 48-49.

[36] Repr. in *The Helping Hand* 8/43 (1967): 91, (1975): 99, (1983): 1.

[37] Report of the Committee on Christian Social Action, Conference Minutes, *SDB Yearbook* (1962) 54-55. Affirmed: Conference Minutes, *SDB Yearbook* (1963) 59-60.

[38] Report of the Women's Society, Conference Minutes, *SDB Yearbook* (1964) 217-19.

churches in the United States and beyond. From the Mission to the World emphasis, sister Seventh Day Baptist Conferences were invited to send delegates to the General Conference sessions in August 1964.[39] That invitation led to the establishment of the Seventh Day Baptist World Federation.[40]

The Program for Advance concluded in 1964 with a cooperative celebration including six other denominations in the Baptist Jubilee Advance; the two-part celebration was held at Atlantic City, New Jersey, in May and at the World Consultation of Seventh Day Baptist Conferences (dubbed "CoWoCo") in Salem, West Virginia, in August. Two years prior to the program's completion, a follow-up program was proposed that would concentrate on the application of Seventh Day Baptist beliefs to the contemporary world.[41] That proposal led to a new initiative called "Mission 65" to be celebrated in the conference year 1964–1965.

Mission 65

Mission 65 invited key laypeople and pastors to volunteer to assist other churches in carrying out "some application of our beliefs in the local community, presenting and sharing our distinctive witness in the local situation."[42] Twenty-three churches reported participation in the program, with six laymen and twelve ministers serving as missionaries. From this experience, a follow-up program was recommended by the Planning Committee for the year 1965–1966 under the title Involvement in Christian Service.[43]

Involvement in Christian Service

The initial success of the SCSC program for young people led to the desire for wider participation in similar dedicated services extending for longer periods of time and making use of experienced lay personnel. By 1967, the Dedicated Service programs included five areas of service: (1) Summer Christian Service Corps, (2) Vacation Church School and Camp Leadership, (3) Extended Dedicated Service, (4) Missioners, and (5) COME, an acronym referencing Acts 16:9, where Paul has his vision of

---

[39] Report of the Commission, Conference Minutes, *SDB Yearbook* (1962) 49.

[40] Report of the First World Consultation of Delegates from SDB Conferences (CoWoCo), Conference Minutes, *SDB Yearbook* (1964) 38-43.

[41] Report of the Commission, Conference Minutes, *SDB Yearbook* (1962) 49.

[42] "More about 'Mission 65,'" *Sabbath Recorder* 176/13 (30 Mar 1964): 9.

[43] Report of the Planning Committee, Conference Minutes, *SDB Yearbook* (1965) 47-48.

the man of Macedonia (Come Over into Macedonia to help us Emphasis). The latter program encouraged extending calls to individuals or families to move to other locations to strengthen existing work or to start new work.[44]

Facing Frontiers with Faith

When Rev. Alton L. Wheeler was employed as general secretary, he developed a new five-year plan called Facing Frontiers with Faith. A "canopy" concept of communication, cooperation, and concurrent planning among the boards and agencies was projected.[45] By year three, the General Conference became involved in the interdenominational emphases "Crusades of the Americas" and "Missions in the 70s."[46] These were followed by a series of yearly emphases such as "Introspect—Prospect," "Era of Action," "Outreach—U.S.A.," "Key 73," and "Reach Out Now" (RON).

Commitment to Growth

In 1975, the Commission initiated a program for church growth in which the General Conference contracted with the Fuller Evangelistic Association—initially with Dr. John Wimber and later Carl George as consultants. Focus for this Commitment to Growth program was initially placed on the development of "growth eyes" through Bible study and the discovery and fuller use of spiritual gifts within the church. Churches were encouraged to establish mission statements and growth goals. Workshops and training sessions were held to equip both laity and pastors for extension.

Several new churches were established as a result of the Commitment to Growth program. The decline in total membership reversed. Some significant changes were made in organization with the formation of the General Council (a merger of the Commission and the Planning Committee) intended to involve the agencies responsible for denominational program in the initial planning stages. Growing out of the changed attitudes toward growth potential, the denomination was better prepared to enter the 1980s, which it termed the "Decade of Discipleship."

---

[44] Report of the Planning Committee, Conference Minutes, *SDB Yearbook* (1967) 33.

[45] Report of the Planning Committee, Conference Minutes, *SDB Yearbook* (1966) 37.

[46] Report of the Planning Committee, Conference Minutes, *SDB Yearbook* (1968) 36.

Decade of Discipleship

The goal to "double in a decade" was an ambitious aim with hopes of doubling not only the total number of Seventh Day Baptists, but doubling the number of churches, the number of active participants in worship and the Sabbath school, as well as doubling missionary activity. The plan involved a continuing process of nurture, extension, and ministry through each year of the decade. To bring each of these into sharper focus, it was recommended that there be a concentration of effort, personnel, and materials according to yearly emphasis: the first year (1980) emphasized the "Decision to Disciple," while the remaining nine years alternated the successive emphases "Disciples in Nurture," "Disciples in Extension," and "Disciples in Ministry."

This program was the most goal-oriented of the century and resulted in increased cooperation among the boards in the budget process with respect to those goals. New concepts of ministry began to focus on urban culture rather than on the rural mindsets that for nearly three centuries had dominated Seventh Day Baptist thinking.

Out of this background of program emphases, a new strategy of motivation was developed for the last decade of the last millennium. MORE 2000 (Mission of Revival and Evangelism 2000) focused the denomination's resources into a unified effort to assist the local church in instructing, motivating, and setting goals and strategies to meet local needs and visions. MORE 2000 was described as a process rather than a program.

Establishing a Denominational Center

At the same time these initiatives were being undertaken, the General Conference was also considering the value of a physical location that could house conference ministries and where such a building should be located. In 1917, a committee appointed to plan a suitable building for the publishing house reported to the General Conference that the time had come to move from the visionary to vision, to "convert the vision into tangible form." What was originally projected as larger and better publishing quarters was now projected as a home for denominational life. "Just as a church expresses the community spirit, so this edifice would be a rallying point denominationally." The committee expressed the hope that the building would cause boys and girls to lift their heads a little higher in the knowledge that it was *theirs* and that the older members would feel still greater pride in a denomination that believed in its future strongly enough to build such an enduring monument.[47] The vision, which became a reality in 1929, was of long standing.

Early Visions

As early as 1852, this vision was expressed in the Publishing Society's proposal for a building "in which the business of our Missionary, Tract, and Publishing Societies may be transacted, provided with a room or rooms for meetings of the Boards of these Societies, with a reading-room for a Sabbatic Library and a collection of Missionary Curiosities."[48] Some initial steps were taken by the societies, but as they expressed the following year, "It is feared that among the able brethren of the denomination generally, the object is not yet fully appreciated, and that some delay may be experienced in their coming forward to aid it."[49] The delay they feared was realized. The Publishing Society was frustrated by the lack of support it received from other societies that were using the rooms of its building not only as centers of business but for storage as well: "It is hardly to be expected of the Publishing Society, the only Society which asks no donations and relies for pecuniary means wholly upon the income of its publications, to furnish such accommodations for the other denominational societies unless the friends and supporters of those societies are willing to lend a helping hand."[50]

Chautauqua: A Rallying Point?

In August 1881, Rev. A. H. Lewis delivered an address at the great Summer Assembly at Chautauqua on the subject "Sunday Laws, Past and Present." An audience of several hundred clergymen listened to the address, which was circulated in printed form to some six or eight thousand people then at Chautauqua. In tract form it reached thousands more.[51] Two years later, George H. Babcock suggested establishing headquarters for the Bible Sabbath in Chautauqua, "where all the

---

[47] Report of the Special Committee on Denominational Publishing House, American Sabbath Tract Society Report, *SDB Yearbook* (1917) 231.

[48] Annual Report of the Board of Managers of the SDB Publishing Society, SDB Publishing Society Minutes (1852), MS 19x.187, V-D file , pp. 132-33, SDB Historical Society Archives.

[49] Report of the Board of Managers to the SDB Publishing Society (1853) 162.

[50] Report of Board of Managers to SDB Publishing Society, 2 (1856) 54.

[51] "Chautauqua Address," Report of the American Sabbath Tract Society, Conference Minutes, *SDB Yearbook* (1882) 25.

publications on the subject could be had by earnest inquirers, and the sign above which could be a constant reminder that there was a Sabbath of Jehovah in contradistinction to the Sunday of pagan Rome."[52]

The General Conference adopted a resolution in 1883 expressing the opinion of many that a Seventh Day Baptist headquarters at Chautauqua would furnish a rallying point and a means of supplying information to those who seek to know the truth. A committee was appointed with power to solicit funds and erect a building for that purpose, with the understanding that the conference would not be involved in any way with the expense.[53] However, subsequent conference sessions reveal no actions and the matter appears to have been dropped.

Five years later, a suggestion was made that the conference itself might establish a permanent conference location that would be "most desirable with reference to means of access, expenses, and convenience for entertainment" and in an area where delegates and other attendees could find accommodations at their own expense.[54] A committee to study this matter reported that "the losses would much outweigh the advantages."[55] Although the idea of a central location was considered periodically, the fear always surfaced that centralization and any concept of a "headquarters" would detract from the idea of local autonomy and the benefits derived from more diverse participation. It was not until 1916, with the beginning of the Forward Movement Program, that the idea of a Seventh Day Baptist Center again received serious consideration.

The Denominational Building: Phase I

The initiative for a denominational building came from the American Sabbath Tract Society, which would benefit most directly from facilities for publishing. In the initial planning and promotion, the publishing aspect was secondary. In their report to the General Conference in 1917, the society maintained that the building could not be justified financially, but that "if it is built it must only be on the highest ground of denominational uplift, on the ground that we have faith in our cause and faith in our future,—on the ground that the time has come to go forward and that this is one step in definite determination to grow."

---

[52] G. H. B., "Letter from Chautauqua," *Sabbath Recorder* 39/35 (30 Aug 1883): 4.
[53] Conferences Minutes, *SDB Yearbook* (1883) 12.
[54] Conference Minutes, *SDB Yearbook* (1888) 23.
[55] Conference Minutes, *SDB Yearbook* (1889) 11.

The society further added that "as a people we have been too prone to think of ourselves as a small people preserved by God for the great purpose of His Sabbath and so it is possible that we have been a little too content to let our faith be the reason for our existence." The report concluded with the declaration, "If we are ever to be anything but a little people we must think big and talk big denominationally; we must have faith to believe that God has a big place for us to fill and that this building is only the beginning of the big things we are going to do."[56]

The Tract Society had envisioned this broader aspect of centralization in its support of the 1915 recommendation for incorporation of the General Conference.[57] A year later, the Tract Board stated that from its point of view a centralized management of our denominational affairs was becoming increasingly desirable, if not necessary.[58] Out of these concerns came the request in 1916 that the Board of Directors prepare a general plan for providing a suitable building for the use of the Publishing House. The plan presented the following year was basically that which was later built in two stages as two connected buildings, a one-story publishing house in back and a three-story office-administrative portion in front. In 1918 Conference encouraged the Tract Society to begin raising money and "proceed with the erection of the denominational building as soon as in its judgment it seems wise to do so."[59]

Open meetings were held by the Tract Society, with invitations sent to members of churches widely removed from Plainfield. One such meeting included a tour of the publishing facilities housed in extremely cramped quarters with rooms scattered from the cellar to the fourth floor in different buildings. The editor's office was in the editor's home; files were stored 5 blocks away; the office of the Memorial Board was on the third floor of another building; and the collection of the Historical Society was stored in safety vaults at Newark, some 18 miles away.[60] At least nine articles appeared in the *Sabbath Recorder* with full discussion of

---

[56] Report of the American Sabbath Tract Society, Conference Minutes, *SDB Yearbook* (1917) 232.

[57] Report of the American Sabbath Tract Society, Conference Minutes, *SDB Yearbook* (1915) 264-65.

[58] Report of the Committee on Denominational Activities, Conference Minutes, *SDB Yearbook* (1916) 52.

[59] Report of the Committee on Denominational Activities, Conference Minutes, *SDB Yearbook* (1918) 63.

[60] "Denominational Building Council at Plainfield, N.J.," *Sabbath Recorder* 83/21 (19 Nov 1917): 642.

the whole issue. There seemed to be little disagreement as to the need for more adequate facilities for denominational publishing, but many questions were raised concerning when, how, and where to build.

At first, the when and the how dominated the discussion. Many who favored building wanted to postpone action until the time was ripe. They argued that it would be unpatriotic to use building materials needed for the war effort. Others saw difficulty in raising money while the government was calling on people to buy war bonds. Still others argued postponement until prices were more in line or until all the funds were in hand. On the other hand, men like Frank J. Hubbard, the treasurer of the Tract Society, spoke in favor of immediate action, recalling that his father had been one of those who, sixty years prior, had urged the building of a suitable facility. "But," he said, "that was given up and the matter dropped from that day until about a year ago, and it is quite probable that will be the fate of this campaign if we drop it now,— that it will drop not for a year or two, but for a generation."[61]

In 1920, the Tract Society reported that "a condition arose in reference to the lease on the property occupied by the Publishing House by which a notice to vacate at any time was imminent." This spurred the Committee on Denominational Building to action. Wishing to involve more people in the decision as to the new building's location, a referendum was advertised and circulated in the *Sabbath Recorder*. Although it was proposed that only the print shop portion of the building be built to meet the emergency, it was realized that the location of that facility would necessarily determine the location of the whole building project.[62]

History, the location of the Tract Society, and the cost of moving equipment and personnel all weighed heavily in the choice of Plainfield as the proposed building site. However, Battle Creek's more central location, generous pledges from the Michigan churches, and the availability of a building in Battle Creek that had initially been used by the Seventh-day Adventists for printing, made that location more economical. When the vote was finally taken, 1,946 were cast for Plainfield and 1,477 for Battle Creek. That which they had hoped would be a uniting factor proved to be divisive, as the closeness of the vote and an extension of the referendum deadline (which allowed the New Jersey

---

[61] F. J. Hubbard, *Sabbath Recorder* 83/21 (19 Nov 1917): 645.
[62] See *Sabbath Recorder* 88/6 (9 Feb 1920).

votes to be counted after the original publicized date) caused some suspicion of unfair manipulation in favor of Plainfield.

In 1921, the Tract Society purchased a desirable site in Plainfield situated almost opposite the city hall on Watchung Avenue, facing the proposed city hall park, and adjoining the plot where the new YMCA building was to be erected.[63] On 9 October 1921, ground was broken for the publishing house portion of the denominational building. On 9 April 1922, after the publishing house was completed and the equipment moved, the building was dedicated. At least the Tract Society had a home with room for editing, printing, circulation, storage, and society business all under one roof. The front half of the lot was held in reserve for the construction of the future denominational building, which for over fifty years after its construction served as a symbol of Seventh Day Baptists as a denomination.

The Denominational Building: Phase II

Two years after the dedication of the publishing house, the Commission recommended that approval be given for the Tract Society to make a separate campaign to raise the needed funds to complete the denominational building.[64] In 1925, the Tract Society reported its plan to erect a memorial building in front of the print shop for offices, committee rooms, and a denominational library. No special campaign had been started, but efforts had been made to increase the general acceptance of the proposition. As the Tract Society noted, "The appealing arguments for the erection of this building are that it will meet an actual present need, that it will be a fitting memorial to a worthy past, and that it will be evidence of our faith in our future."[65]

In 1928, the Tract Society reported its adoption of a specific plan with the note that it did not intend to begin construction until the entire estimated cost of $90,000 had been subscribed.[66] By April 1929, the goal had been reached and the builders broke ground. The society's treasurer for that year listed 690 names of individuals who contributed during a 6-month period. Included in those named were members of the Shanghai

---

[63] Report of the American Sabbath Tract Society, Conference Minutes, *SDB Yearbook* (1921) 185.
[64] Report of the Commission, Conference Minutes, *SDB Yearbook* (1924) 102.
[65] Report of the American Sabbath Tract Society, Conference Minutes, *SDB Yearbook* (1925) 217.
[66] Report of the American Sabbath Tract Society, Conference Minutes, *SDB Yearbook* (1928) 168.

and Liuho churches in China, whose contributions ranged from 1 to 4 cents per week over a 23-week period.

The General Conference dedicated the denominational building on 28 December 1929. (Although to this day the words "Seventh Day Baptist Building" remain formed in concrete above the main entrance, the building was normally referred to as the "denominational building.") At the dedication service, W. L. Burdick, the secretary of the Missionary Board, summarized what he believed the building represented: (1) a home for the boards, (2) better unifying of the denomination's work, (3) increased efficiency on the part of every board, and (4) new courage and enthusiasm with greater results for the Master.[67] To these four representations a young pastor added the perspective of the denomination's youth: "To us young people this building shows that our denomination is a going concern. Hats off to the past and coats off to the future."[68]

In later years, unforeseen circumstances dampened some of the denomination's initial enthusiasm. Some elements of the overall vision of a center for the boards did not materialize, as several boards and agencies maintained their principal offices in other locations. Nonetheless, for the next fifty years, the denominational building served as a center for publishing, financial accounting, historical preservation, and research as well as a hub to coordinate denominational programs. In time, the training of ministers was also centered in this building.

Changing Environment Brings Changed Attitudes

The depression of the 1930s caused a cutback in both programs and personnel. The denomination had a new home but fewer activities to require its centralized facilities. Many who contributed to the construction costs were not as generous in later providing funds for the building's maintenance and operation. In addition, the local and state governments, also in need of money, viewed the entire denominational building as a business and subject to taxation. An editorial in the *Sabbath Recorder* attributed part of the crisis to the fact that "we have allowed to accumulate the taxes for the past three or more years while we have hoped we might escape the necessity of paying." The court ruled otherwise, so the Tract Society was forced to borrow money to pay the

---

[67] "The Building Is Dedicated," *Sabbath Recorder* 108/1 (5 Jan 1930): 5.
[68] Ibid.

taxes.[69] For several years, the problem escalated as interest on loans increased the cost of maintaining the facility.

In 1936, the Commission recommended that the offices of the Recorder Press be removed from the Seventh Day Baptist building to the Publishing House, that the Tract Society be empowered to transfer the title to the front building and transfer title for the grounds exclusive of the Recorder Press to the General Conference, and that the General Conference incorporate in order to hold this property. By this action the society hoped that the denominational building would be exempt from taxation.[70]

The following year, the expenses for the building were removed from the denominational budget and made a matter for a special appeal directed by the Tract Society. The 1938 General Conference, which was set up as a council-conference similar to the Chicago Council of 1890, included one committee devoted to the problems of the denominational building. This committee recognized that the conference had to make a decision that year "whether in its opinion the time has come to relinquish this building—or seek ways and means whereby it may be retained and made to serve the constituency more efficiently." Seven proposals were considered by the committee, including: (1) maintaining the status quo but making the cost of upkeep and operation a preferred claim in the denominational budget; (2) disposing of the building and using the income to provide housing for the interests of the denomination; (3) renting office space to others to generate revenue; (4) making all denominational agencies participants in the cost of maintenance; (5) asking the publishing house and the Recorder Press to assume a considerable share of the cost of maintenance in accord with claims that these agencies made when the campaign for construction funds was in progress; (6) proceeding with a campaign for permanent endowment; and (7) incorporating the General Conference and transferring the title from the Tract Society.

The Council Committee recommended incorporation and suggested that each denominational agency, whether located in Plainfield or elsewhere, be asked to provide displays in the building that would explain the building's mission and create interest in the conference's ministries in the community. It also recommended that a host be posted

---

[69] Theodore L. Gardiner, "The Tax Problem," editorial, Sabbath Recorder 12/42 (25 Jan 1937): 63.
[70] Report of the Commission, Conference Minutes, SDB Yearbook (1936) 53.

in the building to welcome visitors and furnish information concerning the displays and denominational interests.[71]

On 26 September 1938, fully eighteen years after the first committee was appointed to consider incorporation, the General Conference became a legal body with power to hold property and the title to the Seventh Day Baptist Building was transferred to General Conference.[72] The report for 1942 indicated that no taxes had been assessed against the denominational building for the years 1940–1942. Problems still existed over its use and support. Objection was raised over charging denominational boards for space. Since the boards and agencies were independent entities, this could be interpreted as rent, hence a business proposition, and the property could then be placed on the tax roll.[73] The Seventh Day Baptist Building, which had been viewed as a symbol of unity and vitality, survived a major crisis.

In 1950, the Commission recommended that a study be made of ways the building could be made to serve the needs of the denomination more fully. It is unclear whether such a study was ever conducted. The following year, the office of executive secretary was established with the expectation that this office would be located in the building. Yet, it was several years before a secretary had a primary office in the building. Eventually, offices of the General Conference including the Memorial Fund occupied the first floor and those of the Historical Society, including its library and museum, the third floor. The second floor provided a large conference room for use by all agencies. With the closing of the School of Theology at Alfred and the establishment of the Council on Ministry in 1963, the ministerial education program moved to the second floor of the denominational building. Yet, even this addition did not have the impact envisioned by some for increased usage by pastors and denominational leaders, for changes in the program and a decentralization of seminary attendance lessened its use by students.

These factors, increased cost of utilities, and normal depreciation after forty years of use, along with a changed urban environment, led the General Conference to a reconsideration of the best place for a denominational center within a societal organization. Ultimately, the

---

[71] Report of the Conference Council Committee, Conference Minutes, *SDB Yearbook* (1938) 101.

[72] Report of the Treasurer of Board of Trustees of the SDB Conference, Conference Minutes, *SDB Yearbook* (1939) 28.

[73] Conference Minutes, *SDB Yearbook* (1942) 27.

General Conference reviewed its mission with respect to the local congregations and decided a move was necessary.

Move to Janesville, Wisconsin

The Task Force appointed in 1975 to consider more denominational effectiveness and efficiency included the location of headquarters as an item for discussion. A special committee was appointed to study the feasibility, desirability, and possible economics of moving headquarters away from Plainfield.[74] In 1981, the General Council, after study of specific facilities in several proposed locations, presented its recommendation to the conference in session that year that the offices of the General Conference and the offices of the boards and agencies located at Plainfield be moved to a relatively new, energy-efficient building in Janesville, Wisconsin. Factors cited in favor of the relocation included a more favorable environment, better security, lower cost of living, a more modern building, the ease of recruiting personnel, lower utility costs, better schools, a more centralized location, and a strong local church at nearby Milton. Factors considered to be potentially negative to the proposed move included moving costs, the cost to purchase a new facility, the reluctance of some boards and agencies, distance to major travel hubs, and the need to maintain the denomination's heritage or tradition.[75]

When the vote was taken by the General Conference, 235 delegates voted in favor of the move and 67 voted in opposition. The move was made less than a year later, and Janesville became the focal point for many of the same hopes that had accompanied the establishment of the first denominational center. The sale of the Plainfield property to the city and full payment for the new facility were accomplished in three years. Offices that previously had been in Plainfield were relocated to the new facility, while those of the Missionary Society remained in Westerly, Rhode Island, and those of the Board of Christian Education continued in Alfred, New York.

The denomination did not forget its past, however, for soon after the move was made, the city of Janesville honored the General Conference's request to rename two streets that bordered the new property. What became officially known as the Seventh Day Baptist

[74] Report of the Task Force, Conference Minutes, *SDB Yearbook* (1976) 60.
[75] Report of the General Council, p. 49, and Report of the Interest Committee for Reference and Counsel, p. 79, Conference Minutes, *SDB Yearbook* (1981).

Center was thus located on Kennedy Road between Newport and Plainfield Avenues.

Despite protracted discussions, the General Conference took significant steps in the twentieth century in the areas of program development, goal setting, and cooperative ministry. Unified efforts to do cooperative ministry funded by combined efforts of the churches of the conference and its boards and agencies yielded positive fruit and led to more allied efforts. These efforts ultimately led not only to an allied purpose but also to a desire to house these conference ministries in a single location. From this location, Seventh Day Baptists continued to reach out to the wider world.

21

TWENTIETH-CENTURY INTERNATIONAL EXPANSION

John R. Mott expressed both the vision and the hope of Christians around the world in 1900 in his book *The Evangelization of the World in This Generation.*[1] Groups such as the Student Volunteer Movement for Foreign Missions (1886) and the World's Student Christian Federation (1895) stimulated both youth and adults to renew their emphasis on the call to missions at the beginning of the twentieth century. Among Seventh Day Baptists, the beginnings of the Young People's Board and the Woman's Board coincided with these movements, for both the youth and women were very much a part of the missions emphasis of the time.

Some of the American cultural ideas of "Manifest Destiny," which prompted movement and expansion of the nation from coast to coast, were now applied to the expanded boundaries that resulted from the Spanish American War and to the United States' new role in foreign affairs. Robert E. Speer expressed the need for Christians to pick up the pieces following World War I, viewing the Christian Church as an agency of righteousness in an exploited world. He pointed out ways in which political agencies had forced great wrongs on non-Christian people and claimed that the Christian Church alone represented the inner moral character of the Western World.[2]

The *Jubilee Papers*, published by the Seventh Day Baptist Missionary Society in 1892 to commemorate the fiftieth anniversary of the Missionary Society and the centennial of William Carey's foreign mission movement, reflected optimism for the future based on the accomplishments of the preceding periods. The Missionary Society saw the present as a turning point calling for "greater unity in spirit, in purpose, and in organized endeavor."[3] The denomination responded with an active period of missions activity that saw the banner of Seventh

---

[1] J. R. Mott, *The Evangelization of the World in this Generation* (New York: Student Volunteer Movement in Foreign Missions, 1900) 6.

[2] Robert E. Speer, *The New Opportunity of the Church* (New York: Macmillan Co., 1919) 97.

[3] "The Future," in *Jubilee Papers* (Westerly RI: Board of Managers of the SDB Missionary Society, 1892) 160.

Day Baptists fly in Asia, Africa, North and South America, Europe, Australia, and islands of the Pacific and Atlantic.

SEVENTH DAY BAPTIST MISSIONS IN 1900

The Missionary Board in 1901 reported that for the preceding year the denomination had supported 4 missionaries and 11 native workers in China; 2 native workers in Ayan Maim, Gold Coast of Africa; 2 workers in Holland; and 76 workers on the home field. Some of the home-field workers served for the entire year, while others served for only part of the year. Included among the workers on the home field were 27 missionary pastors serving 37 churches, 5 general missionaries serving 5 areas, 4 evangelists, and 9 student quartets. Included in these quartets were those who became leaders of the denomination during the first thirty or more years of the twentieth century.[4]

The board's report visualized a change from a few advocates of foreign missions to a general concern for evangelizing the world. In the midst of the challenges to Seventh Day Baptist churches as a whole, O. U. Whitford, the corresponding secretary of the Missionary Board, raised the following question concerning Seventh Day Baptists: "Shall we rise up to our occasion? Will we enter the doors before us? Shall we improve our opportunities? All our mission fields call upon us for greater labor, greater wisdom, consecration and effort."[5]

THE FIVE "PS" OF MISSIONS

Seventh Day Baptists had to make hard choices in the early years of the new century that affected later generations. Some of these decisions involved the five "Ps" of missions.

(1) Purpose: Why become involved in missions?
(2) Priority: Should home missions or foreign missions have priority?
(3) Place: Where should effort be expended?
(4) Personnel: What personnel and training is needed for a successful mission?
(5) Process: What is the relationship between planting a mission and the cultivation of seed already planted?

---

[4] Missionary Society Minutes, Conference Minutes, *SDB Yearbook* (1901) 24-33.
[5] Missionary Society Minutes, *SDB Yearbook* (1901) 36.

As Seventh Day Baptists entered the twentieth century, the answers they gave to each of these questions would provide a basis for reviewing the work of missions during the century.

1. *The Purpose of Missions.* The Great Commission of Matthew 28:18-20 has urged followers to go, make disciples, baptize, and teach the observance of Christ's command. This urging had long been a foundational conviction of Seventh Day Baptists, and in the early years of the twentieth century, Seventh Day Baptists found purpose for their missions efforts in these verses and others like them. From these verses, they sensed a commission that required obedience, an increased passion for the lost, a sense of expectation for success, the possibility of growth, and an opportunity to share their Sabbath convictions.

Obedience to a Commission—Involved in this commission are the purpose, the power, the process, and the promise. Nearly every mission statement acknowledges or implies this command of Jesus as its purpose for being. The constitution of the Missionary Society states that its object shall be "the dissemination of the gospel in America and other parts of the world, and the promotion of kindred religious and benevolent work."[6] Yet, there can be considerable difference in how people interpret and apply the command of Jesus. For some, obedience is a matter of duty. "We ought to be witnesses because we are told to go." Many missions have resulted from individual Bible study. Baptist missionary William Carey's beginning work came from his conviction that the Great Commission was for all time. In his 1792 publication *An Enquiry into the Obligation of Christians to Use Means for the Conversion of the Heathen*, Carey refuted many of the commonly held objections to missions, pointing out that if we had as much love for the souls of others as merchants "have for the profits arising from a few otter skins…then all these difficulties would be surmounted."[7]

Carey's report of his work in India and that of the Adoniram Judsons in Burma convinced many to take the gospel to other countries. The Seventh Day Baptist mission in China, begun in 1846, was clearly a response to the Bible's command to "Go into all the world." Obedience

---

[6] Article I, "Constitution of SDB Missionary Society," revised 1891. Compare *SDB Yearbook* (1901) 53.

[7] William Carey, cited by Bruce Shelley, *Church History in Plain Language* (Waco TX: Word Books, 1982) 395.

to this call continued to motivate the missions movement throughout the twentieth century.

Passion for Souls—A second purpose for missions is the genuine passion for souls that results from the initial response to duty. Returning missionaries generated a real desire to ease the burden of those who did not know the gospel. After Dr. Rosa Palmborg and Susie Burdick returned to the states in 1900, they visited churches and associations, telling of the needs of the Chinese people. Sabbath school classes, youth groups, and women's societies responded to these firsthand experiences and the mission grew. Other areas, such as the African Gold Coast, might have had an equally open door for the gospel but lacked the personal field reports that inspired people to feel passion for the souls of the heathen. In the end, it was easier to feel passion for lost people who had the benefit of being face to face with a Seventh Day Baptist who could serve as their advocate in the United States.

Investments Pay Dividends—A third purpose for missions is the idea of investment with expected returns, as expressed by the biblical words "Give and it will be given to you." A mission-minded church is generally a healthy church. Investment was seen in the student movement's slogan to Christianize the world in their generation. One way to have peace and justice in a person's own country was to take the gospel to other countries. The isolationism of previous generations was no longer possible in the twentieth century.

Missions Provide Soil for Growth—A fourth purpose is growth. With the closing of the frontier and membership in American churches tapering off, people looked to overseas missions as a place to experience numerical growth. By the closing decade of the twentieth century, close to 90 percent of those claiming to be Seventh Day Baptists lived outside the United States. Not all of these converts were the result of direct missionary activity, but the contacts made and the assistance given as a result of missions activity accounted for a large portion of this outreach during the century.

A Special Mission in Sabbath Reform—A fifth purpose, particularly expressed during the early years of the century, was a part of the Sabbath Reform movement. Convinced that the special mission of the denomination was to bring the Sabbath to all people, many believed that success might be greater among non-Christians who had no established tradition of worship. If one's first introduction to Christ were through the teaching of the Bible, then the acceptance of the biblical Sabbath would be seen as a natural part of a life in Christ.

   2. Priority in Missions: Foreign versus Home Missions. Few Seventh Day Baptists have opposed the concept of missions, but many have expressed considerable difference as to whether the emphasis should be on home or foreign missions. Many argued that interest in foreign missions strengthens the local church. One artist painted a picture of a dying church with a spider web over the slot in the missions box. Others, however, argued that the denomination's small size prevented it from competing in the foreign field against denominations with far greater resources. They argued that the same amount of effort and money going overseas would do more good at home.[8] Statistics were sometimes used to show that there was a larger percentage increase in membership when the emphasis was on home missions.[9] There were those who also claimed that aggressive Sabbath Reform work on the home field resulted in considerable growth; they concluded that "the more we have done for foreign missions the less we have undertaken and accomplished in our home mission work."[10]

   The 1951 study on denominational reorganization called for a division of responsibility whereby the Tract Society would become the Tract and Home Missions Board, leaving the foreign missions in the hands of the Missionary Society.[11] Although the recommendation was not adopted, it shows a division in the thinking concerning missions goals.

   The report of the Commission in 1959 recognized that the increase in growing foreign mission fields required a corresponding increase in annual giving. This left the Commission with the dilemma of not being able to allocate money for even normal increases on the home field at a time when advanced effort at home was imperative. In addition, there

---

   [8] Theodore Gardiner, "Direct Reflex Influence of Foreign Missions," editorial, *Sabbath Recorder* 71/1 (3 Jul 1911): 1-6.
   [9] G. W. L., letter to the editor, *Sabbath Recorder* 72/16 (15 Apr 1912): 494.
   [10] Stephen Burdick, "Lessons of the Past," *SDBs in Europe and America*, 3 vols., ed. C. F. Randolph (Plainfield NJ: SDB General Conference, 1910) 2:1292.
   [11] Dr. Lloyd Seager, unpublished study paper (1951), G-File, Denominational Organization, p. 5, SDB Hist. Soc. Lib.

was little difficulty in challenging dedicated workers to tackle the foreign fields, but a general apathy existed toward challenges at home.[12] The following year (1960), the Missionary Interest Committee of the General Conference was divided into two separate committees "in recognition of the increasing importance of the home missionary field."[13]

3. *Choosing the Place for Mission.* In his president's address to the General Conference in 1912, Boothe C. Davis noted the change in agriculture from "extensive" to "intensive" farming methods. He defined the former as "the careless and slovenly tilling of large areas" in contrast to latter "careful scientific treatment of small areas." Davis appealed for more "intensive" cultivation of carefully selected fields of missionary activity, because even though tilling soil intensively may be more expensive, the dividends are often greater. "It is well to give to missions because it is the Lord's cause, and because we are blessed by giving," he said, "but there is no enjoinment against seeking to make our gifts effective in producing the maximum amount of useful work for the money expended."[14]

From the beginning of the twentieth century, doors for missions were opening faster than Seventh Day Baptists were able to enter. Choices had to be made as to where and how they should enter these God-given opportunities. Although these choices have had to be made in each field of mission, the choice of the place for missionary effort in this study is best illustrated by opened doors in Africa. Two doors opened at about the same time, Nyasaland in the eastern part of Africa and the Gold Coast on the western shore. A history of each gives insight into factors influencing choices and possible reasons for differing results. Response to a third open door a few years later in Nigeria highlights the need for caution and prudence in deciding which "doors" to walk through, as not all opportunities are created equal.

Nyasaland (Malawi)

In July 1898, Joseph Booth, an industrial missionary working in Nyasaland in British Central Africa, preached in the Plainfield Seventh Day Baptist Church. He had established over fifteen industrial missions

---

[12] Report of the Commission, Conference Minutes, *SDB Yearbook* (1959) 48.

[13] Report of the Committee on Home Missionary Interests, Conference Minutes, *SDB Yearbook* (1960) 47.

[14] Boothe C. Davis, "President's Address," Conference Minutes, *SDB Yearbook* (1912) 12.

over the years along Baptist lines. He confessed that he had not been able to read certain Scriptures concerning the Sabbath without experiencing some feelings of unrest. After the service, A. H. Lewis and A. E. Main entered into such persuasive discussion with Booth that he became a Seventh Day Baptist and joined the Plainfield Church just months later in September. This step cost Booth both friends and former colleagues' support. Thus, he turned to Seventh Day Baptists to help carry on the missions work to which he was committed.

Yet, how could the denomination afford another mission? The work in China needed continued support, and other denominational programs needed both financial and personnel assistance. Some of those in the Plainfield area churches proposed forming a Sabbath Missionary Union, but after consulting with the Missionary Society, they determined it was best to incorporate the proposed union as a business organization. Thus, on 30 January 1899, the Sabbath Evangelizing and Industrial Association was incorporated with the specific objective of establishing an industrial mission for educating and training the natives in Christian doctrine and in agricultural and industrial skills. It was hoped that such a mission might become self-supporting.[15]

The association was incorporated as a stock company. After about 3,000 shares were sold at $1 per share, Joseph Booth and his wife left for Blantyre, Nyasaland. Within two years, the association had purchased a coffee plantation that gave employment to as many as 478 workers at one time. A congregation of 300 to 400 natives attended the Sabbath preaching service, although only 29 were members.[16]

Widespread coffee crop failures created serious financial problems. In his haste to see the work accomplished, Joseph Booth had not followed sound business practices and, as a consequence, led the association into debt. Health problems and political involvement made it necessary for Booth to return to America. Jacob Bakker, the son of Pastor J. F. Bakker of the Netherlands, was sent by the General Conference to adjust the affairs. In December 1901, the association terminated its contract with Mr. Booth, leaving the stockholders responsible for the association's indebtedness. Booth entered into an agreement with the Seventh-day Adventists and returned to Africa under their auspices. In

---

[15] Report of Sabbath Evangelizing and Industrial Association, Conference Minutes, *SDB Yearbook* (1900) 18.

[16] Report of Sabbath Evangelization Association, Conference Minutes, *SDB Yearbook* (1900) 19.

Africa, Mr. Bakker was able to negotiate $4,000 for the sale of the plantation that originally had cost $15,000. After three and a half years, the Sabbath Evangelizing and Industrial Association officially disbanded.[17] By most standards the venture was a failure, for it never approached the high aims it had set. Yet some of its converts continued in the faith.

Booth's term with the Adventists was also brief. Several years later, he again secured some Seventh Day Baptist support through the Missionary and Tract Boards for his work in South Africa, where he trained Nyasaland workers to return to pastor independent, self-sustaining native churches. That support was terminated after an investigation in 1912 that revealed Booth's activities were associated with political movement toward African independence.[18] Correspondence continued through the decades between Booth and some Seventh Day Baptist pastors, and forty years later some of the scattered groups of Sabbathkeepers issued a plea for leadership that was answered in 1947 by Ronald Barrar, a Seventh Day Baptist from New Zealand. With the aid of individuals and churches in the United States, England, the Netherlands, and New Zealand, Barrar and his supporters developed the Makapwa Mission Station.

Ronald Barrar's 1953 visit to the United States generated enthusiasm for Seventh Day Baptist involvement in Africa. The Pacific Coast Association gave support for two nurses, Joan Clement and Beth Severe, to accompany Ronald Barrar back to Nyasaland and assist in the work. Upon a petition from the Pacific Coast Association and recognition by the General Conference of these nurses' consecration and decision to become missionaries, the Missionary Board extended a call in January 1953 for them "to serve as missionary nurses and/or teachers under the direction of the Missionary Society."[19]

With the communist party's forced closing of the China mission in 1950, the mission in Nyasaland (later named Malawi) became a primary foreign mission. Joan Clement and Beth Severe were followed by Dr. Victor Burdick, Sarah Becker, Barbara Bivens, and Audrey Fuller in the medical field; Rev. David and Bettie Pearson (who served together for over thirty years) and Rev. John and Joyce Conrod in the teaching,

---

[17] William C. Hubbard, "Sabbath Evangelization and Industrial Association," *SDBs in Europe and America*, 1:582-83.

[18] Harry W. Langworthy III, "Joseph Booth: Prophet of Radical Change in Central and South Africa, 1891–1915," *Journal of Religion in South Africa* 16/1 (1986) 22-43.

[19] Missionary Society Minutes, *SDB Yearbook* (1953) 118.

preaching, and administrative ministry; and Menzo Fuller in a general maintenance ministry. In 1989, Ian and Trudy Ingoe and their family, from Auckland, New Zealand, were jointly commissioned by the Australasian Conference of Seventh Day Baptists and the Seventh Day Baptist Missionary Society to assist the Central Africa Conference in a building ministry in Malawi.

The Central Africa Conference, incorporated in Malawi in 1967, became a charter member of the World Federation; since then it has sent delegates to each federation session.[20] In 1988, the Central Africa Conference reported 31 churches and 63 branches with 4,861 total members.[21] In 2008, the conference's executive director, Nedd Lozani, reported 16,000 members: 10,000 in 140 churches in Malawi and 600 in 30 churches in Mozambique. The conference today operates six primary and two secondary schools, a Bible college, and four health centers.[22]

Gold Coast (Ghana)

At about the same time that the Evangelizing and Industrial Association was deeply involved with the mission of Joseph Booth, a door was opened on the West Coast of Africa at a village known as Ayan Maim, Gold Coast (Ghana). Joseph Ammokoo learned, through *Watson's Theological Dictionary*, that there was a denomination known as Seventh Day Baptist that kept Saturday as the Sabbath. His study of the Bible convinced him that he also ought to keep the Sabbath. He obtained the address of the publishing house and the address of a church in Richburg, New York. Assuming that Richburg was "a wealthy church," he requested assistance to bring two young men to America to be educated in the Sabbathkeeping faith and in English studies. He indicated that he had purchased land for a mission farm and was anxious for a Sabbathkeeping school for the children. This letter, reprinted in the youth page of the *Sabbath Recorder*, generated considerable interest.[23] Many saw this as a door God had opened to Seventh Day Baptists.

[20] David C. Pearson, *Seventh Day Baptists in Central Africa* (Janesville WI: SDB Historical Society, 2003) 45.

[21] Directory, *SDB Yearbook* (1988) B38.

[22] SDB World Federation Minutes, *Report of the SDB World Federation, Seventh Session, July 28–August 1, 2008, Carthage College, Kenosha, Wisconsin USA* (Salem WV: SDB World Federation, 2008) 54-55.

[23] Joseph Ammokoo and sons, letter to Richburg SDB Church, Sep 1898, *Sabbath Recorder* 55/7 (13 Feb 1899): 106.

Late in December, the Evangelizing and Industrial Association secured the services of William C. Daland, the American missionary pastor of the Mill Yard church in England, to visit the Gold Coast and verify whether this would be a fruitful mission field. His first letter from the field was encouraging, as he found a people who were already conscious of the Sabbath.[24] In a later letter written on shipboard, Daland reaffirmed his opinion concerning West Africa as a place for Seventh Day Baptist mission work. He spoke of God's call, "If we hear and heed his call, he will surely bless us. If he has spoken and we do not heed, he may work his will without us, but we shall lose the blessing."[25]

At the General Conference session in 1901, the Evangelizing and Industrial Association handed over the Gold Coast interest to the Missionary Society because it did not fit into the association's industrial plans. Their commitment was to the work in the central and eastern portions of Africa. O. U. Whitford expressed the willingness of the Missionary Board to take up the Gold Coast Mission if people would support it, "but it would require something more than enthusiasm to carry it on." He then added, "The Board had in years past taken up special work under the enthusiasm generated at a General Conference, and after a little the interest had died out, and they were left without support for that particular interest."[26]

Peter Velthuysen, a student at Alfred University and the son of Pastor Gerard Velthuysen of the Netherlands, was interested in the Gold Coast and volunteered to go as a missionary if the General Conference would indicate its desire for him to enter that field. The Missionary Board called him to serve, but severe seasickness and the equatorial climate left him weak and exhausted. On 20 October 1902, he died of tropical fever.

The Missionary Board made other outreach efforts in the Gold Coast, including the education in America of Joseph Ammokoo's son Ebenezer.[27] After attending Tuskegee Industrial Institute in Alabama and Milton College in Wisconsin, he returned to Africa in 1912. He wrote to the Tract Society office frequently requesting books and papers, but it seemed that "his point of view was largely commercial" (as opposed to

---

[24] William C. Daland, letter to the editor, 6 Feb 1900, "Dr. Daland in Africa," *Sabbath Recorder* 56/12 (19 Mar 1900): 181.
[25] William C. Daland, letter to the editor, 25 Feb 1900, "Dr. Daland Returning from Africa," *Sabbath Recorder* 56/17 (23 Apr 1900): 261.
[26] Missionary Society Minutes, *SDB Yearbook* (1901) 2.
[27] Missionary Society Minutes, *SDB Yearbook* (1902) 112.

being spiritual). Since Ebenezer Ammokoo was holding no religious services or Sabbath schools, the Missionary Board stopped sending him money.[28] In 1913, the Missionary Board reported a feeling of "sadness bordering on guilt" that they had failed to establish a lasting mission in the Gold Coast.[29]

Nearly fifty years later, field missionaries reported Sabbathkeeping churches in Ghana and recorded communications with the Tract Society and the Missionary Board. In 1958, Roger Cazziol, a Sabbath convert from Turin, Italy, visited both Ghana and Nigeria, thanks in part to some support from the Mill Yard church in England, where he held his membership. During one sermon he reminded people of the efforts of Peter Velthuysen, who was buried in Ghana, and concluded, "It would be an everlasting memorial to the sacrifice of this missionary if I could establish a Seventh Day Baptist work here."[30] Nearly ten years later, there was an active group in Ghana, identified as Seventh Day Baptists, under the leadership of Ralph Cann. Despite some communication, particularly with European Seventh Day Baptists, they have had no direct ties to either the General Conference or the Seventh Day Baptist World Federation.

The door to the Gold Coast or Ghana remained open for well over half of the twentieth century, but Seventh Day Baptists chose not to enter it because they lacked sufficient support to maintain their work there. There are many "Macedonian calls" that continue to challenge those who would take the gospel to all the world. Which places should be entered and which should be left to others? How should the decision be made? The case of Nigeria poses further questions concerning the decision of where effort and resources can best be expended.

Nigeria

In 1953 the Salem, West Virginia, church received a letter from Nigeria stating that through correspondence and the various tracts the natives had received from "our Salem brethren" and "our London brethren" they had organized a Seventh Day Baptist Church with a total membership of 142, with many more coming to study. They asked for official recognition of the church and its pastor, licensing of evangelists,

---

[28] Missionary Society Minutes, *SDB Yearbook* (1913) 148.
[29] Ibid.
[30] Roger J. Cazziol, "Letter From Ghana" (8 Aug 1958), *Sabbath Recorder* 165/10 (22 Sep 1958): 3.

and tracts and study materials. The General Conference responded with an expression of interest, a suggestion that the group in Nigeria organize into an autonomous conference, the desire to send a representative to study firsthand the work there, and the designation of the Salem church as the official point of contact between the Nigerian and the American churches.[31]

Subsequent correspondence showed considerable growth and activity in Nigeria. The need for on-the-field investigation was again affirmed.[32] This need was further expressed in the Missionary Society's 1955 report, which revealed that, through other missionaries in the area and civil authorities, the society had been warned of possible fraudulent claims and the risk of being saddled with indebtedness. The society also reported that the area was "sufficiently churched." On the basis of this investigation, the Missionary Society recommended that "no one be sent until or unless more favorable reports are received." To send anyone to investigate "would tend to commit the society to assuming responsibility for mission work in Nigeria."[33]

In spite of this recommendation, an unofficial visit was made by Dr. Wayne Rood, who indicated that efforts were being made to comply with some of the probationary standards the Missionary Society had recommended.[34]Rood's overall conclusion confirmed the idea that Nigeria was in fact an open door, but he warned that unless Seventh Day Baptists were prepared to provide *intensive* care, rather than *extensive* or halfway measures, the denomination through the Missionary Society was not in a position to make this a primary field.

The door was not closed, however, for reports continued to come and visits continued to be made throughout the succeeding years. In 1973, Nigeria applied for and was granted admission as a sister conference into the Seventh Day Baptist World Federation. Gershen A. Harrison represented Nigeria at the 1986 session of the World Federation. His report in 1989 listed nine active churches with 2,140 members plus a new field opening with 5 additional churches. Upon Harrison's death, Lawrence Uchegbuonu became the leader and represented the Nigerian conference at the 1992 sessions in New Zealand. Increasing political and religious tensions complicated

---

[31] Conference Minutes, *SDB Yearbook* (1953) 28-29.

[32] Clifford W. P. Hansen, letter from Salem SDB Church to the General Conference, Conference Minutes, *SDB Yearbook* (1954) 23-25.

[33] Missionary Society Minutes, *SDB Yearbook* (1955) 122-23.

[34] Report of the Planning Committee, Conference Minutes, *SDB Yearbook* (1956) 22-23.

communication with the Nigerians, particularly after Uchegbuonu's death in 2007.

4. *Personnel and Leadership in Missions.* The places of missions are important, but so also is the personnel or the leadership within those places selected. This principle is illustrated by the mission to the American Tropics, which was centered in two areas, British Guiana (now Guyana) on the northern coast of South America and Jamaica, an island in the West Indies. Both missions were initially the result of those who had come to the Sabbath through the work of the Seventh-day Adventists but who separated from that body because of disagreement on matters of doctrine and polity.

British Guiana (Guyana)

The work in Guyana began with Rev. T. L. M. Spencer, a native of Barbados who had served as a missionary of the African Methodist Episcopal Church in Trinidad. Around 1902, his attention was called to the Sabbath through an unidentified book published by the Seventh-day Adventists. For several years Spencer served as an Adventist missionary, but "his heart led him toward the Seventh Day Baptists, of whom he had heard very little." He gathered a group of about forty likeminded adults who shared his conviction to worship regularly in Georgetown, the capital of British Guiana. In 1913, he wrote to the United States requesting further information on Seventh Day Baptists. His desire to be identified with Seventh Day Baptists led him to visit the Missionary Board in Rhode Island. He joined the First Hopkinton Church, visited several other churches, and attended sessions of the General Conference.[35]

In 1913, the corresponding secretary of the Missionary Society, E. B. Saunders, reported that this group of Sabbathkeepers living in Georgetown was asking for assistance and that it was "a more Christian act to assist people who have accepted the Bible Sabbath than to persist to carry the special Sabbath to people who care nothing for it and will not accept it."[36] Thirty-five charter members organized a Seventh Day Baptist church in Georgetown on 15 November 1913. Secretary Saunders

---

[35] "Rev. T. L. M. Spencer in Plainfield," *Sabbath Recorder* 75/7 (18 Aug 1913): 193-94.
[36] Report of the Corresponding Secretary, Conference Minutes, *SDB Yearbook* (1913) 160.

proposed that "this should be our center for missionary and Sabbath reform work in South America and the West India islands."[37]

British Guiana became the area's work center for about a decade. With annual assistance from the American Sabbath Tract Society, Pastor Spencer published the *Gospel Herald*, which generated interest in the denomination in Trinidad and the Barbados Islands. Annual reports showed continued interest and growth, along with the desire for more support to increase their ministry capabilities. In 1920, the Missionary Society assisted in the purchase of property in Georgetown for a church building. Foreign corporations were restricted in ownership of property, so the title was at first held individually by Mr. Spencer. Only after considerable legal steps could the Missionary Society obtain title to the land.

Three years later, other complications came to light with respect to the property and Mr. Spencer's work, and the need for sending a missionary from the states became apparent. In 1927, Rev. and Mrs. Royal Thorngate and their daughter were sent as missionaries. After a thorough investigation, Mr. Spencer was dismissed on the ground that he was not dependable, had misused the trust committed to him, and had gained a questionable reputation in Georgetown. It was also reported that he had "done all he could to stir up prejudice against the white race, the board and its representatives." When he withdrew, he took much of the congregation with him. The church reorganized and gradually demonstrated growth, but it felt the loss of effective leadership for many years.[38]

This experience highlighted a problem Seventh Day Baptists have often faced in foreign missionary efforts. In its 1931 report, the Missionary Society stated that all denominations working in the tropics were facing racial, political, and religious problems and that methods that had been followed in the past with a fair degree of success were now failing. The report concluded, "If Christian denominations from the United States help these peoples very much, they must study conditions till they get a telescopic vision of the situation; they must go as brothers and colleagues; they must be patient and forbearing; and above all they must possess something of the love for those to whom they go which prompted Christ to pass through Gethsemane and endure the cross."[39]

[37] Missionary Society Minutes, *SDB Yearbook* (1914) 149.
[38] Missionary Society Minutes, *SDB Yearbook* (1928) 133.
[39] Missionary Society Minutes, *SDB Yearbook* (1931) 162.

Malaria forced Pastor Thorngate to resign as missionary and return to the states in 1930. The Missionary Board reported that although the work in British Guiana was promising, "there are several indications that it has been disintegrating since he left and that it will not succeed without a missionary from the home land to advise and encourage."[40] It was nearly thirty-five years before another missionary was sent. During this interval, general supervision of the mission at British Guiana was often included in the duties assigned to missionaries in Jamaica.

The work in British Guiana continued under native leadership with minimal support from the Missionary Board and the Mill Yard church in England. William Berry, Frederick T. Welcome, Alexander Trotman, and Joseph Tyrrell continued to serve the scattered congregations in a land where the river provided the principal means of transportation. In 1946, following the death of William Berry, his son Benjamin entered the School of Theology at Alfred, New York, where he took special courses to help in his ministry. He returned to British Guiana in 1949 and assumed leadership until 1957, when he terminated his services to the denomination "because of his hope to better his financial situation."[41]

During the next few years, efforts were made to secure missionaries. Two couples accepted the call but because of health and family situations were unable to go. In 1962, Rev. and Mrs. Leland Davis accepted the call and served for four years. They were followed by the Rev. Leroy and Marjorie Bass family from 1966 to 1974. The leadership of these families stimulated activity and expansion, particularly among the youth. Two young people took advanced theological training. Jacob Tyrrell enrolled at the Guyana Bible Institute, graduating in 1968, and Samuel Peters enrolled in Jamaica Theological Seminary, graduating in 1974.

Tyrrell represented the Guyana Conference at the founding meetings of the World Federation in 1964 and as its general secretary through 2002, when he was replaced by Kharlyn Henry. Peters returned to Guyana as a pastor until 1981, when he returned to his wife's homeland in Jamaica. After 90 years, the Guyana Conference reported in 2004 that membership had reached 317 in 10 churches.[42]

Jamaica

---

[40] Ibid.

[41] Missionary Society Minutes, *SDB Yearbook* (1957) 115.

[42] Directory, *SDB Yearbook* (2005) 73.

Of the missionary efforts initiated in the twentieth century, the one in Jamaica has been the most successful. Its close location to the United States made it easily accessible for communication and support with both personnel and services.

Around 1918, a number of Seventh-day Adventists in the British West Indies and the United States withdrew from that denomination "for justifiable reasons" and formed the Free Seventh-day Adventist denomination. Seventeen of those churches were located in Jamaica.[43] About this same time, a publication titled *The Voice* was widely circulated in Jamaica. It was edited by Rev. Robert B. St. Clair, the pastor of a Seventh Day Baptist church in Detroit, Michigan, who was described as being "a conscientious man who frowned upon everything that had a shade of dishonesty."[44] St. Clair had served as an evangelist at camp meetings with the Methodists until he discovered the Sabbath.[45] He recalled that although he had attended Adventist meetings and agreed with them on the Sabbath question, "yet I can find little else that is acceptable to me." After listing a number of disagreements, he commented, "I am afraid that some calamity to the Sabbath cause will occur through some failure either of their 2nd Advent views—or some absurdity of Mrs. Ellen G. White, the so-called Prophetess of the Lord Most High.[46] His fear of some of those teachings can clearly be seen in the pages of *The Voice* as he challenged many of Mrs. White's writings. He particularly challenged writings that appeared to him to be racist. He found ready readers among those who felt the effects of discrimination.

When two churches in Jamaica that had joined the splinter group of Adventists wrote to St. Clair requesting support, he referred the matter to the Northwestern Association. The association urged that two men be sent immediately to the island and began a drive for funds. The Tract Society and the Missionary Board later joined in this effort. Pastor C. A. Hansen of Chicago and W. L. Burdick, the secretary of the Missionary Society, visited this newly opened door in 1923. They found that the Free Seventh-day Adventist Conference of Jamaica was about to break up over dissatisfaction with mismanagement of conference affairs and the polity of the denomination, which was not congregational. In company

---

[43] Missionary Society Minutes, *SDB Yearbook* (1924) 179.

[44] Dr. J. C. Branch, obituary, "Rev. Robert B. St. Clair," *Sabbath Recorder* 105/1 (2 Jul 1928): 17.

[45] Rev. Robert B. St. Clair, letter to Sarah F. B. Hood (postmistress of Ashaway RI), A-File, St. Clair, 12 Oct 1902.

[46] St. Clair, letter to Mrs. Hood, 5 Aug 1903.

with Elder Louie H. Mignott, president of the defunct Free Conference, the two representatives visited discouraged churches and explained Seventh Day Baptist beliefs and practices. Eight additional churches became Seventh Day Baptist, making a total of ten that were organized into the Jamaica Seventh Day Baptist Association. Five other congregations soon joined. Elder Mignott stayed on as the general missionary on the field.[47]

In 1926, the Memorial Fund promised an appropriation, provided a missionary be sent to Jamaica to help in the building of a church in the capital city of Kingston. The Missionary Society voted to employ two missionaries to work in the South American and West Indies mission fields as soon as the matter could be properly arranged.[48] The following year, 1927, D. Burdette Coon was sent to Jamaica and Royal Thorngate to British Guiana. With the exception of the war years, 1942–1945, missionaries were sent regularly during the next three decades. In addition to D. Burdette Coon (1927–1931), the general missionaries in Jamaica included Gerald Hargis (1931–1938), Luther Crichlow (1938–1941), Wardner Fitz Randolph (1945–1956), and Leon Lawton (1956–1964).

In 1929, the Missionary Society adopted the following policy of developing indigenous leaders in the American Tropics. In foreign countries, "native church members shall be encouraged to assume the responsibility of leadership as fast as they shall become able." The board stated further "that the attitude of our missionaries, as far as possible, shall be that of advisers rather than dictators, to the end that native leadership may be brought out and a sense of responsibility created."[49] To implement the policy of developing native leadership and indigenous or self-sustaining missions, education received high priority. In Jamaica, Crandall High School was opened in 1948 on property next to the Kingston church. The supervising principals that led the school through its first thirty years came from the United States and were employed by the Missionary Society. These included Neal Mills, Orville Bond, Grover Brissey, Courtland Davis, Wayne Crandall, and Douglas Mackintosh. A number of others have given dedicated service as teachers. In 1978, Ronald Smith, a product of Crandall High School, became its first Jamaican principal.

---

[47] Missionary Society Minutes, *SDB Yearbook* (1924) 179-80.
[48] Missionary Society Minutes, *SDB Yearbook* (1926) 183.
[49] Missionary Society Minutes, *SDB Yearbook* (1929) 150-52.

The Missionary Society still maintains a small line item in its budget for assistance to special needs in Jamaica, but Jamaica is no longer an official mission field; it is now an independent conference with 32 churches and more than 1,400 members (as of 2006). Instead of receiving support to carry on its work, it is now sending support to other sister conferences. Almost the entire current congregation of the Mill Yard Seventh Day Baptist Church in London, England, is Jamaican in origin. Several of the churches and fellowships in the Seventh Day Baptist General Conference in the USA and Canada are primarily Jamaican. One of the protégés of the Jamaican mission educational program, Rev. Joe A. Samuels, now pastor of the Plainfield Seventh Day Baptist Church, served as president of the 1989 session of the General Conference, USA and Canada, and of the World Federation, 2003–2008. He had been one of the Jamaican delegates to the World Federation's founding body in 1964. The Jamaica Conference hosted the World Federation sessions at Passley Gardens in 1997 with seventy delegates and observers from fourteen member conferences. At the 2008 sessions, its president, Claudia Ferguson reported 35 churches and 6 fellowships with membership of "just under 2,500."[50]

5. *Planning for Missions.* Some of the earliest missionary activity of Seventh Day Baptists was the result of deliberate plans to establish new communities and churches where members could enjoy the advantages of Sabbath worship. Although the underlying reasons for migration may have been economic and geographic, plans for settlement included such ideas as that expressed by the colony association of 1871, which led to the settlement of North Loup, Nebraska: "To give such of our people as observed the Seventh Day of the week as the Sabbath the opportunity to settle together for purposes of convenience to themselves, as well as to avoid molesting others who differ from them in religious faith, while they carry out their convictions of duty in keeping another day than Sunday as the Sabbath."[51]

After such communities were established, associations and the denomination as a whole responded in home mission activity as they sent missionaries and circuit riders to the scattered members of the faith. Similarly, the beginnings of foreign missions in the decade of the 1840s were deliberately planned to take the gospel to such places as China and

---

[50] SDB World Federation Minutes (2008) 43.
[51] Hosea Rood, *A Historical Sketch of the Thorngate-Rood Family* (Ord NE: Horace M. Davis, 1906) 70-71.

Palestine. But the missionary activity of the twentieth century has been almost completely in response to the "Macedonian call": "Come over to Macedonia and help us" (Acts 16:9).

In addition to the early twentieth-century missions in Africa and the American Tropics, Seventh Day Baptists have been involved in assisting a number of other Sabbathkeeping Baptist groups around the world. In most of these Seventh Day Baptist Conferences and missions, help has been given through printed material, correspondence, financial aid, short visits, and the training of local leaders. Only in the Philippines have resident missionaries been sent for any extended period. Even the work of Rodney and Camille Henry from 1979 to 1985 in the Philippines was not the typical mission. The major portion of this ministry was the development of Theological Education by Extension (TEE), a program directed toward equipping native leaders to better train their own pastors and workers. (The support of Dr. Thomas McElwain in Finland and other Nordic areas beginning in February 1987 was a response to one already on the field.)[52]

On the home field, there has been an increased emphasis on church planting. In most situations a new church has been located in response to interest already present. Sometimes the interest has been generated by a person who has come to the Sabbath through Bible study, from reading a tract or other means of written or oral testimony. At other times it has been from a Seventh Day Baptist who moved to a new location. A few new churches have been "transplants" from some other Sabbathkeeping denomination who have found Seventh Day Baptist polity or beliefs more in line with their own convictions. The Seventh Day Baptist Church at White Cloud, Michigan, for example, came into being when the Michigan Conference of the Church of God (Seventh Day) asked for and was granted membership in the General Conference in 1917. The White Cloud church was influenced by an evangelistic team and communications with the Seventh Day Baptist Church of Battle Creek.[53]

Guidelines have been developed by the General Conference to help in church planting efforts. Programs such as Reach Out Now (RON), a 1970s pilot project in church planting; the Commitment to Growth and the Extension Pastor program of the 1980s; and Training in Ministry and Extension (TIME) in the 1990s are all examples of home mission field

---

[52] *Sabbath Recorder*, 209/3 (Mar 1987): 28-29.

[53] D. Burdett Coon, "Two Hundred People in Michigan Affiliated with the Seventh Day Baptists," *Sabbath Recorder* 83/18 (29 Oct 1917): 551-54.

programs in which local churches have been provided with financial and leadership support.

Seventh Day Baptist World Federation

The most significant development in the twentieth century outreach effort has been the development of the Seventh Day Baptist World Federation, a vision of Everett T. Harris, corresponding secretary of the Missionary Society from 1952–1979, and Gerben Zijlstra of Holland. In August 1964, at the invitation of the General Conference, six sister conferences (from England, British Guiana, Germany, Malawi, Holland, and Jamaica) sent delegates to the First World Consultation of Seventh Day Baptist Conferences (CoWoCo) in connection with sessions of the General Conference at Salem, West Virginia. One year later, the World Federation came into being after eleven conferences voted to accept its constitution. By 1984, the number of conferences in the World Federation had expanded to seventeen: Australia/New Zealand, Brazil, England, Germany, Guyana, India (Andra Pradesh), India (Kerala), Jamaica, Malawi, Mexico, Myanmar (Burma), the Netherlands, Nigeria, the Philippines, Poland, South Africa, and the United States and Canada.[54] In 2009, three new African conferences joined: Burundi, Kenya, and Zambia.[55]

The purposes of the World Federation as stated in its constitution are: "(1) to provide increased communication, (2) to stimulate fellowship, (3) to promote evangelism and other projects benefiting from international cooperation, (4) to coordinate mutual endeavors through the office of the executive secretary, (5) to receive and evaluate statements of need, and (6) to act as a liaison for individuals recommended by a group or conference/convention."[56] Sessions of the World Federation have been held in 1971 at Westerly, Rhode Island, with eighteen delegates from nine countries; in 1978 at Alfred, New York, with thirty-four delegates from ten countries; and in 1986, again at Westerly, with sixty-three delegates and observers from sixteen conferences. In the 1990s, the World Federation sessions moved out of the United States; thirty-five delegates from sixteen countries met in

---

[54] Janet Thorngate, "A worldwide witness: the World Federation's first 20 years," *Sabbath Recorder* 209/1 (Jan 1986): 8-11.

[55] *SDB World* (Salem WV: SDB World Federation, Oct 2009) 1.

[56] Article II, "SDB World Federation Constitution," 1973.

New Zealand in 1992[57] and thirty-five delegates from fifteen countries (including one fraternal delegate from Haiti) met in Jamaica in 1997.[58] The first sessions in the new millennium, held in 2003, hosted twenty-four delegates from ten countries in Brazil.[59] In 2008, sessions were again held in the USA with plans to meet in the Philippines in 2013.

Officers of the World Federation have served as volunteers; several of the general secretaries have even served concurrently with an executive position in their own conferences: Alton L. Wheeler (1965–1978), K. Duane Hurley (1978–1981), Dale D. Thorngate (1981–2003), Calvin Babcock (2005–2008), and Jan Lek (2008–). The federation sponsors an annual Seventh Day Baptist Week of Prayer, observed the first week of January since 1966, and each year publishes a devotional booklet translated into several languages.

The following summary information concerns those member conferences not previously covered; these are given in chronological order. (This information should be viewed with caution as reporting methods are not consistent between conferences. For example, as a result of different membership standards and accounting methods, it is sometimes difficult to know exactly how many members or churches a conference might have.)

Holland (The Netherlands)

Aside from England and the United States, the Netherlands has the longest Seventh Day Baptist history. In 1858, Gerald Velthuysen broke from the Reformed Church and established a branch of the "Society for the Propaganda of the Truth," taking the Bible alone as the rule of conduct. Around 1876, he received several tracts about the Sabbath published by Dr. Nathan Wardner, then a Seventh Day Baptist missionary in Scotland. After careful study, Velthuysen became convinced of the Sabbath and with twenty others established a Seventh Day Baptist church in Haarlem, Holland, in October 1877.[60]

---

[57] Janet Thorngate, "'Give Me This Mountain': World Federation Meets in New Zealand," *Sabbath Recorder* 214/3 (Mar 1992): 20-21.

[58] Janet Thorngate, "World Federation Meets in Jamaica," *Sabbath Recorder* 219/11 (Nov 1997): 22-23.

[59] Janet Thorngate, "Freedom for Our World: World Federation Sessions, Feb. 10–16, 2003," *Sabbath Recorder* 225/4 (Apr 2003): 4-12.

[60] Leon Lawton, "SDBs in the Netherlands," mimeographed trifold duplicated by the SDB World Federation (1971), V-D-File, box 0, "Countries" folder.

Pastor Velthuysen was both an evangelist and a social reformer. Under his leadership, the churches in the Netherlands became active in establishing a mission in Java and supporting work in Africa and Australia. Their concern for others in Europe later led to contacts with Germany and Poland. Although the Netherlands Seventh Day Baptist Conference currently list a membership of only sixty in three churches,[61] missionary concern is expressed through the work of Jan Lek and others who have conducted relief and church development work in Poland and, more recently, in the Ukraine and Moldavia. For a period of time, Lek published *The Link*, a European Seventh Day Baptist newsletter carrying English, Dutch, and German translations. From the World Federation's origins, the Dutch have provided leadership, with Lek currently serving as its general secretary.

Germany

Seventh Day Baptist witness in Germany began in the early 1930s when Elder L. R. Conradi left the Adventists and became a Seventh Day Baptist. He attended the sessions of the General Conference in 1932 and soon afterward joined with several others to form the German Union of Seventh Day Baptist Churches, which numbered 8 churches and about 300 members. By 1935, the German Union reported 18 churches and 500 members.

World War II took a heavy toll from which the Germans never recovered. Elder Conradi, then in his eighties, died of natural causes, and other leaders were called to serve in the army. Both military and civilian casualties further diminished the German Seventh Day Baptists' numbers. After the war the partitioning of Germany left several churches in East Germany, where travel and communications were difficult.[62] These churches were represented in the 1986 World Federation session by Alfred Mellmann, but Germany was no longer listed as an active conference.[63]

Australia and New Zealand

Churches in Australia and and New Zealand joined the World Federation as the Australasian Conference, but in 2003 the Federation received the Australia Association as a separate member. The witness in

---

[61] SDB World Federation Minutes (2008) 58.
[62] Lawton, "SDBs in Germany" (Plainfield NJ: SDB World Federation, 1971).
[63] Directory, *SDB Yearbook* (1988) B29.

New Zealand began as a Bible class of Sabbathkeepers, most of whom left the Seventh-day Adventist church. After a study of Seventh Day Baptist beliefs, they organized into a local church in Auckland on the North Island in the 1930s, with Rev. Francis Johnson as pastor. About the same time, another group under the leadership of Rev. Edward Barrar formed on the South Island at Christchurch. By 1940, both groups were in fellowship with the General Conference.

These churches in New Zealand have had a strong missionary zeal. In 1946, Pastor Barrar's son Ronald answered the call from pastors in Nyasaland (Malawi) in Africa and was largely responsible for reactivating that mission.[64] The New Zealand churches continued to support that mission by sending Ian Ingoe in 1989 as a construction missionary. These churches have also given support to missions work in India and Nigeria. The New Zealand churches were instrumental in the establishment of churches in Australia.

In 1975, a young Seventh-day Adventist couple in Bundaberg, Queensland, Australia, saw inconsistencies in Adventist beliefs and teaching and withdrew from that church. In searching for an alternate church with which to fellowship, they remembered having read of Seventh Day Baptists in their Adventist history. From a visiting Baptist from America they received a point of contact. Rev. Alton Wheeler replied with literature and the address of Pastor Francis Johnson in Auckland, New Zealand. As a result of these contacts, a church was organized in Bundaberg on 23 August 1975.

The following October, Pastor and Mrs. Johnson visited Australia and spent two weeks in following other leads with respect to other potential Seventh Day Baptist groups. At about this time, a Seventh Day Baptist immigrant from the Netherlands, Vicky Kube, and her husband Stefan (whose family had been among early Sabbathkeepers in Poland), visited Bundaberg. The Kubes organized a church meeting in their home in Warrimoo, New South Wales, and invited the Johnsons to attend. As a result of this meeting, other churches and fellowships soon organized, including a Spanish-speaking church in Melbourne headed by Pastor Joseph Alegre and, more recently, a Samoan congregation led by Marlo Siolo in Brisbane.[65]

---

[64] Lawton, "SDBs in New Zealand" (Plainfield NJ: SDB World Federation, 1971).

[65] Mavis Rudd, *A Decade in Australia*, 1975–1985, 2nd ed. (Bundaberg, Queensland: M. L. Rudd, 1986).

The Australasian Conference joined the Baptist World Alliance in 1983 and hosted the SDB World Federation sessions in Auckland, New Zealand, in 1992. The Australians contributed much to worldwide communications through the monthly publication *Link*, edited by Stefan Kube. Beginning in 2003, Australian young people were involved in Summer Christian Service Corps (SCSC) projects in the United States. This led to an SCSC training session in Australia under the umbrella of the Seventh Day Baptist General Conference USA and Canada's Women's Society.

Brazil

In 1913, six leaders of the Seventh-day Adventist conference of Brazil withdrew to form a new conference called the Seventh Day Evangelical Adventists (also known as Evangelical Extraordinary). In 1950, after learning of the Seventh Day Baptists from churches of this faith in Germany, these Adventists revised their statutes and adopted the Seventh Day Baptist name "Brazilian Conference of Seventh Day Baptists." In 1965, their General Assembly approved association with the Seventh Day Baptist World Federation and was represented at the 1971, 1978, 1986, 1992, and 1997 sessions before hosting the federation in Bocaiúva do Sul, Paraná in 2003.[66] The 2003 report listed 2,800 members.[67] In 2008 this conference listed sixty-one churches and ten home missions groups.[68]

The Brazil conference translates *The Helping Hand* and other SDB publications into Portuguese for their own use and supplies copies to Portuguese-speaking contacts in Mozambique. In cooperation with the Seventh Day Baptist Historical Society, it also translated the first edition of *A Choosing People* and had it printed in Brazil.

India (Andhra Pradesh)

The earliest known record of a Seventh Day Baptist Church in India is found in an open letter from the pastor of the Seventh Day Baptist Church of Christ in Calcutta; the letter was published in 1925 in *The Voice* edited by Robert St Clair. Churches in Michigan and Ohio sponsored a trip for the pastor of that church, A. P. C. Dey, to visit others in India who were interested in a Seventh Day Baptist witness. Dey reported that

---

[66] Lawton, "SDBs in Brazil" (Plainfield NJ: SDB World Federation, 1971).
[67] Directory, *SDB Yearbook* (1988) B23-26.
[68] Brazil Report, SDB World Federation Minutes (2008) 7, 36-41.

in less than two months' time, four other churches were established.[69] Although this church in Calcutta was accepted in 1925 as a member of the General Conference[70] the name is not carried among the statistics beyond 1927. There appears to be no documented evidence of any connection between either this group or a Seventh Day Baptist church at Nazareth in South India and later Seventh Day Baptists in India.

The current Seventh Day Baptist witness began when a former Catholic priest, Rev. B. John V. Rao, joined with about twenty others to form the Telugu Seventh Day Baptist Mission in 1950. Their first contact with Seventh Day Baptists was with the German Seventh Day Baptist church in Salemville, Pennsylvania. In May 1968, correspondence was made with Rao by the General Conference through the American Sabbath Tract Society that provided funds to publish the statement of beliefs in the Telugu dialect.[71]

John Rao attended the World Federation sessions in 1986, but the Andhra Pradesh Conference has not sent a delegate since then, usually because of visa or travel complications. Rao's son B. Kishor Kumar has led the work since his father's death, receiving some support from the Missionary Society. In 1988 the Andhra Pradesh Conference reported 258 churches with 60 field evangelists, 32 evangelism teams, 33 prayer crusades, 16 youth teams, 15 women's teams, 5 social service teams, and 2 medical centers. Relief projects, some supported by the Baptist World Alliance, have included digging forty-eight irrigation wells and eight drinking water wells.[72]

Burma (Myanmar)

Burma is one of the oldest Baptist mission fields, dating back to 1813 when Adoniram and Ann Judson began their work in that country. Some of the Judsons' reports were widely circulated in the earliest Seventh Day Baptist missionary publications and did much to inspire missionary outreach. However, it was not until 1960 that two native converts to the Sabbath, L. Ngura and C. Khawvelthanga, started a mission in Tahan, Burma. Correspondence with Seventh Day Baptist leaders in the United States led to the formation in 1965 of the Burma

---

[69] "Open Letter from India" *The Voice* 4/11 (Oct 1925), repr. in "Pastor's Whirlwind Evangelistic Tour," *The Voice* 5/11 (Oct 1926): 1.

[70] Conference Minutes, *SDB Yearbook* (1925) 90.

[71] Lawton, "SDBs in India," (Plainfield NJ: SDB World Federation, 1971).

[72] Directory, *SDB Yearbook* (1988) B30-32.

Seventh Day Baptist Conference, which became one of the charter members of the World Federation.

The church in Burma has been hampered by government restrictions that forced all foreign missionaries to leave the country. The government's suspicions of any foreign investments or influence have made communications and assistance difficult. In addition, a disagreement erupted between leaders in the organization of the conference in 1975. It was mediated by the ecumenical Tahan Christian Council and caused one of the original leaders, L. Ngura, to leave. That council also declared, "1960 is not the year of establishment of the Seventh Day Baptist Church in Burma and forbid to use this year within its capacity. The year in which the Seventh Day Baptist Church was first established is 1964."[73]

L. Sawi Thanga represented Burma at the World Federation sessions in the United States in 1986, but increasing political restrictions have prevented travel and hampered communications since then. The Burma Conference's 1988 *Yearbook* report listed fifteen churches with a membership of 811. In 1985 the Burma Conference became a member of the Baptist World Alliance, giving it added status to enhance its witness.

Mexico

The Seventh Day Baptist witness in Mexico originated with a Mexican Baptist minister who became convinced of the Sabbath through Adventist teachings while he was living in San Antonio, Texas. When he moved back to Mexico, he established an independent Sabbathkeeping church. In time, his son Elias Camacho became the leader of a group of twenty-eight churches. Around 1965, Pastor Camacho received two Seventh Day Baptist tracts and wrote to the General Conference requesting more information. After study and contacts with several individuals, he wrote again, saying, "We say that we are not similar; no, we are the same flock and we want to be close to you."[74] In 1965 he attended the Seventh Day Baptist Minister's Conference, and the following year the conference president, Marion Van Horn, and the Director of Evangelism, Leon Lawton, visited the churches in Mexico.

---

[73] "The Tahan Christian Council," 22 Jan 1976, transcript, MS 196x.7, C file, p. 1, SDB Hist. Soc. Lib.

[74] Elias Camacho, quoted in "Mexican Churches of Like Faith and Order," *Sabbath Recorder* 178/11 (15 Mar 1965): 13.

Before learning of Seventh Day Baptists, the group took the name Church of Christ of the Seventh Day as its legally registered name for holding property. Their churches reflect Mexico's economic poverty. They have no paid clergy and ask for nothing but prayers, although some assistance has been sent to help in their work, particularly through a Missionary Society committee within the USA and Canada's Mid-Continent Association. Pastor Camacho attended World Federation sessions in 1986 and in 1988 reported 11 churches with 479 members.[75] Unfortunately, following his death, communication with his son Rosalio has proved problematic, and in 2008 the World Federation removed Mexico from its membership list.[76]

The Philippines

The first contact of Seventh Day Baptists with the leaders in the Philippines was through correspondence beginning in 1971. In 1974, General Conference executive Alton Wheeler and Missionary Society executive Leon Lawton visited the Philippine mission on their around-the-world ambassadorial tour. Soon after this visit, the Seventh Day Baptist Philippine Conference was organized and became a member of the World Federation. The Philippine Conference was represented by its president, Rev. E. O. Ferraren, at the 1978 session of the World Federation.

From 1979 to 1985, Rodney and Camille Henry served as missionaries to the Philippines and developed a program of pastoral training based on a model called Theological Education by Extension (TEE), in which bi-vocational pastors participated in supervised home study and training seminars. In 1981, following a division in the original conference, a new Seventh Day Baptist Philippine Convention was organized with pastors Saubon, Santianez, and Paypa as leaders. Rev. Eleodore Saubon served as the first president. In 1984, Rev. Eleazar Paypa became president and took over the deanship of the TEE program from Rodney Henry.[77] Matthew and Ellen Olson went to the Philippines in 1987 for three months as short-term missionaries, Ellen serving as a medical missionary financed by the Missionary Society and Matt was an

---

[75] Directory, *SDB Yearbook* (1988) B38, B43.

[76] SDB World Federation Minutes (2008) 6, 13, 34.

[77] Janet Thorngate, "Getting Acquainted: SDBs Around the World," *Sabbath Recorder* 208/3 (May 1986): 22.

educational missionary funded by the Board of Christian Education. The 1988 report listed 14 churches and 275 members.

Eleazar Paypa represented the Philippine Convention at World Federation sessions in 1986 and 1992; following his 1997 death in an automobile accident, his son Al B. Paypa became the convention leader and its delegate to the World Federation in 1997, 2003, and 2008. The TEE program, later called TIME (Training in Ministry and Extension), is credited with much of the growth reflected in the Philippine Convention's 2008 report of twenty-two churches and five new groups. Paypa also reported a merger of the conference and the convention, which had been under discussion for several years.[78]

Poland

Branislaw Ciesielski dated the beginning of the Sabbath Day Christian Church in Poland with a separation in 1933 from the Seventh-day Adventists over "noticeable deviations in teaching, morality and organizational structure." Members of the church stress differences with the interpretations of Ellen G. White and the theology surrounding "the investigative judgment." At first they took the name Fellowship of Independent Seventh-day Adventist Churches, but in 1936 they changed their name to United Seventh Day Evangelical Christians. Their current name, the Sabbath Day Christian Church, was adopted and registered with the government in 1961.[79]

About a year later, in 1962, the Polish Sabbathkeepers' first official contact was made with Seventh Day Baptists when Gerben Zijlstra, the secretary of the Conference of Seventh Day Baptist Churches in the Netherlands, made a visit to churches in Germany and Poland. In correspondence with the Missionary Society, he wrote, "In my opinion, we have to do with earnest Christians, simple-hearted men and women, among whom we will feel at home, though they do not call themselves Seventh Day Baptists."[80]

Eighteen years later, in 1980, another secretary of the churches in the Netherlands, Jan Lek, represented the World Federation in a visit to Poland. He reported that the Polish churches were "pleased to be in touch with SDBs from abroad again. All of them hope that this fresh

---

[78] Philippines Report, SDB World Federation Minutes (2008) 60-61.

[79] Bronislaw Ciesielski, "What Everyone Ought to Know about Sabbath Day Christians in Poland," diss., trans. K. W., pub. by author, 1975.

[80] Everett T. Harris, "Secretary Zijlstra Visits Sabbathkeeping Churches of Poland," *Sabbath Recorder* 173/15 (22 Oct 1962): 9-10.

contact will lead to strengthening and enlarging the ties of co-operation."[81] Lek further reported that the door to increased fellowship is tentatively opened, but the initiative must be taken by others. He went on to suggest the need for a general missionary to serve all of Europe.[82]

In 1984, Poland was voted into the Seventh Day Baptist World Federation. The federation's executive secretary Dale Thorngate and his wife Janet officially welcomed the Polish delegates at their conference session in Bydgoszcz in July. Ciesielski represented them at the 1986 sessions and Pawel Bujak in 1992 and 1997. In 1988, the Poland Conference reported eleven churches with a total membership of 455.[83]

South Africa

The newest member of the Seventh Day Baptist World Federation at its 1986 meeting was South Africa. Some trace this conference's roots to 1906, when William Olifan heard about Seventh Day Baptists through the work of Joseph Booth. Thus, the date 1906 appears on the conference's application for membership in the World Federation.

Jacob Bakker of the Netherlands, who was sent in 1910 by the Tract Society and the Missionary Board to visit both South Africa and the Gold Coast, reported that William Olifan, a Baptist who came to the Sabbath through a native Adventist minister, began to observe that day privately while preaching to the Baptists. In 1906 he gathered a church of about eighty members, most of whom accepted the Sabbath but were unable to keep it, for as Olifan explained, "All our people have to work for the white men, and hence are compelled to break the Sabbath most of the time; they are keeping the Sabbath in a poor way."[84] More recent research shows a closer relationship between Olifan and Booth, who was then living in South Africa.[85]

The Missionary Board report for 1954 indicated correspondence with a Seventh Day Baptist in Johannesburg. An article in the *Sabbath Recorder* in 1963 reported that the board had received a copy of the constitution governing the church at Port Elizabeth. The pastor who sent the copy wrote, "I have pleasure to bring to your knowledge that we

---

[81] "Missionary Tour of Germany-Poland," *Sabbath Recorder* 202/3 (Mar 1980): 16-17.

[82] Tom Merchant, "Send Us a Paul," *Sabbath Recorder* 202/4 (Apr 1980): 15.

[83] Directory, *SDB Yearbook* (1988) B41-42.

[84] "Mission of Jacob Bakker," *Sabbath Recorder* 69/22 (28 November 1910): 690.

[85] Harry W. Langworthy III, *Africa for the African: A Biography of Joseph Booth, 1851–1932*, ch. 15, pp. 2-12; "Booth and Seventh Day Baptists Again, 1910–1911," MS 1990.16, SDB Hist. Soc. Lib.

have here converted two different church branches who have now joined the Seventh Day Baptist Church." He indicated difficulty in deciding on a name, as some preferred a slightly longer designation.[86] In 1974, Alton Wheeler and Leon Lawton renewed contact with these churches on their world tour of missions and new contacts.

Personal visits of representatives of the General Conference, the World Federation, and other missionary personnel led to closer cooperation and assistance from sister conferences. Funds were provided by Seventh Day Baptists to assist such projects as the erection of a church building and ministerial training for Pastor Nyaniso James Siwane. In 1995, the Seventh Day Baptist Historical Society, in cooperation with the South Africa Conference, published Siwani's book *The Unknown Made Known: A History of Sabbathkeepers in South Africa.*[87]

The South African church is caught in the country's ongoing problems of social, economic, and political unrest. Apartheid, illiteracy, and poverty affected community and churches alike, leading to division. A serious rift in 1982 among some of the leaders of the Seventh Day Baptist congregation led to questions of facility ownership and organizational legitimacy. Despite these challenges, in 1986, the group led by Pastor Siwane was accepted into the World Federation. In 1988, this conference reported 3 churches and 4 groups with 364 members.[88] The 2006 report indicated there were 5 churches with 300 members.[89]

India (Kerala)

The seventeenth group to become a member of the World Federation was the Malankara Seventh Day Baptist Church of Kerala, India, which was accepted in 1989. The church, located on the west coast of India bordering the Arabian Sea, was independently organized in 1985. Communication with Seventh Day Baptists initially occurred through a member living in Texas and another in California. Other representatives of the General Conference soon made contacts, and visits took place with Rev. B. John V. Rao of the conference in Andhra Pradesh, on the east coast of India. Missionary Society executive Leon Lawton and World Federation president Gabriel Bejjani visited Kerala in 1988. This newest member, at the time of its entrance into the federation, consisted

---

[86] South Africa Church News," *Sabbath Recorder* 175/15 (21 Oct 1963): 15.

[87] Nyaniso James Siwani, *The Unknown Made Known: A History of Sabbathkeepers in South Africa* (Janesville WI: SDB Historical Society, 1995).

[88] Directory, *SDB Yearbook* (1988) B42-43

[89] Directory, *SDB Yearbook* (2006) B75.

of 3 churches and 2 fellowships with a total membership of 170.[90] In 2000, 3 churches reported a total of 400 members.[91] Sosamma Philip and Susamma Koshy, a teacher and an administrator in the school operated by the conference, represented it at 1997 Federation sessions in Jamaica.

OPENING DOORS AROUND THE WORLD

At the beginning of the twenty-first century, Seventh Day Baptists are finding a number of other doors opening to new or renewed Sabbath witness. The dismantling of the iron curtain in Europe has revealed the people's desire to follow the teachings of the Bible in worship on the Sabbath. There are Sabbathkeeping Baptist churches or fellowships in Finland, in Estonia, in Latvia, in Czechoslovakia, and reportedly in Russia at Moscow and Leningrad. Renewed relations with China give some promise of renewed witness among those who were influenced by earlier generations of missionaries. The denomination has also maintained contacts with interested individuals in neighboring Korea. The five Ps of mission—purpose, priority, place, personnel and plan— continue to challenge thought and action in the present and the future.

---

[90] *SDB World* (Janesville WI: SDB World Federation, Dec 1988) 1.
[91] Directory, *SDB Yearbook* (2000) B66.

22

TWENTIETH-CENTURY ECUMENICAL RELATIONS

Seventh Day Baptists have always been ecumenically minded. They have chosen to cooperate with other Christians when possible without compromising convictions. However, when, in the mid-nineteenth century, individual Seventh Day Baptists led efforts to bring all churches together, an editorial in the *Sabbath Recorder* pointed out that "to unite all churches or two of them with conflicting theories or sentiments, is impossible."[1] For Seventh Day Baptists, the Sabbath and believer's baptism have been the "conflicting theories and sentiments" over which compromise is impossible. Yet, this steadfastness has not precluded interdenominational cooperation in other areas.

The noted Baptist historian Dr. Winthrop Hudson called Seventh Day Baptists "Separate but Not Sectarian," describing them as being "separate in organization and practice but ecumenical in spirit." He listed several of their notable features, the first of which he said was their continued existence:

> It is one of the wonders of history that Seventh Day Baptists have been able to survive at all. Small groups usually do not have a long history. They either grow or die. This is especially true of nonsectarian groups like the Seventh Day Baptists who are unwilling to deny the name Christian to those who do not agree with them in all things. Reasonable people appealing to reasonable people do not usually have the stamina to maintain their witness and their existence in the midst of a larger society whose members they are not ready to condemn out-of-hand.[2]

ECUMENICAL CONFERENCE ON FOREIGN MISSIONS

A major portion of the Protestant Christian world entered the twentieth century with an Ecumenical Conference on Foreign Missions, which was held in New York City in 1900. Over 1,500 delegates and 600 missionaries were present representing some 48 missionary boards and societies. The 1899 General Conference voted to endorse the proposed

---

[1] Editorial, *Sabbath Recorder* 14/10 (13 Aug 1857): 37.

[2] Winthrop S. Hudson, "Separate but Not Sectarian," Willis Russel Lecture, Alfred University, 14 Feb 1977, repr. in *Sabbath Recorder* 1994/4 (Apr 1977): 28.

conference "and commend its purpose and work to our churches."[3] The Seventh Day Baptist Missionary Society was represented by four delegates: A. E. Main, George H. Utter, L. A. Platts, and Boothe C. Davis. In addition, the Missionary Society's president, William Clarke, and its corresponding secretary, O. U. Whitford, were members of the General Committee, which organized the conference. Others attended some sessions, including Dr. Phoebe J. B. Waite, who represented Seventh Day Baptist women.

INTERDENOMINATIONAL ORGANIZATIONS

The desire for greater unity and cooperation led many Protestants to call for denominations to send representatives to a conference "for the purpose of organizing a federation of denominations." The General Conference appointed Stephen Babcock, Eli Loofboro, A. H. Lewis, George B. Shaw, and Henry Jordan as its representatives.[4] Many Seventh Day Baptists recommended denominational participation in such an event, particularly in light of their statement that the meeting "shall have no authority over the constituent bodies adhering to it" and that it would have "no authority to draw up a common creed or form of government or of worship, or in any way to limit the full autonomy of the Christian bodies adhering to it."[5]

Federal Council of the Churches of Christ

The first meeting of the Federal Council, as it was called, was scheduled for December 1908, but the Executive Committee of the Federal Council began its work much sooner. Stephen Babcock, the Seventh Day Baptist representative, reported that temperance, immigration, international arbitration, child labor, and the religious training of the young were the leading issues that engaged the attention of the Executive Committee during the first years. "Nothing of importance touching the Sabbath question has engaged the attention of the Federation since its organization in 1905," he added.[6]

Sessions of the Federal Council and the role Seventh Day Baptists played were reported regularly through the pages of the *Sabbath*

---

[3] Conference Minutes, *SDB Yearbook* (1899) 52.

[4] Committee on Petitions Report, Conference Minutes, *SDB Yearbook* (1905) 87-88.

[5] Conference Minutes, *SDB Yearbook* (1906) 101.

[6] Report of the Church Federation Committee, Conference Minutes, *SDB Yearbook* (1908) 82.

Recorder. Topics ranged from unity and cooperation to missions, from immigration problems to modern industry, from temperance to family life, and from religious education to Sunday observance. It was from this last subject that Seventh Day Baptists received the most notice.

Over the next sixty-five years, Seventh Day Baptist participation in the Federal Council and its successor, the National Council of Churches, was active though sometimes controversial. Seventh Day Baptist representatives were respected members of the council. They were allowed to select delegates out of proportion to their membership; as a consequence, their voice was heard on many key issues. They consistently spoke out against attempts at Sunday legislation and often received support of others who respected the right of conscience.[7] Seventh Day Baptist participation provided a forum in which their name and beliefs widely circulated. Of particular importance was the committee's publication of a book titled *The Churches of the Federal Council*. A separate chapter was devoted to the history and principles of each of the denominations represented in the council. Of the chapter on Seventh Day Baptists, prepared by Dean A. E. Main, the committee reported: "Never in our history has such an opportunity been given Seventh Day Baptists to make known to the world the long existence of organized Sabbathkeeping Christians, and to set forth the character of our organization."[8] The report of the Federal Council delegates to the 1917 session of the General Conference indicated that the denomination's participation was not primarily as "Sabbath propagandists," but like that of other denominations, to inspire cooperation; it concluded, "We are there, one of the smallest denominations, to do our bit; to show our interest and do our part in the great task confronting the Christian church.... Connection with the Council has not lessened our denominational loyalty, nor diminished our purpose and effort to promote Sabbath truth, but rather has strengthened our hope that Sabbathkeeping Christians shall have increasing influence in the task of bringing in the kingdom of God."[9]

During the 1920s, the deep theological differences found in the modernist-fundamentalist positions embraced by Protestantism surfaced in ecumenical circles. In general, the council tended toward the liberal

---

[7] Arthur E. Main, "Federal Council," *Sabbath Recorder* 66/5 (1 Feb 1909): 135.

[8] Report of Delegates to the Federal Council, Conference Minutes, *SDB Yearbook* (1916) 26-27.

[9] Report of Delegates to the Federal Council, Conference Minutes, *SDB Yearbook* (1917) 28-32.

position, thus forcing many conservatives to seek withdrawal on theological grounds. In 1929, the General Conference appointed a carefully selected representative committee to study the whole question of the denomination's relationship to the Federal Council,[10] but no action or direction followed.[11]

Economic problems of the Great Depression curtailed some of the denomination's direct participation in the Federal Council during the 1930s, although the need for cooperative action and social concerns increased. To many people, the Federal Council provided a means whereby members could feel that they were in some small way ministering to society as a whole. It was during this same period that the council's strong stands on peace and reconciliation fell under suspicion by those who were strongly nationalistic. As the nation became involved in World War II, the Federal Council took a lead role in helping churches adjust to a changed society. Its Committee on Foreign Relief Appeals in the Churches served to validate appeals to churches and handled funds when they were received.[12] Even in the midst of war, the council's Commission to Study the Bases for a Just and Durable Peace sought ways to wage peace for post-war recovery. This commission's chairman, John Foster Dulles, would later become secretary of state.

Four Seventh Day Baptist ministers—Luther Crichlow, Leon Maltby, Wayne Rood, and Hurley Warren—volunteered for service as chaplains, and several other members of churches served as chaplains' assistants. The Federal Council gave assistance to support those who took stands as conscientious objectors. A. J. C. Bond expressed the value of membership in the council when he wrote that "membership has defined us as a Christian denomination with a background, a message, and a forward look, rather than as a narrow sect willing to avoid the great issues involved in the Church's united challenge to the paganism of our materialistic world."[13] In the years following World War II, the issue of membership in the Federal Council took on added concern as steps were taken toward merging eight national interdenominational agencies into a proposed National Council of Churches.

---

[10] Conference Minutes, *SDB Yearbook* (1929) 45.

[11] Conference Minutes, *SDB Yearbook* (1930) 55.

[12] Report of Delegates to the Federal Council, Conference Minutes, *SDB Yearbook* (1942) 14.

[13] Report of Delegates to the Federal Council, Conference Minutes, *SDB Yearbook* (1943) 22.

National Council of Churches

In December 1950, the Federal Council of Churches merged with several entities: the Foreign Missions Conference of North America, the Home Missions Council of North America, the International Council of Religious Education, the Missionary Education Movement, the National Protestant Council on Higher Education, the United Council of Church Women, and the United Stewardship Council to form the National Council of Churches of Christ in the United States of America, popularly referred to as the NCC. Seventh Day Baptists were represented at the constituting convention, not only because the General Conference was a member of the Federal Council, but also because the Board of Christian Education was a member of the International Council of Religious Education, the Missionary Board was a member of the Foreign Missions Conference, and the Women's Board was a member of the United Council of Church Women.

Many within the denomination expressed opposition over membership in this new organization. An article in the *Sabbath Recorder* in 1950 under the title "The Threat Evangelicals See in the Proposed National Council" expressed these fears, which involved: (1) "the potential of a Protestant monopoly or a 'super church' which can eventually…" rob individual members of their freedom of thought and action; (2) the liberal leanings of the leadership that would propagate "a liberal evangelism which eliminates sin and the need of redemption in the blood of God's Son"; (3) the control of the radio, the press, and community enterprises; and (4) "political pressure programs" and lobbying which would "officially commit the good name of Protestantism and that of each of its component Churches."[14] The debate continued for over two decades, until the General Conference voted in 1973 to withdraw. The vote was a roll-call vote of churches under the unit rule, in which the total votes allotted to each church were cast either pro or con. The vote was 335 for withdrawal and 250 against.

World Faith and Order

The increased world consciousness of the early twentieth century revealed the impossibility of religious isolation. Early in the century, steps were taken to call a World Conference on Faith and Order. The

---

[14] Summarized from "United Evangelical Action," repr. in *Sabbath Recorder* 149/6 (14 Aug 1950): 92.

plan called for consideration of "those things in which denominations differ, from the viewpoint of things in which they agree." Each participating denomination was asked to restudy and prepare its own statement of faith for circulation. By 1912, eighteen denominations had appointed commissions for this purpose.[15] Boothe C. Davis called upon the General Conference to take steps to send representatives when such a conference was held. "Let us take our place here, also, and do our work, and let our voice be heard."[16] The conference responded by appointing a committee of seven with Rev. Edwin Shaw as chairman. Other members included Theodore L. Gardiner, William L. Burdick, Alfred E. Main, Boothe C. Davis, William C. Daland, and C. B. Clark.[17]

The outbreak of World War I delayed the proposed conference. Nevertheless, the committee prepared its statement, which was circulated in the *Sabbath Recorder* and then presented to the 1917 General Conference in session, which adopted it "as a substantial statement of faith."[18] This statement contained three main elements: (1) beliefs that were in harmony with the faith of modern Protestantism; (2) statements of polity and practice that suggested some denominational differences in matters of polity and practice; and (3) a statement on the Sabbath that justified a separate denominational existence.[19]

It was not until 1927 that the first meeting of the long-proposed World Conference was held at Lausanne, Switzerland. A. J. C. Bond was the official representative of Seventh Day Baptists, with Rev. Pieter Taekema of Holland ready to stand in as an alternate. Bond reported that he never felt more certain of the logic of the Seventh Day Baptist position. "It is historically and Scripturally sound. We have a right to become enthusiastic over it.... We have a right to be in every such movement. We are a small people, but with our feet firmly planted on the rock foundation we need not fear."[20]

At the conclusion of the conference, a Continuation Committee was selected to carry on the work during the interim. A. J. C. Bond was one of those selected, even though several much larger denominations were not

[15] Boothe C. Davis, "President's Address," Conference Minutes, *SDB Yearbook* (1912) 17.
[16] Ibid.
[17] Report of the Nominating Committee, Conference Minutes, *SDB Yearbook* (1912) 120.
[18] Conference Minutes, *SDB Yearbook* (1917) 72.
[19] "Faith and Order Movement," *Sabbath Recorder* 82/10 (5 Mar 1917): 293-94. See also Conference Minutes, *SDB Yearbook* (1917) 25-27.
[20] A. J. C. Bond, "The World Conference on Faith and Order," *Sabbath Recorder* 103/10 (5 Sep 1927): 300.

represented. For financial reasons, Seventh Day Baptists could not represent the denomination at either the World Conference on Faith and Order or the 1937 World Conference on Life and Works and thus had little say in the proposals that sprang from them. From these two meetings came the proposal to form the World Council of Churches.

World Council of Churches

In May 1938, a conference of delegates from around the world was scheduled to take place in Utrecht, Holland, so that the new World Council could draft a constitution. Of the eighty total delegates, ten were from the United States, accompanied by an additional ten to serve as alternates. Two Baptists were chosen, Dr. Kenneth Latourette of Yale Divinity School and Professor W. O. Carver of the Southern Baptist Theological School. When Professor Carver was unable to go, his alternate, Dean A. J. C. Bond of the Alfred School of Theology, took his place among the delegates. As it turned out, Latourette and Bond were the only two Baptists attending the constituting conference. Their presence made a difference in several of the constitution's major aspects.[21]

In 1938, the General Conference approved the proposed constitution and accepted membership in the World Council, "provided there is no financial responsibility beyond that already provided."[22] When the constitution was written at Utrecht, it was expected that the first assembly of the World Council would be held in 1941, but the outbreak of World War II forced a postponement. Several preparation meetings were held during the war at which Seventh Day Baptists were represented. Dean Bond expressed an example of Seventh Day Baptists' disproportionately powerful voice in ecumenical affairs when he related the following incident: in one meeting wherein a delegate made reference to the denomination's small size, the presiding officer remarked, "Seventh Day Baptists weigh more than they count."[23]

Dr. Lloyd Seager represented Seventh Day Baptists at the First Assembly of the World Council of Churches held at Amsterdam in 1948. Rev. Clifford W. P. Hansen represented Seventh Day Baptists at both the Second Assembly held in Evanston, Illinois, in 1954, and at the Third

---

[21] A. J. C. Bond, "The Utrecht Conference," *Sabbath Recorder* 124/26 (27 Jun 1938): 414-15.

[22] Conference Minutes, *SDB Yearbook* (1938) 42.

[23] A. J. C. Bond, class discussion in Alfred School of Theology, 1950, attended by the author.

Assembly hosted in New Delhi, India, in 1961. Rev. Alton Wheeler, as general secretary of the General Conference, was the representative at the Fourth Assembly held in Uppsala, Sweden, in 1968, but he opted not to attend the Fifth Assembly held in Africa in 1975 at Nairobi, Kenya because the General Conference's membership in the World Council of Churches was being questioned.

In 1976, the General Conference voted to withdraw from membership in the World Council of Churches. The issue of membership in the council was a natural follow-up to the conference's 1973 vote to withdraw from the National Council. Many of the same arguments, both pro and con, were aired. The reports that came out of the Fifth Assembly in Nairobi probably did much to tip the scales in favor of withdrawal, for they highlighted the perceived changes within the World Council. What had begun out of evangelistic zeal in reaching the world for Christ was largely eclipsed by social and political activism. Representatives of the Third World nations were particularly strong in their denunciation of capitalistic nations while soft-pedaling any opposition to communist governments' denial of human rights. Although some Seventh Day Baptists still felt that one could effect greater change from within an organization than from outside, others felt that the essential freedom of "selective indignation" was no longer present in that organization.[24] The final vote by member churches, which allowed for split votes, was 355 for withdrawal and 227 against.[25]

Despite withdrawal from the National and World Councils, Seventh Day Baptists continued in cooperation with such nondenominational bodies as the American Bible Society. In some ways, separation from the National and World Councils, which were composed of such diverse traditions and theology, allowed for greater concentration of effort with other Baptists in the Baptist World Alliance (BWA), the North American Baptist Fellowship (NABF), and the Baptist Joint Committee on Public Affairs.

COOPERATION WITH OTHER BAPTISTS

Over the years, there have been voices that have urged closer cooperation and union with other Sabbathkeeping churches such as the Seventh-day Adventists and the Seventh Day Church of God. Official

[24] "Open Forum on WCC," *Sabbath Recorder* 198/3–7 (Mar–Jul 1976): 3:7-8; 4:8-9; 5:8; 6:8, 24; 7:26.
[25] Conference Minutes, *SDB Yearbook* (1976) 34-36.

delegates were often exchanged and fraternal relationships have been maintained. But differences of polity, interpretations, and other barriers have prevented any serious moves toward corporate unity. Individual members have actively participated in such groups as the Bible Sabbath Association, which hold to the distinctive doctrine of the Sabbath; however, as a denomination, Seventh Day Baptists have generally found more agreement and basis for cooperation with other Baptists with whom they disagree primarily on one issue, the Sabbath, but find agreement on most other doctrinal questions.

Baptist World Alliance

The Baptist World Alliance was organized in 1905 as an international coordinating organization to "facilitate cooperation, fellowship and proclamation among the national member bodies whose oneness in Christ stretches across different backgrounds, nationalities, economic levels and traditions."[26] It is organized around several divisions working in such areas as evangelism and education, relief in meeting human needs, communications, study, and research, all within the framework of the tradition and identity of Baptists. Within the basic framework there are separate departments for Baptist men, Baptist women, and Baptist youth as well as regional fellowships.

The Seventh Day Baptist General Conference became a member of the Baptist World Alliance (BWA) in 1935. Within the context of the need to express unity in Christ, which led to the formation of the World Council of Churches, there came an increased awareness of those distinctive characteristics that kept Baptists separate.[27] There is little record, however, of any denominational participation in the BWA during the next twenty years.

With the development of the Program for Extension and Growth, Seventh Day Baptists became aware that the American Baptist Convention was producing material for a six-year commemoration of organized Baptist work in America. In 1959, Seventh Day Baptists joined the Baptist Jubilee Advance and modified their program for extension to follow the Jubilee Advance schedule. The book *Baptist Advance*,

---

[26] *Baptist World Alliance* (McLean VA: Baptist World Alliance, 1987) 1.
[27] Report of the Committee on the Baptist World Alliance, Conference Minutes, *SDB Yearbook* (1936) 25.

published in 1964, was a joint effort of seven Baptist denominations. The chapter on Seventh Day Baptists was written by Albert N. Rogers.[28]

Leon Maltby, the editor of the *Sabbath Recorder* and a member of the Baptist Jubilee Advance Committee, attended the 1960 meeting of the BWA Congress in Rio de Janeiro. His attendance provided the opportunity to follow up on correspondence with Brazilian Seventh Day Baptists, thus opening doors for a closer relationship a decade later. Baptist affiliation represented a shift in ecumenical priorities. Maltby reported that ecumenical Baptist contacts were both more pleasant and more profitable than some of the broader-based ecumenical associations. "The fellowship is more intimate, since the aims, polity, and lines of thought are so comparable to ours."[29]

Since that Tenth World Congress meeting in Rio de Janeiro, Seventh Day Baptists have had delegates at each of the quinquennial meetings held in Miami Beach, Florida, in 1965; Tokyo, Japan, in 1970; Stockholm, Sweden, in 1975; Toronto, Canada, in 1980; Los Angeles, California, in 1985; Seoul, Korea, in 1990; Buenos Aires, Argentina, in 1995; Melbourne, Australia, in 2000; and Birmingham, United Kingdom, in 2005. In addition, Seventh Day Baptists have participated in annual meetings of the Executive Committee and on various study groups of the Baptist World Alliance. The Andhra Pradesh, India, conference, though not a member, has received assistance from BWA relief funds to meet disasters of droughts and tropical storms.

North American Baptist Fellowship

In 1963, the seven Baptist denominations that worked together in the Baptist Jubilee Advance (1958–1964) continued their cooperative fellowship after the conclusion of the Jubilee celebration.[30] The Council on Ecumenical Affairs reported in 1966 that the General Conference "along with five other Baptist bodies, met the required number to bring into being the North American Baptist Fellowship (NABF), a regional committee of the Baptist World Alliance." The first vice president of the

[28] Albert Rogers, "Seventh Day Baptist General Conference," in *Baptist Advance* (Plainfield NJ: Recorder Press) 251-60.

[29] Report of the Delegates to the Tenth World Congress of the Baptist World Alliance, Conference Minutes, *SDB Yearbook* (1960) 34.

[30] "North American Baptist Fellowship," *Sabbath Recorder* 175/9 (9 Sep 1963): 15.

General Committee of the fellowship was a Seventh Day Baptist, US Senator Jennings Randolph of West Virginia.[31]

Throughout the succeeding years, the denomination has been well represented both on the NABF administrative General Committee and in such auxiliary organizations as the North American Baptist Men's Fellowship and the North American Baptist Women's Union. The NABF meetings and work are largely done through "kindred" groups such as those held for missions, publications, youth, historians, executives, Christian education, theological training, and women. In 1990, a new constitution was adopted that gave the NABF a status less dependent on the BWA for leadership.

Baptist Joint Committee on Public Affairs

In 1939, the Southern Baptist Convention, the Northern Baptist Convention, and the National Baptist Convention, USA, adopted a joint statement on religious liberty and the separation of church and state that affirmed religious liberty was not only an inalienable right, but also indispensable to human welfare. "A Baptist must exercise himself to the utmost in the maintenance of absolute religious liberty for his Jewish neighbor, his Catholic neighbor, his Protestant neighbor, and for everybody else.... We stand for a civil state, with full liberty in religious concernments."[32]

This joint action led to the proposal for the Baptist Joint Committee on Public Affairs (BJC), in which all national bodies of Baptists of the United States and Canada could participate. The inauguration of the Joint Committee was delayed until after World War II. In 1945, four major Baptist conventions voted to maintain an office in the nation's capital in Washington, DC. Fifty years later, the name was changed to Baptist Joint Committee for Religious Liberty to better specify its main focus. With its office in Washington, DC, the agency serves as an informational and lobbying body in expressing the joint Baptist concerns of its member bodies as well as representing the interests of any one of its members before both state and federal governments. It also serves to inform its member constituents of any governmental movements and measures affecting Baptists, particularly in the area of church-state relations, human rights, and social justice.

---

[31] Report of the Council on Ecumenical Affairs, Conference Minutes, *SDB Yearbook* (1966) 55.
[32] "Purpose and Programs," Joint Committee on Public Affairs, 1980.

Seventh Day Baptists joined the organization by action of the 1963 General Conference.[33] Representatives from the BJC often made presentations to the General Conference in session, and a representative elected by the conference served on the BJC Board of Directors. Early in the twenty-first century, some Seventh Day Baptists' dissatisfaction with positions of the BJC or members of its staff on such controversial issues as educational vouchers or prayer in schools led to a recommendation that the General Conference withdraw from the organization. In 2007, employing the rarely used vote-by-church procedure, the conference voted 279 to 234 not to withdraw its membership.[34]

Conversations with the American Baptists on Union

In the midst of the Baptist Jubilee Advance and the formation of the North American Baptist Fellowship, the Commission reported to the General Conference in 1963 the simultaneous concern they felt over a downward trend in membership and the enlarged vision of Seventh Day Baptists within the world. A recommendation was presented that involved conversations exploring the possibilities of interdenominational cooperation and a merger with the American Baptist Convention. This action was taken in response to an initiative the American Baptists had taken in creating a committee "to enter into any kind of negotiations that might seem appropriate at this time with Seventh Day Baptists if they are at all interested."[35]

A six-member committee was appointed to enter into conversations with the American Baptist Convention. The following year they reported an initial meeting that revealed that the American Baptists were "assured that in their opinion, mutual benefits would be derived, mutual liberties guaranteed, mutual differences respected, and that the barriers which now divide us are not insurmountable." The Seventh Day Baptist committee felt that without a clear indication by the denomination as a whole, there was no point in further conversations with their committee, which was "prepared in principle for organic union."

The action of the General Conference clearly indicated the fact that the conference itself could not make a move in any direction without further study, particularly on the part of the agencies such as the Missionary Society, the Tract Society, the Board of Christian Education,

---

[33] Report of the Commission, Conference Minutes, *SDB Yearbook* (1963) 63.
[34] "Conference votes to remain with BJC," *Sabbath Recorder* 229/9 (Sep 2007): 6.
[35] Report of the Commission, Conference Minutes, *SDB Yearbook* (1963) 62-63.

and the Memorial Board. Thus, they urged the agencies to prepare for the committee "statements of the problems and possibilities and forms of merger with the corresponding American Baptist agencies."[36] After further study it was determined that conversations in terms of merger would not be beneficial. However, it was recommended that the Committee to Conduct Ecumenical Conversations be requested to explore areas in which fuller cooperation might be profitable, and that "exploration of cooperation with other Christian bodies should not be excluded from the thinking of the committee."[37]

By 1966, the committee reported that there was a clear understanding of the three nonnegotiable fundamentals—the seventh-day Sabbath, congregational polity, and the freedom of individual conscience—and that these constituted a basis for, rather than an obstacle to, further conversations. The chairman of the committee then concluded that there appeared to be no ecumenical future for Baptist-oriented churches beyond discrete cooperative venture. However, he proposed that "a different form of interdenominational identification might be pioneered by Baptists which would preserve Baptist principles and create an alternative to the bureaucratic, headquarters-centered, corporation-modeled form of church union thus far attempted among Christian denominations."[38] The committee continued with little or no action until 1975, when it was disbanded, but interdenominational cooperation has continued strong in most churches.

ECUMENISM ON THE LOCAL CHURCH LEVEL

Seventh Day Baptists have often been leaders in interchurch cooperation on the local level in two distinct areas. First, in those communities that have cooperative services on Thanksgiving, World Day of Prayer, Religion in American Life (RIAL), and even Lenten series, Seventh Day Baptists have generally been considered in the mainstream of Protestantism. Ministers frequently are involved in local ministerial associations and councils of churches, sharing in many areas of cooperative witness and service.

Second, many Seventh Day Baptists, both from the lay and the ministerial ranks, have assisted churches of other denominations in their

---

[36] Report of the Commission, Conference Minutes, *SDB Yearbook* (1964) 73.

[37] Report of the Commission, Conference Minutes, *SDB Yearbook* (1965) 68.

[38] Report of the Committee to Conduct Ecumenical Conversations, Conference Minutes, *SDB Yearbook* (1966) 67.

worship. Because their times of worship are on different days, many Seventh Day Baptists have played the organ or piano, sung in the choir, tended infants in nurseries and/or taught classes in Sunday churches. Ministers have frequently filled the pulpits for their Christian brothers; some have served as interim or supply pastors for periods ranging from a few months to years. In one community in New York State there was a time when the Methodist, the American Baptist, and the Presbyterian churches were all served by three different Seventh Day Baptist ministers. Someone suggested that the three churches ought to unite and hire one Seventh Day Baptist minister and then all would be happy. A church in Wisconsin had four of its members serving as organists, another as choir director, and two as interim pastors contributing to worship in seven different churches in the area each Sunday. Similarly, teenage girls from two churches in southern New Jersey provided service as nursing attendants in a local Presbyterian church.

The experience of Seventh Day Baptists in ecumenical relations has been one of continual choices. They have had to face a dilemma in choosing between their commitment to the essential unity in Christ and the admonition to separate from unbelievers. They have sometimes had to choose whether to emphasize their commonality of belief, or the distinctive traits that make them different. Some have felt that they can best effect a change from within an organization, while others see any compromise as essentially evil.

Choosing Priorities

For those in executive positions, ecumenical relations have forced choices in the allocation of time and money. These executives have often had to decide whether participation in committees and commissions of interdenominational organizations should come at the expense of denominational responsibilities. For example, the 1995 Baptist World Alliance Congress meeting in Buenos Aires, Argentina, coincided with a session of the General Conference; thus only one executive was present at the worldwide congress. A shift from an interdenominational focus to a denominational focus led to the disbanding of the Council on Ecumenical Affairs despite the denomination's Commitment to Growth emphasis. On the other hand, work in the expanded level of the Christian community has given some individuals greater meaning and fulfillment in the call to Christian service than has some of the routine work in a more secluded atmosphere, where it is sometimes difficult to see results.

Seventh Day Baptists as a whole have attempted to give meaning to both aspects of the church, as they express in their statement of belief:

> We believe that the church of God is all believers gathered by the Holy Spirit and joined into one body, of which Christ is the Head. We believe that the local church is a community of believers organized in covenant relationship for worship, fellowship and service, practicing and proclaiming common convictions, while growing in grace and in the knowledge of our Lord and Savior Jesus Christ.
>
> We believe in the priesthood of all believers and practice the autonomy of the local congregation, as we seek to work in association with others for more effective witness.[39]

---

[39] "The Church," *Statement of Beliefs of Seventh Day Baptists* (adopted 1987).

23

APPLYING THE GOSPEL TO SOCIAL ISSUES

When A. H. Lewis wrote of the intensity of the political age in the first half of the twentieth century, the Christian church was just entering the period known for its social gospel emphasis. In the midst of a rapidly changing society with its urbanization, industrialization, and increased immigration, there were many voices among Christians calling for the church to leave the security of its stained-glass sanctuaries and enter the marketplace, where its influence might bring about reform. Three voices stand out as particularly significant among Protestants.

Washington Gladden, a Congregational minister in Columbus, Ohio, wrote *Applied Christianity* in 1886. He put his brand of Christianity into practice when he was elected to the city council in 1900. His hymn "O Master Let Me Walk with Thee" is still a favorite among those concerned with service to others. In 1897 Charles M. Sheldon, another Congregationalist, titled his bestseller *In His Steps: What Would Jesus Do?* Sheldon challenged Christians in all walks of life to apply the teachings of Jesus to everyday life. Baptist Walter Rauschenbusch began his career as a professor at a seminary in Rochester, New York, in 1897 and gave theological support to the social gospel in such books as *Christianity and the Social Gospel*, published in 1907, and *A Theology for the Social Gospel*, published ten years later.[1]

SEVENTH DAY BAPTISTS IN MORAL REFORM

In the opening session of the General Conference in 1901, Earl P. Saunders spoke of the achievements of the century past but added a plea for moral reforms as he enumerated many of the ills of the time. These problems ranged from bossism in politics to monopolies in business, from price-fixing and oppression of the poor to mob violence, and from intemperance to impurity of thought. "These and many other evils cry out to us for correction," he said, adding the note that Seventh Day

---

[1] Edwin S. Gaustad, ed., *A Documentary of History of Religion in America Since 1865*, A Documentary of History of Religion in America, 2 vols. (Grand Rapids MI: William B. Eerdmans Publishing Company, 1983) 2:104-132.

Baptists had always stood in the forefront of the battles for reform.[2] Saunders' address raised the question whether opposition can rightly be called reform. Seventh Day Baptists, during the nineteenth century, had passed strong resolutions on a number of moral issues. Yet, despite protests made, could one rightly be called a reformer if no reforms had taken place?

Saunders identified the principal ways in which Seventh Day Baptists have been able to work in the area of social reform. These are to discover "the true Christian attitude toward these questions" and "to encourage and strengthen individual workers in the various departments of moral reform." Because of the individualistic nature of Baptists, it is hard to measure the full extent of their social reform contributions.

BAPTIST PRINCIPLES IN SOCIAL ACTION

Robert G. Torbet suggests four reasons why Baptists have had a less spectacular role in social reform than some other denominations: evangelism priority, separation of church and state, individualism, and the theological liberalism of much of the social gospel.[3] Each of these four observations concerning Baptists in general can be seen in the historic attitudes and actions of Seventh Day Baptists.

Evangelism priority is based on the premise that if a person preaches "Christ, and Him crucified" (1 Cor 2:2), then all the ills of society would be taken care of. Certainly, if all citizens were fully committed Christians, then society would be free of many of its problems. Among some Seventh Day Baptists at the turn of the century (nineteenth to twentieth), the keeping of the Sabbath was thought of as a social reform issue; they argued that if the Sabbath were fully observed, many of the labor-management problems would disappear.

Second, the emphasis on separation of church and state came as a reaction to the state-church concept in England and the continued discrimination in America by the theocracy of Puritan New England. In later years, attempts by the government to enforce "Sunday Blue Laws" made Seventh Day Baptists even more fearful of church-sponsored legislation.

---

[2] Earl P. Saunders, "Moral Reform Needed," Conference Minutes, *SDB Yearbook* (1901) 3.

[3] Robert G. Torbet, *A History of the Baptists*, 3rd ed. (1950; repr., Valley Forge PA: Judson Press, 1963) 524.

Third, individualism is a natural result of the decentralized character of Seventh Day Baptist polity. Attitudes of many individual Seventh Day Baptists have been affected by the church, but because of their small numbers, these individuals have had to work through other organizations to achieve reform. For example, continued resolutions against the use of alcohol and tobacco did very little to reform society, but individuals who joined organizations such as the Women's Christian Temperance Union (WCTU) or the Anti-saloon League influenced the passage of the 18th Amendment in 1919, which, for a time, outlawed the manufacture, sale, and use of alcoholic beverages. Many people have joined special interest groups to meet specific moral problems. This forum has appealed to Baptists because it allows them to choose the areas in which to contribute. The formation of several ecumenical organizations was motivated by a desire for members to have a greater impact on the reformation of society through this corporate expression. Yet, Baptists have often had problems in these groups, because, in an organization composed of member denominations rather than individuals, the corporate body may take a stand that is contrary to the position of an individual.

Finally, the liberal theology of some of the reform movements has caused Seventh Day Baptists to be silent on that portion of the social gospel that has been based on the humanistic belief that man, by his own effort, can bring about the kingdom of heaven on earth. To these individuals, a social gospel that treats morality as relative, that views social ills as the product of environment, and that does not deal with man's sinful nature and his need for a Savior is no gospel at all.

GENERAL CONFERENCE SOCIAL CONCERNS

The president of the General Conference in 1913 reminded the young people that "the purpose of all service is more than a humanitarian one and more than bettering man's physical and material condition. The real purpose is found in the prevention of evil and the reclamation of man from sin. The true dynamic of such service is found in religion through a personal experience of salvation through Christ."[4]

Yet, at that same session of the General Conference, the Committee on Denominational Activities presented a comprehensive list of social action concerns that included complete justice for all, preservation of the family, proper housing, development of each child through education,

---

[4] Conference Minutes, *SDB Yearbook* (1913) 102.

relief from poverty, safe working conditions, health and retirement, rights of labor and management, humans' sense of dignity, and the right of each person to rest one day in seven and be protected against unscrupulous Sunday laws.[5] Other social issues were addressed as new conditions demanded new considerations. The most prominent issues during the twentieth century were matters concerning the handicapped, peace and war, church-state relations, and human rights.

The Handicapped

Concern for the handicapped, particularly children, was an area in which a few individual Seventh Day Baptists became deeply involved in the early years of the century. Beginning in 1897, for example, Rev. Herman D. Clarke, pastor of the Seventh Day Baptist church in Dodge Center, Minnesota, and agent of the Children's Aid Society, placed up to 1,300 orphans in new homes in the Midwest and the West. He not only kept in touch with many of these children, but also influenced many others through his writing and preaching.[6] Lottie Baldwin and her brother James, of Plymouth, Wisconsin, donated their farm for the purpose of founding an orphanage.[7] Their vision of an orphanage was never fulfilled, but their gift continues to serve special needs among Seventh Day Baptists.

Other individuals expressed special concerns through personal gifts, services, or bequests. The will of Nathan E. Lewis, probated in 1960, provided for a fund to benefit the blind.[8] Similar concern for the disadvantaged has been reflected in the vision of the Ralph and Jack Hays families, which led to the 1976 founding of Sunshine Mountain, a home for the handicapped owned and operated by the Chatawa Seventh Day Baptist Church in Mississippi for thirty years.[9] The home had no official relationship to the General Conference, but it had received support from individuals and agencies until it closed in 2006.

---

[5] Report of the Committee on Denominational Activities, Conference Minutes, *SDB Yearbook* (1913) 116.

[6] Clark Kidder, *Orphan Trains & Their Precious Cargo: The Life's Work of Rev. H. D. Clarke* (Bowie MD: Heritage Books, 2001) xvi. See also *Seventh Day Baptist Pulpit* 12/1 (Jan 1917): 14-22.

[7] Conference Minutes, *SDB Yearbook* (1904) 93.

[8] Nathan E. Lewis, Last Will and Testimony, Article 7, Section A, courtesy of the SDB Memorial Fund.

[9] Jack Hayes, "A Welcome to Sunshine Mountain," *Sabbath Recorder* 198/7 (Jul 1976): 29-30.

"Blessed Are the Peacemakers"

World War I brought concern over issues of war and peace. A General Conference resolution in 1918 supported the Boy Scouts as one means of "safeguarding our youth from the dangers of moral laxity and increase in juvenile crimes, incident to war-time conditions."[10] That same year, a denominational War Board was authorized to work with the War-time Commission of the Federal Council to coordinate support for those aiding in the war effort. The Committee on Denominational Activities declared that "We must get into the war denominationally as well as individually," calling for some organization through which contributions could be credited to churches rather than individuals.[11] A War Reconstruction Board provided help to returning servicemen in the name of the denomination to let them know that Seventh Day Baptists were interested in their welfare.[12]

In the postwar period, attention turned toward securing peace. In 1920, the General Conference voted to support the Federal Council of Churches, which encouraged Congress to pass laws enabling the Federal Government "to keep its treaty obligations, to punish violators of such treaties, to deal equitably with immigrants, and to repeal laws that discriminate against and humiliate Asiatic people." The conference took this action in the belief that "the success of missionary work and the hope of averting another world war was dependent upon the Christian treatment of Asia and the Asiatics."[13]

A generation later, as the storm clouds of war again threatened America, the General Conference in 1936 affirmed a strong pacifist statement declaring that war is unchristian and a crime against the human race, that the country should maintain a policy of neutrality, and that legislation should be passed to take the profit motive out of war and the arms race.[14] As the possibility of America's entry into war became more apparent, the conference in 1940 passed affirmations in support of those who declared themselves conscientious objectors as well as those

[10] Report of the Committee on Denominational Activities, Conference Minutes, *SDB Yearbook* (1918) 62-63.
[11] Report of the Committee on Denominational Activities, Conference Minutes, *SDB Yearbook* (1918) 41.
[12] Report of the War-Reconstruction Board, Conference Minutes, *SDB Yearbook* (1919) 82.
[13] Report of the Committee on Reference and Counsel, Conference Minutes, *SDB Yearbook* (1920) 75-76.
[14] Conference Minutes, *SDB Yearbook* (1936) 65.

whose conscience called for entering the military.[15] Throughout the war, Seventh Day Baptists supported both positions.

In post-World War II years, emphasis was directed toward peace, yet it is ironic that a resolution in 1947 urging Congress to set up a Department of Peace with a Secretary at a cabinet-level position was not adopted by the General Conference, even though such legislation was first introduced in the House of Representatives in 1945 by a Seventh Day Baptist, Jennings Randolph.[16] Nearly forty years later in 1984, just before his retirement after forty years in Congress, Senator Randolph was instrumental in the establishment of the National Peace Institute, which carried the name "Jennings Randolph Program for International Peace."[17]

For years individuals have urged the General Conference to take a more positive stance against war. In 1977, the Christian Social Action Committee affirmed that although every Seventh Day Baptist should be urged to live at peace with all men, the denomination as a whole was reluctant to support a resolution that would commit it to the pacifist position, since there was no agreement on the issue.[18] Two years later, that committee presented a resolution declaring that war, with its killing, hatred, and destruction, was at cross-purposes with Christian principles.[19] Subsequent resolutions reaffirmed this position but declared that the only answer to the age-old problem of war was to change the minds and hearts of people and nations throughout the world. The statement called upon all Christians "to support and pray for adoption of public policy which could realistically reduce the likelihood of war."[20]

Church-State Relations

Seventh Day Baptists in America have often taken for granted the separation of church and state. Only when attempts to enforce by law the observance of Sunday as a day of rest has the matter been important enough to demand serious attention by the General Conference. In such

---

[15] Report of the Commission, Conference Minutes, *SDB Yearbook* (1940) 38.

[16] Report of the Committee on Courtesies and Resolutions, Conference Minutes, *SDB Yearbook* (1947) 56.

[17] "Randolph Is Sponsor for Peace Legislation," *Sabbath Recorder* 205/5 (May 1983): 5. See also "Peace Institute Reporter" (Washington DC: National Peace Institute Foundation, Sep 1986) 5.

[18] Conference Minutes, *SDB Yearbook* (1977) 51.

[19] Report of the Christian Social Action Committee, Conference Minutes, *SDB Yearbook* (1979) 57.

[20] Conference Minutes, *SDB Yearbook* (1979) 55.

cases the matter was clear-cut: the state had no right to interfere! But, beginning in the 1930s with the Great Depression and continuing through World War II and the postwar period, both society and the government changed. The trend was toward paternalism as the government took over more and more of the philanthropic or benevolent activities traditionally held to be the responsibility of the church. With such dependency on tax dollars has come the inevitable control and loss of sharp distinction between church and state roles.

COMMITTEE ON CHRISTIAN SOCIAL ACTION

Within the context of change, the creation of a Committee on Christian Social Action was recommended at the Council-Conference session of the General Conference in 1938.[21] Over twenty years later, this committee became an integral part of the conference structure. In 1960, the Missionary Board found it necessary to receive funds from the Nyasaland government to continue and to expand the medical and educational phases of its work in that country. The General Conference recognized this as a deviation from its previous position on separation of church and state and appointed a special committee to develop an interpretation of the issue.[22] That committee recommended those government contributions be listed under "Refunds, Sales and Services," thus preventing any appearance of a contribution from a government to Our World Mission.[23] This incident demonstrated the need for a statement of policy on church-state relations and a recognition of the need for a continuing committee to coordinate the study of social concerns and the implementation of social action.

Statements of Policy

In 1963, a statement of policy was adopted that summarizes the general position of Seventh Day Baptists in many areas of social concerns. It recognized the historic Baptist polity of freedom of conscience, a reluctance to issue authoritative statements on specific public issues that might be considered by some to be binding on individual members, a refusal to recognize the authority of the state over

---

[21] Report of the Council Committee on Christian Social Problems, Conference Minutes, *SDB Yearbook* (1938) 106.

[22] Conference Minutes, SDB Yearbook (1960) 64.

[23] Report of the Committee on Christian Social Action Interest, Conference Minutes, *SDB Yearbook* (1962) 54.

the individual in matters of religious principle, and an absolute separation of the church and the state on theological grounds rather than for practical advantage. The statement recognized that even though principles do not change, forms of government and the claims of civil authority do change, necessitating constant vigilance and study. "Christian people organized into churches have spiritual responsibility for the political conscience, and spiritual loyalties of individuals everywhere, including those in positions of civil authority." This responsibility extends to a creative rediscovery and application of the principles underlying the Baptist heritage of freedom and responsibility in such issues as tax exemption for religious institutions and legal enforcement of religious observances.[24]

Aside from the issue of church-state relations, the first report of the continuing Committee on Christian Social Action included a summary of actions taken on race relations, a recommendation that the General Conference become a member of the Baptist Joint Committee on Public Affairs, and a proposal that the denomination study the issue of birth control.[25] The initial impact of the committee is seen in the actions of the 1964 session of the General Conference, which (1) affirmed its belief that "any limiting qualifications of race as to such membership or attendance are not in harmony with the teachings of Christ, and that new and existing churches be urged to adopt or practice no such limitations"; (2) recommended that a policy statement of principle on race relations similar to that on church and state be prepared; (3) resolved that, in line with the policy statement on church-state relations, "Seventh Day Baptists can not recognize any government agency as properly possessing power to direct Bible reading and the use of prayer in the public school system"; and (4) called for individuals to contribute to the political life by voting intelligently in line with personal Christian convictions by giving praise and support where deserved and criticism where warranted, by participating in office when so talented, and by encouraging talented and interested young people to train and prepare for fields of service in politics and social welfare.[26] The committee also recommended that an issue of the *Helping Hand* be devoted to a

---

[24] Report of the Commission, Conference Minutes, *SDB Yearbook* (1963) 59-60.
[25] Report of the Committee on Christian Social Action, Conference Minutes, *SDB Yearbook* (1963) 77-79.
[26] "Social Action," Report of the Commission, Conference Minutes, *SDB Yearbook* (1964) 73-74.

concentrated study of the Christian's involvement in selected areas of social concern.[27]

The Committee on Christian Social Action, which was initially established for an educational and policy-defining role, soon expanded its function to include response to emergency situations. In 1973, a fund was established through which individuals and churches could channel contributions for relief. This included such ongoing programs as those carried out by the Church World Service and the Baptist World Alliance as well as any emergency situations that might arise at home or abroad.[28] The administration of the United Relief Fund became a major function of the committee.

HUMAN RIGHTS

Seventh Day Baptists' emphasis on the individual has placed them on the side of those who call for human rights for all people. The sacredness of human life is seen as fundamental in the teachings of Christ, and anything that deprives a person of his or her basic rights as a child of God is sin. A statement adopted in 1962 by the General Conference defined Christian Social Action as "personal commitment to God as revealed through Jesus Christ translated into human relationships which interpret the love of God to society and exert righteous influence in the world."[29]

Yet, in a pluralistic society, the church often finds itself in a situation where much of its social action is reactive. Instead of being the dominant force in the prevention of social problems, it has tried to bring healing only after the problem has become acute. Among Seventh Day Baptists, this has been demonstrated in such areas as race relations, right to life, and environmental concerns. In nearly all of these situations, principles have been stated but responsibility and commitment have usually been left to the individual or the state.

Race Relations

Most of the early-twentieth-century statements dealing with racial equality were very general, such as that of the 1913 proclamation in which the General Conference declared "its desire and purpose to stand

---

[27] Report of the Committee on Christian Social Action Interests, Conference Minutes, *SDB Yearbook* (1964) 57. See also *Helping Hand* 82/1 (Winter 1966): 1-8.

[28] Conference Minutes, *SDB Yearbook* (1973) 41-42.

[29] Conference Minutes, *SDB Yearbook* (1962) 51.

in cooperation with other Christian bodies, for equal rights and complete justice for all men in all stations of life."[30] In the mid-1920s, with the admission of the People's Seventh Day Baptist Church of Washington, DC, and the recognition of the Jamaican Association, a committee was appointed to make a careful study of interracial work in the denomination. In 1926, that committee reported that they saw "no occasion to change the present policy of Seventh Day Baptists as to the reception of coloured churches into the General Conference," adding "that when the number of coloured churches shall have so increased as to enable them to maintain a separate Conference, and it should appear that such an organization would greatly promote the work of the common cause, the matter can be adjusted to the mutual satisfaction of all."[31]

It was not until the mid-1950s that race relations again became an item of serious consideration by the General Conference. A resolution in 1956 recognized the issue of civil rights in political discussion and expressed its conviction that Christian love transcends the differences of race, color, and position in life. The resolution also affirmed that it was the duty of Christian people to speak and to act in Christian charity and to deal with all men as their brothers.[32] In 1957, the General Conference recorded its support for the decision of the Supreme Court, which affirmed that the Constitution guarantees equal freedom to all citizens.[33]

Each year for a decade or more, churches were urged to observe "Race Relations Sabbath" on the second week in February as one means of keeping the subject in the minds of the congregation. For a majority of Seventh Day Baptist churches, integration was never a major issue in terms of actual practice because of their geographic locations. It therefore became easy to take comfort in the fact that progress was being made through the government. But for others it became a matter of deep concern that attitudes of prejudice still existed. A few individuals became involved in protest movements, several youth camps made conscious efforts to involve multicultural participation, and in a number of communities congregations participated in intercultural exchanges and visitation. Although some prejudice continued to exist, there were those churches, particularly in urban areas with mixed populations,

---

[30] Conference Minutes, *SDB Yearbook* (1913) 116. See note 6.

[31] Conference Minutes, *SDB Yearbook* (1926) 86. See also pp. 76-77.

[32] Supplement to the Report of the Committee on Courtesies and Resolutions, Conference Minutes, *SDB Yearbook* (1956) 64.

[33] Conference Minutes, *SDB Yearbook* (1957) 50.

where as members ministered to the community, the churches became increasingly diverse.

Right to Life

The need for policy statements on issues other than church-state and race relations became evident soon after the formation of the Committee on Christian Social Action. In 1964, the committee was urged to develop a statement of principles in regard to other specific issues.[34] One of the first such statements dealt with the question of birth control, which had been referred to the committee for study the previous year.[35] Out of this study came the position statement adopted in 1965 under two headings: Birth Control and Extramarital Sex Behavior. Under the first heading, the statement urged each family to make birth control a question of personal concern in the family relationship and suggested that "contraception by methods recognized by the medical profession can be helpful in making birth a voluntary, responsible, creative act, rather than an emotional accident." As to extramarital sex behavior, the committee affirmed that "sex is the God-given drive through which we participate in a continuing creation, and is a mutually enriching blessing within the bonds of matrimony" but added that "sexual intercourse outside the bonds of matrimony is wrong, and that any contraceptive to control pregnancy does not change this basic concept."[36]

As the sexual revolution of the sixties and seventies continued and made its way into the court system, the lines were drawn between "pro-choice," which favored permissive abortion, and "pro-life," which sought to prevent any threat to the life of the unborn. Seventh Day Baptists have had considerable difficulty in formulating a clear position statement on this issue. There has not been the kind of unanimity that existed over the temperance issue of preceding generations when, for a century and a half, action was urged through every avenue, including legislation, to deal with the use and abuse of alcohol and tobacco.

The cherished tradition of freedom of choice and the individual's responsibility for making those choices have led some to take a position of "pro-choice." Others whose personal convictions place them on the side of "pro-life" have been reluctant to make any corporate statement that could not find consensus among the churches or that might deny

---

[34] Report of the Commission, Conference Minutes, *SDB Yearbook* (1964) 74.
[35] Conference Minutes, *SDB Yearbook* (1963) 79.
[36] Conference Minutes, *SDB Yearbook* (1965) 70.

others their right to choose. The treatment of this issue by the General Conference during the 1980s is illustrative of Seventh Day Baptist polity in those areas where there is considerable diversity of opinion. Often, discussions in themselves are valuable in the development of Christian attitudes toward an issue and of compassion for those who differ.

The statement adopted in 1981 did not have unanimous support but reflected the general position of Seventh Day Baptists represented at that year's session of the General Conference. It recognized the sacredness of human life beginning at conception and strongly disapproved of society's gross disregard for this sanctity as reflected in the increase in the number of abortions on demand. It encouraged individuals and churches to promote legislation and policies that would reverse this trend and would discourage immorality, ignorance, and lack of restraint, which produce problem pregnancies. It also called for individuals to set an example to society by living and teaching biblical standards of morality, responsibility, and respect for human life.[37]

ENVIRONMENTAL CONCERNS

The social concerns of Seventh Day Baptists over the environment have been revealed in two major areas—the physical environment in terms of stewardship of natural resources and the moral environment that is so largely influenced by the media.

Physical Environment

Through the first half of the twentieth century, Seventh Day Baptists were largely a rural people, closely linked to the earth. Even those who lived in urban areas were often but a generation from the farm and understood from experience the relationship between man and his environment. Many Seventh Day Baptist farmers were leaders in such movements as the Soil Conservation Service. A Seventh Day Baptist Rural Fellowship was established in 1946 using a logo embracing the three words "Save-Soil-Souls," which recognized that the saving of soil was somehow related to the saving of souls.

As urbanization and industrialization moved society into a "throwaway" culture, environmental problems expanded beyond the mere erosion of the soil. Toxic pollution of the soil, the water, and the atmosphere have brought new challenges that the church has not been

---

[37] Conference Minutes, *SDB Yearbook* (1981) 100-101.

fully prepared to meet. As Leon Wheeler wrote in an environmental issue of the *Sabbath Recorder* in 1989, "We theologize from the safety of our doctrine, and lose sensitivity and compassion."[38]

Moral Environment

Throughout much of Christian history, attention has been given to the moral environment. Sometimes the church tried to control the moral climate by isolating its members from influences it perceived to be immoral. During the nineteenth century, many churches tried to discourage their members from patronizing various secular entertainments, such as the tavern, the dance hall, pool rooms, or places where cards were played. During the early part of the twentieth century, movie theaters were sometimes added to the list of immoral influences to be shunned by the dutiful Christian. The selection of reading material was another area of great concern. With the television's entrance into the home, the focus shifted toward attempts to encourage members to watch only the better programs offered.

Action of the 1989 General Conference urged members to cooperate with other concerned Christians in the midst of society's massive assault on Christian morality. A resolution called for a cooperative boycott of two companies that had been "leading sponsors of programs containing foul language, sleazy sexual innuendo, brutality and anti-Christian characterizations." It also called for a boycott of a leading motel chain considered to be "the largest provider of in-room pornographic movies in the world." Economic pressure was considered the most effective means of reformation, for it was believed that if left to its own devices, the television industry would not clean itself up.[39]

Toward the end of the century, the Christian Social Action Committee's activities focused less and less on promoting education or action on social issues, so that in 2009 General Conference action replaced the twelve-member standing committee with a three-member task force charged mainly with administering the United Relief Fund. It remains to be seen whether the General Conference will continue to issue the types of problem-specific position statements as those noted above.

---

[38] Leon Wheeler, "On Corrupting the Earth," *Sabbath Recorder* 211/11 (Nov 1989): 11.

[39] Resolution from 1989 General Conference, repr. in *Sabbath Recorder* 211/11 (Nov 1989): 2.

The Church and the Individual in Social Action

David Moberg, in his book *The Church as a Social Institution*, noted that the official policy of a church and the opinion prevalent in its membership are not always the same. Several surveys revealed that on certain issues church leadership was more liberal in its policy and more receptive to social change than its parishioners were.[40] This discrepancy can weaken the witness of the church as an institution of reform and put more responsibility on the individual. Resolutions passed by the corporate body will have little effect if the members who pass these resolutions ignore them in personal action. Collectively, the church may be opposed to such things as the lottery as a means of raising money, but if the members buy lottery tickets in the hopes of winning big, lotteries will continue. Among a "choosing people," the choices made by individuals do speak louder than their denomination's corporate speech.

Moberg also suggested that the most important role of the church and the individual Christian may be in their therapeutic and supportive roles, rather than their reforming roles. "In times of rapid social change when all the earth seems chaotic and uncertain, there is refuge in the 'everlasting arms' of a God who is 'the same yesterday, today, and forever.'"[41]

Seventh Day Baptists may have felt powerless in effecting social reform, but many individuals and churches have been effective in therapeutic roles. They have felt that prayer, mercy, hospitality, teaching, counseling in hospital or prison ministries, and setting examples of Christian living can often do more ultimate good than the enactment of a multitude of reform laws. It is the conviction of many that the Sabbath, rightly observed and honored, has the power to bring man into that harmony with God that can bring lasting social values and moral conduct.

---

[40] David O. Moberg, *The Church as a Social Institution: The Sociology of American Religion* (Englewood Cliffs NJ: Prentice Hall, 1962) 385.
[41] Ibid., 165.

24

THEOLOGY IN A SCIENTIFIC AGE

William Brackney, in his book *The Baptists*, identifies three critical points in Baptist history that mark the unique identity of Baptists. Seventh Day Baptists have identified with each of these three, but the third was particularly important in much of the twentieth century.

Three Critical Points in Baptist History

The first critical point was the London Confession of 1644, which linked Baptists with the mainstream of English Protestant life while bringing a concept of association to otherwise independent and autonomous congregations. This confession allowed each congregation the right to freely interpret the Bible while recognizing the value of counsel and cooperation with others of similar faith.

The second critical point was the creation in 1792 of the English Particular Baptist Society for the Propagation of the Gospel Among the Heathen, an organization that later became known as the Baptist Missionary Society. Not only was this significant in its world evangelistic outreach, but also it brought the societal principle to the churches as voluntary societies were created "to fulfill the extra-congregational visions of their leadership."

The third critical point was the establishment of the Baptist Bible Union in 1923, which Brackney describes as the "fundamentalist reaction to modernization forces in polity and the intellectual life of the denomination." Its effect for most Baptists was to emphasize "the complete loyalty to Scripture and the autonomy of the Church, even at the cost of missions, fellowship, and unity as a denomination." Differences in interpretation brought differences in both theology and polity. "The distance between many Baptists increased, and became greater than between some Baptists and non-Baptists, as the result of the formation of the Baptist Bible Union."[1] The differences surrounding this union were largely responsible for the description that Henry Warner

---

[1] William Henry Brackney, *The Baptists* (New York: Greenwood Press, 1988) xix-xxi.

Bowden gave of Baptists as "a denomination known for ideological squabbling and institutional splintering."[2]

Effects on Seventh Day Baptists

Each of these three critical points is reflected in Seventh Day Baptist history. The London Confession of Faith in 1644 helped define a climate in which Seventh Day Baptist congregations, with their interpretation of the biblical Sabbath, were able to develop as a legitimate fellowship composed of independent congregations. The influence of the Baptist Missionary Society of 1792 encouraged Seventh Day Baptists to adopt the societal form of organization through which autonomous societies have carried on much of the denomination's work.

The ideas surrounding the Baptist Bible Union of 1923 did not cause the same degree of "institutional splintering" among Seventh Day Baptists that was found in several other Baptist groups. Seventh Day Baptists' small size, common heritage, family relationships, and commitment to the distinctive doctrine of the Sabbath prevented the formation of separate denominations to express theological differences. However, Seventh Day Baptists did have their share of "ideological squabbling" that affected their work and witness in the twentieth century. In 1924, a year after the formation of the Baptist Bible Union, some Seventh Day Baptists formed a Bible Defense League, which published a bimonthly magazine called the *Exponent* "to reaffirm, restate, re-emphasize and maintain the historic faith of Seventh Day Baptists *within* the Seventh Day Baptist denomination."[3] Seventh Day Baptists did not escape the fundamentalist-modernist controversy.

FUNDAMENTALIST-MODERNIST CONTROVERSY

Any controversy that involves a person's beliefs frequently becomes more acute by the emphasis on what one does *not* believe. Thus, the modernist who attempted to make theology conform to conclusions of scholarship and science was often characterized by the fundamentalist as one who did not believe in the inspiration of the Bible, and who thus rejected such other "fundamental" beliefs as the creation of man, the virgin birth of Jesus, miracles, the necessity of the cross, the physical resurrection of Jesus, and the second coming of Christ. The fundamentalist, on the other hand, whose faith and belief were based

---

[2] Henry Warner Bowden, "Series Forward," quoted by Brackney, *The Baptists*, xii.
[3] Alva L. Davis, "Eight Questions," *The Exponent* 1/1 (May 1925): n.p.

wholly on the Bible as the infallible word of God to be interpreted literally in all circumstances, was viewed by the modernist as being anti-intellectual, blind to facts, and intolerant.

Roots of the Controversy

The critical study that precipitated the modernist-fundamentalist controversy was the publication of two books by Charles Darwin, *The Origin of Species* in 1859 and *The Descent of Man* in 1871. Darwin's basic premise was known as "evolution," the theory that all life began millions of years ago in some simple-celled organism and slowly developed into higher, more complex forms. "The last and most advanced forms of pre-human life to appear were the large monkeys and apes, which needed only the luck to be born with a bigger than average brain and the ability to walk on two legs to qualify as human beings." Involved in this process was what Darwin termed "natural selection" and the "survival of the fittest."[4]

The theory of evolution stood in sharp contrast to the biblical concept of special creation as recorded in Genesis. Yet, it was nearly fifty years after the publication of his first book before Darwin became generally recognized as the archenemy of the religious fundamentalist. During the first quarter of the twentieth century, the controversy over evolution festered within the church until it reached its peak in 1925 with the trial of John Scopes of Dayton, Tennessee. This trial brought national attention not only to questions of creation, but also to the extent to which the state, in its control of public education, could determine the nature of religious instruction given in its schools.

There were those, particularly in academic circles, who early recognized the potential threat on orthodoxy posed by the theory of evolution. Yet, it was not until the end of the first decade of the century that it became a matter of deep concern in the vast majority of churches. This delay was due to several major factors.

First, Darwin's method was not unique, for it grew out of the spirit of the time. The new enlightenment, with its investigation and experimentation, was found in nearly every phase of man's quest for knowledge. Many of the improvements in man's daily life were the result of the application of science to life. Science was acceptable to most people, for it was viewed as beneficial.

---

[4] James O'Hern, *This Is Our World* (Morristown NJ: Silver Burdett Co., 1981) 178-79.

Second, Darwinism was introduced primarily in the academic circles of colleges and universities, often among men who were able to sift fact from theory. Jonathan Allen, the president of Alfred University in New York state from 1867 to 1893, used science as evidence of the order of the universe. In 1874 he wrote, "God specializes all providences, yet grounds them in general laws. Instead of dead mechanisms, and insensate forces, there is everywhere the living presence, the conscious spirit, the pervading God."[5] He called religion the "vital relationship and communion with the divine," stating that religious certainty does not come by either logic or historic testimony, but by a personal relation.[6]

The influence of teachers such as Allen greatly affected Seventh Day Baptist thought for several generations. Most of the ministers and many other leaders received at least part of their training at Alfred either under Allen's tutelage or under that of his disciples. They did not feel threatened by scientific investigation but used it as further evidence of God's presence in the universe.

A third reason for a delay between the introduction of Darwinism and the fundamentalist-modernist crisis of the 1920s was the fact that evolution was not the primary issue that caused the division. Biblical criticism was the real issue. Conservative religionists could ignore Darwin and his theories in their preaching and teaching, but when "higher criticism" applied the scientific method and evolutionary theories to the study of the Bible, it was seen as an attack on the fundamentals of evangelical Christianity. The fundamentalist believed the Bible to be the Word of God; the liberal viewed it as containing the Word of God, which implied that parts of the Bible might not be the words of God, but the words of men.

Seventh Day Baptist Action and Reaction, 1900–1923

"Religion in the twentieth century cannot live in a cloister," wrote A. H. Lewis. "The minister for that age cannot spend all his time in the quiet of his library, nor in the secret retreat for prayer. As a man of God commissioned to defend and sustain the highest and most important interests that touch human life, he must be, to some extent, a man of the world, carrying his Godliness into the current of the world's life."[7] Lewis

---

[5] Jonathan Allen, *Allen of Alfred*, ed. Edwin H. Lewis (Milton WI.: Davis-Greene Corp. Press, 1932) 76-78.

[6] Ibid., 80.

[7] Abram Herbert Lewis, *Letters to Young Preachers and Their Hearers* (Plainfield NJ: American Sabbath Tract Society, 1900) 224-25.

himself, in his study and his writing, was very much a man of the world. He was familiar with the writings of philosophers and scientists as well as theologians. Like Jonathan Allen, he sought to bring harmony between science and religion by elevating both to a spiritual level that dealt with eternal rather than temporal values.

Lewis was aware of the conflict that was seriously threatening Seventh Day Baptists in the wake of the application of scientific study and its methods to the Bible. He condemned the inflexibility of literalism in both science and religion. His last book *Spiritual Sabbathism*, published after his death in 1908, called for the placing of the Sabbath on a higher spiritual level that would not be affected by "the materialistic philosophy and 'scientific' untruth" that called for "immediate tests and demonstrated finality." He recognized that many considered anything that could not be verified in the laboratory nor cashed at the bank as being irrelevant.[8] To the geologist and the biologist, with their multitude of observations, Lewis pointed out: "Geology does not deal with the beginning, but with the long process of becoming."[9] He saw science as attempting to deal with the process or the "how" of creation, whereas religion deals with the purpose or the "why" of it.

Lewis avoided the "either/or" approach to the scientific age with a "both/and" concept similar to that of the poet Ralph W. Seager, who demonstrated that the mind of the scientist and that of the poet operate in different realms and are not necessarily contradictory. Seager said, "Ask a scientist what is water, and he will tell you it is H_2O; ask a poet what is water, and he will tell you it is wet. Which one is right?"[10] A. H. Lewis had the mind of the poet and saw the spiritual value of the Sabbath without discrediting the work of the scientist.

Dr. A. E. Main, dean of the Alfred University School of Theology from 1901 to 1933, was viewed as one of the principal spokesmen for the modernist view. In a sermon published in the *Seventh Day Baptist Pulpit* in 1907, he referred to the early chapters of Genesis as "a most wonderful piece of religious literature," comparing it with other cultures' accounts of creation. His comparison was for the purpose of showing the biblical record's supremacy, but many were critical of any suggestion that the

---

[8] Abram Herbert Lewis, *Spiritual Sabbathism* (Plainfield NJ: American Sabbath Tract Society, 1910) vi.

[9] Ibid., 77.

[10] Ralph Seagar, lecture, Christian Writers and Editors Conference, Green Lake WI, Jul 1959.

account had a human rather than a divine origin.[11] Main generated even more criticism among the conservative Seventh Day Baptists when he wrote: "We must not forget that the face of divine truth may shine through myth, fable, and symbol, through the figures of rhetoric and the beauty of poetry."[12] Some Seventh Day Baptists interpreted this statement to mean that some of the biblical truths, even that of the Sabbath, might be contained in myth, fable, or symbol. To the literalist, all else that Dean Main had to say in terms of spiritual value was largely lost, and with it some of the credibility of the school in which he taught.

The writings of men like A. H. Lewis and A. E. Main, which sought to bring modern scholarship to religious study, were not accepted by many within the church. Rev. Elston Dunn published a sermon titled "Biblical Criticism" in which he pointed out that even though there may be value in criticism that corrects error and demolishes superstition, the net result is often destructive; this is particularly the case as it is reported in the press that "the difficulties and objections to the Bible become more familiar to the unthinking mass than the Bible itself.[13]

An editorial in the *Sabbath Recorder* for 16 August 1909 prompted a series of articles that brought the issue more sharply into the consciousness of both the laity and the clergy. Theodore Gardiner, the editor, maintained that one could be a true Bible Christian without denying the well-established facts of modern science: "The Christian may stand among modern thinkers and accept everything that has been thoroughly proved by the study of history, science, or by higher criticism and not be worried or frightened over any of it. The verities of the Christian's Bible shall remain unscathed."[14] Not all Seventh Day Baptists agreed with Gardiner's premises. Several made their feelings of dissent known in succeeding articles in the *Sabbath Recorder*, which became a forum for debate.

In 1910, after several months of debate between the modernists and the fundamentalists, Theodore Gardiner, as editor, closed the columns of the *Recorder* to further debates. He wrote that he had given equal opportunity for both sides to express their views in the hope that some common ground might be found, but the time had come for arguments to close "simply because there is no prospect, so far as we can see, of

---

[11] A. E. Main, "A Study in Genesis," *Seventh Day Baptist Pulpit* 5/1 (Feb 1907): 10.
[12] Ibid.
[13] Elston M. Dunn, "Biblical Criticism," *Seventh Day Baptist Pulpit* 7/2 (Mar 1909): 26.
[14] Theodore Gardiner, "Science in the Bible," *Sabbath Recorder* 67/7 (16 Aug 1909): 195.

finding common ground on which the two sides, composed of men who are equally sincere, may harmonize."[15]

That decision did not end the struggle. The *Seventh Day Baptist Pulpit*, a monthly publication designed to assist pastorless churches, provided a vehicle through which the attempt to bring harmony between the divergent views continued. Sessions of the General Conference also provided a sounding board for theological dialogue. The president of the General Conference in 1919, Rev. William L. Burdick, recognized that part of the crisis of change was the fact that many had been unable or unwilling to see any problem at all.[16]

Beginning in 1922, the *Sabbath Recorder* again became a vehicle for discussion when Dean A. E. Main published a series of articles titled "The Book of Books." In his in-depth study of both the text and the context of the Scriptures, he made such statements as: "the Bible writers were human and fallible.... There are imperfections in the records, from our point of view.... We understand, as our fathers did not, how this revelation is sometimes stated in the form of legend or myth...." He stated that the Old Testament was influenced by the ideas, religion, traditions, and writings of non-Hebrew nations and that the books as they exist today are the result of compilation and editing. "Old Testament history is not good history according to modern standards, in respect to exactness, comprehensiveness, and orderly or scientific arrangement.... Let us admit but not magnify its imperfections."[17]

The reaction to these articles from conservatives was predictable, and the *Recorder* carried a representative cross-section of opinions. Finally, in the last issue of 1923, the editor again closed the pages of the magazine to debate, pointing out that its effect on other denominations was filling the outside world with disgust and driving many away from the Christian church. "No one is likely to be won to Christianity by quarreling Christians," he wrote, as he referred to the history of allowing freedom of conscience in matters of doctrine. "The more we forget the controversial spirit, and the more we can unite in the work of evangelism, striving to win souls to a loving Savior, the better it will be

---

[15] Theodore Gardiner, editorial, "Why Not Stop Now?" Sabbath Recorder 69/11 (12 Sep 1910): 321.

[16] William L. Burdick, "President's Address," *SDB Yearbook* (1919) 5.

[17] A. E. Main, "The Book of Books I," *Sabbath Recorder* 92/18 (1 May 1922): 546.

for us, and the better it will be for our good cause in generations to come."[18]

It is one thing to tell people to forget differences and quite another thing to dismiss differences easily. The president of the General Conference in 1924, Rev. Alva L. Davis, was the recognized spokesman for the fundamentalists. In the closing remarks of his president's address, he threw out Joshua's challenge, "Choose you this day whom you will serve" (see Josh 24:15), adding that it was up to each one to decide "whether to join with the exponents of modernism who rebel against the constituted authority, human or divine; or whether in response to the divine purpose and in harmony with the divine will to look up into the Father's face and say, 'Bless the Lord, O my soul.'"[19] It was at this session of the General Conference, in after-hours meetings, that the Bible Defense League was organized.

Bible Defense League

Beginning in May 1925, the Bible Defense League published a bimonthly magazine called *The Exponent*. An article in the first edition stated that the League was organized at Milton, Wisconsin, at the time of the General Conference session "when a group of ministers and lay workers met to discuss ways and means of meeting the present day modernist movement. The meetings were called between the sessions of Conference by the president of the General Conference who also presided over them."

That first issue of *The Exponent* also explained that the Bible Defense League was an organization within the Seventh Day Baptist denomination, for Seventh Day Baptists, and by Seventh Day Baptists. The organizers further emphasized that they had no thought of leaving the denomination or of seeking to drive others out. They expressed love for their brethren and for the Master's work but felt that "Seventh Day Baptists ought to be big enough, wise enough and Christ-like enough to throw off the incubus of rationalism which threatens the very life of present-day Christianity."[20]

In spite of their declaration of unity, the Bible Defense League was viewed by many within the denomination as being divisive, intolerant,

---

[18] Theodore Gardiner, "Sad Indeed is the Bitter Controversy," *Sabbath Recorder* 95/27 (31 Dec 1923): 833-34.

[19] Alva L. Davis, "President's Address," *SDB Yearbook* (1924) 20.

[20] Davis, "Eight Questions," *The Exponent* 1/1 (May 1925): 1.

and unduly influenced by members of other denominations. In answer to the charge of divisiveness, league members contended that it was others who brought division to the denomination: "Rather, we are seeking to preserve denominational unity by removal of the evils which promote division." As to being intolerant, they responded: "Just why preaching the Sabbath makes one a Christian reformer, but preaching the Deity of Christ an intolerant dogmatist, does not appear clear to us.... Let us remember, we have been preserved as a denomination through the centuries not simply because we honored God in keeping the Sabbath, but honored His Word by believing it." They also held that most of the converts to the Sabbath from other denominations were not modernists. "So far as we are able to judge, only people of simple faith in the Bible as the Word of God ever come to accept the Bible truth."[21]

The debate continued with little constructive effort to resolve differences until 1927, when the Committee of Six on Denominational Harmony was appointed. The membership of the committee—Edwin Shaw, Alva L. Davis, Lester G. Osborn, Lely D. Seager, J. Nelson Norwood, and Loyal F. Hurley—represented a wide spectrum of belief. Their report recognized that differences existed, that the right of private judgment should be freely exercised, and that the grounds of unity were in Christ. They expressed a desire to unite in a comprehensive program to save lost souls and concluded with the recommendation "that a page or two of the *Sabbath Recorder* be given weekly to a setting forth under two separate editors, of the positions and beliefs of the modernists and the fundamentalists."[22]

In spite of some reluctance on the part of the editor of the *Sabbath Recorder*, who at one point stated that, as editor, he and he alone determined what material went in it,[23] the plan was implemented. Rev. A. L. Davis was given responsibility for the fundamentalist page while J. Nelson Norwood was asked to edit the modernist position. Articles from the modernist side began in January 1928 with a series written by Norwood appearing as letters from a father to a son.[24] These were followed by a series by August Johansen, who was particularly concerned for the young people "who find they can no longer honestly

---

[21] Ibid.

[22] Report of the Commission, *SDB Yearbook* (1927) 96.

[23] Alva L. Davis, *Autobiography*, transcript, MS 1952.1, pp. 80-81, SDB Hist. Soc. Lib.

[24] J. Nelson Norwood, "Modernism," *Sabbath Recorder* 104/5-12, 5:138, 6:173-74, 7:204-205, 9:259-60, 12:365-66.

accept the tenets of fundamentalism." He wanted to confirm them in their hope that they might still call themselves Christian.[25]

The "Fundamentalist Page" 1929–1931

The first "Fundamentalist Page" in the *Sabbath Recorder* appeared 7 January 1929. In that column, A. L. Davis explained the "Why of the Department" with a summary of the history of the *Exponent* and its opposition to modernism, which he viewed as the greatest menace confronting the Church of Jesus Christ. He wrote that its deadening, paralyzing effects were seen in every evangelical Christian denomination.[26] The column ran every week until 15 June 1931. In his final editorial, A. L. Davis affirmed his conviction that modernism had reached its zenith and was waning, and that the future of fundamentalism was "as bright as the promises of God." This optimism was based on several factors: (1) issues had been clarified so there was no longer any doubt about the difference between modernism and fundamentalism; (2) modernism was less militant, in part because the most militant advocates of modernism had left the evangelical churches for Unitarianism or complete rejection of their Christian faith; and (3) there was a great increase in the number of fundamentalist schools and seminaries, publications, and organizations, both within denominations and outside them.[27]

Wayne Rood, in a chapter of his book *The Lesson For Tomorrow* titled "The Great Test," summarized this controversial period as being one in which freedom of thought revealed strength as men who had trained in Seventh Day Baptist colleges and served on their faculties took opposite sides in the intellectual quest. "If the people and the ministry as a whole had not been at least sympathetic with the freedom of real scholarship, the denomination might have split on the issue, or it might have emerged completely reactionary," he wrote, adding further that if the educators had run riot, the denomination might have turned to an equally unsatisfactory radicalism. "None of these disastrous extremes came to pass. The wisdom with which the Seventh Day Baptist schools had used their traditional freedom was demonstrated."[28]

---

[25] August E. Johansen, "Other Fruit," *Sabbath Recorder* 105/18 (29 Oct 1928): 548-51.

[26] Alva L. Davis, "Fundamentalist Page," *Sabbath Recorder* 106/1 (7 Jan 1929): 25.

[27] Davis, "The Future of Fundamentalism," *Sabbath Recorder* 110/24 (15 Jun 1931): 760-63.

[28] Wayne R. Rood, "The Great Test," in *The Lesson For Tomorrow: The Story of Education Among the Seventh Day Baptists* (N.p., 1944) 123-24.

The closing of the "Fundamentalist Page" in 1931 is sometimes considered the close of a crisis period in Seventh Day Baptist history. However, the effects of the controversy continued through the rest of the century in several ways.

The economic problems of the depression at home and growing nationalism abroad shifted much of the thought of the 1930s away from the theological controversy of previous decades. Other areas of concern demanding close cooperation provided a climate for healing some of the scars. The completion of the Seventh Day Baptist Building in Plainfield, New Jersey, held potential as a visible sign of unity. Economic restraints forced some consolidation of efforts. The decade saw new and renewed efforts in education, particularly among the young people as youth camps were being organized and promoted.

In 1929, the General Conference appointed a Committee to Promote the Religious Program (later named Committee on Religious Life) with evangelism as its ultimate objective. At first this committee was comprised of those who already had responsibilities for denominational programs with the Missionary Society, the Tract Society, and the Sabbath School Board,[29] but in 1933 the committee suggested that it might be better to appoint on this committee persons who did not already hold official positions within the denomination.[30] The appointed committee included pastors in the Central Association. It is significant that the chairman was Rev. Alva L. Davis, who had been the spokesman for the fundamentalists. He now put his evangelical zeal into united programs to further the denomination's religious life.

A New Statement of Belief

The Committee on Religious Life recommended that the General Conference and the associations give a prominent place in their programs for 1934 to "the great doctrines of our faith, our history, and the how and why of personal evangelism." They suggested that study groups be held on specific subjects related to these issues. They asked the Sabbath School Board to depart from the International Lessons and devote a quarter's issue of the *Helping Hand* to a study of denominational

---

[29] Report of the Commission, Conference Minutes, *SDB Yearbook* (1929) 64.
[30] Report of the Committee on Religious Life, Conference Minutes, *SDB Yearbook* (1933) 17.

beliefs.[31] This study was partly responsible for the drafting of the Statement of Belief adopted by the General Conference in 1937. Care was taken to express both the liberal and the conservative viewpoints, resulting in a statement that was "an exhibition of the views generally held by Seventh Day Baptists and is not adopted as having binding force in itself."

The 1937 statement has been criticized as being too vague and general in certain areas. The General Statement and the section on Polity, which served as a preface, were particularly ambiguous, for they tread a narrow line between "cherishing liberty of thought" with "no binding creed" while holding to "certain beliefs and practices having the support of Scripture and adhered to by followers of Christ through the centuries" as being "binding upon all Christians."[32]

Coming as it did so soon after the theological differences of the preceding decade, it is remarkable that a statement of faith could be adopted that was acceptable across the spectrum of belief. It is also understandable that fifty years later, in a considerably different theological climate, the need was felt for a new, more definitive statement.[33]

Higher Education

Most of the spokesmen for the modernist or liberal theological views were connected with the denominational colleges at Alfred, New York; Milton, Wisconsin; and Salem, West Virginia. Early in the century, many Seventh Day Baptist students from across the country completed at least part of their training at one of these schools. The fear that students might be exposed to the teaching of evolution and the critical study of the Bible or other non-fundamentalist positions caused some students to enroll in more evangelical schools that had been established by other denominations. This siphoning off of students and support because of theological differences was one factor that hastened the day when these colleges could no longer be considered Seventh Day Baptist schools.

---

[31] Report of the Committee on Religious Life, Conference Minutes, *SDB Yearbook* (1934) 21.

[32] *Seventh Day Baptist Beliefs: A Manual For Study* (Plainfield NJ: American Sabbath Tract Society, 1941) x.

[33] "Seventh Day Baptist Statement of Belief," adopted August 10, 1987, *SDB Yearbook* (1987) A45-46, B19-21.

That which was true for the colleges was even more pronounced in the seminary. For over thirty years (1901–1933), Arthur E. Main was the dean of the Alfred University School of Theology. During this time he was closely identified with the modernist view, as he brought the tools of the academic studies to his theological and biblical teaching and writing. In 1930 Everett Harris, who had been reared in a very conservative church, wrote a letter for the *Sabbath Recorder* in which he stated that he had come to Alfred to take the seminary courses bringing with him distorted ideas concerning the seminary, but with the purpose of discovering if there were any basis for those ideas. After two years he had discovered that Dean Main was the most deeply religious man, without exception, he had ever known. His associations with Dean Main had also made him realize the great need for more Christian ministers, the high calling of the ministry, and that the so-called "higher criticism," as taught in the seminary, was merely the application of good sense to religion.[34]

Main's successor in 1933 was Dean A. J. C. Bond, who had served the denomination effectively as pastor, as the leader in Sabbath Promotion, as director of the Forward Movement, and as a primary promoter of youth camps and teenage conferences. He had not been as involved in the theological disputes as his predecessor had been and thus was able to help draft the 1937 Statement of Belief, which received denomination-wide acceptance. Nonetheless, because of his involvement in such ecumenical organizations as the Federal and World Councils of Churches, he was associated with the non-fundamentalist position. The School of Theology thus became branded as a liberal school.

The School of Theology did contain many of the traits associated with liberalism. Considerable freedom of thought was granted. Biblical criticism and other modernist ideas were introduced along with fundamentalist ideas, but it was left to the student to develop his own doctrinal beliefs. This was done in an atmosphere of deep Sabbath convictions and in a community with Sabbath opportunities for worship and service. Some students who came from conservative backgrounds left seminary with a more liberal theology, while others from liberal backgrounds became more conservative.

The choice of some students to go elsewhere for theological training had several direct effects on the future. First, it deprived the school of some of the evangelistic fervor that was more characteristic of the

---

[34] Everett Harris, "Letter to the Editor," *Sabbath Recorder* 108/10 (10 Mar 1930): 290.

fundamentalist position. In the give and take of the classroom and other face-to-face experiences of a seminary setting, the conservative voice was often absent.

Second, the bond of fellowship among the ministers and their families that was often established during seminary days was not as inclusive in later years. When the choice of seminary was made on theological grounds, these differences tended to persist through the years of pastoral service. During much of the 1950s, considerable time and energy was expended in the debate over the seminary.

A third result of the choice to attend other seminaries was economic. It became increasingly difficult to maintain an adequate staff when the faculty at times outnumbered the students. In order to meet the increased demands of academic accrediting agencies, it was necessary to enter into agreement with the Methodist conference in the area to provide both students and staff. The crisis came when the Methodists decided to open their own seminary. However, even with the denomination's full support, it is doubtful the seminary could have existed much beyond 1963, when its doors were closed and a new program was instigated.

The Center on Ministry

The new program for ministerial education, which began in fall 1964 with Rev. Victor W. Skaggs as dean, was centered in the Seventh Day Baptist Building in Plainfield, New Jersey. Students enrolled in the program received support from the denomination to attend accredited seminaries of their choice located within an area close enough to Plainfield that they could attend weekend retreats and longer institute seminars where denominational distinctives were taught. Several seminaries granted academic credit for work done at the center, and the dean was listed on the faculty of at least one of those seminaries. The dean reported to a Council on Ministrial Education (COME) elected by the General Conference.

In reviewing the advantages of the new program, Rev. Albert N. Rogers, who had succeeded Bond as dean of the Alfred School of Theology in 1952, listed the opportunity for students to study in larger, fully accredited seminaries and to study with students from varied backgrounds. In addition, students coming to Plainfield had exposure to denominational leaders and activities of the headquarters. "Best of all," he noted, "the Center is free from the dead hand of theological dispute which had continued at the seminary long after the Fundamentalism controversy was stilled."[35]

Rev. Rex E. Zwiebel succeeded Skaggs as director (1970–1974), and the program was expanded so that students attending any accredited seminary in the United States could be included in the Center's Program and receive its benefits. The denominational distinctives were then taught in three three-week summer institutes at Plainfield: Seventh Day Baptist History, Seventh Day Baptist Polity, and Sabbath Philosophy. [36] About the same time, the dean's responsibilities were revised to include "support, recruitment, education, pastor-church relations, and ministerial retirement," and the body he reported to was renamed Council on Ministry (COM).[37] During the deanship of Rev. Herbert E. Saunders (1974–1981), the courses in history and polity were combined "as both an economy move and as an opportunity to relate the two aspects of history and polity into an understanding of modern Seventh Day Baptist history."[38]

With the 1982 move of the General Conference offices to Janesville, Wisconsin, the Center on Ministry, with Rev. J. Paul Green Jr. as the newly appointed dean, was the first agency to occupy the new facility. When Rev. Rodney L. Henry succeeded Green in 1988, the title officially changed to Director of Pastoral Services. Under the direction of the Council on Ministry and the Missionary Society, Henry developed and implemented an alternate training program for those who could not attend seminary. The Training in Ministry and Extension program (TIME) was specifically designed "to provide effective training in ministry for those who must continue their present occupation or who are retiring and feel the call to pastoral ministry."[39]

Rev. Gabriel Bejjani served as dean of the School of Ministry and as Director of Pastoral Services from 1999 to 2003, when he was succeeded by Rev. Gordon Lawton.

---

[35] Albert N. Rogers, "Ministerial Training and Seventh Day Baptists," *Foundations* 16/1 (Jan–Mar 1973): 67.

[36] Report of the Committee on Ministerial Interests, Conference Minutes, *SDB Yearbook* (1972) 72.

[37] Report of the Commission, Conference Minutes, *SDB Yearbook* (1971) 51.

[38] Report of the Council on Ministry, Conference Minutes, *SDB Yearbook* (1979) 7G.

[39] Report of the Council on Ministry, Conference Minutes, *SDB Yearbook* (1988) J5.

Ecumenical Relations

Seventh Day Baptist relationship with other churches is the third area affected by the theological differences of the early part of the century. This was particularly true of such organizations as the Federal Council, the National Council, and the World Council. As noted in chapter 22, although the initial objections to membership in some of the organizations were over questions of polity and church autonomy, growing concern was expressed over the ecumenical leadership, which was often dominated by the more liberal theologians. Several churches and individuals threatened to withdraw from the denomination rather than be listed in fellowship with churches that questioned such doctrines as the virgin birth or the deity of Christ.

EVALUATION

In spite of half a century's passage since the intense theological controversy of the twentieth century's first two decades, it is still difficult to make a full assessment of the debate's impact on the denomination. Where some see obvious cause-effect relationships, others see multiple causes, or in some cases an in-spite-of relationship. For example, a statistical decline in membership began at the same time that modernism and liberal theology came to schools and churches. David Moberg, in *The Church As A Social Institution*, has pointed out that by its very nature, fundamentalism is more adept at contending for the faith, for "Fundamentalists know exactly what they believe and are not merely seeking truth.... Nothing is more difficult for the outsider to sympathize with than the attempt to combine two loyalties; nothing is harder to understand than the man who recites the creed with mental denial."[40]

Among Seventh Day Baptists, the theological wrestling included the Sabbath principle. In evaluating the theological stance of Seventh Day Baptists at about the midpoint of the century, Loyal Hurley remarked, "We are basically a liberal denomination with a conservative doctrine in the Sabbath." This reality posed a dilemma at times, for as will be considered more fully in the next chapter, many of the more theologically conservative denominations are the most liberal in their interpretation of the biblical Sabbath. That is, some who hold most strongly to the literal interpretation of the inerrancy of the Scriptures rely

---

[40] David O. Moberg, *The Church as a Social Institution: The Sociology of American Religion* (Englewood Cliffs NJ: Prentice Hall, 1962) 283-84.

most completely on tradition and ecclesiastical authority for their position on the Sabbath.

25

THE SABBATH IN A SABBATHLESS AGE

A. H. Lewis, in *Letters to Young Preachers*, warned young theological students of the difficulty of their work in what he characterized as a "Sabbathless Age" at the opening of the twentieth century. "There are too many churches to which you will be called to minister which are not ready for higher views, broader plans and more consecrated Sabbathkeeping," he warned, pointing out that many members have been influenced by the prevailing influences of society. "You must start life with the truth fully recognized that our history is inseparably connected with the Sabbath question. Our future cannot be separated from it. As the combined influences which oppose Sabbathism increase, the evidence of this close relation between our denominational life and Sabbath Reform will become yet more apparent."[1]

A MAJOR CONCERN TO SOCIETY

Lewis's concern over the problem of the young minister's work in a Sabbathless age grew out of his own experience and the change he saw at the turn of the century. In his earlier years of Sabbath Reform work, Lewis believed that once people were convinced that the seventh day was the true biblical Sabbath, they would simply switch from Sunday to the Sabbath. This was the approach he made in the *Outlook* (1882–1893). But in his later years, he observed that the problem was much deeper, for it involved the whole concept of Sabbathism. This observation prompted not only the book *Spiritual Sabbathism*, but also another that dealt more specifically with the lack of reverence for any day.

In 1899, Lewis published *Swift Decadence of Sunday. What Next?* In this book he cited the concern of Baptists, Methodists, Congregationalists, Presbyterians, and Episcopalians over the loss of Sunday's religious significance as a day of worship. They decried the shift of that day from a holy day to a holiday and society's fastening "a giant's grasp upon it as a day of leisure." Much of this desecration, Lewis believed, could be traced to the Puritans, who stopped short of their break from

---

[1] Abram Herbert Lewis, *Letters to Young Preachers and Their Hearers* (Plainfield NJ: American Sabbath Tract Society, 1900) 227.

the Roman Church by the compromise that applied the name Sabbath to Sunday.[2] Lewis was convinced that the basic problem of this secularization stemmed from the lack of biblical support for Sunday as a day of worship and the attempt to apply biblical Sabbathism to a day that is not the Sabbath. He saw this unfair way in which the Bible has been interpreted as having done more to break down the authority of the Scriptures than the "higher criticism" of the time.[3]

Lewis was not alone in this contention, for he quoted several others who cited the role of tradition in this matter. Doctor A. S. Hobart, for example, said that if Baptists give up tradition as a source of authority, then they must give up worship on Sunday to begin with. Yet, Hobart acknowledged that preaching and quoting from the Bible "won't make any impression at all toward changing the practice of the church, for they would say grandpa did it that way, and it is good enough for us."[4]

On the other hand, Lewis also cites a Presbyterian, Rev. I. W. Hathaway of the American Sabbath Union, who in 1897 noted confusion over the validity of the Fourth Commandment as a reason for the downward trend of Sabbathism: "While a majority of men in Christian lands admit, without question, the law of the Decalogue, as related to idolatry, murder, theft, and adultery, they question the authority of the fourth commandment, and appear to use or abuse the Sabbath-day, disobey this law, as their feelings or inclination may prompt, without realizing that they are doing violence to their moral and spiritual being."[5]

Lewis believed that if Seventh Day Baptists were to be successful, they must do more than show that others are wrong. New ground must be broken that involves the concept of Protestantism itself. This new ground must begin with Christ's concept of the Sabbath.[6] "When Pagan philosophy and prejudice against the Jews began to teach the falsehood that the Sabbath was only a 'Jewish affair' and that it was not binding on Christians, the spiritual life and power of the church declined in swift and increasing ratio. This was especially true after Christianity became a

---

[2] Abram Herbert Lewis, *Swift Decadence of Sunday: What Next?* (Plainfield NJ: American Sabbath Tract Society, 1899) ii.

[3] Ibid., 131.

[4] A. S. Hobart, quoted in ibid., 16.

[5] I. W. Hathaway, "Have We an American Sabbath?" *Christian Intelligencer* (8 Dec 1897), quoted Lewis, *Swift Decadence*, 107-108.

[6] Lewis, *Swift Decadence?*, 235-36.

religion of the Roman Empire by civil law, and Sunday and other festivals appointed by the state-church were exalted and fostered."[7]

Other Seventh Day Baptists expressed the same concern over this Sabbathless age. In 1904, Rev. L. A. Platts published a sermon titled "The Outlook for Sabbath Reform" in which he viewed the nature of the Sabbath Reform movement as an attempt not only to restore the Sabbath to its proper place in the divine calendar but to see it as God's appointment. "Loyalty to the Sabbath law, because it is God's law becomes a test of loyalty to God and his word in other matters—in all other matters."[8]

Platts listed four conditions or groups that react to a movement of this kind: (1) the irreligious who have no regard for any religious observances; (2) the religionists such as the Roman Catholics to whom the Sabbath in any proper or biblical sense has no meaning; (3) the Protestant Christians who have felt the need for a Sabbath and have invented the civil Sabbath, a legal rest day for which they invoke the civil law for authority and defense; and (4) those who "recognize in the Sabbath Law the voice of God speaking with the authority of Sinai, and with the compassion of Calvary; who know no better way of expressing their loyalty to God than by keeping his commandments, or of showing their gratitude for the great salvation than by joyfully following in the footsteps of Him whose life was devoted to the accomplishment of His Father's will."

STEPS TO REFORMATION

Platts affirmed that God works through human agencies to achieve reform among men. "If Seventh Day Baptists have been raised for this Sabbath Reform work," as he believed they had, "how shall they best do their part to hasten the reform?" He suggested five steps, each of which echoed in some fashion through much of the century.

1. Greater spirituality: "God gave the Sabbath not primarily because the body needs rest, but because the soul needs the divine uplifting. When this comes to be the meaning of the Sabbath to us, and when the fellowship of our life with God is the sweetest joy we know, we shall be just where God can use us for his truth."

---

[7] Ibid., 236-37.
[8] L. A. Platts, "The Outlook for Sabbath Reform," *Seventh Day Baptist Pulpit* 2/5 (Jun 1904): 83-87.

2. Personal loyalty to God and his word: "If we love God with all our hearts, and his Sabbath as the promoter of our religious life, all God's truth will be precious to us and obedience to all his will will be our joy."
3. Sabbath evangelism: "We ought more systematically, more earnestly and more lovingly to press its claim upon the attention of others."
4. Mutual support in Sabbathkeeping: Platts cited the relationships between employers and employees so that a person is able to support himself and his family and keep a clean conscience toward God.
5. The removal of any barriers: There are both real and imagined hindrances that make Sabbathkeeping difficult.

Seventh Day Baptists in the twentieth century pursued each of these five steps in their attempts to preserve and elevate consciousness of the Sabbath in a Sabbathless age.[9]

Greater Spirituality

Throughout the twentieth century, the refrain of greater spirituality was the essential ingredient for Sabbath Reform, yet many found it difficult to attain. Too often the challenge was theoretical or even theological without touching the everyday lives of the people.

Less than eighteen months later, W. D. Burdick also wrote for *The Pulpit*, pointing out the need for the same keen watchfulness over spiritual matters as one has over such things as market conditions, weather, politics, fashions, and amusements. He was greatly concerned over the accommodations that many were making to a materialistic and pleasure-loving age, the religious indifference masked under the guise of tolerance, and the neglect of parents to talk with their children about habits and beliefs.[10]

A. H. Lewis's book *Spiritual Sabbathism* was one of the most influential Seventh Day Baptist publications of the century in setting a tone for the Sabbath as a spiritual experience. In his preface, Lewis maintained that "Sabbathism no longer appears a small or legalistic, or casuistic, or ceremonial issue. It becomes, not a question of formal deeds, but a question as to what men shall be at heart.... It is a question whether

---

[9] Ibid.
[10] W. D. Burdick, "Signs of the Times," *Seventh Day Baptist Pulpit* 3/8 (Sep 1905): 139-43.

men can transcend time by consecrating it, and live in the eternal while yet in time."[11]

Many of the sermons and reports at sessions of the General Conference and articles in the *Sabbath Recorder* reflected the need for greater spirituality in Sabbathkeeping. Tracts carried such titles as "The Sabbath and Spiritual Christianity" and "Have You Made the Wonderful Discovery of a Spirit-filled Sabbath?" During the theological controversy between modernists and fundamentalists, the two sides expressed different views on the manner in which the Sabbath came to man, but all were united in the fact that the Sabbath was given by God for man's spiritual development and communion. The programs considered in chapter 20 all included emphasis on spiritual growth as a basis for any numerical growth.

Sabbath Philosophy was one of the pivotal courses in the School of Theology. Even those who chose not to attend were expected to take work in this field before they could be accredited by the General Conference.[12] With the development of the Center on Ministry, the course on Sabbath Theology was offered during the Summer Institute and was required of all ministers seeking accreditation.[13] The expectation that ministers representing the denomination be grounded in a strong spiritual basis for the Sabbath was reinforced through and at ministers' conferences and retreats.

One of the most significant books on the Sabbath by a Seventh Day Baptist in recent history grew out of a series of lectures at a Ministers' Conference in 1969. Rev. Herbert E. Saunders, in his book *The Sabbath: Symbol of Creation and Recreation*, challenged his readers to spiritual growth in Sabbathism as he stated that "Seventh Day Baptists ought to stand in unique contrast to the present world's preoccupation with busyness and its over-emphasis on the material. We ought to stand for spiritual life and a personal encounter with God in contrast to concern for wealth, prestige and social recognition." He viewed the Sabbath as placing Seventh Day Baptists in a "unique position of being instruments through which a new spiritual life can be born in twentieth century

---

[11] Abram Herbert Lewis, *Spiritual Sabbathism* (Plainfield NJ: American Sabbath Tract Society, 1910) iii-xii.

[12] Report of the Committee to Consider the Theological Training of Our Ministers, Conference Minutes, *SDB Yearbook* (1953) 22-23.

[13] Wayne R. Rood, ed., *A Manual of Procedures for Seventh Day Baptist Churches* (Plainfield NJ: SDB General Conference, 1972) 61.

man." The Sabbath affords a time set apart for renewal and spiritual exercise, bringing a new emphasis on personal identity and worth.[14]

Two other significant books on the Sabbath were written by a new generation of writers. The first work, *The Sabbath: God's Creation for Our Benefit* by Rev. Rodney L. Henry, Director of Pastoral Services, was published in 1996 with funds donated in memory of former General Conference president George E. Parrish, who had expressed a desire for Sabbath teaching materials. Two years later, Rev. Larry Graffius, chairman of the Conference Tract and Communication Council, authored *True to the Sabbath, True to Our God*, a practical guide to Sabbathkeeping.

Obedience: A Response to God's love

It has not always been easy to distinguish between obedience as a loyal response to God's love and obedience as response to a legalistic command. At issue is the difference between a covenant and a command. Seventh Day Baptists began the century with a strong emphasis on a covenant theology. The essential nature of the covenant was viewed as the solemn agreement between God and his people, ratified by obedience and love. God took them as His chosen people, and they, on their part, accepted the conditions He imposed. One of the principal signs of that covenant was the Sabbath. The Chicago Council of 1890 affirmed that "the keeping of the covenant is the highest expression of the soul's allegiance and love to God. And the maintenance of the covenant is vitally necessary to the Christian life and growth." Furthermore, the council declared that it was "the neglect of covenant-keeping that makes the Christian world so indifferent to the commands of God, that makes some of our people careless about the Sabbath, that is preventing spiritual development, and is sapping the Christian life."[15]

Nearly all of the churches had within their congregational covenants some agreement to observe the Sabbath as a condition of the covenant relationship. In some covenants, keeping the Sabbath was implied by such phrases as that found in the covenant of the old Newport Seventh Day Baptist Church: "...and give up ourselves to God and one another, to walk together in all God's holy commandments and holy ordinances."[16] Others often added specific mention of the Sabbath

---

[14] Herbert E. Saunders, *The Sabbath: Symbol of Creation and Recreation* (Plainfield NJ: American Sabbath Tract Society, 1970) 10.

[15] Committee on Spiritual Life and Religious Development, *Proceedings of the Seventh-day Baptist Council, Held at Chicago, Ill., Oct. 22–29, 1890* (n.p., n.d.) 49-50.

[16] Covenant, Newport Seventh Day Baptist Church, see ch. 7 of this book.

by an agreement "to keep the appointments of God's house by a regular attendance upon the Sabbath service."[17] Some more recent covenant expressions have been personalized with the statement, "I covenant and agree to faithfully keep the Sabbath of the Bible, the seventh day of the week, as a sacred time, a gift of God, instituted at creation, affirmed in the Ten Commandments and reaffirmed by Jesus and the apostles."[18] Since many of the covenants also contained the agreement "to watch over each other for good," with the provision that discipline would be administered in accord with Matthew 18:15-17, the practice of "churching" or "laboring with" an individual was often practiced during the early years of the century. Sometimes the basis for such action was a failure to keep the Sabbath as determined by the congregation.

Over the years, as society in general emphasized the rights of the individual, the covenant concept became less important in members' thinking. Thus, in the minds of many, particularly among the younger people, the Sabbath was seen as a time of prohibitions, or "Thou shalt not...." This idea was reinforced by the efforts of other churches to create civil laws to enforce Sunday prohibitions.

Some of the attitudes and ideas that came out of the theological controversies of the first half of the century influenced thinking in regard to Sabbath obedience. The affirmation that the Bible "is our final authority in matters of faith and conduct"[19] was often interpreted to mean that the Bible was a spiritual guide to relationship with God rather than a rulebook to dictate behavior. This ambiguity is demonstrated in the statements that prefaced the 1937 Statement of Belief. In the General Statement there is an emphasis at the beginning on "liberty of thought" and a lack of any "binding creed to which members must subscribe." Yet, this was followed by the statement that "certain beliefs and practices, having the support of scriptures and adhered to by followers of Christ through the centuries, are binding upon all Christians." The statement on Polity also gave emphasis to Baptist congregational polity that grants "freedom of conscience in all matters of religion" and calls the Statement of Belief "simply an exhibition of the views generally held by Seventh Day Baptists and is not adopted as having binding force in itself."[20]

---

[17] Covenant, Seventh Day Baptist Church, Riverside CA (1896).
[18] Covenant, Seventh Day Baptist Church, Battle Creek MI (12 Jul 1987).
[19] "The Bible," SDB Statement of Belief, Article IV (1937).
[20] "General Statement and Polity," SDB Statement of Belief (1937).

Fifty years later, when a new statement was adopted in 1987, this ambiguity was removed. The Introduction reaffirmed "liberty of thought under the guidance of the Holy Spirit to be essential to Christian belief and practice." It encouraged the "unhindered study and open discussion of Scripture" and granted "the individual's freedom of conscience in seeking to determine and obey the will of God." The statements that followed were considered as "expressions of common belief derived from understanding of Scripture."[21]

Obedience was still expected, but on a level of one's personal commitment that was further exemplified in the statements concerning the Sabbath. The 1937 statement on the Sabbath ends with the words, "it should be faithfully kept by all Christians as a day of rest and worship, a symbol of God's presence in time, a pledge of eternal Sabbath rest."[22] The corresponding article in 1987 ended with the recognition that "in obedience to God and in loving response to Christ, the Sabbath should be faithfully observed as a day of rest, worship and celebration."[23]

Pressing the Claims of the Sabbath

Chapter 13 pointed out that during the first half of the nineteenth century, Seventh Day Baptists had four basic target options for missionary activity: (1) to strengthen scattered members, (2) to go to other Christians, (3) to take the Gospel to Sabbathkeeping Jews, and (4) to break new ground among non-Christians.

At the beginning of the twentieth century, the Seventh Day Baptists' major emphasis in Sabbath promotion was in pressing the claims of the Sabbath on other Christians. During the years of the most aggressive Sabbath promotion, a number of books and other publications were addressed primarily to other Christians. Much of the early effort during the century was directed toward proselytizing from other denominations. One of the major reasons cited for participation in ecumenical organizations was that it gave a platform for witnessing to the Sabbath.

The most consistent effort, however, was strengthening scattered members. Even some of the efforts to reach other Christians with the Sabbath was for purpose of self-survival. The Committee on Sabbath Reform at the Chicago Council reported that "if Christian people in general cannot be brought to the observance of the seventh day Sabbath,

<hr>

[21] "Introduction," SDB Statement of Belief (1987).
[22] "The Sabbath," SDB Statement of Belief, Article X (1937).
[23] "The Sabbath," SDB Statement of Belief, Article IX (1987).

there is danger that the coming generations of our own people will be swept away with the over-whelming tide of no-Sabbathism, so that the work of saving our own people to the Sabbath largely depends upon our success in bringing other Christians into its observance."[24]

Articles about the Sabbath that appeared in the *Sabbath Recorder* and sermons of the period that have been preserved were largely addressed to those who already were connected to the church. The evangelistic quartets of the last decade of the nineteenth century, which continued into the twentieth century, went primarily performed for communities where there was a sponsoring Seventh Day Baptist church. This ministry of music was revived in later years when Loyal Hurley worked as an evangelist with a quartet during the summers of the mid-1950s. A more extensive year-round evangelistic music ministry was established in 1972 with the formation of Light Bearers for Christ under the direction of Rev. Mynor Soper. A generation later, another musical group, Stained Glass, presented the gospel under the direction of Mrs. Dede Mackintosh. Each of these efforts provided training and experience in evangelism, but the local church was the target most often reached.

Subconsciously, there may have been a limited concept of those who could be reached. H. Leon McBeth reflected in his book *The Baptist Heritage* that Seventh Day Baptists might have grown more in this country "but for the rise of Seventh-day Adventism in the 1840s which drew off many of their converts, actual and potential. American religion apparently offers only a limited market for seventh-day worship, and the Adventists have captured the lion's share."[25]

Whether a limited market is real or imaginary may be debated, but there is no debate that a great deal of concern by Seventh Day Baptists in the twentieth century was directed toward gaining identity and recognition. Many of those who claim they have never heard of Seventh Day Baptists mistakenly identify them with the Adventists. Letters written on printed letterheads with clear identification were often answered addressed to the Seventh-day Adventist church. Even in communities where Seventh Day Baptists have been present for over 100 years, similar slips were sometimes made in newspaper items. This identity has been further complicated by certain Sabbathkeeping sects or denominations that have, without true historical basis, claimed much of the early Seventh Day Baptist history as their own.

---

[24] Committee on Sabbath Reform, *Proceedings of the SDB Council*, Chicago, 61.
[25] H. Leon McBeth, *The Baptist Heritage* (Nashville: Broadman Press, 1987) 706.

When Seventh Day Baptists entered into the Commitment to Growth program in 1976, the fourth target area came into sharper focus: choosing to break new ground among non-Christians. Dr. John Wimber, Director of Church Growth for the Fuller Evangelistic Association, emphasized that the greatest potential for growth lay in reaching those who have no church affiliation. If a person who has never known Christ is brought to salvation in Christ, he will be very likely to accept the religious beliefs and practices of the church that was responsible for his conversion. Those churches that have practiced this premise in their ministries found new life and new growth.

Mutual Support in a Sabbathless Age

The fourth step suggested by L. A. Platts for Sabbath Reform work was strengthening the relationship between employers and employees, enabling mutual support. Not only did this call for employers within the church to give special consideration to the hiring of Sabbathkeepers, but also it implied that "those who have service to give in exchange for wages ought to bring such talent and such conscience to their work that, from the worldly point of view, employers cannot afford to pass them by."[26]

In 1918, the General Conference Committee on Denominational Activities recommended the appointment of a Committee on Vocational Opportunities to help young people train for and find employment in areas where they could be free to observe the Sabbath.[27] That committee recommended denominational surveys of opportunities for employment in Sabbathkeeping communities, vocational training in communities where Seventh Day Baptist churches were located, the establishment of a vocational advisory department among Seventh Day Baptist schools, and that adequate space provided in the *Sabbath Recorder* for the work of a department editor.[28] Very little action was reported by the committee over the next few years, in part because of the wide geographic distribution of its members.

In 1923, Rev. Robert B. St. Clair of Detroit became chairman of the Vocational Committee. His report for 1924 showed an aggressive program that included an urban ministry. Concerning the urban

---

[26] Platts, "Outlook," 86.

[27] Report of the Committee on Denominational Activities, Conference Minutes, *SDB Yearbook* (1918) 64.

[28] Report of the Committee on Vocational Opportunities, Conference Minutes, *SDB Yearbook* (1919) 63-64.

migration that was drawing many young people away from their home churches, St. Clair declared that the church had no right to allow her inexperienced children to be lost in the maze of a great city but must anticipate their arrival and make it easy to do right and hard to do wrong. He described the Detroit plan whereby members of that church made an extensive survey of vacancies in the city and its environs that offered Sabbath privileges. The report ended with a plea for an aggressive plan to "drive our stakes" in a number of urban areas where people were going anyway without aid from the denomination. "How long will it be before some of these people cease to be 'our' people?"[29] In 1924, Robert St. Clair was employed fulltime by the Missionary Board in recognition of what he was doing "from the standpoint of vocational needs and from the standpoint of extending our influence to people with whom we are not now acquainted, as well as in other missionary lines."[30]

In 1925, the committee's list of activities included securing from the Detroit City Council an exemption for Sabbathkeepers that defined the seventh day from sunset Friday to Saturday sunset. This exemption allowed labor and business to be performed on Saturday evenings. The committee also proposed entering into the production phase of employment with the building of a health food plant, but this phase was never carried out.[31] Serious problems of unemployment in the Detroit area created a condition that Pastor St. Clair reported the "committee was unable to overcome, being the tail and not the dog." The committee received many requests from people looking for work, but often applicants did not specify their skills or capabilities.[32] The untimely death of committee chairman Robert St. Clair at the hands of unknown assailants in June 1928 greatly curtailed the work of the scattered committee.

The Vocational Committee continued as a part of the General Conference until 1965, when its duties and responsibilities were incorporated within the structure of the Board of Christian Education.[33] A number of different emphases were made during the years to assist in providing employment in Seventh Day Baptist communities. These ranged from articles in the Sabbath Recorder, aptitude tests for youth

[29] Report of the Vocational Committee, Conference Minutes, SDB Yearbook (1924) 58-60.
[30] Report of the Commission, Conference Minutes, SDB Yearbook (1924) 102-103.
[31] Report of the Vocational Committee, Conference Minutes, SDB Yearbook (1925) 45-47. See also SDB Yearbook (1926) 47.
[32] Report of the Vocational Committee, Conference Minutes, SDB Yearbook (1927) 49.
[33] Report of the Vocational Committee, Conference Minutes, SDB Yearbook (1965) 54.

groups (particularly at camps), a "Who's Who and What They Do" directory, counseling for vocational opportunities, and attempts at job placement.

The results of these efforts were less than spectacular for two main reasons. First, it is difficult to do denominationally that which needs to be done locally. The time between job openings and their publication, coupled with the lack of personal information or recommendations, made job placement by a scattered committee difficult. Second, there remained through most of the twentieth century a colony mindset that viewed Sabbath observance in terms of existing Seventh Day Baptist churches.

Barrier-Free Environment for Sabbath Observance

The fifth step for encouraging Sabbath observance in the twentieth century, identified by Dr. Platts, was the removal of, or at least diminishing of, the barriers erected and maintained by a Sabbathless society. He pointed out that there were many who were ready to acknowledge the truth of the Sabbath but who felt unable to follow their belief for economic reasons, because jobs required work on the Sabbath. He asked the question, "Are we doing all we can to remove these barriers by which many, who would otherwise embrace the truth, are now hindered from doing so?"[34]

Legislative Barriers

One of the barriers to Sabbath observance is the tradition of Sunday observance often reinforced by civil law. The so-called Sunday Blue Laws[35] have persisted in many states even after their religious significance has been lost. This is best illustrated by a 1961 Supreme Court decision.

In 1959, several employees of a large discount store in Maryland were indicted for violating the state's Sunday closing law. The employees' conviction in state court worked its way to the Supreme Court, where, along with three other cases, it received a hearing in 1961. Chief Justice Warren, in delivering the majority opinion of the court, declared that there was no dispute that the original laws that dealt with

---

[34] Platts, "Outlook," 86-87.

[35] It is uncertain where the name "Blue Laws" originated. One theory states that it was derived from the fact that the law books of Connecticut that included harsh Sunday legislation were bound in blue.

Sunday labor were motivated by religious forces. The question was whether they still retained their religious character. After tracing some of the historical background in the inception and the application of these laws, the court upheld the Blue Law concept by concluding that it was common knowledge that the first day of the week had come to have special significance as a rest day in this country as "people of all religions and people with no religion regard Sunday as a time for family activity, for visiting friends and relatives, for late-sleeping, for passive and active entertainments, for dining out and the like.... Sunday is a day apart from others. The cause is irrelevant; the fact exists."[36]

Seventh Day Baptists have been among those who have protested that the cause *is* relevant. They sided with the lone dissenter on the Supreme Court, Justice William Douglas, who criticized his colleagues' action in his dissenting opinion by claiming, "No matter how much is written, no matter what is said, the parentage of these laws is the Fourth Commandment; and they serve and satisfy the religious predispositions of our Christian communities."[37]

In his closing argument, Justice Douglas quoted a Presbyterian pastor who said that "though Sunday-worshiping Christians are in the majority in this country among religious people, we do not have the right to force our practice upon the minority. Only a church which deems itself without error and intolerant of error can justify its intolerance of the minority." The pastor then cited from his experience a small Seventh Day Baptist church that met around the corner. He said that while he disagreed with them on points of doctrine, including the "seventh-day worship," he respected them. He pointed out that it was easy for the people of his congregation to set aside their jobs on the first of the week and gather in God's house of worship "since Sunday-closing laws—inspired by the Church—keep them from their work." But, he noted, "it takes real sacrifice at the Seventh Day Baptist church where the people set aside their jobs on Saturday to worship God because Saturday is a good day for business." He concluded by saying that he did not believe that "because I have set aside Sunday as a holy day I have the right to force all men to set aside that day also. Why should my faith be favored by the state over any other man's faith?"[38]

---

[36] *McGowen v. Maryland*, 366 U.S. 420.

[37] Justice William Douglas, "The Douglas Dissent," quoted by Warren Johns, *Dateline Sunday, U.S.A.* (Mountain View CA: Pacific Press Assoc., 1967) 153-54.

[38] Ibid., 158-59.

Seventh Day Baptists stood with Jews, the American Civil Liberty Union, Adventists, and others in opposition to the enactment of Blue Laws and the Supreme Court's upholding of them. A number of individual Seventh Day Baptists, including Senator Jennings Randolph from West Virginia, were able to influence legislation and secure exemptions of some of the Sunday laws passed by various states. The influence of Seventh Day Baptists in ecumenical organizations has been able to enlist support from the larger segment of the Christian community in their struggle against legal barriers to Sabbathkeeping.

Social Barriers

It has not been legal restrictions that have created the most difficulty for Sabbathkeepers in society but social and economic barriers. In a society that for years operated on a six-day work week, many Seventh Day Baptists felt limited in their choice of occupations and workplaces. The teaching profession, which traditionally operated on a five-day work week, drew a disproportionately high number of Seventh Day Baptists. Yet, even in education, young people and teachers have had to make hard choices in relation to school activities, for centralization of school systems has lowered the proportion of Sabbathkeepers in a district and lessened their influence on school schedules.

With the wide acceptance of the 40-hour work week, the number of positions with a five-day work week increased. However, many workers do not have a choice of which days they have off. With the rapid increase in the service industries, both Saturday and Sunday are the busiest days of the week. To accommodate those who treasure weekends for recreation, workers are often forced to work on a rotation basis that may allow only one or two Sabbaths free per month.

Rural Orientation

For nearly two centuries in America, Seventh Day Baptists were able to follow the colonial type of society in which a homogeneous community could observe the Sabbath. The pattern of migrations during those years resulted in a number of communities in which Seventh Day Baptists were either in the majority or comprised a large enough segment to command consideration from others. For example, Robert St. Clair, in giving the Vocational Committee report at the 1926 session of the General Conference in Alfred, began by commenting that the atmosphere would be conducive to awakening a larger interest in the work at hand, since he and his colleagues were meeting in "a town where since 1812 the Sabbath of Jehovah has been honored, and where post office, drug store, bank and all other places of business are closed by sunset of the Sixth Day and not opened again until the Sabbath of Christ is ended."[39]

During the pre-World War II years, St. Clair's description of Alfred fit many other communities in which Seventh Day Baptist churches were located. Of the 106 churches reported in 1900, there were only 9 churches in cities that by the 1910 census had more than 5,000 inhabitants. The rural mentality of the denomination was well illustrated by the General Conference session of 1912, when President Boothe C. Davis stated that Seventh Day Baptists "have no assured future existence, growth or prosperity independent of our rural churches. There are fundamental reasons why we can never do our greatest and our best work among city populations." He called for special training of ministers for leadership in country districts. "Rural sociology, economics and pedagogy must be understood by such ministers and our Theological Seminary is striving to meet this new demand."[40] Forty years later, the seminary at Alfred was still offering a course in Rural Sociology but nothing to equip ministers for urban pastorates.

A seminar on the Opportunities and Obligations of the Vocational Committee was held at the 1942 session of the General Conference. Paul Hummel, a rancher from Colorado, stated that it was a sorry day for the churches and for the denomination when Seventh Day Baptists began to educate their young people away from agriculture. "We as a people were unwise to stress the desirability of white collar jobs and the undesirability of farming and it is our loss and the loss of agriculture that so many of the cream of our farm raised young folks were lured away to other callings."[41]

This highlighted the denomination's dilemma during the middle part of the century. Farming did provide an environment in which one could arrange his schedule to fit in with Sabbath observance. But the number of farms had decreased to the point that there were fewer family farms on which one could make a decent living, and the migration

[39] Report of the Vocational Committee, Conference Minutes, *SDB Yearbook* (1926) 45.
[40] Boothe C. Davis, President's Address, *SDB Yearbook* (1912) 9-10.
[41] Paul Hummel, "Opportunities and Obligations of the SDB Vocational Committee from the Standpoint of the Real Estate and Agricultural Interests," *Sabbath Recorder* 133/11 (14 Sep 1942): 198.

pattern of the twentieth century was away from the farm to urban areas and urban culture. Some religious groups, such as the Mennonites and Amish, have been able to maintain a rural homogeneous society in which their distinctive lifestyle can be practiced with little outside interference. However, to maintain this environment, education has often been downplayed and an isolation policy has remained in effect.

Seventh Day Baptists have chosen to uphold education and encourage young people to excel in whatever field they select to make their living. At that same session of the General Conference in which Paul Hummel spoke for the farm family, John Reed Spicer addressed the question from the standpoint of the professional man. He recognized that there was a higher proportion of college graduates among Seventh Day Baptists than in most other denominations. They had founded and maintained an active interest in three colleges from which a high proportion of the Seventh Day Baptist graduates had come. Each of these schools had been concerned with broad or liberal education, which tended to direct graduates into the professions rather than agriculture or industry.[42]

Many of the suggestions for dealing with the observance of the Sabbath in a Sabbathless society leaned toward the colonial solution of making a safe sanctuary for Sabbathkeeping. Seventh Day Baptists have tended toward a maintenance ministry of retaining members; as a result, growth was limited to biological growth. With the development of "growth eyes" and the denomination-wide "Commitment to Growth" study of the 1970s, there came a slow awakening to new possibilities. The denomination began to look to the urban areas not only for potential growth, but also as areas most in need of the Sabbath.

SABBATH NEEDS IN AN URBAN SOCIETY

Seventh Day Baptists are not alone in the recognition of the great need for Sabbatic quality in modern society. In 1976, the editor of *Christianity Today*, Harold Lindsell, argued that the developing natural resources crisis required prompt action. He suggested that all businesses in the nation be closed one day a week and suggested Sunday as the logical day for this respite. Response from Sabbathkeepers caused him to rethink the issue, and thus, in the 5 November 1976 issue of that magazine, his editorial was titled "Consider the Case for Quiet

[42] John Reed Spicer, "Opportunities...from the Standpoint of the Professional Man," *Sabbath Recorder* 133/17 (26 Oct 1942): 296-97.

Saturdays." He wrote again of the need for conservation and the option of closing down all energy-consuming businesses for one day but recognized the sticky point to be the day, for no decision would please everyone. He suggested that Saturday be set aside as the day of rest for all people. Those who chose to join in the corporate worship of God on that day could do so, while others could spend the time in other ways. Lindsell then pointed out that Jews and other Sabbatarians would be served by this decision and that "for Protestants and Catholics it should prove no theological hardship: apart from the fact that our Lord rose from the dead on the first day of the week, there is nothing in Scripture that requires us to keep Sunday rather than Saturday as a holy day." He called for responsible leaders to discuss the possibilities.[43]

The executive secretary of the General Conference, K. Duane Hurley, wrote to leaders of other denominations suggesting that they engage in dialogue on the subject. "At issue is not the proper day for worship, but whether America will accept, in her need, God's gift." The reaction was varied, ranging all the way from the simple statement, "I am sure that the Lord knows we need more rest and quiet than we are getting these days," to voices echoing general assent to the idea but recognizing that "There is no reason to believe that our nation would be any more ready to accept a quiet restful Saturday than a day of rest on Sunday."

One of the most significant responses was from an unidentified Baptist who suggested that "we might well begin with our Baptist household in considering such a conference." He proposed that it be a topic of discussion at the North American Baptist Fellowship. At the October 1977 meeting of that body, K. D. Hurley, Herbert Saunders, and Thomas Merchant presented a panel discussion on "Quiet Saturdays" and Sabbathkeeping. Dr. Hurley wrote that it would be exciting "if we as the oldest Sabbath keeping denomination could capitalize on the current focus of attention on 'Quiet Saturdays' to enhance our Sabbath keeping and cause other conscientious Christians not only to strengthen their own religious convictions but to see the validity of our unique Bible-oriented heritage."[44]

---

[43] Harold Lindsell, "Consider the Case for Quiet Saturdays," *Christianity Today* 21/3 (5 Nov 1976), repr. by permission in *Sabbath Recorder* 198/12 (Dec 1976): 30.

[44] K. Duane Hurley, "An Accident (?)—in Human History," *Sabbath Recorder* 199/2 (Feb 1977): 6-7, 20.

Other writers have expressed similar needs for a Sabbath concept in the contemporary world. Harvey Cox, in his book *Turning East*, published in 1977, noted the need of a form of Sabbath observance that could be practiced in the modern pluralistic world and that could function on an individual or small-group basis.[45] Similarly, Gordon MacDonald in 1984 wrote in his book *Ordering Your Private World* that the person who establishes a block of time for Sabbath rest on a regular basis is most likely to keep all of life in proper perspective and remain free of burnout and breakdown. He further emphasized that "the world and the church need genuinely rested Christians who are regularly refreshed by true Sabbath rest, not just leisure or time off."[46]

In 1988, *Christianity Today* asked a random sample of readers to rate the importance of a series of religious and theological questions. To the surprise of the editors, the highest rating was given the question, "Should Christians take the Lord's Day observance more seriously?" In response to this finding, Eugene Peterson wrote "Confessions of a Former Sabbath Breaker," in which he called breaking the Sabbath "the willful violation of the fourth commandment...the American bargain-basement sin, on sale in virtually every American church." Peterson spoke of an entire culture living on the edge of panic with "a mind boggling technology that could do almost anything in and with space, but fidgety, nervous, and spastic with time." To find a solution, he called for "some first-class looking and listening, the kind of first-class looking and listening that Sabbath keeping nurtures and matures."

As a pastor, Peterson felt particularly robbed of any Sabbath observance because Christians often cover the sin of Sabbathbreaking with "a smoke screen of activity," pretending to keep a Sabbath by Sunday churchgoing "and then stuff the day with meetings, responsibilities, committees, and concern until it looks (and feels) tight as a German sausage. Pastors are usually in charge of the stuffing." Since Sunday was a workday for most pastors, he and his wife observed Monday as a time when they could experience the presence of God in contemplation and the combination of work and play that he saw as essential for good Sabbathkeeping.

---

[45] Harvey Cox, *Turning East: Why Americans Look to the Orient for Spirituality—And What that Search Can Mean to the West* (New York: Simon & Schuster, 1977) 71. See also *Sabbath Recorder* 209/5 (May 1987): 9.

[46] Gordon MacDonald, *Ordering Your Private World* (Nashville: Thomas Nelson, Inc., 1985) 162, 175.

In conclusion, Peterson wrote that any effort to recapture the Sabbath would not come by "bully preaching or blue laws. But as a few Christians in a few churches in a few communities in America keep a Sabbath, pockets of resistance are formed that provide access to leisured and loving time for the people around them, in the same way that national parks preserve access to the beauties of wilderness space. These pockets of hidden holiness preserve our American days and keep each week accessible to creation work and resurrection appearances."[47]

In reviewing Peterson's article in *Lead-Line*, Janet Thorngate asked: "Are Seventh Day Baptist churches such pockets of resistance—pockets of hidden holiness?"[48] If so, they would take it one step beyond that suggested by Peterson; they would not substitute a Monday or some other time for the Sabbath experience, but rather demonstrate this experience in the only time that receives God's blessing, the Sabbath of the Bible.

Furthermore, it became apparent that the pockets of holiness must not be completely hidden but must be found in those places where most needed—not in isolated rural areas but within the urban society. The thrust into the cities by a previously rural-dominated branch of the Christian Church grew from such reasoning.

Entering the Urban Areas

In a fourteen-year period from 1975 to 1989, thirty-four churches were officially organized as compared to twenty-two in the previous fifty years. Twenty-eight, or 82 percent, of these churches were located in metropolitan areas. Of those thirty-four new churches, twenty still appeared in the 2006 *Yearbook*. Since 1989, an additional thirty-six new churches and fellowships have been organized, twenty-one (or 58 percent) of which are in urban areas, including two Spanish-speaking churches in the Washington, DC, area.

It is in this new field Seventh Day Baptists have chosen to enter that the greatest hope for the future appears to rest. In contrast to Boothe C. Davis's 1912 concerns that "Seventh Day Baptists are not assured a future existence, growth and prosperity independent of our rural churches" and that "we can never do our greatest and best work among

---

[47] Eugene Peterson, "Confessions of a Former Sabbath Breaker," *Christianity Today* 32/12 (2 Sep 1988): 25-28.

[48] Janet Thorngate, editorial, "Confessions of a Former Sabbath Breaker," *Lead-Line* (Sep 1988) 2.

city populations," Seventh Day Baptists are discovering that their best work is still ahead and that there is a future apart from the rural churches.[49]

---

[49] Boothe C. Davis, President's Address, *SDB Yearbook* (1912) 9-10.

26

SUMMARY:
CHOOSING PATHS ALONG HISTORY'S WAY

Robert Frost, in his poem "The Road Not Taken," expressed poetically the experience of both individuals and society in the choices they make.

> Somewhere ages and ages hence:
> Two roads diverged in the wood, and I—
> I took the one less traveled by,
> And that has made all the difference.[1]

For ages, in similar fashion individuals and churches have had to make many choices. Some have chosen the well-worn way of the majority; others have taken the "one less traveled." Seventh Day Baptists have often taken that less-traveled road.

Sometimes the choices are relatively minor. At other times, the choices are like those forks in the road to which one never returns to try "the road not taken." Throughout history there have been many critical forks that have determined other choices further down the road. In this history of the Seventh Day Baptists as a "choosing people," several of these forks in the road have been lifted up as being particularly significant in directing them down the road less traveled.

THE REFORMATION TRAIL

As part of their spiritual heritage, Seventh Day Baptists count the great reformers of the sixteenth century. Luther, Zwingli, and Calvin all reached forks in the road that led away from the papal system of indulgences and authority. Yet, in terms of organization, the new, less-traveled road often ran parallel to the state churches they had left. The Anabaptists reached another fork and saw the church as a covenant relationship that could be entered only by a profession of faith.

During this same period of reformation on the Continent, a political crisis brought the English people to a similar fork in the road. Although

---

[1] Robert Frost, "The Road Not Taken," in Louis Untermeyer, *A Pocket Book of Robert Frost's Poems* (New York: Washington Square Press, 1960) 223.

some continued their allegiance to Rome, the Act of Supremacy in 1534 declared the King of England, through his ministers, to be the titular head of the church. Along with this change came a great increase in the availability of translations of the Bible in the language of the people. Armed with this "road map," it was not long before many people began to explore paths that led to the concept of the "priesthood of all believers," the idea that one could have direct access to God without intercession from a network of priests and bishops. The most radical of these individuals were called Separatists or Dissenters.

Among those who took this separatist view were those who followed the lead of men such as William Brewster and John Robinson. These separatists gave rise to the Congregationalists. Others who read the Bible carefully felt led to make additional choices: John Smyth and Thomas Helwys discovered nothing in Scripture to support infant baptism and noted that the commands of Jesus were to teach and then baptize. Early in the seventeenth century, they took the road leading to the Baptist doctrine of adult, or believer's, baptism.

DISCOVERING THE SABBATH WAY

With the Bible as their principal guide, some Christians discovered the seventh day Sabbath and chose that path. John Traske in 1617 followed the path but a short way, then reverted back to the more heavily traveled road. Theophilus Brabourne gazed down the Sabbath path and tried to persuade the established church to take that route, but in his personal life that way remained "the road not taken" as he continued on the well-worn road of tradition.

With the execution of King Charles I in 1649 and the establishment of the Commonwealth under the Protectorate of Oliver Cromwell, England faced a climate in which choices could be made more easily. During the "Great Decade" from 1650 to 1660, a number of Baptists chose the Sabbath. Among those were James Ockford, William Saller, Dr. Peter Chamberlen, John Spittlehouse, and Henry Jessey. The oldest existing Sabbathkeeping Baptist church, later named Mill Yard, resulted from some of their choices.

With the restoration of the monarchy in 1660, both political and religious barriers were erected along the separatist road that greatly affected those who had accepted the Sabbath. One Sabbathkeeping Baptist pastor, John James, was martyred in 1661 on charges of being a Fifth Monarchist. Because of his Sabbath convictions, Edward Stennett was forced to change his profession and worship behind closed doors. Francis Bampfield came to the Sabbath while in prison and gathered a congregation following his release. From this beginning, the Pinner's Hall Seventh Day Baptist Church was founded and continued for over 175 years. Around 1665, two Sabbathkeeping members of the Baptist congregation at Tewkesbury, Stephen and Anne Mumford, chose to seek their lot in America, where they were instrumental in leading others on that less-traveled road of the Sabbath in Rhode Island.

PATHFINDING IN COLONIAL AMERICA

Several moments of decision stand out in Seventh Day Baptist history during the colonial days in America. The decision of Samuel and Tacy Hubbard to accept believer's baptism in 1647 led to their subsequent choice to move to Newport, Rhode Island, where religious freedom had been granted. In 1665, they, along with several other members of Dr. John Clarke's Baptist Church, accepted the Sabbath. When two couples who had walked the way with them made the decision to return to the more traveled path, the five remaining Sabbathkeeping members felt they could no longer take communion with those who had once walked with them, instead giving up their belief. Thus, in 1671 they covenanted together with the Mumfords to follow the path less traveled. This choice gave birth to the first Seventh Day Baptist church in America.

In Pennsylvania, during the last decade of the seventeenth century, Abel Noble, a Keithian Quaker, was drawn to the Sabbath through his study of the Bible. Others who were in the habit of referring to the days of the week by their numerical name of first, second, or third day, saw the inconsistency of worshipping on the first day when their scriptures called for a remembrance of the seventh day as the time to keep holy. Between 1700 and 1725, several Seventh Day Baptist churches were organized in the Philadelphia area. Through their influence, Conrad Beissel became a Sabbathkeeper and led a settlement of German Pietists to form the German Seventh Day Baptist monastic order at Ephrata in about 1728.

In Piscataway, New Jersey, a deacon in the Baptist Church, Edmund Dunham, faced a fork in the road when he was challenged to prove by Scripture why working on Sunday was wrong. Deacon Dunham studied the matter with his class. Since he found no biblical proof, he with seventeen others withdrew from the Baptist church in 1705 to form the Seventh Day Baptist Church of Piscataway.

From these three forks in the road, paths led to the establishment of other churches in Rhode Island, Pennsylvania, and New Jersey. As the frontier opened following the Revolutionary War and vast new territories were added to the United States, the paths of choice led to New York, Wisconsin, West Virginia, Ohio, and points both west and south.

The struggle for national independence brought many challenges to those on this "less traveled way." Some, such as the Wards of Rhode Island, became involved politically; many were involved militarily. A few, such as those who had Quaker roots, tried the path of neutrality. Nearly all were affected by occupation forces and the devastation of war.

NINETEENTH-CENTURY CROSSROADS

For Seventh Day Baptists, the nineteenth century was particularly marked by their attempts to find identity as a people and determine the best means for carrying out their mission. In 1802, eight churches took steps leading to the formation of the General Conference. Since they respected the congregational polity of local autonomy, the conference was organized as an association of churches that served largely in an advisory capacity: (1) to give Seventh Day Baptists an identity, (2) to define doctrinal standards, (3) to facilitate communications, (4) to stimulate thought, and (5) to develop program. Although the initial impetus for this corporate body was missions, it soon became apparent that the voluntarism of the people could best be harnessed in societies to serve particular causes.

Several missionary societies were organized beginning in 1818. As new fields of mission were considered, new societies formed to direct the work. Initially the missionary activity was among the "scattered of the brethren," but as new settlements were made along the frontier, missionary efforts followed these new byways of opportunity. In keeping with the missionary spirit of the time, the Seventh Day Baptist Missionary Society amended its constitution in 1844 to include the words "and other parts of the world," opening up a century of foreign mission work in China and Africa.

Similarly, members and churches within the General Conference saw the need for work in publishing and tract distribution and formed societies through which to fulfill this work. These efforts produced such periodicals as the *Missionary Magazine*, the *Protestant Sentinel*, the *Seventh Day Baptist Register*, and the *Sabbath Recorder*, a nearly continuous thread of denominational communications since 1821.

Since the process of decision-making relied on an informed populace, education received a high priority. Seventh Day Baptists were among the leaders in the church school movement as Sabbath schools were considered a vital part of each church. The need for teachers and educated leaders in the church and community led to the founding of academies years before public school education was available or affordable. The most notable of these academies were at DeRuyter and Alfred in New York, Milton and Albion in Wisconsin, and Salem in West Virginia. Three of these schools, Alfred, Milton, and Salem, were later granted college or university charters. The desire for a well-educated ministry led to the establishment of the School of Theology at Alfred in 1871.

In that same year, in commemoration of the 200th anniversary of the founding of the Newport Seventh Day Baptist Church, a Memorial Fund was established to support higher education. Some of these funds are still earmarked to aid young men and women preparing for the ministry. The Memorial Fund has become the investment arm of the denomination.

Efforts to develop closer cooperation and fellowship among churches in specific geographical areas produced a system of associations that organized following the decisions of the General Conference in 1834. Out of some of these associations came suggestions for a hymnbook, local societies for missions, and the recognition that women and youth needed some means by which to implement their particular gifts. In 1884, the Woman's Board formed and later took the name Women's Society. Five years later, in 1889, a Young People's Board was added to the General Conference. A concern for the preservation and communication of history led to the formation of a Committee on Denominational History in 1863. Over fifty years later, the Historical Society was incorporated in 1916 to continue and to expand this interest.

During the last quarter of the nineteenth century, a sense of urgent mission culminated in the Sabbath reform work led by A. H. Lewis. Those involved were not satisfied in treading the poet's "less traveled way" alone and were determined to advertise and post road signs to direct more people onto the Sabbath path. Although the vast majority of people continued to travel the traditional "well traveled road," a sufficient number were persuaded during this period to give Seventh Day Baptists their largest number of churches and members.

TWENTIETH-CENTURY INTERCHANGES

The opening of the twentieth century brought to Seventh Day Baptists a myriad of new choices. Unlike the simple fork in the road that Robert Frost envisioned, this century's options were more like the fast-approaching, multilane cloverleaf intersections of a busy modern highway. The three basic options presented to Joshua and the Israelites still remained: (1) accept traditions of the past, (2) accommodate to the mores and customs of the land in which one dwells, or (3) constantly follow God's lead. Off each arterial road were side roads and conflicting signs. Even a simple right turn might be a part of a traffic circle that could take one in the completely opposite direction.

The questions for a choosing people during such a century were not so much questions of ultimate goals, but rather how best to reach those goals with the resources available. The resultant tensions proved healthy or unhealthy depending on how they were resolved. Constructive tensions can keep people alert and, when resolved, bring unity. However, those tensions are deadly and bring about disunity when the "way" becomes more important than the goal.

For Seventh Day Baptists, the century began with the 1902 centennial celebration of the General Conference. The previous century had witnessed a slow but steady growth in both numbers and areas of mission and service. That growth showed signs of plateau and decline. Some of the enthusiasm of individuals in the societies, which had spurred missions, schools, and publications, decreased as efforts became so institutionalized that sometimes their primary functions appeared to be maintaining what had already been undertaken.

The field for missions was wide open, with many doors opening in underdeveloped areas of the world, but resources of personnel and money were not readily available. Choices had to be made as to which door to enter. The choices of Nyasaland (later Malawi) in Africa and Jamaica in the Caribbean proved most fruitful, leading to mission activity on six continents. Even the concept of the church's mission presented a whole new set of choices. The home missions program could no longer be limited to the rural frontiers but faced the social, economic, cultural, and environmental problems brought on by urban and global industrialization. The movement into urban settings was at first gradual and halting but eventually deliberate as new programs for church planting evolved.

The enormity of some of these problems was such that individuals, local churches, and even denominations could not possibly tackle them alone. Thus, the twentieth century became a century of ecumenical cooperation that at times became competitive. Tension increased between the societal structure, which was task-oriented, and the associational structure, which was concerned with the total mission of the body of Christ.

To ease some of this tension, many leaders of the General Conference who were successful businessmen sought to bring principles of efficient management to denominational structure. The choices made through preceding centuries had rejected any authoritative organization that threatened local autonomy, leaving the General Conference as essentially an advisory body. To give greater meaning and representation to this advisory function, various forms emerged, ranging from an Advisory Board of over thirty in 1909 to a Commission of six in 1938 and to a General Council of twelve in 1978. In some of these structures the societies were directly represented, while in others they were excluded.

One of the main functions of these structures was to focus effort on ultimate goals. From the Forward Movement program of 1915 to the Decade of Discipleship in the 1980s and a MORE 2000 emphasis leading into the twenty-first century, the ultimate goal was bringing people to the saving knowledge and experience of Christ. There was never much disagreement concerning this goal, but the methods of achieving it presented many choices. Issues arose concerning allocation of resources and personnel, location of centers of activity, relationship to others of similar or divergent views, and theological bases for distinctives.

During the twentieth century, the power of the purse represented for many Seventh Day Baptists their most direct voice in the denomination's corporate decisions. Programs of systematic giving were introduced early in the century, gradually developing into attempts to unify the budgets of the agencies charged with carrying out the denomination's mission.

A desire for greater unity and identification, coupled with the need for printing facilities, led to the construction in the 1920s of the Seventh Day Baptist Building in Plainfield, New Jersey. The first phase was a printing plant; the second phase was an office edifice that served the denomination in many ways for over fifty years. In 1981, economics, demographics, and other factors contributed to the decision to move the hub of General Conference activity to a more central location. The Missionary Society and the Board of Christian Education continued to be centered in their places of incorporation, but the General Conference, the Council on Ministry, the Tract Society, the Historical Society, and the Memorial Board all moved their offices to Janesville, Wisconsin.

During the first half of the century, efforts to consolidate related functions led to the merging in 1940 of the Education Society, the Sabbath School Board, and the Young People's Board into the Board of Christian Education. With the closing of the School of Theology in 1963, a Council on Ministry was formed as a direct agency of the General Conference to provide for the education of ministers and assist in church-pastor relations. Shortly after the relocation of the publishing interests to Janesville, the American Sabbath Tract Society became the Tract and Communications Council of the General Conference. The Historical Society, which began as a standing committee of the General Conference in 1863, was incorporated as a society in 1916 and continues as a membership corporation today. The Missionary Society and the Board of Christian Education, with periodic modifications to their structural connections to the conference, remain independently incorporated agencies.

The world consciousness of the twentieth century and the need for cooperation was demonstrated by Seventh Day Baptist participation in many ecumenical movements, from the Federal Council of Churches in 1908 and the World Council of Churches in 1948 to the North American Baptist Fellowship and Baptist World Alliance in the post-World War II era. Withdrawal from the first two allowed concentration of effort with those groups that shared Baptist polity. In 1965, the formation of the World Federation of Seventh Day Baptists solidified the global fellowship and mission of the denomination located on six continents.

Throughout the century, individual churches and members found a sense of participation in what are referred to as "parachurch" (alongside the church) groups that are specific-task oriented. These included such groups as local ministers' councils, the Christian Endeavor Society, Campus Crusade, the American Bible Society, the Gideons, the Bible Sabbath Association, the Women's Christian Temperance Union, World Vision, and a host of other organized groups ministering to particular needs. Some of these groups provided outlets for Seventh Day Baptists to apply Christian principles to social, economic, and cultural problems while maintaining individual freedom and church-state separation. Statements of principles were frequently made, encouraging individuals to become involved in areas of concern without committing others to support ideas or practices with which they disagreed in principle or method.

The scientific and educational explosion that opened the twentieth century brought divergent theological thought that culminated in the modernist-fundamentalist controversy of the 1920s. This caused a serious rift and actual division in several denominations, but the Sabbath provided a common bond that allowed the denomination to weather the storm and provided it the opportunity to sharpen its focus on the ultimate goal. Instead of the legalism that had marked so much of the Sabbath observance of the past, an attempt to recover a spiritual Sabbathism has sprung up—a Sabbathism that brings meaning to the very presence of God in time.

BIBLIOGRAPHY

The Act Concerning Toleration. MD, 1649.

Address of the Executive Committee. *The American Tract Society Documents, 1824-1925.* New York: Arno Press, 1972.

Address to the All-Asian Consultation, Seoul '73, Korea, August 27-September 1, 1973. Quoted by Ralph Winter. *The Two Structures of God's Redemptive Mission.* South Pasadena, Calif.: William Carey Library.

Alderfer, E. Gordon. *The Ephrata Commune: An Early American Counterculture.* Pittsburgh: University of Pittsburgh Press, 1985.

Allen, Abigail A. *Life and Sermons of Jonathan Allen, Ph.D., D.D., LL.D., President of Alfred University.* Oakland, Calif.: Pacific Publishing Co., 1894.

Allen, Jonathan. *Allen of Alfred.* Ed. E. H. Lewis. Milton, Wis.: Davis-Greene Corp. Press, 1932.

Armitage, Thomas. *A History of the Baptists; Traced by Their Vital Principals and Practices, from the Time of Our Lord and Saviour Jesus Christ to the Year 1886.* New York: Bryan, Taylor, & Co., 1887.

Ashley, Maurice. *England in the Seventeenth Century.* 1952. Hutchinson & Co. Ltd., 1978.

Association Records of the Particular Baptists of England...., ed. B. R. White. London: Baptist Historical Society, [1971-1974], 190-195.

Auren, Jonas. *Noah's dove. Leed's Almanac.* N.p., 1700.

Backus, Isaac. *A History of New England with Particular Reference to the Denomination of Christians Called Baptists.* Newton, Mass: Backus Historical Society, 1871.

Bailey, James, ed. *Biographical Sketches and Published Writings of Eli S. Bailey, Physician and Minister of the Gospel.* Toledo, Ohio 1871.

---. *History of the Seventh-day Baptist General Conference: From Its Origin, September, 1802, To Its Fifty-third Session, September, 1865.* Toledo, Ohio: S. Bailey & Co., 1866.

Bampfield, Francis. *All in One: All Useful Sciences and Profitable Arts In One Book of Jehovah Aelohim, Copied Out, and Commented Upon in Created Beings.* [London], 1677.

---. *A Name, an After-one.* London, 1681.

---. *The Seventh-Day Sabbath the Desirable-Day.* [London], 1677.

Baptist Advance. [Plainfield, N.J.: Recorder Press, (c.1964)].

Baptist Quarterly. 1928-.

Baptist World Alliance. McLean, Va.: Baptist World Alliance, 1987.

Barrows, C. Edwin, ed. *The Diary of John Comer.* Collections of the Rhode Island Historical Society, vol. 7. [Newport], R.I., 1893.

Barrows, C. E[dwin]. *History of the First Baptist Church in Newport, R.I.: A Discourse Delivered on Thanksgiving Day, November 30, 1876.* Newport, R.I., 1876.

Bartlett, John Russell, ed. *Records of the Colony of Rhode Island and Providence Plantations, in New England.* 10 vols. Providence, 1856.

Bettenson, Henry, ed. *Documents of the Christian Church.* New York: Oxford University Press, 1947.

Bicknell, Thomas William. *The History of the State of Rhode Island and Providence Plantations.* 3 vols. New York: American Historical Society, 1920.

Billington, Ray Allen. *The American Frontier Thesis: Attack and Defense*. Washington, DC: American Historical Association, 1971.

Bindoff, S. T. *Tudor England*. The Pelican History of England 5. Middlesex, Eng.: Penguin, 1979.

Black, Jeannette D. and William Greene Roelker, eds. *A Rhode Island Chaplain in the Revolution: Letters of Ebenezer David to Nicholas Brown, 1775-1778*. Providence: Rhode Island Society of the Cincinnati, 1949.

Black, William Henry, ed. *The Last Legacy: Or, The Autobiography and Religious Profession, of Joseph Davis, Senior,... with Public Documents Relating to Him and to His Benefactions*. London: Mill Yard Congregation, 1869.

Boccaccio, Giovanni. *Decameron*. Trans. John Payne. Ed. Charles S. Singleton. Berkeley: University of California Press, 1982. 1 (Days I-V): 40-45.

Bock, Jerry. *Fiddler on the Roof*. New York: Crown, 1965.

Bond, A. J. C. Class discussion in Alfred School of Theology, 1950, attended by the author.

Bonham, John H. Notebooks of John H. Bonham, Shiloh, N. J., 1880-1952. SDB Historical Society Library.

Bownde, Nicholas. *The Doctrine of the Sabbath: Plainely layde forth, and soundly proved by testimonies both of holy Scripture, and also of olde and ecclesiasticall writers*. London, 1595. 2 sections. See also: SDB Hist. Soc. Lib.

Brabourne, Theophilus. *An Answer to Two Books on the Sabbath...Ives...Warren*. London, 1659.

---. *A Defence Of that most Ancient, and Sacred ordinance of Gods, the Sabbath Day*. 2nd ed. [London], 1632.

---. *Of the Sabbath Day, Which is now the highest controversie in the Church of England*. N.p., 1660.

Brackney, William Henry, ed. *Baptist Life and Thought: 1600-1980*. Valley Forge, Pa.: Judson Press, 1983.

---. *The Baptists*. New York: Greenwood Press, 1988.

Bradley, Phillips, ed. *Democracy in America*. New York, 1945.

A Brief and faithful relation of the Difference between those of this church and those who withdrew their Communion from it with ye causes and reasons of the Same... Newport, R.I. First Baptist Church Records, 1725. Ms., Book #1167. Newport Historical Society, Newport, R.I.. 137-53. [See also: Newport, RI SDB Church Records, 1692-1846. MS 19x.78. SDB Hist. Soc. Lib. 109-36.]

A Brief Summary of the Principles of the Christian Religion, Expounded by Way of Questions, with Answers in the Words of the Sacred Scriptures with an Appendix, Containing an Exposition of the Ten Commandments, for the Instruction of Youth. New-Brunswick, N.J., N.p., 1814. [Bound with Sabbatarian Tracts. BV125.A3. SDB Hist. Soc. Lib.]

[Brown, Thomas B.], ed. *An Appeal for the Restoration of The Bible Sabbath: in an Address to the Baptists, from the Seventh-day Baptist General Conference*. New York: American Sabbath Tract Society, 1852.

Bunyan, John. Questions about the Nature and Perpetuity of the Seventh-day Sabbath; and Proof that the First Day of the Week is the true Christian Sabbath. London, 1685.

Burdick, Oscar. *The Great Decade, 1650-60*. June 1984 draft, ms. SDB Historical Society Library.

---. *The Great Decade, 1650-60*. 1989 draft, ms. MS 1989.28. SDB Historical Society Library.

---. Letter to SDB Historical Society. 20 November 1982. SDB Historical Society Library.

---. Research Trip to England and Germany 1988. MS 1988.56. SDB Historical Society Library.

---. Sleuthing the Origins of English SDBs in the 1650's: A Bibliography. *Summary Proceedings of the 38th Annual Conference of the American Theological Library Association.* Ed. Betty A. O'Brien. Holland, Mich.: Western Theological Seminary, June 1984.

---. The Stennett Family. Master's Thesis. Alfred University, School of Theology, 1953. [MS 195x.3. SDB Historical Society Library.]

Calamy, Edward. *The Nonconformist's Memorial: Being an Account of the Lives, Sufferings, and Printed Works of the Two Thousand Ministers Ejected from the Church of England, chiefly by the Acts of Uniformity, Aug. 24, 1662.* 3 vols. London, 1802.

Camenga, John H., comp. *History of the Seventh Day Baptist Church of Shiloh, New Jersey, Prepared for the Two Hundred-Fiftieth Anniversary, 1737-1987.* Shiloh, N.J.: Shiloh SDB Church, 1987. MS 1988.2. SDB Historical Society Library.

Campbell, Alexander. *Autobiography of Rev. Alexander Campbell.* Ed. C. A. Burdick. Watertown, N.Y.: Post Printing House, 1883.

Centennial Drama of Milton SDB Church. Ms., MS 1983.46.3.2. SDB Historical Society Library. 1940.

Chapman, Bernice B. and Maleta O. Curtis, eds. *History of the Riverside Seventh Day Baptist Church.* Riverside, Calif., 1979.

Church Letters to the Seventh-day Baptist General Conference, and Other Papers, 1746-1835. Ms., bound. MS 19x.181. SDB Historical Society Library. Note: Ts. copy, BX6393.C57. SDB Historical Society Library.

Clark, John. *Ill Newes from New England: Or, A Narrative of New-Englands Persecution wherin is Declared That while old England is becoming new, New-England is become Old.* London, 1652.

Clarke, Henry. *A History of the Sabbatarians or Seventh Day Baptists, in America Containing Their Rise and Progress to the Year 1811, with Their Leaders' Names, and Their Distinguishing Tenets, etc.* Utica, [N.Y.], 1811.

Comer, John. History of Baptists in Newport. 1728. Isaac Backus Papers. Cs. mss. 1984-1. Box 6. Franklin Trask Library. Andover-Newton Theological School, Newton Center, MA. 2. See also: MS 1989.30. SDB Historical Society Library. 2. [Note: There are slight variations between the two extant copies of the Newport SDB covenant.]

---. Newport Baptist History. Isaac Backus Papers. Vault M-Ba-1, F. Rhode Island Historical Society, Providence. (16) 30. See also: MS 1989.29. SDB Historical Society Library.

Cox, Harvey. *Turning East: Why Americans Look to the Orient for Spirituality--And What That Search Can Mean to the West.* New York: Simon, 1977.

Cox, Robert. *The Literature of the Sabbath Question.* 2 vols. Edinburgh: MacLachlan & Stewart, 1865.

Davis, Alva L. *Autobiography.* Ts., MS 1952.2. SDB Historical Society Library.

---. Eight Questions. *The Exponent.* Ashaway, R:I. The Seventh Day Baptist Bible Defense League. 1 (May 1925) n.p.

Davis, Boothe C. *Memoirs of Boothe C. Davis and Estelle Hoffman Davis.* Ts., LD131.A317. SDB Historical Society Library. 1937.

[Davis, Elizabeth Fisher]. *A History of the Seventh Day Baptist Mission School at Fouke Arkansas.* Ts., n.p. BX6394.A7D3. SDB Historical Society Library.

Davis, Tamar. *A General History of the Sabbatarian Churches; Embracing Accounts of the Armenian, East Indian, and Abyssinian Episcopacies in Asia and Africa, the Waldenses, Semi-*

Judaisers, and Sabbatarian Anabaptists of Europe; with the Seventh-day Baptist Denomination in the United States. Philadelphia, Pa.: Lindsay and Blakiston, 1851.

Dawn, Marva J. *Keeping the Sabbath Wholly: Ceasing, Resting, Embracing, Feasting.* Grand Rapids, Mich.: William B. Eerdmans Press, 1989.

Denison, Charles H. and John Ward. *Governor Samuel Ward of Rhode Island, 1725-1776.* Plainfield, N.J.: SDB General Conference, 1907.

Dennison, James T., Jr. *The Market Day of the Soul: The Puritan Doctrine of the Sabbath in England, 1532-1700.* Lantham, Md.: University Press of America, 1983.

Dexter, Henry Martyn, and Morton Dexter. *The England and Holland of the Pilgrims.* Boston: Houghton, 1905.

Dickens, A. G. *The English Reformation.* 1964. Glasgow, Scotland: Fontana, 1967.

Disraeli, Benjamin. *Life of Charles I.* London, 1851.

Douglas, Justice William. The Douglas Dissent.

Dunham, Isaac Watson, comp. *Dunham Genealogy: Deacon John Dunham of Plymouth, Massachusetts, 1589-1669, and His Descendants.* Norwich, Conn.: Bulletin Print, 1907.

Edwards, Morgan. *Materials Towards A History of the Baptists.* Eds. Eve B. Weeks and Mary B. Warren. 2 vols. Danielsville, Ga.: Heritage Papers, 1984.

Evangel and Sabbath Outlook. Ed. A. H. Lewis. 1-4 (June 1893-June 1897).

Evans, John. *Sermon...Oct. 18, 1795 Being a Tribute of Respect to the Memory of the Rev. Samuel Stennett....* London, 1795.

A Faithful Testimony Against the Teachers of Circumcision.... [1667]. Originally bound as an appendix to Edward Stennett's *The Royal Law....* 2nd ed. London, 1667.

Fox, John. *...Acts and Monuments of Martyrs....* 9th ed. 3 vols. London, 1684.

Furthey and Caps. *History of Chester Co.* Philadelphia, J. B. Lippincott & Co., 1881.

Gaustad, Edwin S., ed. *Baptist Piety: The Last Will & Testimony of Obadiah Holmes.* Grand Rapids, Mich.:   Christian University Press, 1978.

---, ed. *A Documentary of History of Religion in America Since 1865.* A Documentary of History of Religion in America 2. Grand Rapids, Mich.: William B. Eerdmans Publishing Company, 1983.

---, ed. *A Documentary of History of Religion in America to the Civil War.* A Documentary of History of Religion in America 1. Grand Rapids, Mich.: William B. Eerdmans Publishing Company, 1982.

Greaves, Richard L. *Saints and Rebels: Seven Nonconformists   in Stuart England.* Macon, Ga.: Mercer University Press, 1985.

Greene, C[harles] H. The Keithians. 4 mss. & 1 ts. drafts. MS 19x.178.1-5. SDB Historical Society Library.

---. The Keithians. *Sabbath Recorder* 63 (8 April 1907): 235.

---. C. H. Greene Papers, ms 1918.2. SDB Historical Society Library.

Griffiths, Thomas S. *A History of Baptists in New Jersey.* Hightstown, N.J.: Barr Press, 1904.

Hessey, James Augustus. *Sunday: Its Origin, History, and Present Obligation Considered in the Bampton Lectures.* 3rd ed. London, 1866.

Historic Roadsides in New Jersey. Plainfield, N.J.: Society of Colonial Wars in the State of New Jersey, 1928.

Holland, W. Lancelot. *Bunyan's Sabbatic Blunders.* London: Madgewick, Houlston & Co., n.d.

Hubbard, Samuel. Register *of Mr. Samuel Hubbard.* (transcription of excerpts with notes by Isaac Backus, ca. 1775). B 136 i Mss. Rhode Island Historical Society Library,

Providence. [Microfilm copy, MF 1989.4. SDB Historical Society Library.] [Note: This
ms. is the source of several later transcriptions including the typed transcript: Samuel
Hubbard's Journal, circa 1633-1686. R.I. Historical Records Survey, Works Projects
Administration, Providence, 1940. MS 194x.6. SDB Historical Society Library.]

Hudson, Winthrop S. Separate but Not Sectarian. Willis Russell Lecture. Alfred University.
14 Feb. 1977. Reprinted in *Sabbath Recorder* 199:4 (April 1977): 28.

Huling, Ray Greene. *Samuel Hubbard, of Newport: 1610-1689.* N.p.: n.p., n.d. Reprint from
Narragansett Historical Register 5:4 (December 1887).

Hurley, Loyal F. The Liberal-Conservative Division. Ms., MS 1970.18. SDB Historical
Society Library. N.p.

Iddings, Richard. Will, No. 1485. Chester County Archives, West Chester, Pa.. Filed 20 July
1753.

Ivimey, Joseph. *A History of the English Baptists: Comprising the Principal Events of the History
of the Protestant Dissenters, During the Reign of Geo. III....* 4 vols. London, 1830.

Johns, Warren. *Dateline Sunday, U.S.A.* Mountain View, Calif.: Pacific Press Assoc., 1967.

Johnson, Nellie (Willard), comp. *The Descendants of Robert Burdick of Rhode Island.* Norwich,
NY, 1937.

Jubilee Papers. Westerly, R.I.: Board of Managers of the SDB Missionary Society, 1892.

Katz, David S. *Philo-Semitism and the Readmission of the Jews to England, 1603-1655.* Oxford:
Clarendon, 1982.

Kidder, Clark. *Orphan Trains & Their Precious Cargo: The Life's Work of Rev. H.D. Clarke.*
Bowie, Md.: Heritage Books, 2001.

Langworthy, Harry. [W.]. *Africa for the African: The Life of Joseph Booth.* Kachere Monograph
No. 2. Blantyre, Malawi: Christian Literature Association of Malawi, 1996.

Langworthy, Harry W. *Africa for the African: A Biography of Joseph Booth.* MS 1990.16. SDB
Historical Society Library.

---. Joseph Booth: Prophet of Radical Change in Central and South Africa, 1891-1915. *Journal
of Religion in Africa,* 16 (1986): 22-43.

Lee, Francis Bazley. *New Jersey as a Colony and as a State.* 4 vols. New York: Publishing
Society of New Jersey, 1903.

Lewis, A[bram] H[erbert]. *A Critical History of the Sabbath and the Sunday in the Christian
Church.* Alfred Centre, N.Y.: American Sabbath Tract Society, 1886.

---. *Letters to Young Preachers and Their Hearers.* Plainfield, N.J.: American Sabbath Tract
Society, 1900.

---. *Spiritual Sabbathism.* Plainfield, N.J.: American Sabbath Tract Society, 1910.

---. *Swift Decadence of Sunday; What Next?* Plainfield, N.J.: American Sabbath Tract Society,
1899.

Liechty, Daniel. *Andreas Fischer and the Sabbatarian Anabaptists: An Early Reformation Episode
in East Central Europe.* Studies in Anabaptist and Mennonite History 29. Scottdale, Pa.:
Herald, 1988.

Light of Home. Eds. A. H. Lewis, and C. D. Potter. 1-5 (1885-1889).

Lindsell, Harold. Consider the Case for Quiet Saturdays. *Christianity Today* (5 November
1976).

Littrell, Franklin. *The Free Church.* Boston: n.p., 1957.

Luchetti, Cathy. *Under God's Spell: Frontier Evangelists, 1772-1915.* San Diego, Calif.:
Harcourt Brace Jovanovich, 1989.

Lunt, W. E. *History of England.* 3rd ed. New York: Harper, 1945.

Lutz, Donald S., and Jack D. Warren. *A Covenanted People: The Religious Tradition and the Origins of American Constitutionalism.* Providence, R.I.: John Carter Brown Library, 1987.

McBeth, H. Leon. *The Baptist Heritage.* Nashville: Broadman, 1987.

---. *A Sourcebook for Baptist Heritage.* Nashville: Broadman, 1990.

MacDonald, Gordon. *Ordering Your Private World.* Nashville: Thomas Nelson, Inc., 1985.

McGowen V. Maryland 366 U.S. 420. 6 L.Ed. 2nd 393 (1961).

McLoughlan, William G., ed. *The Diary of Isaac Backus.* Providence: Brown University Press, 1979.

McNeill, John T. *The New Schaff-Herzog Religious Encyclopedia.* Grand Rapids, Mich.: Baker, 1955.

Manwell, Reginald D., and Sophia Lyon Fahs. *The Church Across the Street.* Boston: Beacon, 1947.

Maring, Norman H. and Winthrop S. Hudson. A *Baptist Manual of Polity and Practice. Valley Forge, Pa.*: Judson Press, 1963.

Marshall, Peter, and David Manuel. *From Sea to Shining Sea.* Old Tappan, N.J.: Fleming H. Revell Company, 1986.

The Maryland Act Concerning Toleration. Maryland Legislature, 1649.

Maxson, William B. And William Parkinson. *A Discussion of the Original Institution, Perpetuity, and Change of the Weekly Sabbath....* Schenectady, N.Y., 1836.

Merrill, Georgia Drew, ed. *A Centennial Memorial History of Allegany County,* New York. Alfred, NY: W. A. Ferguson & Co., 1896.

Mill Yard, London, Eng. SDB Church Records, 1673-1845. Ms., CRR 1932.1. SDB Historical Society Library.

Milton, John. *A Treatise on Christian Doctrine: Compiled from the Holy Scriptures Alone.* Trans. Charles R. Sumner. 2 vols. Boston: Cummings, Hilliard & Co., 1825.

Minard, John S. *Allegany County and Its People: A Centennial Memorial History of Allegany County, New York.* Ed. Georgia Drew Merrill. Alfred, N.Y.: W. A. Ferguson & Co., 1896.

Missionary Magazine. 1-2:1-7 (August 1821-September 1825). Morrisville, N.Y.: SDB Missionary Society Board.

Moberg, David O. *Church as a Social Institution: The Sociology of American Religion.* Englewood Cliffs, N.J.: Prentice, 1962.

The Moralite of the Fourth Commandment. 1652. M2617A. UMI.

Mott, J. R. *The Evangelization of the World of This Generation.* New York: Student Volunteer Movement in Foreign Missions, 1900.

Newport, R.I. First Baptist Church. Letter to Newport, R.I. SDB Church. 24 Apr. 1726. Isaac Backus Papers. Vault-Ba-1. Rhode Island Historical Society Library, Providence, 1: 6. See also: MS 1989.32.1. SDB Historical Society Library.

Newport, R.I. First Baptist Church Records, 1725. Ms., Book #1167. Newport Historical Society, Newport. A Brief and faithful relation... 137-53. See also: Newport, R.I. SDB Church Records, 1692-1846. MS 19x.78. SDB Historical Society Library. 109-36.]

Newport, R.I. SDB Church. Letter of response to Newport, R.I. First Baptist Church. 6 May 1726. Isaac Backus Papers. Vault-Ba-1. Rhode Island Historical Society Library, Providence. 1: 5. See also: MS 1989.32.2. SDB Historical Society Library.]

Newport, R.I. SDB Church Records, 1692-1846. Ms. copy by Thomas B. Stillman and Joseph Stillman. 1850. MS 19x.78. SDB Historical Society Library. Note: Incl. Newport, R.I. First Baptist Church Records, 1725.

Newport, RI SDB Church Records, 1708-1817. Book #1400. Newport Historical Society Library, Newport, R.I. See also: Negative microfilm copy, MF 1957.10. SDB Historical Society Library.

Nicholson, Susie Davis. *Davis: The Settlers of Salem, West Virginia: Their Ancestors and Some of Their Descendants.* 3rd ed. Salem, W.Va.: Salem SDB Church, 1992.

Norwood, J. Nelson. *Fiat Lux*, The Story of Alfred University. Alfred, N.Y.: Alfred University, 1957.

O[ckford], J[ames]. *The Doctrine of the Fourth Commandment: Deformed by Popery; Reformed & Restored to its Primitive Purity.* London, 1650. Only known copy: Christ Church College, Oxford, Eng. [Microfilm copy, MF 1986.76. SDB Historical Society Library.]

O'Hern, James. *This Is Our World.* Morristown, N.J.: Silver Burdett Co., 1981.

Old South Leaflets. Vol. VI: 126-50. Research and Source Work Search Series 106. [New York: Burt Franklin, n.d.].

Otis, Amos. *Genealogical Notes of Barnstable Families.* 2 vols. Barnstable, Mass.: F. B. & F. P. Goss, 1888.

Pastorius, Francis Daniel. Henry Bernhard Koster, William Davis, Thomas Rutter & Thomas Boryer, Four Boasting Disputers of this World briefly Rebuked, And Answered according to their Folly, which they themselves have manifested in a late Pamphlet, titled, Advice for all Professors and Writers. New York, 1697.

Payne, Ernest. More About the Sabbatarian Baptists. *Baptist Quarterly* 14 (1951-52): 161-66.

Pearson, David C. *Seventh Day Baptists in Central Africa.* [Janesville, Wis.]: SDB Historical Society, 2003.

[Penn, William]. The Frame of the Government of the Province of Pennsilvania in America: Together with   Certain Laws Agreed Upon in England by the Govenour and Divers Free-Men of the Aforesaid Province. London, 1682.

Peterson, Eugene. Confessions of a Former Sabbath Breaker. *Christianity Today.* (2 September 1988) 25-28.

Pinners' Hall, London, Eng. SDB Church Records, 1686-1863. Ms., CRR 1951.9. SDB Historical Society Library.

Piscataway, New Jersey, Marriage and Death Records. *Proceedings of the New Jersey Historical Society.* 4:1-4 (new series 1919) 33-43.

Piscataway, N. J. SDB Church Records, 1705-1836. Ms., CRR 1956.9.1. SDB Historical Society Library.

Plymouth Church Records 1620-1859. 2 vols. Cambridge, Mass: Cambridge University Press, 1920.

Proceedings of the Seventh-Day Baptist Council, Held at Chicago, Ill., Oct. 22-29, 1890. N.p., n.d.

Protestant Sentinel. Ed. John Maxson. Vol. 1-8 (1830-1839).

Randolph, Corliss Fitz. A *Century's Progress: An Historical Sketch of the First SDB Church of New York City.* Plainfield, N.J.: Recorder Press, 1948.

---. *A History of the SDBs in West Virginia Including the Woodbridgetown and Salemville Churches in Pennsylvania and the Shrewsbury Church in New Jersey.* Plainfield, N.J.: American Sabbath Tract Society, 1905.

---, comp. *Seventh Day Baptist Conference.* Newark, N.J.: Committee on Denominational History, 1907.

---. Seventh Day Baptists in the British Isles. Unpublished essay. Notebook 42, ts. 1950. SDB Historical Society Library.

Randolph, Oris H. F., comp. *Edward Fitz Randolph Branch Lines, Allied Families, and English and Norman Ancestry: A Family Genealogy, 860-1976.* Ann Arbor, MI: Edwards Brothers, Inc., 1976.

Register. Eds. J. Greene, A. Campbell, and James Bailey. 1-4 (Mar. 1840-Feb. 1844.).

Report of the Commissioners Appointed in Pursuance of An Act of Parliament... Mr. Humphrey's Report on Joseph Davis Endowment for Sabbatarian Protestant Dissenters. London: W. Cloves & Son, 1840.

Rhode Island for Museum Mansions. New *York Herald Tribune.* 14 July 1963, Sec. 4, 13.

Ringer and Glock. The Political Role of the Church... *Public Opinion Quarterly* 18 (Winter 1954-55): 337-47.

Rogers, Albert N. Ministerial Training and Seventh Day Baptists. *Foundations.* American Baptist Historical Society. 16 (Jananuary-March 1973): 67.

Rogers, Thomas. *The Catholic Doctrine of the Church of England: An Exposition of the Thirty-nine Articles.* Ed. J. J. S. Perowne. Cambridge: Cambridge University Press, 1854.

Rood, Hosea W. *A Historical Sketch of the Thorngate-Rood Family Descendants of George Thorngate, Senior and Matilda Blanchard, 1798-1906.* Ord, Neb.: Horace M. Davis, [1906].

Rood, Wayne R. *The Lesson for Tomorrow: The Story of Education Among the Seventh Day Baptists.* N.p., [1944].

---, ed. *A Manual of Procedures for Seventh Day Baptist Churches.* Plainfield, N.J.: SDB General Conference, 1972.

Sabbatarian Tracts. Plainfield, N.J.: American Sabbath Tract Society, n.d. BV125.A4. SDB Historical Society Library.

Sachse, Julius Friedrich. *Benjamin Furly, An English Merchant at Rotterdam, Who Promoted The First German Emigration to America.* Philadelphia, 1895.

---. *The German Pietists of Provincial Pennsylvania (1694-1708).* Philadelphia, 1895.

---. *The German Sectarians of Pennsylvania, 1742-1800: A Critical and Legendary History of the Ephrata Cloister and the Dunkers.* 2 vols. Philadelphia: n.p., 1900.

---. The *Monument on Zion Hill: An Address Delivered at Ephrata, Lancaster, Pa., on Patriots' Day, Wednesday, September 11, 1895.* Lancaster, [Pa.], 1895.

---. Sabbath Keepers of the Seventh Day Baptists of Chester County. Copyrighted story published February 1888. 1:7. PP1916.5

Saeger, Ralph. Lecture. Christian Writers and Editors Conference. Green Lake, Wis., July 1959.

Saller, William. *Sundry Queries`tendred to such as are, or profes themselves to be ministers of Jesus Christ, for clearing the doctrine of the Fourth Commandment. And the Lord's Sabbath Day....* N.p., c.1653.

---, and John Spittlehouse. *An Appeal to the Consciences....* N.p., 1657.

Sanford, Don A. *A Free People in Search of a Free Land.* 1976; Janesville, Wis.: SDB Historical Society, 1987.

Sanford, Don A. *Conscience Taken Captive: A Short History of Seventh Day Baptists.* Janesville, Wis.: SDB Historical Society. 1991.

Saunders, Herbert E. *The Sabbath: Symbol of Creation and Recreation.* Plainfield, N.J.: American Sabbath Tract Society, 1970.

Sawyer, Joseph Dillaway. *History of the Pilgrims and Puritans.* 3 vols. New York: Century History Co., 1922.

Scott, James Leander. *A Journal of a Missionary Tour.* March of America Facsimile Series 80. Ann Arbor, Mich.: UMI, 1966. Reprint from 1843 edition.

A Series of Questions on the Historical Parts of the New Testament; Embracing the Gospels of Matthew, Mark, Luke and John, and the Acts of the Apostles for the Use of Sabbath Schools and Bible Classes. DeRuyter, [N.Y.], 1837.

Seventh Day Baptist Beliefs, A Manual for Study. Plainfield, N.J.: American Sabbath Tract Society, 1941.

Seventh Day Baptist Pulpit. 1-12 (1903-1917). Westerly, R.I., Missionary Society.

Seventh Day Baptist Structure Study. Commissions Study Guide. *General Conference Task Force Notebook.* Ts., MS 1990.3. SDB Historical Society Library. 4 (February 1966): 3.

Seventh Day Baptist Memorial. 1-3 (1852-54). Eds. Lucius Crandall, Walter B. Gillette, and Thomas B. Stillman. New York: Seventh Day Baptist Publishing Society.

Seventh Day Baptist Missionary Magazine. (Morrisville, NY: Seventh Day Baptist Missionary Society Board). 1:1-2:7 (August 1821-September 1825).

Seventh Day Baptist Publishing Society Minutes. Mss., MS 19x.187. V-D-file. SDB Historical Society Library.

Seventh Day Baptist Pulpit. 1-12 (1903-1917). Westerly, R.I.: SDB Missionary Society.

Seventh Day Baptists in Europe and America. Plainfield, N.J.: American Sabbath Tract Society, 1910, 1972. 3 vols. Vol. 1 and 2 paged continuously. Vol. 3: 1900-55, by Albert N. Rogers.

Shelley, Bruce. *Church History in Plain Language.* Waco, Tex.: Word Books, 1982.

Shrewsbury, N.J.-Salem, W.Va. SDB Church Records, 1745-1834. Ms., CRR 19x.121. SDB Historical Society Library.

Siwani, Nyaniso James. *The Unknown Made Known: A History of Sabbathkeepers in South Africa.* Janesville, Wis.: SDB Historical Society, 1995.

Smith, Kenneth E. *Sam: Ward, Founding Father.* Plainfield, N.J.: SDB Historical Society, n.d.

Speer, Robert E. *The New Opportunity of the Church.* New York: MacMillan Co., 1919.

Stennet[t], Edward. The Royal Law Contended For.... 2nd ed. London, 1658. PP 1987.66, SDB Historical Society Library.

---. *The Seventh Day is the Sabbath of the Lord: Or, An Answer to M. William Russel his Book, Entituled, No Seventh Day Sabbath Commanded by Jesus Christ in the New Testament.* [London], 1664.

Stennett, Joseph. *The Works of the Late Reverend and Learned Mr. Joseph Stennett.* 4 vols. London, 1732.

Stennett, Samuel. An Answer *to the Christian Minister's Reasons for Baptizing Infants in a Series of Letters to a Friend.* London, 1775.

---. *Remarks on the Christian Minister's Reasons for Administering Baptism by Sprinkling or Pouring of Water in a Series of Letters to a Friend.* London, 1772.

Sweet, William Warren. *Religion in the Development of American Culture.* New York: Scribner's, 1952.

---. *The Story of Religion in America.* 1930. New York: Harper, 1950.

Tertullian. *Apology. The Ante-Nicene Fathers.* Eds. Alexander Roberts & James Donaldson. Buffalo, N.Y.: Christian Literature Publishing Company, 1885. 3: 55.

Test Act. *Narragansett Historical Register* 6:138.

Thomsen, Russell J. Seventh-day Baptists--Their Legacy to Adventists. Mountain View, Calif.: Pacific Press, 1971.

Thorngate, Janet. Confessions of a Former Sabbath Breaker. Editorial. *Lead-Line* (September 1988).

Tillam, Thomas. *The Lasher Proved Lyar.* N.p., c.1658.

---. *The Seventh Day Sabbath Sought Out and Celebrated*. London, 1657 edition. [At Regents Park, Oxford.]

---. *The Temple of Lively Stones*. N.p., 1660.

Torbet, Robert G. A *History of the Baptists*. 3rd ed. 1950. Valley Forge, Pa.: Judson Press, 1963.

Transactions of the Baptist Historical Society, 7 vols. London: Baptist Historical Society, 1911.

The Trial of John James at the King's-Bench, for High-Treason, November 14, 1662. A Complete Collection of State-Trials, and Proceedings Upon High-Treason, and Other Crimes and Misdemeanours from the Reign of King Richard II to The End of the Reign of King George I. 2nd ed. 6 vols. London, 1730.

The True and Perfect Speech of John James,... London, 1661. Ann Arbor, Mich.: UMI. Wing. J430-J431.

Turner, Daniel. Sermon *Occasioned by the Death of Rev. Mr. Joseph Stennett*. Abingdon, 1769.

Turner, Frederick Jackson. *The Frontier in American History*. 1920. New York: Holt, 1947.

Tyndale, William, and John Frith. *Works of English Reformers: William Tyndale and John Frith*. Ed. Thomas Russell. 3 vols. London, 1831.

Ussher, J. *Works*. Eds. C. R. Elrington and J. M. Todd. Vol. 16. Dublin, 1847-64.

Utter, George B. *The Seventh-day Baptist Praise Book*. New York, 1879.

Walker, Williston. *A History of the Christian Church*. 3rd ed. New York: Scribner's, 1970.

Ward, John. *The Life and Services of Governor Samuel Ward, of Rhode Island, A Member of the Continental Congress in 1774, 1775, and 1776*. New York, 1877.

---. *A Memoir of Lieut.-Colonel Samuel Ward*. New York, 1875.

W[histon], E[dward]. *The Life and Death of Mr. Henry Jessey*. N.p., 1671.

White, B. R. *The English Baptists of the Seventeenth   Century*. Ed. B. R. White. A History of English Baptists 1. 3 vols. London: Baptist Historical Society, 1983.

Whitley, W. T. *A Baptist Bibliography*. 2 vols. London: Kingsgate Press, 1916.

---. *The Baptists of London, 1612-1928*. London: Kingsgate P, n.d.

---. *A Century of Sabbath doctrine, 1595-1695*. 1911. Ms. copied by Charles Henry Greene. [C. H. Greene Papers, Notebook #10, p. 80-178. SDB Historical Society Library. A later version is W. T. Whitley. Men of the Seventh Day. [Ms. at Regents Park College, Oxford.]

---. *A History of British Baptists*. London: Charles Griffin & Co., 1923.

---, ed. *Minutes of the General Assembly of the General Baptist Churches in England, with Kindred Records*. 2 vols. London: Baptist Historical Society, 1910.

---. SDBs in England. *Baptist Quarterly*. 12:8 (Oct. 1947) 252.

Williams, Roger. *The Bloody Tenent of Persecution for Cause of Conscience Discussed: and Mr. Cotton's Letter Examined and Answered*. Ed. Edward Bean Underhill. London: Harserd Knollys Society, 1848.

Winter, Ralph D. The Two Structures of God's Redemptive Mission. American Society of Missiology, 1974.

Winthrop, John *Winthrop's Journal: History of New England, 1630-1649*. Ed. James Kendall Hosmer. 2 vols. New York: Scribner's, 1908.

INDEX

Clark, C. B., 324
Clark, Francis, 227, 228
Clarke, Bethiah (Hubbard), 106
Clarke, E. Lua, 197
Clarke, Henry, 128, 137, 140, 142, 146, 147, 154, 179, 198, 231
Clarke, Herman D., 337
Clarke, John, 74, 80f, 86, 87, 88, 89, 91, 106, 387
Clarke, Joseph, 88, 106, 108
Clarke, Joshua, 204
Clarke, Wiliam, 320
Clement, Joan, 295
Cohansey, New Jersey, Baptist Church, 109
Colchester, Essex, England, 32, 50, 52, 53, 54, 67, 68, 70
Collins, Arnold, 115
Collins, Henry, 115, 203
Colorado, 156, 157, 226
Columbus, Ohio, SDB Church, 157
Comer, John, 74, 86, 89, 90, 91
Commission, SDB, 260ff, 264, 265, 267, 268, 273, 274, 276, 284, 285, 292, 330, 391
Commitment to Growth, SDB, 249, 276f, 306, 332, 374, 380
Committee on Christian Social Action, 248, 274, 339, 340ff
Committee on Denominational Activities, SDB, 260, 270, 336, 338, 374
Committee of Six on Denominational Harmony, 356
Committee on Ecumenical Affairs, SDB, 328
Committee on Missions, SDB, 293
Committee on Nominations, SDB, 161
Committee on Reference and Counsel, 260
Committee on Religious Life, 358
Committee on the State of Religion, SDB, 145
Committee on Vocational Opportunities, 374
Congregational polity, 21, 23, 30, 35, 51
Congregationalists, 28, 102, 111, 365
Connecticut, 105, 152

Conogocheage, Pennsylvania, 100
Conradi, L. R., 309
Conrod, John, 295
Conrod, Joyce, 295
Constantine, 12
Constitution, SDB General Conference, 138, 140, 141, 142, 149, 160, 161, 167, 173, 258, 259,
Constitution, United States of America, 78, 113, 133, 134, 153, 343
Continental Congress (First and Second), 115, 116, 117
Conventicle Act, 56
Coon, D. Burdette, 230, 267, 304
Coordinating Leadership Team (CLT), SDB, 265
Coppinger, Matthew, 52
Cornthwaite, Robert, 68
Corporation Act, 56
Council on Ministry, SDB, 209, 285, 361f, 369, 392
Coverdale, Miles 2, 19
Cowell, John, 57, 68, 87
Cox, Harvey, 382
Cramner, Thomas, 2, 19, 232
Crandall High School, Jamaica, 304
Crandall, Ben, 272
Crandall, Grace, 177, 222
Crandall, Henry, 212
Crandall, John, 81, 82, 106
Crandall, Joseph, 91, 107, 108
Crandall, Lucius, 186, 201
Crandall, Wayne, 304
Crichlow, Luther, 304, 322
Crofoot, A. Burdett, 248, 262
Crofoot, Jay W., (Mr. and Mrs.), 177
Cromwell, Oliver, 32, 44, 46, 53, 59, 82, 386
Cuba, New York, 167
Curtis, Jonathan, 100
Cyprian of Carthage, 8
Czech Republic (part of former Czechoslovakia), 7, 318
Dakota, Wisconsin, SDB Church, 157
Daland, William C., 172, 184, 210, 296, 324
Darwin, Charles, 350

James I (of England; VIII of Scotland), 4, 25, 26, 32
James II (of England), 33, 63, 64
James, John, 32, 47, 57, 58f, 67, 70, 71, 386
James, William, 100
Janesville, Wisconsin, 235, 249, 263, 286f, 392
Java, 308
Jerusalem, Israel, 172
Jessey, Henry, 32, 51, 203, 386
Jesuits, 83
Johannesburg, South Africa, 316
Johansen, August, 356
John Myles Company, 109
Johnson, Francis, 309, 310
Jones, William Mead, 66, 69, 171
Jordan, Henry, 320
Jubilee Papers, 199, 233, 246, 288
Judaism (Jewish), 36, 37, 39, 40, 47, 52, 53, 61, 68, 169, 170f, 329, 366, 378
Judson, Adoniram, 164, 180, 290, 312
Kansas, 157
Keach, Elias, 84f, 111
Keith, George, 94f, 96, 98, 99
Keithians, 74, 93, 95, 98, 100, 387
Kelpius, Johannes, 93
Kentucky, 156
Kenya Conference, SDB, 249, 307
Kenyon, William C., 205, 206, 208
Kerala, India SDB Church (Malankara), 317
Khawvelthanga, C., 312
Kiangnam Arsenal, Shanghai, China, 176
Killingsworth, Thomas, 84, 93, 96, 99, 102, 109, 111
King James Bible, 26
King Philip's War, 105, 109
Kingston, Jamaica, SDB Church, 304
Knox, John 2, 22, 25
Koshy, Susamma, 317
Koster, Heinrich Bernhard (Henry), 95, 96, 98
Kube, Stefan, 310
Kube, Vicky, 310
Kumar, B. Kishor, 312
Lancaster, Pennsylvania, 119

Langworthy, Andrew, 106
Langworthy, Rachel (Hubbard), 90, 106
Lanphere, Ethan, 199
Lathrop, John, 51, 104
Latimer, Hugh, 20
Latourette, Kenneth, 325
Latvia, 318
Laud, William, 41
Lausanne, Switzerland, 324
Lawton, Gordon, 362
Lawton, Leon, 304, 313, 314, 316, 317
Lee, Captain Henry ("Light Horse Harry Lee"), 121
Lek, Jan, 308, 309
Leningrad, Russia, 318
Leonardsville, New York, 254
Lesson Leaves, 196
Letter to the Baptists (1843), 144
Letters to Young Preachers, 251, 365
Lewis, Abram Herbert, 37, 149, 184, 200f, 228, 242, 246, 251, 257, 278, 294, 320, 334, 351f, 365, 389
Lewis, Edwin H., 200
Lewis, Nathan E., 337
Lexington and Concord, Battle of, 119
Liechty, Daniel, 12
Light of Home (*The*), 185
Lightbearers for Christ, 373
Lihue, China, 177
Lihue, China, SDB Church, 283
Lindsell, Harold, 249, 380
Link (The) (European), 309
Link (The), (Australian), 310
Little Genesee, New York, SDB Church, 167
Little Wild Street Baptist Church, 65
Littell, Franklin H., 23
Livingston, William, 123
Lollards, 2, 18f,
London Confession of Faith, 348, 349
London, England, 50, 51, 52, 53, 54, 57, 62, 63, 64, 67, 80, 81
Long Island, New York, 93
Loofboro, Eli, 159, 320
Los Angeles, California, 328
Los Angeles, California, SDB Church, 159

Mott, John R., 288
Mozambique, 296, 311
Mumfords (Stephen and Ann), 33, 47, 74, 85, 86, 87, 90, 387
Myanmar (Burma), 164, 180, 248, 290, 312
Myanmar (Burma) Conference, SDB, 307, 312
Nairobi, Kenya, 326
Narraganset, 80, 105
National Council of Churches, 247, 248, 321, 322, 323, 363
Natton, Gloucestershire, England, 66, 70
Nebraska, 157
Netherlands, The (Holland) 13, 26, 27, 28, 29, 186, 238, 289, 295, 297
Netherlands SDB Conference, 307, 308f
New Delhi, India, 326
New Enterprise, Pennsylvania, 155
New Forward Movement, 246, 261, 270f
New Hampshire, 102
New Jersey, 78, 84, 92, 93, 96, 101ff, 107, 108, 112, 123, 135, 138, 152, 181, 234, 235, 332, 388
New London, Connecticut, 90, 107
New Market Academy, 216
New York (state), 74, 134, 151, 152, 153, 154, 155, 169, 181, 195, 204, 208, 210, 332, 388
New York, New York (city), 119, 170, 182, 183, 187, 192, 193, 197, 228, 254
New York, New York, SDB Church, 172, 223
New Zealand, 247, 295, 299, 307, 309
Newark, New Jersey, 111, 280
Newgate Prison, England, 57, 61
Newport, Rhode Island, 33, 74, 80, 85, 87, 90, 109, 111, 115, 124, 387
Newport, Rhode Island, First Baptist Church, 74, 81, 82, 86, 87, 88, 89, 91, 93, 105, 387
Newport, Rhode Island, SDB Church, 57, 58, 74, 85, 86f, 103, 105ff, 109, 113, 114, 115, 119, 123, 137, 138, 203, 370, 387, 389
Newport, Rhode Island, "Six Principle" Baptist Church, 89

Newtown, Pennsylvania, SDB Church (Upper Providence), 74, 84, 97f, 99
Ngura, L., 312, 313
Nigeria Conference, SDB, 298f, 307
Noble, Abel, 85, 93f, 97, 101, 387
Norfolk, England, 67
North American Baptist Fellowship (NABF), 248, 326, 328f, 330, 381, 392
North Carolina, 135, 156
North Central Association, 157
North Hampton, Ohio, SDB Church, 135
North Loup, Nebraska, SDB Church, 157, 305
Northern Association, 157
Northern Baptist Convention (NBC), 329
Northwest Association, 159
Northwest Ordinance (1787), 134
Northwest Territory, 151
Northwestern Association, 156f, 161, 213, 230, 231, 303
Nortonville, Kansas, SDB Church, 157
Norwich, England, 27, 68
Norwood, J. Nelson, 146, 209, 356
Nottingham, Pennsylvania, SDB Church, 100f, 110
Nova Scotia, 101
Ockford, James, 32, 48f, 203, 386
Ohio, 135, 151, 155, 156, 157, 166, 169, 311, 388
Ohio Association, 155
Olifan, William, 316
Olson, Ellen, 314
Olson, Matthew, 314
Onward Movement, 247, 261, 271f
Ordination of Ministers, 22, 27, 91, 108, 135, 143, 162, 180, 206, 222, 242
Oregon, 156, 159
Osborn, Lester G., 356
Our World Mission, SDB, 248, 268, 273f,
Outlook (The), 129, 184f, 365
Oxford University, England, 60, 63, 96
Pacific Coast Association, 158f, 295
Paine, Thomas, 133
Palestine Mission, SDB, 129, 171
Palmborg, Rosa, 177, 222, 225, 231, 291
Parkinson, William, 200
Parrish, George E., 370